The Democratic Dilemma

Religion, Reform, and the
Social Order in the Connecticut
River Valley of Vermont, 1791–1850

RANDOLPH A. ROTH

The Ohio State University

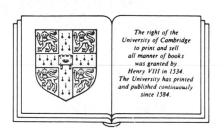

The right of the
University of Cambridge
to print and sell
all manner of books
was granted by
Henry VIII in 1534.
The University has printed
and published continuously
since 1584.

CAMBRIDGE UNIVERSITY PRESS

Cambridge
New York   New Rochelle   Melbourne   Sydney

Published by the Press Syndicate of the University of Cambridge
The Pitt Building, Trumpington Street, Cambridge CB2 1RP
32 East 57th Street, New York, NY 10022, USA
10 Stamford Road, Oakleigh, Melbourne 3166, Australia

First published 1987

Printed in the United States of America

Library of Congress Cataloging-in-Publication Data
Roth, Randolph A.
The democratic dilemma.
Bibliography: p.
1. Connecticut River Valley – Politics and government.
2. Vermont – Politics and government – 1775–1865.
3. Connecticut River Valley – Social conditions.
4. Vermont – Social conditions.   5. Connecticut River
Valley – Church history.   6. Vermont – Church history.
7. Christianity and social problems.   I. Title.
F57.C7R67   1987   974.3   86–28391

British Library Cataloguing in Publication Data
Roth, Randolph A.
The democratic dilemma : religion,
reform, and the social order in the
Connecticut River Valley of Vermont,
1791–1850.
1. Northeastern States – Politics and
government
I. Title.
974'.03   F106

ISBN 0 521 30183 1

The Democratic Dilemma

Religion, Reform, and the Social Order
in the Connecticut River Valley of Vermont,
1791–1850

Contents

Tables and maps

Tables

Maps

Acknowledgments

I would like to thank some of the many people who helped me to complete this study over the past twelve years. I am sorry that I cannot describe more than a small part of their contributions here, and I only hope they will find this work somehow useful or enjoyable, so that it might serve in a very limited way as a partial return for their many kindnesses to me. I wish first to thank Reidun Nuquist, Laura Abbott, Mary Pat Brigham, Edwin Hoyt, Charles Morrissey, and the staff of the Vermont Historical Society; Kevin Graffagnino and the staff of the Wilbur Collection at the University of Vermont; and John Hench and the staff of the American Antiquarian Society, for their generous help. I was aided too by the staffs at the Baker Library at Dartmouth College, the New Hampshire Historical Society, the Sterling Library at Yale University, the Grinnell College Library and Computer Services office, the Vermont State Papers, the Department of Public Records of the State of Vermont, and the National Archives.

I would also like to thank the contemporary inhabitants of the valley – the town officers, church members, and citizens who gave me access to the historical records in their care and lent their time and good offices to help me locate seemingly lost documents. My thanks, too, to the American Council of Learned Societies and to the American Antiquarian Society for research fellowships, to Yale University for my graduate fellowship, to the Humanities Grant Board of Grinnell College for research support, to the Department of History at the University of Vermont for employing me as a visiting instructor, and to the federal government and its taxpayers for my student loans, which together enabled me to finance this project. Mr. and Mrs. Robert A. Sincerbeaux and Mr. Frank H. Teagle, Jr., have kindly supported the publication of my book, as have the members of the Humanities Grant Board of the Ohio State University, who helped me meet the costs of preparing the manuscript for publication.

My debts extend to my former students, Janet Welsh, Sarah Berger, and Stuart Yeager, who helped gather and computerize the data for this study with uncommon energy and skill; to Daniel Wagner, who drew the maps; to my social scientific friends, Ed Barboni, Paul Munyon, and Jon Andelson, who taught me much about quantification, theory, economy, and community; and to my former colleagues in the Department of History at Grinnell College, particularly Don Smith, Alan Jones, and David Jordan, who waded through the entire manuscript and yet never lost hope. Among my friends who helped and do not live in Grinnell, Iowa, are Bill Gilmore, Jan Lewis, Patty Nelson Limerick, Dick Shiels, and my editor at Cambridge, Frank Smith (who used to live in Grinnell, Iowa). They too read the manuscript and blessed me with their insight and wise counsel. Philip Lampi gave me access to his data on early gubernatorial elections in New England. My fellow historians of Vermont, Tom Bassett, Hal Barron, Bill Gilmore, and Donald Smith, shared their knowledge and research generously. My study would not have been possible without the help of their imaginative studies of material and cultural life, of postbellum communities, and of revolutionary Vermont, nor would it have been possible without the work of David Ludlum, whose pioneering study of religion and reform in antebellum Vermont inspired and guided my own.

I would like to thank Howard R. Lamar for his unfailing generosity, appreciativeness, and patience over my entire graduate career; and especially for the way his clarity of mind and concern for narrative helped me make this study more comprehensible to myself and to others. I wish to thank too David Brion Davis for his contagious enthusiasm for the study of antebellum reform and for his probing criticism, his concern for careful, comparative explanation, and his thoughtful suggestions for expanding the focus of this study – as well as his willingness to discuss my hunches, however far afield they strayed. And my appreciation to Paul E. Johnson, for the example of his own work on religious and reform movements, as well as his attention to the details of this one. I learned a great deal from each of these people, and found them ever respectful of my labors.

Finally, I would like to thank Allison Sweeney. She summed up her contribution to this study better than I could ever hope to do. As we shipped off one of the many final drafts of this manuscript, Allison patted me on the shoulder and said, "I just want you to know, I never could have done it without you."

Introduction

The Age of Democratic Revolution, which spanned the period between the end of the Seven Years' War in 1763 and the middle of the nineteenth century, altered forever the terms upon which governments governed and the ways in which religious institutions shaped the morals and spiritual beliefs of the societies that surrounded them. Established churches and unrepresentative governments, whose vitality and legitimacy had already been undermined in many nations for a generation or more, suddenly confronted ideals and social conditions that they were ill-prepared to meet. Belief in equality, democracy, and religious dissent spread, at times lessening the willingness of whole peoples to accept established authority. Population pressure and economic change altered social arrangements and expectations that had provided the foundation for old religious and political institutions.

These changes in belief and society produced a dramatic transformation of religion, morality, and politics on the revolutionary frontier of the United States, especially on the northern edge of that frontier, which extended some 600 miles from the upper Connecticut River Valley of Vermont and New Hampshire to the Western Reserve of Ohio on the southern shore of Lake Erie. This region was settled primarily by New Englanders in the years immediately before and after the American Revolution. Here a society arose that was truly the child of the revolutionary age: a society that was formally committed to the ideals of democracy, equality, and religious freedom and that rejected slavery, monarchy, established churches, and imperial domination. Its members aspired to economic independence and self-employment and dedicated themselves with extraordinary fervor to making it the most perfect society on earth.

This society fell short of fulfilling much of its original promise, however. Despite its formidable achievements, it never became the tolerant, egalitarian society that many thought would arise as a result of popular government and voluntary religion, and by the 1830s and 1840s it could no longer give many of its inhabitants what they wanted most — independent shops and farms for themselves and their descendants. Still, it was less deeply divided, more prosperous and stable, and more firmly committed to democracy, equality, and tolerance than the societies of Europe and most other regions of the United States. It was also markedly more successful in creating churches that received the enthusiastic, voluntary support of a high proportion of the citizenry and in erecting republican governments that could be reformed and that were willing to play leading roles in the effort to reform society.

The new relationship that arose on the frontier between church and government and the citizenry was both a cause and a consequence of the region's most distinctive trait in that era: the frequency with which its inhabitants organized and joined religious and reform movements. They embraced, and in some instances invented, most of the eccentric "isms" of the period (Mormonism, Adventism, perfectionism, millennialism, communitarianism) and they furthered mainstream movements (revivalism, sabbatarianism, abolitionism, Antimasonry, temperance, benevolence) with unparalleled zeal. Indeed, by the mid-1830s the inhabitants had been so far "consumed" by the flames of religious passion and moral fervor that these areas of the frontier were dubbed "burned-over districts." By that time, the region had achieved the highest levels of active church membership and of enrollment in reform societies in the world. Its citizens led the national crusade to make the United States the first truly Christian, reformed republic, one that conformed to God's laws and embodied transcendent moral values.[1]

That is not to say that the people of the northern revolutionary frontier stood alone in their commitment to religious and reform movements. They were part of a wider Anglo-American community that supported religious revivals and reform movements throughout the period in many regions of the United States and Great Britain. The Celtic Fringe of Great Britain, which comprised Wales, Cornwall, and Scotland, was especially burned-over by religious revivals and vied closely with the northern frontier of the United States for leadership in church membership and religious enthusiasm.[2]

The fact that many movements rose and fell simultaneously in the burned-over districts and in the Anglo-American community at large testifies to the close ties and communications among religious enthusiasts and reformers in the English-speaking world and suggests that many movements arose not simply from the peculiar conditions that prevailed on the revolutionary frontier, but from conditions that prevailed throughout the Western world during the Age of Democratic Revolution. Nevertheless, that frontier provided the most fertile ground for these movements: better, for instance, than southern New England or the areas of the revolutionary frontier to the immediate south that were settled by

New Yorkers, Germans, Scotch-Irish, and Dutch, and far better than most of the British Isles and the Continent.

Why did the reserved, industrious inhabitants of northern New England, upstate New York, and northeastern Ohio embark upon the most tumultuous religious and reform crusades of the revolutionary age? The interpreters of America's republican tradition, following Tocqueville, point to the tension between republican ideals and liberal reality in the young nation and argue that Christians and reformers acted as they did because they were afraid that their neighbors were becoming a "liberal" people – individualistic, pluralistic, capitalistic, and partisan – and were not living up to the republican ideals of the Founding Fathers. Those ideals entailed not only the establishment of a republican form of government that vested power in representatives elected by the people and that guaranteed the rights and property of all citizens. They presumed a commitment to the public good before private interests. Some historians contend that Christians and reformers were responding to the specter of corrupt materialism looming over the burned-over districts, breeding tyranny and faction. They saw their unifying communitarian traditions succumbing to the influence of the Revolution and fierce economic competition on the frontier and worked feverishly to constrain those of their fellow countrymen who were ill-disciplined, selfish, and impious.[3]

There is an ambiguity in the republican–liberal interpretation of the history of the burned-over districts that has led advocates of this interpretation to mistake the source of the tension that lay at the center of society in the early republic. That ambiguity stems from a failure to determine what is meant by "liberalism." Liberalism is at once the inevitable product of an irresistible force like the market revolution or human nature, the undesirable fruit of ideals and social changes unleashed by the Revolution, and the tragic consequence of republicanism's problematic effort to reconcile the public good with the private pursuit of happiness.[4] The concept has been used to describe a wide range of changes in values, habits, and institutions in the burned-over districts. Among them are the rise of individualism, evident in a growing emphasis on the rights and freedoms of individuals, as well as in an increase in self-interestedness, isolation, self-expression, and assertiveness; the growth of pluralism, a heightened anxiety among members of particular religious, economic, and social groups to defend their peculiar values and interests, and a corresponding fragmentation of society into conflicting groups; the development of capitalism, attended by an increased attachment to material values, and a deepening involvement in an impersonal market economy dominated by entrepreneurs and financiers who increasingly controlled exchange and production; and the rise of political partisanship, of personal commitment to sustained political activity and of formal political parties that represented the increasingly disparate interests of individuals and social groups.[5]

Historians of the burned-over districts assert that liberalism fostered a privatism that carried the districts and their inhabitants away from the republican ideals of community, cooperation, and equilibrium. Yet it is clear that, on New England's revolutionary frontier, each assertion of individual rights resulted eventually in new claims on individuals, claims that most citizens met willingly. Almost every fragmentation of the society into conflicting groups ended in reunification around new shared values and interests. Despite changes in the structure of the economy, especially in manufacturing centers and in regional markets, the vast majority of the inhabitants remained committed over the entire period to the same goals and strategies, to securing prosperous shops or farms for themselves and their children, and to ensuring that virtue prospered and rough equality prevailed. Control over production and exchange was still widely diffused, and people continued to exchange capital, goods, and services primarily with friends and relatives in protected town and neighborhood markets. Each period of intense political mobilization and conflict, including that which pitted Whigs against Democrats, ended in political reunification and a decline in political participation and party identification.[6]

The emphasis of the republican–liberal interpretation on the tension between ideals and reality also obscures the complexity of republican aspirations themselves. Recent works on revolutionary America demonstrate that republican ideology meant various things to various people.[7] As Donald Smith has shown in his study of revolutionary Vermont, the differences among adherents of the balanced, classical republic of George Washington and John Adams, and people who supported the evangelical republic of the Calvinist clergy, or the radical republic of Thomas Paine, were so pronounced that these factions actually rioted against each other during Vermont's struggle for independence from New York.[8] Each faction propelled society in a potentially liberal direction by advancing regard for individual rights, economic opportunity, personal freedom, and popular government. Some proponents of individualism or capitalism believed that they could unleash the young nation's creative and productive energies by relaxing community restraints. Some advocates of pluralism or partisanship believed that they could prevent any one faction from dominating society by encouraging antagonistic groups to compete for power.

Such people remained a tiny minority, however. Few revolutionary frontiersmen wanted to create a liberal society, and virtually all would have been frustrated had such a society arisen. By embracing republican ideology, the vast majority of people in the burned-over districts committed themselves formally to values that could promote liberalism, but they also committed themselves to other, contrary values, which favored the restraint of liberties for the good of community, and encouraged a sense of mutual obligation among citizens.

These differences among people who espoused republican ideology make it clear why every conscious effort to fashion society after a particular republican vision failed, and why most settlers on New England's frontier were frustrated by the society that emerged after the Revolution. They also indicate that most people on the frontier were firmly set against the liberalization of their society. The social order that they struggled so persistently to create was liberal neither in theory nor in fact.[9]

The mystery behind the widespread participation of New England's revolutionary frontiersmen in moral and spiritual crusades is thus more easily resolved if the central tension in early republican life is located not between republican ideals and liberal reality, but among the diverse and contrary aspirations of revolutionary Americans.[10] Those who settled the burned-over districts embraced the idea of democratic revolution more thoroughly than anyone else in the Western world. Frustrated in their efforts to protect their values and interests by limited economic opportunities, religious controversy, and political strife, most revolutionary frontiersmen blamed their problems on the ecclesiastical and aristocratic establishments of southern New England and Great Britain and vested their trust in a social order whose institutions rested on the principles of consent of the governed and of equality of citizens before the law. They were inspired by what R. R. Palmer terms a "democratic" vision, founded on dissatisfaction with existing social inequities and on an insistence that neither political nor religious power resides in any privileged or closed body of men.[11]

Their revolution was thus a recoiling from old evils as much as a venture toward a specific social order, and it is clear that not all the inhabitants of the burned-over districts wished to press the democratic revolution to its fullest extent. After all, for many people the word "democracy" still had negative connotations. What made the burned-over districts remarkable, however, was that few people shrank from the revolution's radical faith in the equality of mankind. All but a handful of these pioneers dedicated themselves as revolutionaries to bringing toleration, freedom, economic opportunity, and popular government to the frontier and the world. They embedded those ideals in their institutions and their society. Yet in so doing they eliminated almost every instrument they could use to secure their most cherished ideals and interests: economic independence and security, moral and spiritual unity, and political harmony. Together those ideals embodied the New England way of life, which was what they wished most to protect and to share with the world. New England's revolutionary frontiersmen faced a dilemma from which they could not escape: how to reconcile their commitment to competition, toleration, and popular sovereignty with their desire to defend an orderly and pious way of life.

The people of the burned-over districts shared that dilemma with democrats throughout their own nation and the Western world. Yet they experienced it with peculiar intensity, for they were at once the world's most radical democrats and the latest conservators of New England's communitarian traditions. They were on the whole a devout people, and an ambitious one, and they refused to relinquish their desire to create a society that would allow them to save what they valued in their way of life and still enable them to realize dreams long frustrated in America and Europe. That refusal to compromise one aspiration for the sake of another led them to invest their democratic enterprise with singular energy. It was what attracted them to republican ideology, which promised to enable them to realize all their aspirations.[12]

To resolve their dilemma these New Englanders tried to create a Christian, reformed republic. Their goal remained elusive, however. They found that the ideas and social changes brought into being by the Revolution compounded their difficulties and rendered calculated remedies useless. The problem was not that they had become a liberal people. The problem was that they remained, despite social and intellectual change, a people who were democratic by conviction and predicament, but whose aspirations and society were jeopardized by diversity, by partisanship, and by a simultaneous commitment to equality of condition and equality of opportunity. Because almost every event or change that occurred after 1775 seemed to threaten their way of life, they considered themselves in a perpetual state of crisis.

They were delivered by the burst of religious and reform activity that swept the region in the years following the War of 1812. Those crusades were abetted by contemporaneous campaigns for economic and community development that encouraged citizens of different neighborhoods and diverse interests to work together to improve their communities. Through these movements the people of the burned-over districts created the institutions, habits, and ideas that enabled them to cope with the problems of denominational and political strife, ungovernable townspeople and church members, and diminished opportunities for youths – problems that generated an apparent increase in irreligious and immoral behavior. Through these movements, New England's frontiersmen worked to create a new kind of society: not a liberal society whose worst tendencies were checked or controlled by Christians and reformers, but a society that embodied the principles of Christianity and reform.

Those who shaped the postrevolutionary society through the spiritual, moral, and economic campaigns that pervaded the burned-over districts were not always able to understand or articulate that society's workings or their contributions to it, particularly because their new social order succeeded as often by obscuring and begging the dilemmas at the heart of democracy as it did by addressing and resolving them. The methods Christians and reformers devised for controlling youths, diverting discontent into safe political channels, and helping their children succeed economically relied to no small degree on informal coercion, manipulation, and discrimination, even though Christians and reformers committed themselves formally to an open society that eschewed such behavior. They drew creatively on a multiplicity of theological and political traditions to transcend the contradictions between their methods and their democratic values. Yet few of these New Englanders sympathized with the self-conscious builders of new orders in their midst, like Joseph Smith or John Humphrey Noyes; and they themselves had their clearest successes when they were least self-conscious in their efforts to refashion their society.

The Connecticut River Valley of Vermont is an ideal place to study the postrevolutionary order these New Englanders created. There the dilemmas of democratic life presented themselves in their starkest form. Because the valley's settlement began in the 1760s, at the onset of the revolutionary era, its early inhabitants had firsthand knowledge of prerevolutionary southern New England and carried most of its traditions, controversies, and ideals with them to the frontier. Ties of kinship, commerce, and geography linked them to the inhabitants of Massachusetts, Connecticut, and New Hampshire. Yet the valley's settlers also experienced the full force of the democratic revolution, on a frontier contested not only by Great Britain, but by New York and New Hampshire, states vying to impose their own laws and institutions on the valley. By striking out for independence from all three powers, the valley's settlers fought a revolution that was in some ways broader in its aims than the American Revolution. Theirs was a fight against tenancy, unrepresentative government, and religious establishments. It was a fight to determine the character of their way of life and to free themselves from the need to compromise on that score with southern New Englanders and Yorkers.

The Connecticut River Valley itself comprises roughly the eastern half of Vermont, stretching from the Connecticut River in the east to the Green Mountains in the west and the Granite Hills in the north. With

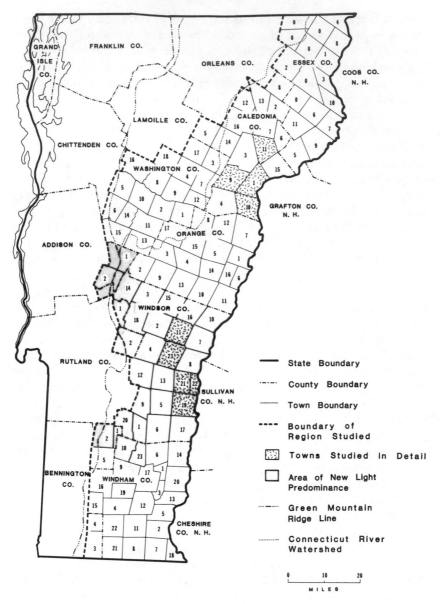

Map 1. Area of study, Vermont

Towns in the Connecticut River Valley of Vermont

Addison County
1. Granville
2. Hancock

Bennington County
1. Landgrove
2. Peru
3. Readsboro
4. Searsburg
5. Winhall

Caledonia County
1. Barnet
2. Burke
3. Danville
4. Groton
5. Hardwick
6. Kirby
7. Lyndon
8. Newark
9. Peacham
10. Ryegate
11. St. Johnsbury
12. Sheffield
13. Sutton
14. Walden
15. Waterford
16. Wheelock

Essex County
0. Not settled
1. Bloomfield
2. Brighton
3. Brunswick
4. Canaan
5. Concord
6. Granby
7. Guildhall
8. Lemington
9. Lunenburg
10. Maidstone
11. Victory

Orange County
1. Bradford
2. Braintree
3. Brookfield
4. Chelsea
5. Corinth
6. Fairlee
7. Newbury
8. Orange
9. Randolph
10. Strafford
11. Thetford
12. Topsham
13. Tunbridge
14. Vershire
15. Washington
16. West Fairlee
17. Williamstown

Rutland County
1. Pittsfield
2. Sherburne

Washington County
1. Barre
2. Berlin
3. Cabot
4. Calais
5. Duxbury
6. Fayston
7. Marshfield
8. Middlesex
9. Montpelier
10. Moretown
11. Northfield
12. Plainfield
13. Roxbury
14. Waitsfield
15. Warren
16. Waterbury
17. Woodbury
18. Worcester

Windham County
1. Athens
2. Brattleboro
3. Brookline
4. Dover
5. Dummerston
6. Grafton
7. Guilford
8. Halifax
9. Jamaica
10. Londonderry
11. Marlboro
12. Newfane
13. Putney
14. Rockingham
15. Somerset
16. Stratton
17. Townshend
18. Vernon
19. Wardsboro
20. Westminster
21. Whitingham
22. Wilmington
23. Windham

Windsor County
1. Andover
2. Barnard
3. Bethel
4. Bridgewater
5. Cavendish
6. Chester
7. Hartford
8. Hartland
9. Ludlow
10. Norwich
11. Pomfret
12. Plymouth
13. Reading
14. Rochester
15. Royalton
16. Sharon
17. Springfield
18. Stockbridge
19. Weathersfield
20. Weston
21. West Windsor
22. Windsor
23. Woodstock

Washington County, part of which lies in the Lake Champlain watershed, it includes six full counties and parts of three more (Map 1). Its inhabitants clearly thought of themselves as a unique people, and of the valley as an important and distinctive region. Whether they lived in a marketing or manufacturing center, an agricultural community, or a backwoods hill settlement, they referred to themselves as "valley" residents. Many of them pointed to the differences between themselves and western Vermonters, whom they considered "wild," and western New Hampshire residents, whose courage and revolutionary fervor they doubted.

The inhabitants of the nine towns whose history is examined here in depth (Map 1) were a varied lot. Some came from hill towns (Peacham or Pomfret), some from prosperous farming communities (Weathersfield, West Windsor, Barnet, Ryegate, or St. Johnsbury), and some from large commercial centers (Windsor or Woodstock). Many of Weathersfield's early settlers were antievangelical Calvinists, or Old Lights, and a number of them opposed both the American Revolution and Vermont's revolution against New York and were less hostile to southern New England's Calvinist establishments and the Federalist Party than other Vermonters. The settlers of the other communities in Windsor County — Windsor, West Windsor, Pomfret, and Woodstock — included a disproportionate number of zealous Calvinist evangelicals, or New Lights, who gave Vermont's revolution and the early Republican Party their wholehearted support. The settlers of the four towns in Caledonia County, most of whom arrived after the Revolution, were more heterogeneous in their political and spiritual convictions. Among their number were the Presbyterian dissenters from Scotland and northern Ireland who settled in Barnet and Ryegate. Unique in their customs and religious beliefs, they were the only large body of immigrants not native to New England to settle in the valley.

The histories of these nine towns were otherwise largely representative. Their populations grew rapidly during the 1790s and early 1800s, and more slowly thereafter, until growth stopped in most valley towns in the 1840s. Caledonia County towns continued to grow in the 1840s, particularly St. Johnsbury, which became a major manufacturing center, and Barnet and Ryegate, where Scots inheritance practices helped young people to continue to establish themselves at home. Windsor County towns grew smaller, however, as the population of these older communities aged and as young people moved away in search of opportunity (Table 1). Along with the rest of the valley, these nine towns moved to Antimasonry in the early 1830s and to Whiggery by the 1840s (Table 2). They shared in the increase in the number of meetinghouses and churches, particularly non-Calvinist churches (Table 3), and issued a steady stream

Table 1. Population of the Connecticut River Valley of Vermont
and of Selected Towns, 1790-1850

	1790	1810	1830	1850
Selected Caledonia County towns				
Barnet	477	1,301	1,764	2,521
Peacham	365	1,301	1,351	1,377
Ryegate	187	812	1,119	1,606
St. Johnsbury	143	1,334	1,592	2,758
Selected Windsor County towns				
Pomfret	710	1,473	1,867	1,546
Weathersfield	1,146	2,115	2,213	1,851
West Windsor/Windsor	1,542	2,757	3,134	2,930
Woodstock	1,605	2,672	3,044	3,041
Connecticut River Valley of Vermont				
	44,664	108,701	142,984	147,774

of petitions. These towns also left the most complete records in the valley
(Appendix A) and thus provide an opportunity to examine in detail the
causes and consequences of the valley's extraordinary moral, spiritual,
and political movements and the ways in which family, church, community, and class relationships changed as the valley's postrevolutionary
order took shape.

Western New Hampshire, southern New England, and other burned-
over districts can furnish some evidence that illuminates the valley's peculiarities, particularly the evangelical and revolutionary fervor of its
earliest inhabitants, and the extraordinary strength of its later commitment to Antimasonry and antislavery. To show that Vermonters faced a
problem of democratic order that was but one manifestation of a more
general problem faced by people throughout the Western world, and that
Vermonters' commitment to religious and reform movements was rooted
as much in that general problem as in the peculiar problems of democratic
life, evidence must come from farther afield. That is why Wales and
Württemberg, two other predominantly rural, Protestant areas with
strong pietistic traditions, are examined briefly in the conclusion to this
study. Those two regions provide evidence that churches and reform
societies gained strength not only where the democratic revolution

Table 2. Party Vote in the Connecticut River Valley of Vermont
and in Selected Towns, 1806-1844

	Median percentage Republican, 1806-17	Median percentage Antimasonic, 1830-34	Median percentage Whig, 1836-44
Selected Caledonia County towns			
Barnet	24	74	59
Peacham	10	66	58
Ryegate	51	77	47
St. Johnsbury	34	77	62
Selected Windsor County towns			
Pomfret	92	55	65
Weathersfield	38	49	82
West Windsor/Windsor	63	49	74
Woodstock	82	54	80
Connecticut River Valley of Vermont			
	53	46	54

triumphed, but wherever revolutionary ideas and social changes disrupted town life and politics. This was particularly true in Great Britain and America, where townspeople and middle-class elites found themselves bereft of effective formal means of securing their values and interests, and most especially true in Vermont, where frontier life and two revolutions (one against government by Great Britain, the other against government by New York) made it difficult to reconstruct laws, institutions, and traditions.

Among the burned-over districts of the revolutionary frontier, the state of Vermont has a strong claim to preeminence. It would become, in fact as well as in fiction, the symbolic fount of the young nation's truculent egalitarianism, militant faith, and crusading idealism. It was home in the antebellum period to unsurpassed religious revivals and temperance crusades and to the strongest antislavery, Antimasonic, and free-soil sentiment in the nation. It was the birthplace of an army of moral and spiritual leaders who attained greatness elsewhere, from Thaddeus Stevens, the fire-eating radical Republican, to Joseph Smith and Brigham Young, the fathers of Mormonism. Vermont's Green Mountain Boys became in

Table 3. Churches and Union Meetinghouses
in the Connecticut River Valley of Vermont, 1791-1843*a*

	1791	1800	1815	1828	1843
Selected towns in Caledonia and Windsor counties					
Calvinist churches	6	9	14	14	18
Non-Calvinist churches	1	2	5	11	15
Union meetinghouses	0	0	0	0	3
Connecticut River Valley of Vermont					
Calvinist churches	35	83	134	170	177
Non-Calvinist churches	1	26	52	114	173
Union meetinghouses	0	1	4	19	40
Number of inhabitants per church or Union meetinghouse	1,241	724	615	460	374

a The data include only churches and interdenominational meetinghouses supported by voluntary contributions. The data do not include town meetinghouses that were supported by taxes. See Appendix A for the sources of the data.

American historical mythology the archetypal revolutionary frontiersmen, defying the land-jobbers and patroons of colonial New York. They surprised the British at Fort Ticonderoga and wrote a constitution in 1777 that outlawed slavery and enfranchised every male who paid his poll tax. Vermont's women supplied authors like Harriet Beecher Stowe, Henry James, and Owen Wister with models for the forthright Yankee women who populated their novels, eager to carry their moral and spiritual influence to benighted places like the West, the South, and Europe.

Of course, such facts and fictions tell only part of the story. Every moral and spiritual crusade inspired strong opposition, and Vermont was as renowned for its satirical wits, profane pranksters, and rough-and-ready woodsmen as for its statesmen, Christians, and reformers. It was the birthplace not only of crusaders, but of wheeler-dealer pragmatists like Stephen Douglas, the popular-sovereignty Democrat, who would turn his back on Vermont when its self-righteous refusal to compromise helped ruin his plan to beg the moral question of slavery. Despite Vermont's enshrinement of Ethan Allen as a freedom fighter, the vast majority of his contemporaries feared him as a freethinker and a leveler and did their utmost to prevent the rise of the open, progressive society he envisioned. And although Vermont's women were generally esteemed as educators, missionaries, and inspirational poets who could enlighten the darkest corners of the globe, they were often frustrated at home and struggled for years to gain a modicum of influence and standing beyond the confines of their homes and churches.

Not all Vermonters wanted to shape Vermont after the visions of church members and reformers, and church members and reformers themselves had no unified idea of the social order they hoped to create. Vermonters contested their society's future hotly, above all because they could not agree upon a common response to the central dilemma of democratic life: how to reconcile their desire for security, moral and spiritual unity, and political harmony with their revolutionary commitment to competition, toleration, and democracy. But through conflict, through diverse religious and moral efforts to address this dilemma, Vermont's postrevolutionary order gradually took shape. That order would rest on Christian and reform principles and center on churches and reform organizations. It was not wholly faithful to the visions of Vermont's founders, nor ever wholly popular or secure, but it did bring unity and stability to town life and politics. It also encouraged Vermonters, as creators of what they thought was the most Christian and democratic society on earth, to believe that they had been chosen to be the custodians of America's (and indeed the world's) moral, spiritual, and political heritage and to take it upon themselves to see that that heritage never became a thing of the past.

1

The revolutionary frontier, 1763–1800

The first patents for settlement of the Connecticut River Valley of Vermont, which was then a part of what was known as the New Hampshire Grants, were issued by Governor Bennington Wentworth of New Hampshire in 1749. Wentworth claimed title on behalf of his colony to the land that lay west of the Connecticut River and east of Lake Champlain, and by 1764 he had placed three million acres – nearly half the future state of Vermont – into the hands of speculators and prospective settlers. Few people dared come to the valley at first, however, because until 1763 it was little more than a battleground for the English, the French, and their Indian allies. It was not until the Seven Years' War ended that the floodgates opened and thousands of settlers came driving north and west from Connecticut, Massachusetts, and New Hampshire.[1]

The valley remained a violent place for many years. Its proximity to Canada meant that settlers were vulnerable to attack throughout the American Revolution. The worst such attack took place in 1780, when the British and their native allies raided the frontier settlement of Royalton. They killed four men, seized twenty-five prisoners, burned twenty homes, and slaughtered nearly 150 cattle. Similar, if less devastating raids occurred through 1782. Settlers were terrified by these attacks – so much so that when the inhabitants of Athens, a small town in Windham County, heard Indian warwhoops issuing from the woods one day they ran for their lives, leaving Athens a ghost town. The alarm spread from town to town, and at length the Windham County militia was sent to engage the Indians in battle. They discovered the cause of the panic to have been a party of young surveyors, idling away the afternoon with a contest to see who could do the best Indian war cry.[2]

New Hampshire and New York had disputed ownership of the Grants for many years. In 1764 British authorities decided that dispute in favor of New York. All New Hampshire titles were suspended, and New York's laws and institutions were imposed upon the settlers of Vermont. There ensued twenty-seven years of litigation, controversy, and armed conflict. The majority of the valley's inhabitants were enraged when New York's "land schemers" attempted to seize the property of settlers who held New Hampshire titles; matters were made worse by the Westminster Massacre of 1775, at which a pro–New York posse killed two protestors and wounded others who had gathered to halt foreclosure proceedings at a court New York had established in the Grants. Most Vermonters cheered when the independent Republic of Vermont was created in 1777. The contest between Vermont and New York was far from over, however. Vermont's militia, the Green Mountain Boys, did not rout the last band of Yorker rebels from the valley until 1784, and Vermont was not truly safe from Yorker interference until it entered the Union, over New York's objections, in 1791.[3]

The decades-long dispute over Vermont's territory did not substantially affect its settlement. Settlers came to the valley in deliberate defiance of New York and Great Britain, seeking unsettled land, which had become scarce in southern New England by the 1760s. By 1777, when Vermont declared its independence from New York, all the lowlands had been penetrated; by 1791, when Vermont was granted statehood, there were settlers in all but the highest and most desolate country. When the first federal census was taken in 1790, the valley's population stood at 45,000. In 1800 it was 80,000.

By the time Vermont became a state, the valley had been divided into 116 townships, each approximately six miles square. Their character varied widely. In townships on good land, near the Connecticut River or one of its major tributaries, the farm population grew rapidly. The fertile strip of floodplain along the Connecticut River, which stretches from the Massachusetts border north to Barnet, supported very large and prosperous farms, many of them owned by wealthy gentlemen farmers like William Jarvis, former U.S. consul to Portugal, who bought up much of the floodplain in Weathersfield and there bred the famous merino sheep that he had smuggled out of Spain. Most farms in the valley were modest, however. They spread out across the high rolling ground above the river, leaving untouched only the swamps and the steepest mountainsides.[4]

Small villages sprang up in the midst of these farms to cater to the farmers' immediate needs. There were usually several to a township, located at the geographical center of the township, at crossroads, or at more arbitrary sites built up by enterprising families of traders, taverners, or blacksmiths, like the Shedds of Sheddsville in West Windsor. These villages were usually composed of a few small buildings: a meetinghouse or church, a general store, a forge, and perhaps a post office or tavern. Craftsmen/farmers generally had their shops on their farms, but a few did settle on the edge of these small villages.

Greater concentrations of population arose along streams and rivers, where water power or navigation expanded the horizons of manufacturers and traders. Stevens Village in the northern township of Barnet, for example, was located on bluffs high above the Connecticut to take advantage of a stream that ran down to the river. Sawmills, flour and oat mills, carding and cloth-fulling mills, and an assortment of shops related in one way or another to the mill trades clustered on the banks of the stream, and the small homes of workers arose nearby. A more commercial village, with more taverns and merchants, arose on the floodplain in southeast Barnet at McIndoes Falls, which marked the last point of the Connecticut navigable by flatboat.

In the early years of settlement these villages were not much like the picturesque Vermont small towns of our imagination. Their streets were often muddy, their buildings rude and unpainted. Yet the availability of lumber, carpenters, and even painters and masons in some cases, made for a steady increase in the number of neat, whitewashed frame houses. Material progress inspired citizens in townships such as Hartford, which straddled the junction of the White and Connecticut rivers, to entertain grand dreams of monopolizing commerce and manufacturing, while civic leaders in the villages of Westminster and Putney made bids for political prominence by launching newspapers. These and most other villages in the valley remained small, however, and the townships in which they arose retained their predominantly agricultural character. Soon after 1800 a few villages with minor advantages did become more important politically or commercially. Newfane, Guilford, and Chelsea, although landlocked, were named shire towns. Chester and Randolph attracted some trade, for Chester was the largest village on the Green Mountain Turnpike and Randolph the largest on the White River. Both were important transportation routes to the interior. Norwich also attracted commerce, because it was situated at a convenient stopping point on the Connecticut River between two very important townships, each over twenty miles away. Still, the influence that these towns exercised did not extend beyond townships in their immediate vicinities.

By 1800, the population of townships located on good land and near major waterways varied from about 400 in Ryegate, one of the northernmost towns in the valley with good land, to 1,800 or more in long-settled towns to the south like Weathersfield. Towns in the rolling uplands a township or two removed from the Connecticut River, like St. Johnsbury, Peacham, or Pomfret, had an average of about 600 inhabitants. Most towns to the north, in Essex or northern Caledonia counties, or in rough areas, like the interior of Orange County, or farther inland from the Connecticut, close to the spine of the Green Mountains, had fewer

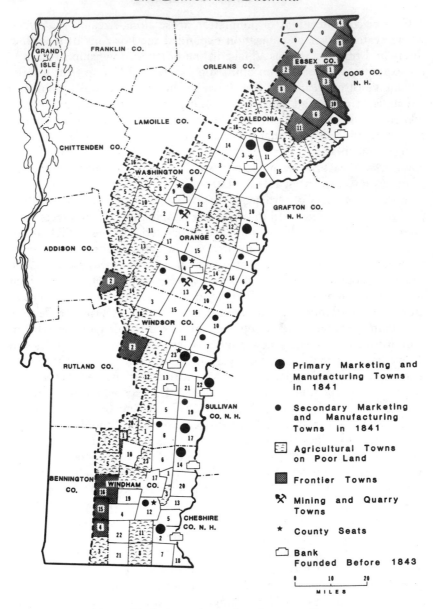

Map 2. Marketing and manufacturing towns, Vermont

Towns in the Connecticut River Valley of Vermont

Addison County
1. Granville
2. Hancock

Bennington County
1. Landgrove
2. Peru
3. Readsboro
4. Searsburg
5. Winhall

Caledonia County
1. Barnet
2. Burke
3. Danville
4. Groton
5. Hardwick
6. Kirby
7. Lyndon
8. Newark
9. Peacham
10. Ryegate
11. St. Johnsbury
12. Sheffield
13. Sutton
14. Walden
15. Waterford
16. Wheelock

Essex County
0. Not settled
1. Bloomfield
2. Brighton
3. Brunswick
4. Canaan
5. Concord
6. Granby
7. Guildhall
8. Lemington
9. Lunenburg
10. Maidstone
11. Victory

Orange County
1. Bradford
2. Braintree
3. Brookfield
4. Chelsea
5. Corinth
6. Fairlee
7. Newbury
8. Orange
9. Randolph
10. Strafford
11. Thetford
12. Topsham
13. Tunbridge
14. Vershire
15. Washington
16. West Fairlee
17. Williamstown

Rutland County
1. Pittsfield
2. Sherburne

Washington County
1. Barre
2. Berlin
3. Cabot
4. Calais
5. Duxbury
6. Fayston
7. Marshfield
8. Middlesex
9. Montpelier
10. Moretown
11. Northfield
12. Plainfield
13. Roxbury
14. Waitsfield
15. Warren
16. Waterbury
17. Woodbury
18. Worcester

Windham County
1. Athens
2. Brattleboro
3. Brookline
4. Dover
5. Dummerston
6. Grafton
7. Guilford
8. Halifax
9. Jamaica
10. Londonderry
11. Marlboro
12. Newfane
13. Putney
14. Rockingham
15. Somerset
16. Stratton
17. Townshend
18. Vernon
19. Wardsboro
20. Westminster
21. Whitingham
22. Wilmington
23. Windham

Windsor County
1. Andover
2. Barnard
3. Bethel
4. Bridgewater
5. Cavendish
6. Chester
7. Hartford
8. Hartland
9. Ludlow
10. Norwich
11. Pomfret
12. Plymouth
13. Reading
14. Rochester
15. Royalton
16. Sharon
17. Springfield
18. Stockbridge
19. Weathersfield
20. Weston
21. West Windsor
22. Windsor
23. Woodstock

people, and they were generally poorer than people who lived closer to the river. They owned small parcels of land, lived in isolated log houses, and carried maple sugar, potash, and cider and drove livestock over rough paths to exchange for goods or cash at river or shire towns. Pockets of poverty also existed in more densely settled areas. A ridge isolated the northwest corner of Peacham, for example, the township just inland from Barnet, and a poor settlement arose there that would be variously known as the Gypsy Camp, Stovepipe Alley, Rouser Town, and Paradise Alley.

There were seven towns in the valley – Brattleboro, Bellows Falls, Windsor, Woodstock, Newbury, Danville, and Montpelier – which, because of their location, their status as shire towns, or the aggressiveness of their community leaders, became the primary centers of the valley's economic and political life (Map 2). The four that lay on the Connecticut River were crossed by major roads to the east and west, and thus situated to take advantage of trade both by land and by water. Windsor, the largest of these towns, with a population of 2,100 in 1800, stood on a terrace between the Connecticut River and Mt. Ascutney, astride a main road to Boston. Almost everyone who traveled to New Hampshire or eastern Massachusetts passed through Windsor and crossed the toll bridge over the Connecticut there. Windsor had also been the state's first capital and since the 1780s had attracted many wealthy people, who made the town the social center of the valley. In 1800 it was a bustling center of artisan, mercantile, and financial activity, with its own newspaper, three bookshops, and the valley's most active presses. It also had three mansions and a church designed by the promising young New England architect, Asher Benjamin.

The three other principal towns – Woodstock, Danville, and Montpelier – lay inland from the Connecticut. Their prosperity, which arrived in earnest only after 1800, derived from trade with their relatively large and productive hinterlands and from their status as shire towns (an honor that came to Montpelier only in 1810 with the creation of Washington County, the last to be formed in the valley). Woodstock, for example, was a large and comparatively wealthy town, with a population of 2,200 in 1800. Its central village lay nine miles west of the Connecticut, on the powerful Ottaquechee River, and in 1794, much to Windsor's distress, it became the shire town of Windsor county because of its central location. Woodstock had many small craft shops, but its wealth, unlike Windsor's, stemmed from trade with the back country, and from publishing, medicine, and the law. The valley's great lawyers, like Charles Marsh and Titus Hutchinson, lived there, and their elegant Federal-style homes made Woodstock the showplace of the valley.

With towns differing so widely in size and sophistication, it was natural that there would be a large degree of variation in local economies. For the most part, however, the level of production and exchange was simple, although not primitive. Most goods were produced in households, where the presiding farmers and craftsmen worked alongside family members and perhaps a hired hand or servant girl. Most labor went to provide food, clothing, and shelter. Men cut timber for fuel and buildings and raised grain and grasses to feed their families and livestock; women tended gardens and dairy animals, prepared and preserved foodstuffs, and produced homespun clothing. Households were not entirely self-sufficient, however. Families had to trade with neighbors to meet their basic needs. They paid most of their debts in labor, sending sons or daughters to work off the price of a horseshoeing or the loan of a span of oxen. Each household produced one or more items for trade with neighbors, which they exchanged for goods, labor, or credit, and thus neighborhoods of only a dozen households produced a surprising range of goods and services. In South Woodstock, for example, Stephen Smith, a pioneer farmer, tanned hides, taught his wife and children to make shoes, and had his eldest son Elias trained as a carpenter. He traded leather goods and his son's labor for help in clearing and fencing his land, for construction of a bark roof for his log cabin, and for flour after his first harvest fell short. Other neighbors contributed to the local economy by building furniture, framing houses, forging tools, loaning breeding stock, or repairing wagons and sleighs.[5]

Because exchange was common, families kept detailed accounts of their debts and credits. Farmers and craftsmen noted the cash value of the goods and services they exchanged with each neighbor and issued promissory notes. Accounts were settled infrequently, often not until neighbors were separated by death or migration. Families seldom had enough cash or commodities on hand to settle debts without calling in credits from other neighbors, and demands for settlement could cause distress and inconvenience. Reciprocity ensured that neighbors were seldom far ahead or behind in the community, but stability depended ultimately on the law. Because a single default could ruin dozens of interdependent households, settlers insisted that debtors meet their obligations. Vermont law refused to forgive bankrupts their debts, and Vermont courts jailed scores of debtors each year on behalf of creditors both rich and poor. The law forbid the imprisonment of propertyless debtors, who were allowed to repay their debts as free laborers; but debtors who owned property worth more than twenty dollars and who could not pay their debts could convey their assets to their creditors and work to repay uncovered debts, or they could go to jail and hope that their families could eventually repay their debts.[6]

Despite the complexity of local exchanges, neighborhoods were not self-sufficient. Families needed to raise money for taxes and to buy what neighbors did not produce – rifles, gunpowder, paper, fine cloth, needles, thread. A farmer or craftsman would also need money to finance the acquisition of land, buildings, or tools and to buy the occasional luxury. Families aimed to produce a marketable surplus (usually wheat, lumber, potash, cloth, yarn, cider, or maple sugar) that they could exchange for cash, credit, or imported goods, but they could seldom trade these goods with neighbors. According to William Gilmore's study of commerce in the valley, roughly one-fifth of all households in the 1780s traded at least once a year with a village merchant. That proportion rose to about one-third by 1800. Most families could not afford to buy or sell goods at store prices. Demand for the valley's products was still weak in southern New England and in the valley's major towns in the 1780s and 1790s, and merchants had their own risks, transportation costs, and profit margins to consider. Most farmers and craftsmen carried their own goods annually to markets on the river or in Boston, Springfield, or Hartford or to their hometowns in southern New England, where friends and relatives could hold goods for timely sale. Lumber moved in the spring, when rivers were high; other goods moved in the winter, when snow made roads passable for heavy sleighs and farmers could spend time away from their farms. The regional trade was a vital source of cash, credit, livestock, and trade goods for the valley's inhabitants, but it yielded its benefits grudgingly.[7]

Most people in Vermont had common goals. They wanted to acquire or improve farms and shops for themselves and their descendants. Many Vermonters were able to exchange small farms and shops in southern New England for undeveloped land or promising commercial sites in the valley. Others had to wait until they had accumulated cash for a downpayment. Then they went to a neighbor or large landowner (there were no banks in the valley prior to 1806) who was willing to sell land or buildings on contract, put down a large downpayment, and paid the balance in installments over five years. Interest rates varied with market conditions, but could not exceed a maximum rate set by the state assembly, which made it a crime for creditors to exploit cash-poor debtors by charging exorbitant rates. It was not difficult to get credit – hundreds of such mortgages were recorded in town land records in the 1790s and early 1800s – or to find land available for purchase, since land speculators on the Vermont frontier, unlike many of their counterparts in New York, preferred to sell their holdings quickly and in fee-simple rather than retain their land and induce new settlers to become tenants.[8] The result was that by 1800 three-fifths or more of the adult male inhabitants of the valley were self-employed farmers, shopkeepers, or mechanics – a rate higher than in southern New England, where crowding was a problem, or in Nova Scotia and the Hudson-Mohawk Valley of New York, where rentier landowners forced settlers to become tenants.

Vermonters set great store by self-employment. That so many southern New Englanders migrated, and consciously avoided moving to landlord-ridden portions of the revolutionary frontier, is indicative of their strong feelings, but they proved their devotion to the ideal of self-employment repeatedly.[9] On several occasions between 1770 and 1775 mobs turned against New York courts that were seeking to evict New Hampshire grantees and to impose quitrents on properly patented land. "Every man's estate, honestly acquired, is his own," declared protestors from Chester in 1774, "and no person on earth has a right to take it away without the proprietor's consent." A county convention in 1775 opposed all foreclosures for debt, concluding that such proceedings were part of a Yorker plot "to bring the lower sort of the people into a state of bondage and slavery" by destroying their economic independence. Vermont's constitutional convention abolished slavery in 1777 to prevent the rise of a labor-degrading, slaveowning aristocracy. In 1786 and 1787, when farmers in western Massachusetts joined Daniel Shays's rebellion after that state's deflationary currency policies forced a rash of farm foreclosures, many Vermonters took up their cause without hesitation, harboring fugitives from the rebellion and staging riots of their own against Vermont courts that foreclosed on farmers.[10]

Not all those who came to Vermont established themselves successfully, of course. Some could never afford to buy property. Samuel and Lucy Scott of Brookfield and Berlin fled southern New England with too many mouths to feed. "They were moving planets," their son Orange wrote in later years. Each season they packed up their scant belongings and moved to another neighborhood in search of better wages. Some people took on too much debt and suffered foreclosure and imprisonment. Some were simply victims of misfortune. Relief Brownson of Stockbridge was reduced to poverty by the death of her husband. She had no choice but to place the two youngest of her six children with a childless couple in Royalton, in hopes that she and the other children could feed themselves once free of the burden of caring for the smallest.[11]

There were also some two hundred and fifty blacks in the valley who remained poor because they were denied credit and shunted into menial jobs in large towns, where they catered to the needs of the wealthy. They were not recognized as equals by other Vermonters. Public records seldom noted their surnames, referring instead to "Susie" or "Edmund, a negro." Although slavery had been abolished in Vermont in 1777, the town of

Windsor argued in court in 1802 that "Dinah," an indigent and blind house servant bought as a slave in 1783 and carried to Vermont by her owner, Stephen Jacob, was still a slave and therefore the responsibility of Jacob, not the overseers of the poor. The town lost its suit, but blacks remained members of a servant caste in white eyes, and most opportunities were closed to them.[12]

The valley's precarious economy at times also threatened those who had gained an economic foothold. It was not insulated from the vicissitudes of New England's economy as a whole. The fortunes of the valley's settlers, especially those just entering the land market, depended heavily on interest rates, currency values, land prices, wages, and commodity prices in southern New England, all of which fluctuated violently between 1775 and 1793 with the American Revolution and the ebb and flow of international trade. The fluctuations ruined some settlers and injured others by inhibiting economic growth in the valley.

The poor and the frustrated were outnumbered, however, by those whose ambitions were fully realized on the Vermont frontier. The Smiths of South Woodstock were typical of families that came to Vermont with very little money and yet prospered in the end. The family barely survived its first years in the valley. Stephen and Irene Smith sold nearly all the family's movable property in 1783 to make the final payment on their hundred-acre farm, only to have the next two harvests fail and the cow die. The family's reputation for being good, frugal, churchgoing folk brought help from neighbors, who extended credit and loaned a cow. That assistance enabled the family to keep the farm, but it was a talent for making maple sugar that brought prosperity. The sugar income enabled them to buy warm winter coats, and eventually to build a frame house and to send eldest son Elias to singing lessons and advanced grammar classes, so that he might become a "public man." The Smiths did not want to be rich. They were content with a middling farm and the promise of a secure future. The bulk of their income was spent on South Woodstock's schools and meetinghouse and on farms and dowries for their children.[13]

For those who came to Vermont with more capital than the Smiths, prosperity was easier to attain. People who could afford large tracts of unimproved land often worked their way to better or larger farms by selling their excess land to newcomers at a profit and by marketing the timber they cleared away as lumber or potash. The valley also provided opportunity for a number of people who wanted much more than economic independence and modest prosperity. Capitalists were present in every town, although Windsor, Woodstock, and Brattleboro had more than their fair share. Foremost among them were the merchants, large landowners, and lawyers who held key positions in the network of economic exchange. Many merchants, especially those in the larger towns, wanted to improve transportation to markets in southern New England and to control that trade. They invested in the toll-road companies chartered by the state legislature in the 1790s and early 1800s, and in the Bellows Falls Canal Company, which in 1802 successfully bypassed the falls at Bellows Falls with nine locks and opened the Connecticut to continuous navigation as far north as McIndoes Falls in Barnet. Along with other wealthy men, they speculated in land, and extended credit to buyers and reaped the interest rewards. Approximately 60 percent of the mortgages in the valley were written by such men.[14]

Naturally, with so many deeds and mortgages changing hands and so many contracts, partnerships, and financial disputes needing supervision, lawyers did well for themselves and were quick to join the ranks of those whose wealth stemmed from financial manipulation rather than physical work. Their increasing numbers reflected a belief, widely held by ambitious young men in southern New England, that Vermont was a good place to make one's fortune. Yet such people were a small minority of the settlers who came to the valley. They were greatly outnumbered by those whose primary ambition was independent proprietorship and the establishment of a robust economy that would provide large, stable markets for their products.

Tension existed between capitalists and the valley's other settlers and was reflected in public hostility toward New York speculators, usurers, and wealthy bankrupts. Settlers feared that covetous elites would exploit the valley and its inhabitants and that they would lose control over politics and the economy, as the people of southern New England and New York had. Despite their divergent interests, however, capitalists and settlers were able to find common ground in the 1780s and 1790s. Both wanted development. To capitalists, it promised wealth, power, and prestige; to other settlers, it promised prosperity, self-employment, and an abundance of reliable, hardworking neighbors with whom they could trade. Although the relationship between capitalists and other settlers was more paternal than cooperative and inspired feelings of deference or condescension more often than fellowship, few settlers chafed under the relationship. As long as people were certain that the profits and undertakings of capitalists posed no threat to rough equality or self-employment and that competition among towns and neighborhoods would not undermine the rough parity that existed among frontier communities in the 1780s, the vast majority of the valley's inhabitants accepted capitalist leadership of the campaign for development.

The people who settled the Connecticut River Valley of Vermont were not solely attracted by the opportunity to better their material circumstances. Many of them aspired to create, or recreate, a particular way of life. When Vermont became independent from New York in 1777, radical democrats and freethinkers who had been frustrated elsewhere in New England by restrictive voting laws and entrenched elites saw an opportunity to establish a truly popular government based upon the principles of natural law. Along with a handful of radical evangelicals, they wanted a chance to separate church and state completely, to rid themselves of the religious establishments that existed everywhere but in Rhode Island. The vast majority of the settlers had had a surfeit of Congregational establishments and unrepresentative institutions and supported the constitution that undid both in 1777, but they did not embrace the social vision or the schemes of the radicals.

Most of these settlers would fall into two groups. There were fervently evangelical Calvinists, who came to the valley with the intent of constructing a web of family, church, and community ties that would establish order in society and fulfill their covenant obligations to God and to each other. The second group would include Christians from all denominations, Calvinist and non-Calvinist alike, who, even if they were not formally attached to any church (although many were) or interested in an intimate Calvinist commonwealth, supported and attended church and believed that religion was important to social order. Led by members of the valley's nascent political and economic elite, this group would seek to establish a political order that would preserve political calm and deference to the leadership of respected, well-to-do Christians and would further the Christian faith, which they felt was vital to securing those ends. In southern New England, these people had been unable to sustain unifying bonds within their families, congregations, and towns and to maintain political order in the face of contentiousness, sectarianism, and the pressures of increasing population.[15] They hoped that the opportunities and even the hardships of the frontier of northern New England would help them to realize their ideals and bring them together again under God's care.

By the late 1770s the majority of all settlers – perhaps two-thirds – were New Light Calvinists. Like other Calvinists, these fervent evangelicals belonged to Congregational, Baptist, or Presbyterian churches, thought it desirable to live in communities that observed their covenant obligations to God, and assented to Calvinist doctrines, particularly those relating to the sovereignty of God, the depravity of man, and the predestination of the elect. They believed that God had chosen certain men and women to receive salvation through the gift of unmerited grace and that, because of humanity's disobedience, all others were destined for eternal damnation.

Unlike other Calvinists, the New Lights interpreted Calvinist doctrines strictly and did their utmost to fulfill the covenant obligations their faith imposed on them. Inspired by the Great Awakening that swept southern New England in the 1730s and 1740s, they were convinced that God saved sinners only through dramatic conversion experiences of the sort that occurred during revivals and insisted that people show visible signs of spiritual rebirth before they could receive holy communion and be full church members. They believed that the Christians of southern New England had impeded the progress of revivals in the 1750s and 1760s by neglecting their covenant obligations and supporting unconverted ministers. Their own ministers were zealous critics of the established churches of Massachusetts and Connecticut and were eager to recast New England's spiritual institutions and communities in the strict evangelical mold.[16]

Of course, these devout Calvinists were not all cut from the same cloth. Only a minority of those who adhered to New Light doctrines were full church members, permitted to receive communion because they were visibly among God's elect; and as they entered the valley they were at odds with each other over the particulars of their beliefs and practices. Most Presbyterian and Congregationalist New Lights were moderates. They had been willing to compromise with so-called Old Lights in southern New England and to accept gradual reform of established churches. They moderated their demands to prevent their campaign for ecclesiastical reform from dividing Christians and transforming churches into exclusive sanctuaries. Indicative of their concern for unity and inclusiveness was their commitment to the Halfway Covenant, an institution that was popular among less rigorous Calvinists. Although not precisely scriptural, the Halfway Covenant brought more people under the watch and care of the church. It allowed not only the unconverted children but the grandchildren of full church members to receive baptism and subjected them to the ameliorative influence of church discipline.

To the strictest Congregationalists the Halfway Covenant was unacceptable, and the moderates' willingness to remain affiliated with corrupt establishments was a shameful thing. They separated from those establishments (thus earning the name Separate Congregationalists), reserved church discipline for full members and infant baptism for their children only, and refused to look (as moderates did) to the faculty of Dartmouth College for guidance in theological matters. Baptists went one step further, baptizing only full members upon their admission to church and refusing the guidance of any college, believing that the Book of Acts called upon each congregation to choose its doctrines through prayer and its ministers on the basis of their piety and preaching, not their learning.

The devout Calvinists of southern New England realized that the struggle between New Hampshire and New York for ownership of Vermont had opened an opportunity for them to shape a commonwealth and to live where they were a majority rather than an endangered minority. They surged into the state in great numbers in the 1770s and early 1780s. Once they had settled there, however, and were free of established religion, they came to recognize that their communal ideals would perish unless they formed a united front. Quietly they put aside their differences, drawing together to support revivalism and religious purity and joining hands in both personal and nonpersonal spheres: in marriage, business, politics, and even in worship.[17] The moderates and Separates of Pomfret, and the Separates and Baptists of Berlin, for example, chose to tolerate one another's baptismal practices and formed united churches.

What enabled these diverse New Light Calvinists to stand together in Vermont was a shared interpretation of the covenant between God and man that was revealed in the Bible. To them, the covenant was an injunction to watch over God's elect. They "labored" to recall people to the church, repeatedly visiting people who had sinned – and not only those guilty of "grosser evils," but those who committed sins that threatened their cherished harmony: gossip, quarreling, breaking promises, and maintaining an "unbecoming hard Sperit" toward others. Calvinists also took more positive steps toward "continewing the Love and unison and fellowship of the Bretherin" by helping one another meet the challenges of the Vermont wilderness, and by insisting that church members act with charity and propriety in the neighborhood economy. The Baptised Brethren of Royalton, a rude frontier town in the 1790s to the north of Woodstock, settled economic grievances and unpaid debts among church members before the church rather than the law. They arranged for a financially solvent member to pay the note of another that was "already in the hand of lawyer Smith to collect." In another case, a member was reproved for selling a note against another member to a creditor who intended to sue for immediate payment. The Baptised Brethren also sought to share the economic burdens of the frontier by establishing their own store to supply cheap goods and credit, by supplementing the meager relief that two indigent widows received from the austere town government, and by levying taxes for the support of worship on the basis of a detailed assessment of each church member's property. That assessment included debts, credits, and even produce on hand.[18]

These Congregationalists, Presbyterians, and Baptists were not trying to shut out the rest of the world. The covenant demanded that they extend their saving and regenerating influence beyond their own churches. In the primitive north-woods town of Berlin, the Church of Christ enjoined its members to spread the word: Heads of families had to promise to read scripture daily to their households and to forbid "dancing, gaming, carousing, or excessive drinking." Members were instructed to use their influence "in the society where we dwell" to "relieve all proper objects of charity," to "bear testimony against every corrupt doctrine and all vicious practices," and to "seek the peace and welfare of this church, and not of this church only, but of the whole Israel of God."[19]

The New Lights were not alone on the frontier, however, and that complicated their efforts to shape the valley according to their ideals. Their principal antagonists were Old Light Calvinists, who urged their rival interpretation of Calvinism upon the early settlers. These Calvinists also wanted to live by the covenant and spread righteousness through society. Yet they understood their faith and their social mission differently.

The Old Lights, so called by contemporaries because they adhered to the calm (and they believed more reasonable) faith that prevailed in New England before the Awakening spread its "new" spiritual light among Christians, also detested spiritual laxity. But they feared that the New Lights' interpretation of conversion and their close supervision of their membership would undermine Christian brotherhood and transform church members into spiritual elitists. They did not demand elaborate proof that prospective members had experienced spiritual rebirth and favored gradual conversions, as likely to be more lasting, over sudden ones. They extended church membership and communion to more people and tolerated minor theological differences among their members. Old Lights were not indifferent to the need for sound doctrine and spiritual zeal, but they gave the community's need for stability, order, and unity a higher place in their hierarchy of values. When the New Lights attacked corruption in the establishment, the Old Lights accused them of wanting to tear down the proper authority of ministers and governments. Charles Phelps, an Old Light from Marlboro, claimed that prominent Separates in neighboring towns believed it "blasphemy against the g-d given law for anybody or bodies of men to make any laws and sinful to obey such laws when made" and blamed them for "creating and keeping up" factions in New England. Old Lights insisted on strict obedience to public officials and established clergymen on matters of colonial and church government. In Massachusetts and Connecticut, where they spoke for the majority, they used the established Presbyterian and Congregational churches to levy sanctions against the New Lights, their ministers, and the revival meetings they held to foster conversions among prospective members. They intended to restore the Christian harmony the New Lights had disrupted.[20]

Old Lights came to the valley in particularly large numbers in the 1760s and early 1770s, when it had not yet become apparent that Vermont extended special promise to dissenters. They planned to erect a Congregational establishment in the valley with the help of the strong church-state laws of New Hampshire or New York. They were soon a majority of the inhabitants of the southernmost county in the valley, Windham, and endeavored with some success to impose their Calvinistic views on its churches and communities.

The Old Lights could not form an effective alliance against the New Lights, however. Once Vermont broke from New York and New Hampshire in 1777 and declared the church–state laws of those states in abeyance, the Old Lights were left without the legal and financial privileges they had expected to enjoy as the founders of Vermont's establishment. Their tolerance made their churches the spiritual home of many who found the New Lights particularly objectionable or had strayed from Calvinism but as yet had no desire to quit the Congregational and Presbyterian churches of their ancestors. Some, who found Calvinism's spiritual elitism distasteful, embraced universalism and claimed Christ's death had purchased salvation for everyone. Some turned to Arminianism and claimed that God's saving grace was given not to a predetermined elect but to all who took Christ as their personal savior. Others, who felt that Calvinism took too dim a view of human nature, became religious liberals, for whom grace played a smaller role than human effort in salvation. They saw God as a benevolent father who gave humanity all the spiritual aid necessary to its moral improvement, rather than as a wrathful God eager to scourge depraved mankind.[21]

A small minority of these dissidents quit the Calvinists entirely and joined the valley's small bands of Universalists, Freewill Baptists, Anglicans, and deists, but most remained nominal Old Lights. They attended services dutifully and did nothing to defy or demean the church, but they seldom partook of communion or became full church members. Nor were they enthusiastic about living by the covenant, even if it was only the Old Lights' version. Their lack of ardor did not concern the Old Lights much; by the late 1770s and early 1780s they accepted whatever support they could get. But the New Lights were sorely grieved by it, because they could not realize their communal ideals or foster a spirit of mutual love and concern without the support of the great majority of Christians.

Thus the New Lights did not monopolize the frontier, and their attempts to do so only met with greater resistance in the mid-1780s, as migration to the valley from Old Light areas in southern New England increased and threatened their majority. They confronted opposition almost every time they sought to organize a church or call a minister, for like other settlers they were as yet too poor to support the gospel without the financial help of settlers who did not share their religious views. They had to settle for itinerant preaching at town meetinghouses, where towns allowed their ministers to occupy the pulpit on a majority of Sundays, but not every Sunday, thereby guaranteeing that minority views would be heard.[22] That did not dishearten the New Lights, however. They fought hard for their beliefs, and at times they found common ground with their adversaries, especially on the issues of church discipline and supervision of public morals. Moderate New Lights proved especially successful at drawing Calvinist Old Lights into union churches and then winning them over to New Light doctrines, as they did in Woodstock. They also kept some predestinarian Universalists and Freewill Baptists loyal to their communal vision, if not to their theology.

New Light Calvinists controlled most town meetinghouses and most of the thirty-six churches that had been formed in the valley by 1791 (only one was non-Calvinist) and organized most of the forty-eight additional Congregationalist, Presbyterian, and Baptist churches formed between 1791 and 1800.[23] They added full members steadily to their churches, although the great majority of their adherents remained nonmembers; and they remained hopeful that the religious freedom that had appeared in the valley as a result of the dispute between New York and New Hampshire would allow them to realize their covenant ideals by freeing them from the persecution that had impeded their evangelical efforts in southern New England. Still, they were not pleased by the valley's spiritual diversity. They blamed the existence of so many sects on the evils of southern New England's establishment, which they believed had driven many Christians away from the pure faith through its poor example and persecution of dissenters. They believed that God had meant the valley for them, and they intended to unify it in His name.

At the same time that the New Lights and their allies were pursuing their ideal of a covenanted community, they were also aligning themselves with a broader group of Christians from a wide range of denominations. This group was trying to erect a political order that would stand strong in defense of Christianity, morality, and harmony in the valley. The Reverend Gershom Lyman, an Old Light minister from Marlboro, expressed their aspirations in an election sermon he delivered before the Vermont state legislature in 1782. He prayed that legislators might see their way clear to passing laws that would suppress "vice and immorality" and promote "the interest of religion," while encouraging "quiet and peaceable" obedience to ministers and public officials.[24] The words were less emotional and the aspirations less intimate than those in Calvinist church covenants, but they testified nonetheless to a commitment that Calvinists shared with many non-Calvinists and with many who attended church regularly but did not formally belong in full membership to a church: a commitment to a standing order, to a government that would supervise public morals, require regular worship in each community, and demand that citizens respect both civil and ecclesiastical authority.

The extent to which the mass of settlers shared that commitment is unclear. A small minority of zealous evangelicals and political insurgents rejected it outright. Some of these people were followers of freethinkers Ethan Allen and Thomas Paine or of millenarian visionaries like Reuben Jones of Rockingham and Abijah Lovejoy of Westminster; others were victims of religious or political persecution under the orders of southern New England and New York.[25] All possessed a radical faith in the powers of God or nature to orchestrate human activity in service of the common good. They believed that strong government generally disturbed the natural or providential order of society and felt that the government that governed least would best serve piety, morality, and deference to authority.

The Reverend Lyman's call for a standing order was nevertheless echoed around the state by other settled ministers, by legislators, by Governor Thomas Chittenden, and by prominent men from all walks of life. Regardless of their religious affiliations, they all shared Governor Chittenden's belief, expressed in his Thanksgiving Day address in 1794, that both "reason and revelation" taught the necessity of strong government and state-supported churches, which would uphold order and restrain the passions and the selfishness that lay in the human heart. They all spoke out in favor of a standing order, calling for government action to preserve religion, morality, and order on the Vermont frontier.[26]

The standing orders of southern New England, which had taken years to develop, were complex blends of laws, institutions, customs, and attitudes that stood in defense of Christianity, right conduct, public leadership by propertied Christians, and, above all, order in politics and society. The standing orders of Massachusetts, Connecticut, and New Hampshire rested upon a foundation of, first, an established Congregational church supported by religious taxes imposed on all adult taxpayers, church members and nonmembers alike (the laws had been altered, however, to exempt certified members of dissenting churches); second, laws against every act conceivably proscribed by the Ten Commandments; third, property requirements for voting and officeholding; and fourth, a fairly strong tradition of deference by voters to the judgment of their betters, both in the colonies and in Great Britain.[27]

A minority of all ministers, public officials, and well-to-do citizens, primarily Old Lights and Anglicans, hoped to carry the orders of southern New England to the frontier with little revision. As seasoned opponents of the Great Awakening, they resented popular insurgency. Even the Arminians and liberals among them demanded an order that would restrain the activities of religious and political dissidents and that could command deference to settled ministers and to Christian men of property and education. Despite their faith in human ability, they recognized that men and women were liable to cast off the guidance of grace and reason, as they had during the Awakening. Most of these settlers supported the American Revolution, convinced that Great Britain, through its tyranny and corruption, had become a threat to law, order, and piety; and some favored Vermont's independence from New York and New Hampshire on similar grounds, believing that those states, under the control of high-handed placemen and speculators, saw the valley only as a source of profit and did not care whether their rivalry jeopardized the land titles of settlers or instigated land wars. Yet those Old Lights and Anglicans who supported America's and even Vermont's revolution feared that insurgency would stir popular passions and remained at best moderate revolutionaries. At a county convention in 1774 a group of Old Lights passed a resolution claiming that true patriots followed "a uniform, manly, steady, and determined mode of procedure" and denouncing "all riotous, tumultuous, and unnecessary mobs" that injured "the persons or properties of harmless individuals." Such rioters were "loathesome animals not fit to be touched or to have any society." Like John Adams and other American adherents of radical Whig traditions, these Old Lights wanted to wrest power from monarchs and aristocrats, whom they considered inherently corrupt; but they wished to minimize change and disruption at home and sought a republican standing order that would keep power in responsible hands.[28]

Among the proponents of a standing order, these people were greatly outnumbered by the New Lights, who felt that most features of southern New England's orders were undesirable, or at least in need of modification. Their belief in human depravity made them advocates of strong government, but having been persecuted during the Great Awakening, they knew that governments could use their powers to oppress Christians. Peter Powers, a New Light minister from Newbury, wrote a pamphlet in which he made it clear that the New Lights considered the persecution they had suffered in southern New England to be of a piece with New

York's effort to seize control of Vermont and with British atrocities like the Boston Massacre, the Intolerable Acts, and the Toleration Act for Catholics in Quebec. All were parts of a broad conspiracy against "the Holy Covenant," a conspiracy sponsored by "wicked persons" who could not endure "the strictness and severity of the divine rules that were given them." The minister observed that the Tory "miscreants" who had sought "Offices of Profit, Places and Pensions, to gratify their Pride and Avarice," relied on a restricted franchise, weak legislatures, appointed judges, and corrupt religious establishments to keep themselves in power in New York and southern New England.[29]

Almost to a man, the New Lights threw themselves into the struggle against the despotic rule of Britain and New York. Their ministers, like David Avery of Windsor, served as chaplains of the revolutionary army, and their laymen filled virtually the entire ranks of every mob and every Green Mountain Boys regiment that arose in the valley and served with an eagerness that frightened the few moderate allies they had. They saw their revolution as an opportunity to establish the reformed order they had long sought in New England and fought to realize an evangelical republican vision so radical, so dedicated to rooting out every impediment to religious liberty and popular rule, that it threatened to crush every moderate hope of bringing a standing order to the valley. Their closest ally in revolution was the Arlington Junto, a heterogeneous group of radicals from western Vermont that included Thomas Chittenden, Separate leader Moses Robinson, and Ethan Allen's orthodox and acquisitive brother, Ira. The Junto worked with the New Lights to eliminate from Vermont's government every instrument of the existing standing orders that threatened, according to an anonymous New Light tract published in the valley in 1776, to "set up the avaricious over the head of the poor, though the latter are ever so virtuous."[30]

The New Lights, who dominated Vermont's constitutional convention, drew upon Pennsylvania's enlightened constitution of 1776 and the Dartmouth faculty's New Light manifesto, "The People the Best Governors," to create the most democratic constitution of the Revolution. The Windsor convention of 1777 suspended property requirements for voting and officeholding, abolished slavery and the imprisonment of debtors who had surrendered all assets to creditors, vested power in a unicameral legislature subject to only a supervisory veto by the governor and council, subjected all judges to annual election or legislative recall, granted access to all government meetings and records, gave towns control over land transactions and power to instruct assemblymen, and allowed citizens complete liberty of conscience in religion and politics, with the right to worship as they pleased.

The constitution shocked many Old Lights and Anglicans, who were afraid that it ended all hope for strong government. The New Lights, inspired by the Revolution and frustrated by governments that had limited their liberty, were no longer so apprehensive about the people or mistrustful of the effects of freedom. Aaron Hutchinson, a New Light minister from Pomfret who gave the election sermon of 1777, was so intent on criticizing the powerful that he lost all critical perspective on the middling and poor, who he believed would create a near-perfect commonwealth in Vermont by following a "well-tempered self love" in politics. That ran counter to the Calvinists' belief in human depravity and in restraint of the human will. Nathaniel Niles, a New Light minister from Connecticut who would serve in the Vermont assembly, claimed that freedom would reduce disorder, by ridding men of the "dumb, sullen, morose melancholy" spirit that prevailed under tyranny. It would transform them into "calm, resolute, and stable" citizens who sought in every action "the collective happiness" of the community.[31]

Yet most of the leading New Lights were not perfectionists. Even during the headiest days of the revolution, they did not jettison their distrust of man, nor did they, in the words of Baptist elder Caleb Blood, "countenance those who through fear of religious tyranny despise good order in society." They desired laws that actively promoted morality, order, faith, and respect for wealth and office. The Arlington Junto's decision to pursue statehood rather than seek an independent republic or continue revolutionizing the frontier by trying to annex western New Hampshire and northeastern New York was meant to help ensure that Vermont would emerge from the chaotic conditions that prevailed on the revolutionary frontier a stable, Christian society.[32]

The New Lights were joined by Old Lights and Anglican moderates in the assembly in the effort to secure Vermont's revolution and to strengthen its government, as far as was consistent with democratic principles. In 1779, the legislature took its first step toward a standing order and passed a comprehensive code of laws for the preservation of public morals. Based on the Connecticut Law Book of 1769, the code proscribed immoral conduct ranging from levity, lying, intemperance, and fornication, to Sabbath travel and blasphemy. The legislature acted to assure settlers that they could maintain order and avoid God's wrath by imposing the letter of God's law on citizens who had not "the fear of God before their eyes."[33]

In 1783, the legislature passed a complementary act that provided state support for public worship, "that the Precepts of Christianity and the rules of Morality [might] be publickly and statedly inculcated on the minds of the Inhabitants." The act represented an honest attempt to accommodate religious diversity and protect the rights of dissenters while retaining support for a general Protestant establishment. It empowered towns to tax their inhabitants to erect meetinghouses and hire ministers favored by a two-thirds majority of the townspeople. It absolved from church taxes those people "of differing sentiments in religious duties, which lead moral and peaceable lives," provided they filed certificates from their churches testifying that they were of a "different persuasion." Although the act did not seek to control honest dissenters or to "dictate the conscience of a single individual," it did seek to control those "who pretend to differ from the Majority with a design only to escape Taxation." Slackers who could not obtain certificates had to support the majority church. The intent of the act was furthered in a number of areas by people who formed "Catholick" religious societies to support public worship for all denominations where the inhabitants were of many sects but of one mind in supporting religion and morality.[34]

Settlement and election laws also served to maintain political and social order in the valley. As in southern New England, towns reserved the right to warn strangers out of town, and in fact town overseers did warn almost every newcomer who seemed likely to stay more than a few weeks. The purpose was to show outsiders that they could not gain residency merely by staying in town: They had to win approval at a freemen's meeting before they could become citizens, qualify for poor relief, vote, or stand for office. Those who bought property were accepted quickly, but those liable to become public charges were held at arm's length and as a consequence were disfranchised.

The end of property requirements did not make voting free. All male residents between the ages of twenty-one and sixty had to pay an annual poll tax of $10 – the equivalent of a month's wages for a farm laborer – or perform alternative service in the militia, which required militiamen to equip themselves with their own guns and ammunition. Virtually everyone met these requirements, but they were hard on the poor, who had an incentive to avoid tax collectors and move along to the next town. The constitution also prescribed a religious test for officeholders that excluded Jews, Roman Catholics, and deists, because they had not embraced "the protestant religion." The freethinking Ethan Allen was forced to entrust his legislative schemes to his brother Ira and to associates like Thomas Chittenden who could take the oath in good conscience. The officeholders' oath raised problems for Universalists as well, because they did not all believe that God was the "rewarder of good and the punisher of the wicked" in the afterlife. The legislature thus circumscribed the political power of worrisome social elements without enacting definite property requirements or imposing religious tests on voters (as opposed to candidates).[35]

In 1782 the assembly passed one more law that helped bring order to the revolutionary frontier: an act to provide district schools in every township. Of course, people supported common schools primarily to ensure that their sons and daughters would learn to read, write, and calculate with sufficient skill to ensure their economic independence and the success of family enterprises. Yet they also wanted to mold children into responsible citizens and to ensure that they received a basic knowledge of the Bible, morality, and republican institutions. The Reverend Gershom Lyman, who addressed the first meeting of the legislative session that established Vermont's educational system, expressed the beliefs of the majority of Vermonters when he referred to ignorance as "a natural source of error, self-conceit, and contracted, grovelling sentiments," both in religion and politics. Ignorance made people "difficult" to rule and ever ready to "find fault with public men and measures, and thwart them in all their power." Education promised to create an electorate that would choose its representatives wisely and then defer readily to the judgment of those they had placed in power over them. Whether it would fulfill that promise remained to be seen; however, the common schools did flourish, and by the turn of the century, the valley had one of the highest literacy rates in the world – approximately 95 percent for men and 85 percent for women.[36]

Few people were certain that a standing order would survive in Vermont. The order that had been so cautiously constructed by the legislature rested on faith more than law – faith that its adherents could preserve morality, unity, and respect for wealth and office in a society formally dedicated to spiritual freedom and popular government. Yet by the mid-1780s there was hope that the harmony and order it sought to foster would prevail. It was not until 1794 that the legislature was asked by petitioners to repeal the certificate system. That does not mean that the system had been universally approved until that time. Non-Calvinists may have remained silent because they did not feel as jeopardized by Vermont's standing order as they had by the orders of southern New England or because they were too few and powerless to entertain hopes of redress. For their part, Calvinists were often unable to agree upon compromise candidates for town ministries (thereby leaving a number of seats vacant for years) or to abide the candidates they did hire. Most towns could not even afford settled ministers before 1791 and had to rely instead on itinerants, part-time ministers, and lay readers for services. And fears persisted among non-Calvinists and Baptists that the valley's

Congregational majority would use the church–state laws to erect a de facto Congregational establishment and to deprive others of their share of pews and Sunday sermons. Nevertheless, by 1800 most towns were conducting regular services, and many Christians willingly put aside their differences in an effort to make Vermont's system work.[37]

The signs in politics were less hopeful. Political strife persisted long after the Yorkers' final rebellion was crushed, because Vermonters still hoped to realize diverse ideals and ambitions through Vermont's standing order. Rival factions of leading citizens vied for power. The Arlington Junto of western Vermont pretended to leadership on the basis of their relationship with Ethan Allen (whom they championed on the basis of his record as a soldier, not a philosopher), their war experience, and their landed wealth. Members of the Junto also claimed that their interests and those of Vermont's farmers and mechanics were identical, primarily because they traded in land and because one of their number, Matthew Lyon, was involved in nail and paper manufacturing.[38]

Although a member of the Junto – Thomas Chittenden – held the governorship almost every year between 1777 and 1797, the group gradually lost support in the assembly, and most especially in the valley. The valley's New Light and Old Light leaders questioned the sincerity of the Junto's professed commitment to Christianity and state-supported religion, the Old Lights because of the Junto's association with Ethan Allen, and the New Lights because of the latitudinarianism of Chittenden and his inner circle. Nor did they fail to observe that while speaking in defense of New England and the common man, the Junto had consorted with British agents in Canada (offering neutrality in the American Revolution in return for open trade) and had speculated in land with an abandon that suggested the free soil of Vermont was nothing more than a commodity to them.

Chittenden and the Junto were turned out of office temporarily in 1789 and 1790, when New and Old Light opponents in the assembly produced evidence of their high-handed offer to betray the American Revolution to the British and revealed that Chittenden had granted an entire township to his political crony, Ira Allen, without legislative approval. Yet the Junto remained powerful, because the opposition was divided. Most Old Lights looked for leadership to Isaac Tichenor and Nathaniel Chipman, college-educated lawyers who lived in western Vermont. Like many Old Lights, they were cultivated men who believed firmly in their superiority and their right to rule. With some justice, Ira Allen called them leaders of a pack of "state politicians" who had come to Vermont only to profit politically from its separation from New York. Chipman had moved to Vermont because he believed he would be, as a lawyer, "rara avis in terra" and thought it would be easy to get elected to some political office. ("Ha ha ha!" he wrote a friend, "I cannot but laugh when I think what a flash we shall make, when we become members of Congress.") But Tichenor, Chipman, and their predominantly Old Light adherents did have a higher mission. It was to bring Vermont's revolution against New York to a quiet end by leading the crusade for statehood and by restoring men of property, breeding, and knowledge to office.[39]

Tichenor, Chipman, and their supporters won the gratitude of the federal government, which lavished federal patronage upon them when statehood was finally granted, but they remained suspect, not only in the eyes of Junto supporters, but in the eyes of many New Lights, who called the Princeton-educated Tichenor "Jersey Slick." Tichenor and Chipman were not wholly unpopular among New Lights, who rightly saw in them firm advocates of a strong standing order in Vermont. Both men occasionally drew the ire of New Lights down upon them, however, as in 1785, when they and their followers in the assembly insisted that Tories receive compensation for improvements on all property seized from them during the Revolution, and in 1786–7, when the drastic postrevolutionary deflation that had provoked Shays's Rebellion in Massachusetts spread to Vermont, and forced a number of farmers into bankruptcy. Virtually every leading citizen and minister denounced the mob, composed primarily of New Light farmers, that turned out in Hartland in 1786 to prevent court-mandated foreclosures. The militia, under Governor Chittenden's orders, quickly suppressed the uprising; but many New Lights, together with Governor Chittenden, blamed the Tichenor-Chipman faction for the trouble, because it had opposed relief for the hard-pressed. The controversy quickly died down with the demise of Shays's Rebellion. A referendum in 1787 on currency reform and debtor relief drew only 2,400 voters to the polls. Still, the potential for insurgency remained.[40]

By the early 1790s, however, the valley's leading citizens had reason to hope that political harmony would prevail. The revival of New England's economy after 1789 stabilized prices and markets in Vermont, and lessened interest in divisive economic issues. No one questioned the assembly's willingness to entrust the valley's economic future to its wealthiest citizens, who received generous charters for toll roads and townships, so that they might improve transportation and hasten settlement of Vermont's northern lands. The town-building mania of the 1790s conferred such prestige on these men that few settlers doubted that the valley's capitalists sought charters for public rather than private ends. The granting of statehood eliminated another divisive issue from politics. The leaders of Vermont's stalemated factions were persuaded to set aside their differences and do their utmost to preserve political tranquility, which they believed was characterized by low voter turnout, largely un-contested elections, and deference to their collective leadership.

They achieved that end by 1791. Political activity was then nearly nonexistent, and support for the state's incumbent leaders was so wide-spread that voter turnout reached a new low. The Windsor *Vermont Journal* observed that in one town of 300 voters only nineteen men turned out to elect a delegate to the state's constitutional convention. The state's leaders recognized that such calm would not continue unless they worked to preserve it. They knew that their order rested not so much on law or on the strength of churches or schools, as on their own willingness to settle differences among themselves before they became political issues and on the willingness of Vermonters, in the words of the election sermon of 1797, to "remove any prejudice against the order, on account of dissentions, uncharitableness, or want of union among ourselves."[41]

For a time it seemed that the valley's settlers might succeed in bringing a covenanted community and a standing order into being. With the climax of the town-building campaign, the closing of the frontier, the stabili-zation of the valley's economy, the expulsion of many Tories and Yorkers, the end of hostilities between Vermont and its neighboring states, and the first tentative moves toward rapprochement between New and Old Lights, many of the sources of conflict had been eliminated. It appeared that the tensions between the settlers' desire for toleration, equality, and popular government, and their desire for order, morality, and political harmony, would be resolved through voluntarily supported Calvinist churches and strong government. Those institutions seemed powerful enough to maintain in equipoise the principles of freedom and unity that were so dear to Vermont's founders. Those desiderata, thus juxtaposed, became the state motto and in 1779 were engraved on the state seal.

Most settlers still believed that they could attain that condition of "perfect liberty" envisioned by the Reverend Nathaniel Niles, in which individuals were "all of one mind" in important matters, each willing to move "in his proper sphere" and to "unite in the same grand pursuit, the highest good of all."[42] Vermont would never achieve that felicitous state, however. The communal ideal shared by Calvinists and the political ideal of the standing order quickly lost their tentative hold on the settlers. The adherents of the covenanted community and the standing order were compelled by divisive ideas and social changes to retreat in the battle against sin and schism and in the struggle to create religiously harmonious and politically uniform communities.

2

The failure of the covenanted community and the standing order, 1791–1815

In the years following statehood, settlers who wanted to reconcile their conflicting ambitions through the ideals and institutions of the covenanted community and the standing order met with nothing but frustration. Defenders of the covenanted community confronted an influx of settlers from southern New England who were less committed to the ideals of evangelical Calvinism than settlers in the past. They also had to deal with the effects of the Revolution's liberating ideas and the dangers presented by plentiful economic opportunities, which made the valley's residents unwilling to abide by the sanctions and strictures of the covenant. Calvinists could no longer discipline those who were not church members, and even church members rebelled against the watch and care of the church. Young people presented a serious problem, as did the trend toward sectarianism.

Maintaining the standing order proved equally difficult. Even the relatively mild legal and institutional supports that had been erected in its defense came under attack, and the unity, tolerance, calm, and deference that was vital to its success began to evaporate. Political leaders faced growing opposition within the valley. They fell to bickering among themselves, and joined in a party struggle that destroyed their hopes of harmony. By 1815 both the covenanted community and the standing order were in ruins. Friend and foe alike were left to wonder what ideals and institutions could replace them.

Ungovernable townspeople and church members

In 1779, the assembly of the newly formed Republic of Vermont had heartened the defenders of the covenanted ideal and the standing order by passing a body of laws for the preservation of public morals. Justice and state court records show, however, that morals laws were not enforced in most towns during or after the Revolution. There were exceptions. In a few small farming communities with strong New Light churches, like Pomfret, just north of Woodstock, morals laws were strictly enforced into the 1780s and 1790s. Swearing, drunkenness, and neglect of the Sabbath were the common crimes. The offenders were most often youths who misbehaved on Sundays: children who giggled in church, boys caught "going from home a Strawberrying" on a sunny Sunday in June, or two young men and four young women surprised at a secret party. Most remanded themselves to the court or were turned in by a relative and willingly confessed their crimes before Justices John Throop and John W. Dana, who were deacons in the Congregational church and were also the wealthiest men in town.[1]

Sabbath laws were also taken seriously in Barnet and Ryegate, which were settled not by New Englanders but by Presbyterian dissenters from Scotland. They adhered proudly to their covenanting traditions and prosecuted offenders well into the nineteenth century. These towns were atypical, however. Because of the peculiar zeal and religious solidarity of their inhabitants, they resembled longer-settled towns in Massachusetts and southwestern New Hampshire, where morals prosecutions persisted into the nineteenth century not so much because of the voluntary efforts of citizens and magistrates, but because of the pressures that well-established Congregational churches and local elites could bring to bear on sinners.[2]

Most towns in the valley witnessed few, if any, prosecutions after the Revolution. There was no intent on the part of the community to eradicate sin through the law or to impose standards on individuals who did not abide by them willingly.[3] Cases were brought to court only when moral transgressions led to concrete acts that harmed society. Immorality in itself was not sufficient grounds for indictment. For example, adultery was nearly the sole justification for divorce, and most divorced spouses had to prove a partner's infidelity. Yet there is no evidence that the courts ever convicted anyone of adultery or fornication. In the sole case in which an indictment was handed down, in Ryegate in 1805, the prosecution dropped charges as soon as the offending pair admitted their guilt and allowed the aggrieved wife to obtain her divorce.[4]

Generally, the courts concerned themselves only with the social problems caused by adultery, abandonment, and nonsupport. For that reason only male heads of households were formally charged with intemperance, because their drinking threatened to make their families public charges. Thomas Prentice, a justice of the peace in Weathersfield, accused one man in 1804 of "spending his time in Idleness Mismanagement and Intoxication." Yet Prentice asked not for a conviction for immoral conduct, but for the appointment of a guardian over the tippler's estate, to prevent him from "rapidly dispensing with his property to his own disadvantage and the disadvantage of his family." Occasionally towns assisted women in bringing paternity suits to court, not to discover the sinner, but to relieve the town of child-support costs. One unwed mother in Springfield was exempted from all costs in prosecution, in hopes that the town could recoup its expenses by getting the father to pay all legal fees and child support. Neither party was indicted for fornication.[5]

In 1806, the Council of Censors, empowered by the state constitution to study Vermont's laws, decried the state's failure to enforce laws against profane swearing, gaming, Sabbath breaking, and intemperance. The council, which included both Calvinists and non-Calvinists, declared the enforcement of these laws "necessary toward ensuring and continuing" divine blessings, and vital to the "concerns of the commonwealth."[6] Yet legal authorities and the voters who elected them remained reluctant to equate legal and moral matters. Nearly all Vermonters demanded that authorities defend innocent families and children – and tax revenues as well – from the consequences of sin. Apart from those Calvinists who adhered strictly to covenant theology, few wanted to prosecute immorality itself.

Why these kinds of prosecutions ceased in most towns in the valley is unclear. Although they declined after the 1780s, they persisted in southern New England. One evangelical supporter of morals prosecutions claimed that settlers in the valley "were immoral and irreligious, almost to a man" and that they preferred "hunting, fishing, and visiting" to Sunday worship; but such charges were unfair to the great majority of frontier people.[7] Most disapproved of sin and its effect on the sinner and feared its potential for creating social disorder. They could have invented practical, noncovenant reasons for continuing prosecutions, as did the non-Calvinist churchmen on the Council of Censors in 1806 who supported the Calvinist majority. But they did not.

No record of their rationale has survived. They may not have wanted to declare openly their intention to tolerate all misbehavior that did not harm the persons or property of others for fear of encouraging sin or because they did not want to forfeit the option of prosecution in certain cases. Such concerns were probably prevalent in Cabot, where for several years the town's elected tithingmen arrested and fined all swearers, revelers, and Sunday tourists and sportsmen, in order to make the town's point, and then at freemen's meetings remitted the fines of the guilty, thus embarrassing but not "coercing" sinners. It is possible that Vermonters may have feared that someday their freedom as dissenters could be circumscribed if a single sect or political faction were to capture the legal apparatus and harass others into an acceptance of the dictates of their particular faith. Such persecution had appeared sporadically during the Revolution. Those opposed to prosecutions may also have believed that they would have provoked nonreligious people, jealous of their newly won rights, to political and social insurgency.[8]

Those Calvinists who took seriously their duty to abide by their covenant with God had some success in disciplining sinners within their churches, a covenant obligation of importance both to New and Old Lights. Even there, however, difficulties arose. In cases concerning gossip, slander, or business disputes, the accused challenged with increasing frequency their fellow members' right to inquire into their actions. After all, who was to say whether the accused or the aggrieved was the wronged party? Was the person preferring charges helping a fallen Christian regain the holy path or jealously persecuting a rival?

Despite the difficulties inherent in prosecuting such cases, church members did not shirk them. Cases involving personal disputes were three times more frequent in Congregational and Baptist churches during the 1790s and early 1800s than were straightforward cases involving the breaking of the Sabbath, intoxication, or other falls from rectitude (Table 2.1). Unfortunately, these cases began to cause even more problems for Calvinist congregations in Vermont than they had in southern New England, where their disruptive potential had been acknowledged for more than a century. Church members under investigation increasingly rebelled against the questioning of fellow members. Helen Dole of the Congregational Church of St. Johnsbury complained in 1820 that, despite her honest recounting of a dispute, church members continued to pursue her "as a pack of hounds pursue the innocent hare." She refused to have anything more to do with the church. Cyrus Taft of Royalton withdrew from the Baptised Brethren in 1795, complaining of the way that church dealt with personal disputes. Taft noted that the church continued to prosecute two women who had resolved their differences to their mutual satisfaction two years earlier. The majority of church members refused to believe that neither of them had intended to injure the other. Charges led to bitter countercharges, until the hostilities engendered by the case overshadowed those involved in the case itself. Taft could only shake his head at the church's lack of "Charety," and say that "the Conduct of the Church has bin Straing indead upon it."[9]

The complaints of Taft and Dole were typical. Dissatisfaction with disciplinary proceedings and with meddling church members was intense in this period. One-fourth of all disciplinary cases in Calvinist churches prior to 1811 concerned disputes over disciplinary proceedings (Table 2.1). Disgruntled members resigned and on occasion published small tracts to tell their side of the story. Certain churches, having failed to convince the accused to accept their findings in grave cases concerning economic deceit, rumors of carnal relations between a church member and a black servant

Table 2.1. Disciplinary Cases
in Congregational and Baptist Churches in Selected Towns
in Caledonia and Windsor Counties, 1790-1859[a]

	1790-1810	1811-29	1830-44	1845-59
Cases concerning interpersonal and personal sin				
Interpersonal sin (gossip, slander, interpersonal conflict, economic disputes)	74	50	28	60
Personal sin (intemperance, Sabbath breaking, profanity, levity)	26	50	72	40
N =	50	82	82	20
Cases concerning neglect of church and discontent with discipline				
Neglect of church	12	10	34	61
Discontent with discipline	26	9	6	8
All other sins	62	81	60	32
N =	81	101	137	64

[a] The records of the following Congregational churches were studied: Barnet, 1829-59; Peacham, 1794-1859; St. Johnsbury Center, 1809-59; East St. Johnsbury, 1840-59; Weathersfield, 1801-59; West Windsor, 1790-1824; and Windsor, 1790-1859. The records of the following Baptist churches were also studied: Danville, 1792-1841; Royalton, 1791-1806; Weathersfield, 1835-59; and Windsor, 1835-59.

girl, accusations that a pastor had lied, and complaints over the size of assessments for support of worship and indigent members, ended by splitting or even disbanding entirely, with the congregation scattering to other churches and the minister left to look for a new position.[10]

That church members would go to such extremes did not mean that there was a new persecuting spirit within congregations. Church members readily forgave most people who confessed their crimes before the congregation, and they entreated sinners repeatedly to return to the path of righteousness. They were not perfectionists. Sin was human; it plagued even the elect. The Baptists of North Danville tried for three years to reclaim a member guilty of a sin as indisputable as drunkenness. They asked the sinner to "consider the wound" his sin had given their hearts and wrote to him "in the bowels of love" to persuade him to repent. "We do not want to cruch you but we want to help you up." Their letter was not a stiff, formulaic accusation, but an entreaty that revealed how sin truly hurt the congregation. Church members labored with this sinner, visiting him each month, asking only that he return so that all might be forgiven.[11]

What had changed in the churches was the attitude of the fallen toward discipline. They saw petty malice in the actions of their fellow members, and became incensed when their accounts of their own actions were criticized or refused. This attitude might have stemmed from new social or political antagonisms within congregations, but there was no evidence that such antagonisms existed. It is possible that the Revolution provided ideas that sinners translated into legitimations for their opposition to disciplinary proceedings. Perhaps by asserting the right of citizens to their own political opinions, or by undermining unquestioning faith in the good intentions and omniscience of authority, the Revolution inspired the fallen to defend their own opinions against those of deacons and disciplinary committees. By setting new bounds to the interference citizens would tolerate in their lives from governmental authority, the Revolution may have encouraged sinners to limit the right of their churches to oversee their economic dealings and personal relationships.

These legitimations were not consciously expressed. The accused and their supporters saw themselves as biblical Christians who eschewed innovation. They did not attack the prerogatives of their accusers, which were, according to Calvinist orthodoxy, outlined specifically in the Book of Acts. Instead, they complained with increasing frequency and vehemence of a lack of charity and understanding.[12]

The adherents of the communal ideal found their efforts checked again. They responded by retreating before the opposition, by tolerating more honest differences and minor disputes among members, and by shifting their disciplinary emphasis toward lapses in personal behavior (Table 2.1). But these shifts took stalwart Calvinists farther from a realization of their ideals and signaled an increasing inability to use church discipline – not to speak of the law – to coerce others into an acceptance or observance of their moral obligations.

Wayward youths

The Calvinists of southern New England, both Old and New Light, had had difficulties for decades with young members and prospective or potential members of their churches. As always, the problem was the youthful penchant for mischief and for experimentation with alcohol, tobacco, gambling, and sex. Young people also had difficulties transforming their youthful religious zeal into mature piety. Adult Calvinists, north and south, tried to deal with these problems straightforwardly, doubling their efforts to supervise, discipline, and convert the young. Despite exhortations to righteousness, however, they could not bring even penitent youths to give up their irreverent attitudes toward certain sins. Nor could they sustain or moderate the intense outbursts of moral fervor and religious conviction that occurred at intervals throughout the period among young people. This was especially true if these outbursts got out of hand, and the young converted before reaching moral maturity or – what was worse – turned their perfervid enthusiasm against adult church members, condemning them for inconsistent doctrines and lack of piety. These problems were not in themselves new, but adult Calvinists seemed to be at a loss as to how to deal with them.

Henry Stevens, a farmer and innkeeper from Barnet, demonstrated how reputable, churchgoing young people could impede the Calvinist cause by at once delighting in and repenting the wrongfulness of their escapades. Stevens began a diary in 1811 at age twenty. He expressed regret about not going to meeting more often and lamented that he lived in a place "inhabited by many young people and Devilish proud." As he began to confess his misdeeds, however, Stevens often forgot to be remorseful. His accounts of his "boyish courtships" turned into "some fine stories about some Lyman [New Hampshire] ladies," the girls across the Connecticut River with whom Henry and his friends most often dallied (the Barnet boys preferred to risk their reputations a safe distance from home). Later in the diary, a regretful account of youthful "scrapes" was interrupted by the entry of July 4, 1812, passing judgment on a day that saw Stevens and several young friends drink grog all morning, offering seventeen patriotic toasts to their country "in less than an hour," and march to the town's Liberty Pole to offer seventeen more "in presence of a Large company. Done well."[3]

How could reputable youths like Stevens, dedicated to their churches, simultaneously lament and delight in their misdeeds? That question confounded Calvinists throughout the valley. They knew that human nature allowed contrary impulses to reside together in weak souls. What they did not want to acknowledge was that young people lived by two standards and felt the continual pull of two lives and two sets of values.

Like all but the most otherworldly of their friends and relatives, young people dwelt in at least two overlapping but distinct spheres of social life, one within their churches and one outside in the community at large.

Both spheres offered the young people of the valley opportunities to meet with neighbors, to test their attractions on the opposite sex, to court, and to forge and express loyalty to their neighborhoods, communities, and nation. Whereas one centered on the church, however, on displaying moral and spiritual maturity, on striving for unity, on observing Christian rituals and Christian holidays – in other words, on realizing the Calvinist communal ideal – the other sphere centered on the tavern, on displaying physical strength and beauty, on working with neighbors at raisings and bees, and on militia training and the Fourth of July.

For men in particular, social life outside the churches revolved around the many taverns of the valley. There people could congregate casually, gossip, exchange business information, play cards or quoits, while away inclement weather, celebrate personal triumphs, and mull over failures. Of course, churches offered some of these attractions, and were the only places where most women could find them outside their own homes. But the churches were not as numerous as taverns. In 1815, the nine towns studied here had thirty-two licensed inns and taverns and only twenty-six churches. Nor could churches keep the hours, offer the comforts, gather the range of neighbors, or provide the atmosphere of easy camaraderie that taverns could. Most devout Calvinists, not to speak of those who were not regular churchgoers, probably spent more time in taverns than in churches.

The sphere of social life outside the churches attracted more inhabitants, including women, to festive gatherings around the taverns. Sporting events were especially popular, even though they sanctioned ostensibly immoral behavior. A wild title match for the wrestling championship of St. Johnsbury, held by lantern light on a Saturday night, carried on so late that the referee set back his watch as midnight approached, so that no one who stayed for the conclusion would "violate" the Sabbath. Horse racing on St. Johnsbury's main street was also popular; especially memorable to residents of that town was "the superior equestrienneship of Sally Tute...who leaping on a barebacked horse called for a glass of stimulant and challenged any man of the crowd to overtake her." These contests drew admiring throngs eager to cheer their neighborhood champions onward, and to pay homage to the physical strength, horsemanship, courage, and tenacity so admired on the farming frontier.[14]

Most frequent of all social events in the valley were the various raisings and bees held to make light work of arduous physical tasks. The major events, however, were the patriotic holidays, the militia training days, and the Fourth of July. Those days were the high points of the year in the towns of the valley, provided that tragedy did not strike in a firearms accident, as it too often did. Such accidents were common because drunkenness was widespread on these occasions. Not only was it the custom for captains to "treat" their men from early morning on to sustain their strength and enthusiasm, but drunkenness allowed the men to level all distinctions among themselves and to celebrate their liberty in intoxicated abandon. Like patriotic songs and martial fervor, alcohol drew townspeople together. But the celebrations served other purposes as well, particularly for the younger participants. Young men took the opportunity to show they could outdrink, outdrill, and outsloganize any patriot in the valley and took pride in having "done well" before friends, neighbors, and most especially, the young women in the crowd.[15]

This sphere of valley life, and that which centered on the church, were inhabited by much the same people. Most church members, including non-Calvinists, participated in the social life outside their churches, and most people were included to some degree in the circle of a church. The spheres were not necessarily inimical to each other. Calvinists young and old felt it possible to be pious and at the same time patriotic, good-natured, and neighborly to those outside their churches. Still, the spheres were distinct, and potential for antagonism was great. In the church's circle, patriotism and good fellowship were not to be sought (and were indeed censured) as ends in themselves. Conversely, in the community sphere, where patriotism and good fellowship were valued as ends in themselves, rectitude and piety were admirable, but there was a point where quibbling over the morality of a national policy or a neighbor's actions became bad manners.

These spheres posed a perpetual problem for the adult Calvinists in the valley, whose mission "to be in but not of the world" required them to participate in the social life outside their churches without becoming creatures of that life. The burden of that problem rested most heavily, however, on the young people of the valley who were of an age to be attracted by the worldly sphere and who were all too ready to place camaraderie ahead of their duty to God. The young also had to face temptation without having mastered the subtle code that told adult Calvinists when they had partaken enough of revelry, when they had shown enough charity toward human frailty, when they should chastise, when they should let matters pass.

Thus it was not strange that young people like Henry Stevens were doomed to repeat what in more sober moods they knew to be sins. As a tavern owner and a promising Presbyterian, Henry Stevens epitomized the dilemma, for he lived in two worlds, amidst piety and promiscuity, and knew the attractions of both.

Drinking and carousing among young people were not the only problems that confronted the Calvinists. Fervent Calvinist evangelicals also faced problems that had their source solely in the religious sphere – in particular, too-early conversions. It was natural for evangelical parents to tell their children at an early age how Christ had died for their sins and how only conversion – the evangelical experience of being "born again," in which God fills the sinner's soul with saving grace – could bring peace and salvation. They meant to shake children into seriousness and to encourage them to think and pray about their own souls. Such conversations produced the desired effect with surprising frequency. Children would try immediately to improve their behavior and would sit down with their friends and play preacher to them – a common enough pastime before the games of cowboys and Indians or cops and robbers came into being. But at times young children were terrified. They hid during thunder and lightning storms for fear of dying before receiving God's grace. Some even made mild attempts at mortification of the flesh. As Joel Winch, a young Hartland boy, recalled in his memoirs (written at the age of twenty-one), he thought "much about dying" after such a conversation with his father, and would "git alone and cry."[6]

Few parents knew what to make of children who were so desperately concerned about their souls. Joel Winch's parents, being dedicated New Lights and full church members, had no wish to discourage their twelve-year-old son from seeking God, but they had hoped he would be a little older before he found Him. Joel did not yet know, they thought, what real sin or real religion was about. His mother tried to reclaim her son and, as Joel wrote later, "being a quick woman twitted me of my pretending to be good." She was none too gentle in her teasing, however, and Joel was crushed. "O how it sunk me down," he wrote. For three years he lived with the knowledge of his own sinfulness. When at last the Lord "broke into" Joel's soul at age fifteen, "the Congregationalist professores would take no notis of that which the Lord had don for me." It was not at that time customary for the church to accept young people as full members.

Joel did gain admittance to the church while still a teenager, as did a number of other young people, even though "it made some talk" among church members. Their elders feared that no matter how fervent the religious commitment the young professed, it was at bottom unreliable. At the age of fourteen, fifteen, or sixteen, young people, particularly those from farm, artisan, and laboring families, were entering the most difficult years of their lives. It was then that they would begin working, often for long periods away from home – the girls as domestics, the boys as farmhands or apprentices. Their wages would go toward augmenting the family income, building dowries, or, in the case of males, toward saving for a farm or a shop. Once they reached the age of twenty-one, young people were responsible for themselves and could "journey" where they wished to find suitable employment. Until then, however, their parents controlled their destinies.

It was the prevailing notion among Calvinists and non-Calvinists alike that responsible relatives, neighbors, and fellow church members handled young people better than did parents, because they did not face rebellion against specifically parental authority and because they were not reluctant to administer strict discipline out of the "false" love that sometimes prevented parents from correcting their children.[17] Putting children out was not always a solution to disciplinary problems, however. There is little evidence that masters and mistresses actually had any less trouble than parents in governing young people. Then, too, even if parents were careful in their selection of an employer, the moral and spiritual lives of their children were sometimes neglected. Masters and mistresses might prove more lukewarm toward the church than parents expected and allow their wards to stay home on the Sabbath or to strike up friendships with freethinkers. Under these circumstances young converts would quickly become backsliders.

The greatest problem for those who converted at a young age, however, was the temptation to cast off godliness for a while and return to carefree, reckless ways. A few truly rebelled against religion, indulging in drunkenness or fornication; others sought release in flirtation, playing pranks, or vandalism. Upon his return from journeying in the fall of 1800, Joel Winch fought with his parents and fell headlong into sin. He stayed out nights, leaving his parents to fear that he had compromised several young women in the neighborhood. In fact he and his friends were trying to start a witchcraft scare. They opened people's doors, made "all manner of noises," threw carts down wells, and put hogs in cow pens and cows in hog pens. The seriousness of what he was doing did not strike Joel until he tried to seduce a young Baptist girl at a party and was repulsed. Her righteous rejection of him made him realize that he had become an ally of the Devil. In his own defense, he protested that he was not as bad as some of his friends. He did not dance, swear, or play cards, for he knew he "could not have the name of being religious" if he did so.

Joel's behavior was typical of many young converts who backslid. They behaved frivolously or wickedly, but were careful not to do anything that would injure their churches. Their sins were committed in secret and were usually minor, having to do with wasting time, gossiping, daydreaming about parties and courting, or fishing when there was work to be done (one young man confessed to catching 1,117 fish in two years). They suffered remorse periodically and rededicated themselves to Christ for weeks or even months, only to lapse again. Unable to live in two worlds at once, they traversed the cycles of sin and salvation.[18]

Even when young people turned to Christ for good, they often confounded their friends, relatives, and congregations with rigorous searches for doctrinal truth and purity. They could do so privately, or they could do so openly and aggressively. Unwilling to confront the leaders of her church, or perhaps merely loath to make trouble, Lois Leverett of Windsor decided secretly that predestination and infant damnation were unscriptural foolishness. There were a great many young people in the valley who went so far as to leave their churches over some difference in scriptural interpretation. Twenty-year old Elias Smith of South Woodstock, distressed at not finding the Baptist doctrines he learned as a child supported by the Bible, demanded that open discussion of complex theological questions be allowed in his church. When his request was denied, he quit to found a church that would allow honest disagreements among sincere Christians.[19]

Backsliding and overzealousness presented enduring problems for Calvinists and their communal ideals. In part, of course, the problem was that young people were just that – young and immature. They had none of the attachments of adulthood that provided a firm basis for social, moral, and spiritual maturity: a spouse, a household, a shop or farm, respectable friends, and a commitment to the community and its values. It took time to acquire such connections and commitments. The young people of the valley remained half in and half out of the adult world at least until their mid-twenties or early thirties.

Adult church members in the valley deliberately chose to let the young mature in their own good time. In a radical departure from the ways of their fathers, they decided not to subject the young to anything more than gentle moral suasion. Moderate New Lights and Old Lights abandoned efforts to discipline the young by the 1790s, the Woodstock Congregationalists in 1783 being the last to omit those baptized, but not converted, from the watch and care of the church. In addition, the churches began to allow applicants for admission to omit confessions of their past sins, except when the sins had been committed so recently as to place the sincerity of the person's change of heart in doubt. Only the Scottish Presbyterians in Barnet and Ryegate continued this practice beyond 1810, because they had brought it with them from Scotland in the 1790s, and all but one of their churches would soon stop.[20]

Most important, the New Lights decided not to encourage or press for youthful conversions. The data on ages at conversion for males show

Table 2.2. New Members
in Congregational and Baptist Churches, 1791-1843[a]

	1791-1815	Revivals, 1816-21	1816-28, except revivals[b]	1829-43
New male members				
Median age[c]	32	25	26	22
Mean age	34	29	29	27
Married and/or household heads (percent)	72	47	36	37
N =	142	197	53	582
New female members[d]				
Married (percent)	80	37	55	37
N[e] =	153	251	198	915

[a] Unless specified otherwise, data in all tables are from Barnet, Peacham, Pomfret, St. Johnsbury, Weathersfield, West Windsor, and Windsor.
[b] The Pomfret data from 1828, and the Barnet, Peacham, and St. Johnsbury data from 1827 and 1828, are included with the data from all towns from 1829 to 1843, because the great revival began in those towns in those years, not in 1829.
[c] Converts of unknown age who were taxed are estimated to have been twenty-five years old; those who were not taxed are estimated to have been eighteen years old. The trends in the data are similar even if these converts are excluded.
[d] The data are from the catalogues of the Congregational churches of the following towns, which noted the marital status of women upon their admission to the church: Barnet, Bethel, Bradford, Chelsea, St. Johnsbury (Second), Vershire, Waitsfield, Wells River, Westminster, Williamstown, and Windsor. Data are also included from the records of the Windsor Baptist Church.
[e] The median age of the fifty-five male converts who joined the Associate Presbyterian church in Barnet from 1791 to 1815 was only twenty-seven, as was the mean age. Only 38 percent were married or household heads. The median age of the forty-one male converts who joined from 1827 to 1843 was twenty-six, the mean age twenty-eight. Forty-four percent were married or household heads. These ages and percentages held steady throughout the period. That was not the case for converts in Congregational and Baptist churches. The data from 1816 to 1826 are missing.

that even during revivals, the typical convert was well into maturity in this period and far older than typical converts during southern New England's Great Awakening (Table 2.2). Eighty percent of new female members were married by the time they entered the church. (The Scottish Presbyterians in Barnet differed; among them the mean age at conversion remained below thirty prior to 1815.) Church members did not censure or disregard all youthful conversions, for they believed that God elected souls when He pleased; still, they were wary of them. Several churches had to vote down, as scripturally unsound, efforts to deny admission to converts solely on the basis of their youth.[21]

The retreat spread as Calvinists, New and Old Light, began grudgingly to tolerate a greater range of excesses, particularly by young people, on public occasions. They issued no audible protests against the continuation of the wrestling match in St. Johnsbury into the Sabbath or the rowdiness among young people that accompanied the raising of that town's meetinghouse. Members of one church actually sided against their minister in favor of several young converts who had "returned to their sports, carousing, and dancing," maintaining "that abstinence from mirthful recreation could not be expected of those who were in the heat and vigor of youth."[22] A new balance of power had been struck between the Calvinists and their young and potential members.

There were now religious and political movements in the valley that were hostile to the Calvinists and their idea of a covenanted community, and adults recognized that they could drive the young into those movements if they pressed them too hard or if they failed to take them seriously. That was precisely what happened to Lois Leverett and Joel Winch. Alternately pressured and chaffed by their elders, they were driven further away from their parents' faith: Lois toward Episcopalianism, and Joel toward Methodism (he was eventually to become a Methodist minister).

In addition to there being new alternatives available, the attitudes of young people seemed to have undergone a change. Relative to southern New England, workers were in great demand in the valley and opportunities for marriage and for independent proprietorship were plentiful. The young considered their futures secure. Therefore they may have been truly less careful of their reputations than before.[23] It is also possible that the Revolution compounded the Calvinists' problems by leading young people to confuse their right to hold their own religious and political opinions with their ability to arrive at opinions that were as valid as those of their elders. Young people had on occasion challenged the beliefs of authorities in southern New England before the Revolution, but on a less widespread basis.

The Calvinists had been deeply frustrated by the young people who were to inherit the ideal of the covenanted community. Not until the 1830s, however, when threats from youthful disorders in their midst increased, would they risk trying to force young people to behave themselves or move to press them wholesale into the churches.

Denominational rivalry

The young, and those who refused to accept discipline, posed a threat to the ideal of the covenanted community, but a greater threat arose from people who were dissatisfied with Calvinism spiritually and who felt that they had no place in the communities the Calvinists tried to create. These discontented Christians, most of whom had been nominal Calvinists when they came to the valley, frustrated the communal ambitions of devout Calvinists, both Old and New Light, by rejecting the Calvinists' right to speak for and impose their standards and beliefs on others. Their numbers grew rapidly. Whereas in 1790 there had been only one non-Calvinist church in the valley, by 1815 there were fifty-two, and although the number of full church members they could claim was not large, services were very well attended. The influence of the churches was augmented by missions in dozens of towns that had yet to establish non-Calvinist churches of particular denominations.

Some of the increase in the number of non-Calvinists stemmed from migration from southern New England, where established churches were still persecuting non-Calvinists as late as 1833. However, the causes of discontent among Christians in the valley were primarily indigenous. They stemmed from tensions that arose from the appearance of an established hierarchy of towns and neighborhoods within the valley after 1790 and from resentment of the Calvinists' conception of the Christian way of life.[24] Methodism and Universalism (along with the minor non-Calvinist evangelical sects, the Freewill Baptists and Christians) took hold quickly in agricultural areas removed from the Connecticut River, where residents felt that post-frontier economic developments had left them increasingly outside the centers of wealth and power. These denominations offered more egalitarian doctrines of grace and more congenial styles of worship than those offered by the Calvinists. Episcopalianism and Unitarianism prospered especially in major marketing centers. They provided a genteel alternative to Calvinism to people who felt that bigotry and narrow-mindedness were impeding their efforts to cultivate a cultured social life to complement the prosperity of their towns.

The non-Calvinist denominations, and the tensions and resentments they addressed, arose first in the valley in the 1790s and grew rapidly and with great consistency. Episcopalianism and Unitarianism were "liberal" denominations that did not view God as wrathful or humanity as innately depraved, that emphasized humanity's ability to improve itself morally and spiritually by following God's benevolent commandments. These denominations gradually displaced Calvinism among the genteel.

Genteel Christians, who tried to pattern their lives after the British gentry and read more widely in both modern and classical literature than other Vermonters, often found Calvinist dogma inimical to intellectual vibrancy, Calvinist intimacy inconsistent with graceful manners, and Calvinist disciplinary proceedings threatening to their standing in society. Although they considered themselves believers and attended church faithfully, they had trouble experiencing conversion and disliked the unsolicited intrusion of the church into the personal lives of church members. Some had found a degree of safety and comfort in Old Light churches, which did not require prospective members to testify to their spiritual rebirth or discipline members for mildly unorthodox views. Yet these people recognized that Old Light churches offered them no permanent home. The Old Lights were still strict with sinners, uneasy with theological innovation, and insistent that prospective members proclaim themselves elect by virtue of some work of grace, something many people could not do. It was no coincidence that marketing and manufacturing towns with Old Light churches spawned the valley's strongest Episcopalian and Unitarian churches. Old Light churches attracted genteel Christians, but could not hold them.[25]

Episcopalians and Unitarians did not, as New and Old Lights charged, deny the importance of piety or the need to watch and assist fellow Christians who had fallen into sin. Both denominations had their share of former Calvinists who had proved unable to demonstrate their election or who had fled from the prospect of undergoing discipline, but their intention was not to harbor fugitives from God. They sought to cultivate a distinctive religious style, one that stressed civility, good manners, and a spirit of tolerance, forbearance, and mutual aid. In their opinion, conversion and discipline did not signal and sustain faith, but rather hindered it by leading to overzealousness, backsliding, and meddling. Many agreed with Thomas Thomas, bookseller and chairman of the council that organized the Episcopalian church in Windsor in 1816, when he said that he had had enough of the Calvinists' "thorough-going, rigid, and bigotted" faith. He felt sure that only a temperate faith, one that did not rely on lightning from heaven to ignite it or formal persecution to sustain it, could represent the true way of Christ.[26]

Thomas was not exaggerating as much as might be expected when he asserted that his faith appealed to "the liberal and most intelligent" people, nor was his arch foe, the Reverend Fowler of the Windsor Baptist church, entirely wrong when he blamed the "fashionables of the village" for the rise of liberal heresy. Both the Episcopalians and the Unitarians had disproportionate support from merchants, professionals, financiers, and clerks (Table 2.3), and from women of similar social standing, es-

Table 2.3. Occupations
of Members of Protestant Denominations, 1830[a]

	Episco-palians	Unita-rians	Congre-gation-alists	Baptists	Univer-salists	Methodists/Freewill Baptists/Christians
Occupations (percent)						
Businessmen/ professionals	32	14	3	5	1	0
Master craftsmen	16	32	10	12	5	9
Small proprietors	11	3	2	2	2	3
Millers/taverners	2	11	1	0	3	2
Clerks	3	0	2	0	1	0
Journeymen/laborers	3	5	13	15	12	14
Commercial farmers	3	27	7	6	6	2
Family farmers	6	0	19	17	23	27
Subsistence farmers	13	3	21	24	23	20
Farm tenants	2	0	1	2	1	3
Farm laborers	8	6	19	18	23	20
N =	62	37	201	66	188	64
Generic occupations						
Marketing/ professions	47	17	8	6	3	3
Manufacturing	19	37	23	27	17	23
Agriculture[b]	34	47	69	67	80	74

[a] The data on Unitarians are from 1840, because no records are available before that date.
[b] Millers and taverners are included in the agricultural group. Ninety-five percent of the Reformed Presbyterians who can be identified (N = 19) were in agriculture, as were 97 percent of the Associate Presbyterians (N = 61).

pecially in the marketing towns of the lower valley. The only nonmarket towns that had liberal churches were Bethel, Royalton, Weathersfield, and Guilford, where early settlers had come from Episcopalian regions in western Connecticut. Yet professionals and businessmen in the principal commercial centers embraced liberal religion not because they were cosmopolitan intellectuals, but because they were more likely than other people to be concerned with gentility. There were those who were intellectually troubled by spiritual questions and who looked to Harvard Unitarians, British moral philosophers, and European romantics for enlightenment. Still, it was gentility or the desire for it that united the members of liberal denominations, gave them their sense of being a people apart, and caused their problems with conversion and discipline.

Why did the genteel have difficulty with conversion experiences? The reason that the Calvinists gave is a likely one: They were too proud. Few professionals or highly educated people had the intense awareness of personal sinfulness and of the consequences of sin that was generally a prerequisite for successful conversion. Their lives did not often admit of the powerful cycles of sin, conviction, and remorse that could have given them such an awareness and that conversion experiences embodied in formal religious terms.

The genteel did not spend their time in rounds of hard physical work and sinful release at taverns and sporting events. Their lives were less frequently interrupted by journeys from shop to shop, farm to farm, household to household, because their families were often wealthier and capable of providing for them at home until they launched careers or set up households. If they did leave home, they might do so to enter private academies and colleges or to take up positions in the firms or households of the valley's merchants, lawyers, and doctors, where they learned both practical and social skills. They traveled not in the company of hired hands with rude manners and educations, but almost exclusively in the genteel social circles of their employers and teachers, where they received more supervision and instruction and progressed more persistently and easily toward full inclusion in the mature adult world around them. Their already strong position in society gave them confidence in their ability to control their lives. Seldom did past transgressions haunt them or burden them with feelings of insecurity and unworthiness. Under certain circumstances, of course, susceptibility to conversion increased. Reversals in personal life or upheavals in society could lead to a sudden awareness of dependence on God and a bewildering sense of helplessness. Without such reversals conversions were rare.

It was possible, naturally, for people who were not raised in genteel circumstances to discipline themselves by genteel standards: to work steadily, keep good company, restrict themselves to proper amusements, and put leisure time to good use. The contrasting spiritual lives of two brothers from a farm family in Reading illustrate how hard work and the avoidance of pitfalls could instill confidence and how that hard-won confidence could militate against conversion. Elmer Townsend, the eldest of eighteen children, had dedicated himself from an early age to the task of helping to provide for his parents and his siblings. Without money or connections, he went to Boston in 1827 to work as a clerk, saving his money, and resisting the "contaminating influence" of the city. He refined his manners and his prose style by joining the Boston Lyceum and the Mercantile Library. Within ten years, he had won the confidence of "respectable men" and had become a full partner in a major mercantile firm. He provided dutifully for his relatives and married into a prominent Connecticut family. Despite his serious and pious character, however, he remained the only member of his devout Congregational family who did not undergo conversion. He felt neither sinful nor totally dependent on God for the work he had accomplished. "We can govern ourselves. We have the *power* to do and not as we please." Everyone faced the same choice: to be "despised by everybody" or to "live a good moral life and a Christian life and be esteemed by everybody that we wish to be esteemed by."[27]

Elmer's wayward brother William did not share these sentiments, nor did he share Elmer's self-control or his desire to better himself. By the time William came reluctantly to Boston to work for his brother as a clerk, he had already learned too well the unsteady work habits, unrefined manners, and coarse humor characteristic of young farm laborers in Vermont. William worked with great industry, but only by fits and starts. He constantly requested the rest periods and holidays he had come to expect on the farm as a reward for work well done and provoked Elmer to complain that his brother was "wild." Rather than help out his family in Vermont, he made it his ambition to impress the boys back home. He hoped to go back in a few years "as big as a junk bottle," "swelling and busting" with wealth, and planned to show his old friends that he was "something more powerful than small trash." Eventually, however, he grew ashamed of his failings and began to lament that he was "not an example" for his brothers and sisters to follow.[28] A short time later, during an effort to break with his past and cleanse his soul, William converted and joined the Congregational church.

The genteel were not incapable of serious sin, of course. Simeon Ide, who rose through apprenticeship and the patronage of important citizens to become the valley's leading newspaper editor, was apt in his younger days to drink too much. Once, when he came home drunk from a political meeting, he was confronted by his wife. "I shall never forget the look on [her] face," he wrote later. He felt no guilt, but recognized his folly and resolved to mend his ways. The next morning he broke all his wine bottles, decanters, and glasses and never drank again. Soon afterward he published a manual on good manners, wrote a biography of Ben Franklin to instruct children in the industrious life, and joined Windsor's Episcopal church.[29]

Women, genteel or not, were less likely than men to have difficulties with conversion. They joined Calvinist churches as full members at a rate nearly twice that for men, and they experienced conversion more often even if for theological or family reasons they became Episcopalians or Unitarians. (There was nothing in liberal doctrine that declared spiritual rebirth unchristian.) They did not convert more readily because they experienced more powerful cycles of sin than men. Although women committed their share of sins and felt particularly guilty about gossip, frivolity, and flirtation, their crimes were not as destructive to self or society as those of men. Yet women were subject to feelings of unworthiness and helplessness that could lead to a strong sense of personal sin and inadequacy. Lucy Gibbs, a young woman of twenty who lived at home in Randolph and had no prospects of marriage, saw nothing but "sin and vanity" in her conduct, even though it appeared to be above reproach. Although she did not specify in her diary what she meant by "sin and vanity," it is evident that she was discontented with her humdrum domestic life and considered that discontent sinful. She felt useless and longed for some way actively to shoulder her "duty" to Christ, but the more she longed to do something, the more sinful she felt. She concluded that God was teaching her "forcibly [her] own insufficiency and dependence."[30]

Conversion could alleviate such feelings of helplessness and worthlessness by drawing women closer to God and allying them with divine power. God's power seemed more immediate to women than to men; women asked God more frequently in their writings for particular favors. Conversion also united a woman with other Christian women who shared her problems and who worked to affirm the sacrifices she made for family and home.

For many well-educated women, however, intellectual pride and a strong sense of self interfered with the conversion process and drew them toward nonevangelical religion. Lois Leverett of Windsor was one such woman. In religion, as in love, she would not allow herself to be "smitten," and she opined that Windsorites caught up in the frenzy of a revival in 1810 were "almost crazy," adding that the revivalists "work too much on the passions of the people." A voracious reader, she thought deeply about religious issues and had a clear sense of her own sinfulness, but shrank from discussing religion with the pious Mrs. Niles, whose submissive acceptance of the contradictions implicit in faith made her uneasy. She relied strongly on intellect to resolve religious questions; after all, she wrote, "the design of religion was not to bewilder, but enlighten our understandings and the plea of ignorance will not avail us." Not to exercise the intellect on any matter would result, she felt, in a "relapse into female style."[31]

The experiences of the Townsend brothers and Lois Leverett seem to confirm that a strong sense of pride and personal accomplishment were not conducive to conversion. Most people who belonged to liberal churches lived in a world that not only encouraged pride, but instructed them in it. Most were avid readers, who lived in or near the villages that had numerous print shops; and whether they were from business and

professional families or prosperous artisan or farm families, many possessed or had access to private libraries. They read a great many didactic
works that encouraged self-reliance and self-improvement. Popular works
like Defoe's *Robinson Crusoe*, Goldsmith's *Vicar of Wakefield*, Franklin's
Autobiography, or even Scott's novels, taught them that a clear conscience
and no small measure of temporal happiness could be theirs if they
disciplined themselves, cultivated good manners, avoided false pride, and
stood by worthy principles. Conversion was unnecessary; one had only
to look deeper into oneself, as did Simeon Ide, in search of the will to
make oneself a model of gentility, decency, and success.[32]

Pride raised difficulties with other aspects of Calvinism as well. The
intimacy of the Calvinist churches and their intrusions into the personal
lives of members were distasteful to the genteel. They did not dislike
close relations with fellow church members; they were, as church members, more likely than Calvinists to name their children after each other
and to form business alliances together. However, they perceived themselves as a union, not of saints, but of decent, refined people with common
interests in religion, culture, and business. They bound themselves in
relationships based on mutual admiration, respect, and trust and dis-
dained love as too capricious a force to unite polite people in so public
an institution. Their churches did not call the saints to love and watch
over one another and to spread Christ's word; they called upon the
civilized to spread the gospel of culture as well as the gospel of Christ.
When Thomas Thomas and the Windsor Episcopalians made their "mas-
termove" in 1817 and attempted to establish Episcopalian churches in
all the important towns of the valley, they did not try to enlist the
spiritually elect, but "the most influential and prominent characters for
all Political Juridical and domestick Objects in the state."[33] The Calvinists
must have shuddered at the thought of gathering a church on such a
worldly basis.

Genteel Christians also hated to see decent, often prominent men
and their families subjected to the humiliation and distress of Calvinist discipline cases. They gladly received the victims of these cases,
like deacon William Tileston of the Windsor Congregational Church.
Tileston, a bookseller and saddler, was incensed at gossip that had
been circulated about him and his daughter Abigail, by his daughter's
sister-in-law, Sabra Hall. Hall had told nearly every woman in Windsor that Abby "did not help her mother, but tended to her cat," that
she was incapable of running a household without two or three hired
girls, that Hall's brother, in marrying Abby, had forfeited a chance to
marry a wealthy Unitarian heiress from Boston, and that Tileston
himself had left town to flee his business debts.[34] Tileston brought

charges against Sabra Hall in church, but the ensuing discipline case (which lasted over two years) injured everyone involved. Every member of good society in Windsor was forced to testify and to choose sides. In the end, Sabra Hall fled from Windsor, and Tileston, disgusted with the way in which his family life had been dragged through the mud, resigned his position as deacon, left the Congregationalists, and joined the Episcopalian church, where he found relative tranquility and a tacit agreement to respect the privacy of others.

One group of well-educated professionals, however, showed little interest in liberal religion: the more arrogant and rakish of those young college graduates who came to the valley prior to 1815 to teach school, study law, and make their fortunes. These young men were often contemptuous of the poorly lettered people they instructed. They delighted in playing practical jokes on the ignorant and trading on their status as "college men" to seduce local girls, in imitation of the jaded villains of Samuel Richardson's novels, which they did not read for moral elevation. They boasted to their intimates of clandestine meetings with young women, joked cruelly about unmarried women who became pregnant, expressed a longing for encounters with "negro wenches, who were keen as briars," and bragged unceasingly of their sexual prowess. "You must prepare your girls for my reception," one wrote a friend in Rockingham on the eve of a visit. "As my stay will be short I must fuck them in a hurry therefore they must be ready on my arrival." For all their ribald bravado, they were careful about appearances and attended church regularly, in part to meet eligible young women. They were not temperamentally liberals, however. They usually felt more guilt than pride about their activities, and most later converted and joined evangelical churches.[35]

The Calvinists also lost support, for very different reasons, among those who felt themselves outside the centers of power and who wished to assert the fundamental equality of all men and women before God. Methodism and Universalism spread like wildfire in the valley. Between 1795 and 1803 the Universalists organized fourteen churches and another nine by 1815. The Methodists increased their ministerial circuits from four to twelve between 1800 and 1815 and quintupled their membership. At one revival meeting in 1800 in the rural Orange County town of Vershire, they drew a thousand people – an astonishing crowd for that time and place. In rural areas the Calvinists also lost members to the Methodists and Universalists' nearest rivals, the Freewill Baptists and Christians. These minor sects never equaled the Methodists or Universalists in support (they had established only seventeen small churches between them by 1815), but they often drew enthusiastic crowds where they did minister.[36]

By rejecting the Calvinist belief in a firm, predetermined line between the elect and the nonelect, Methodists and Universalists appealed to Christians who felt that the doctrine of predestination was really only another Calvinist device to raise artificial distinctions among men. Some of these people had felt a kinship with New Light Calvinists and had admired the New Lights' revolutionary fervor, concern for community, and disdain for southern New England's establishments. Their churches arose primarily north of Windham County, in communities that had been dominated initially by New Lights, who had shown the valley's inhabitants during the Revolution that piety and egalitarian conviction could coexist. Still, even those who had admired certain New Light traits could not abide the New Lights' de facto establishment or loyalty to the doctrine of election, which by the 1790s had made their commitment to equality and freedom of worship seem suspect to many people.[37]

The Methodists and the Universalists did not attract people bent on abolishing all inequities among men, however. Many of them were prosperous commercial farmers, although they were less likely to be proprietors than were members of other denominations (Table 2.3). What distinguished these Christians most was where they lived. Methodist and Universalist churches were prevalent in the upland hills and valleys. Their only urban footholds were in inland marketing towns like Woodstock and Danville, and even there, most members lived in the countryside. Although there were Methodists and Universalists throughout the valley, they were concentrated more heavily in the hills of the south and the agricultural towns of the north – this in marked contrast to the areas in which Episcopalians and Unitarians lived. In these areas, the Methodists and the Universalists appealed to Christians both rich and poor by helping them to express in religious terms their sense of themselves as members of neglected communities.

The appeal of both religions may have stemmed from the compelling constructions they placed on social relations and on personal moral development, constructions that revealed similar attitudes toward worldly wealth and power. The Methodists were aggressive in their appeal to those who, like most Vermont farmers, were outside the mainstream of society, and whose chances of rising to great heights in the world were slim. They promised spiritual peace, deliverance, and riches through Christ and guaranteed that those who had been rich and powerful on earth would be humbled or damned – although, barring the onset of the millennium, these promises were to be fulfilled in the afterlife. In their hymns they spoke of their belief that God would compensate them for the limitations of their lives on earth: "Our troubles and our trials here, Will make us only richer there." The "Gospel Market" of heaven would provide them with food, health, clothing, shelter, golden crowns, and grace, all for free. The Methodists' intellectual world may have been largely circumscribed, like that of other evangelicals, especially Freewill Baptists and Christians, by the Bible, hymnals, and Christian lore; but it was boundless in its promise of blessings through grace.[38]

The Universalists did not offer this kind of redress in heaven, having promised salvation to everyone, nor did they pay as much regard to the miraculous, having imbibed from popular currents of the Enlightenment a more demystified view of the world. Their foremost authors, like Hosea Ballou and Lucy Barns, portrayed the world as just and well-ordered, and declared that it would bring men and women great happiness if they only understood and appreciated it. They took pains to emphasize the spiritual and material comfort believers could obtain on earth and claimed that the mighty, self-righteous, and wicked would pay for their sins on earth through spiritual torment and an inability to enjoy the worldly blessings God had bestowed upon man.[39]

Like the Methodists, the Universalists felt that strict Calvinism appealed primarily to those whose position in the world convinced them that they stood in a special relationship to God. In effect, both the Methodists and Universalists appealed to the outsider, but in distinctive ways: the Methodists by rejecting predetermination and offering grace and deliverance to all willing to repent and accept it; the Universalists by assuring salvation to all and by approving the appreciation of God's gifts to man on earth.

Of course, the rhetoric of resignation and content cannot be taken at face value. For all their visions of heaven and disavowals of earth, the Methodists were not especially otherworldly, and despite their professed certainty that the high and mighty were not as happy as God's children, the Universalists were admittedly "sensitive and jealous" of the wealthy and the powerful. The Revolution, by heightening the ambitions and discontents of common people, may well have spurred the growth of these denominations. Both the Methodists and the Universalists would prove ardent champions of the rights of the common man. Along with Freewill Baptists and Christians, they increased rapidly on New England's revolutionary frontier, except in places where the Revolution took a moderate or antiegalitarian course, as in Old Light–dominated Windham County. Where there was no revolution, as in Nova Scotia, neither denomination flourished.[40]

The Universalists had a special appeal to the rural intelligentsia. Largely self-taught and usually employed as teachers, clerks, or printers, these people were proud of their accomplishments, and that pride interfered with conversion, just as it did for their genteel contemporaries in Windsor or Woodstock. For young school teachers like Pamela Brown of Plymouth, who found moral inspiration in Shakespeare's plays and detested the condemnatory tone of evangelical sermons, Universalism was a rural variant of religious liberalism. Brown was pleased that the Universalists did not insist on conversion experiences, and she appreciated their interest in rational theology. Because Episcopalian and Unitarian churches were scarce in the countryside, the rural intelligentsia did not often make common cause with religious liberals; besides, they often resented the village merchants, well-born professionals, and fashionable society women who set themselves up as superior to country people. Justin Morrill, a young clerk from Strafford, wrote that Episcopalians and Unitarians set up "selfishness as one of the noblest qualities of the human breast." Morrill preferred Universalism, which accepted radical democrats and deists like himself as Christians and did not offer spiritual shelter to fashionable young women who feigned "bashfulness" before inquiring disingenuously into his "pedigree." A sense of estrangement, an appreciation of the common man, and a gift for satire often led young Universalists like Morrill to careers as insurgent editors and politicians.[41]

Despite their disagreement over issues like the necessity of conversion and man's capacity for sin, Universalism and Methodism attracted primarily the same people: farmers and rural artisans. The Methodists, who believed in original sin and in conversion, appealed directly, like the Calvinists, to people with a strong personal sense of sin, to people who were likely to have served and journeyed as youths and to have done physical work, as farmers and artisans certainly did. In sermons and hymns, they explicitly addressed young people who lived "in sin and folly" and adults who were troubled by the sins of their youth. They spoke to those who doted on beauty, and reveled in dancing and gambling, and who were exiles from the "shady bowers" of their parents' homes.[42]

The Universalists rejected the doctrines of innate depravity and conversion, yet they too appealed powerfully to people with a strong sense of guilt and inadequacy. Although an increasing number of Universalists considered their faith to be rationalistic and nonevangelical, it had arisen in the 1780s as an evangelical movement that was keenly aware of humanity's failings. This was a theological legacy Universalist ministers never fully repudiated. Still, they seldom spoke of rebellious sinners and wayward youths saved from perdition only through Christ's mediation.

Instead they spoke of weak and vulnerable children who were guided and protected by a forgiving God who loved unconditionally. In Universalist hymns, God consoled without threats and encouraged personal reformations arising from gratitude, love, and embarrassment over sins, rather than from fear of punishment:

> Oppressed with grief and shame, dissolved
> In penitential tears,
> Thy goodness calms my rising doubts,
> And dissipates my fears.[43]

The Universalist image of the sinner was that of a child who has disappointed his parents, but knows they are forgiving and wishes to improve to please them. It may be that Universalism, with its pervasive imagery of close child–parent relationships, spoke to the moral experience of farm youths who did not endure long journeys away from loved ones, who remained under the guidance and protection of their families until their parents could help them get a farm of their own, and who therefore did not perceive youth as a difficult time of separation from respectable society and from home. It is equally possible, however, that Universalism was compelling because it admitted of a variety of paths to moral and spiritual maturity. Although conversion and divine wrath played no part in Universalism, as they did in evangelical denominations, Universalist imagery did speak to people who had a deep sense of sin and desperately wanted consolation and assurance; and although the moral strength of humanity did not figure in Universalism as it did in liberal religions, Universalist imagery did address people who had a sense of their own worth and hoped to progress gradually toward righteousness with the support of their elders. The appeal of such imagery allowed the Universalists to cast a wider net in the countryside than their evangelical rivals could.

In response to the gains of the non-Calvinist denominations, a number of Congregational and Presbyterian ministers urged Old and New Lights to settle their differences and to intensify their efforts to convert sinners and defeat their common spiritual enemies. These ministers looked for leadership to Timothy Dwight, president of Yale College. Dwight developed a moderate evangelical theology that he hoped would reunite Calvinists and win them new members. He emphasized the importance of conversion, as did the New Lights; but he transformed conversion into an orderly, manageable process that Old Lights could accept. Although he believed in human depravity, Dwight insisted that God intended to save many sinners and that Christians were meant to use practical means, like prayer meetings, pastoral visits, and evangelical missions, to save souls. That doctrine heartened New Lights, by promising an increase in conversions, and pleased Old Lights, particularly those who had drifted toward Arminianism, by encouraging them to believe that conversion could be managed to some extent. More important, it helped Calvinists present their religion to non-Calvinists and nominal Calvinists as a doctrine of hope, which, despite its insistence on predestination, extended hope of salvation to the vast majority of mankind.[44]

Dwight toured the valley four times to spread his centrist doctrines, in 1797, 1803, 1812, and 1813; and he cofounded the Connecticut Missionary Society, which lent financial and ministerial support to Congregational and Presbyterian churches in the valley. His efforts bore some fruit. His ministerial disciples were accepted in a number of towns, mostly in central Caledonia and northwestern Washington counties, which were settled after the Revolution, primarily by Old and moderate New Light migrants from Connecticut. There were also minor Calvinist revivals in the valley during the winters of 1800–1 and 1809–10, which echoed revivals fostered by Dwight's adherents in Connecticut and Massachusetts. Joseph Clark, a Methodist minister in Barnard, complained that the Baptists in his town were "catching [my] chickens and making ducks of them."[45] As yet, however, not even Timothy Dwight could heal the conflict between Old and New Lights, which actually intensified between 1800 and 1815, as Baptists increased in number and grew restive in churches where they were united with Separates or moderate New Lights and as the conflict between the Federalist and Republican parties divided Old and New Lights politically.

Dwight could not stem the anti-Calvinist tide, either. Baptist and Congregationalist churches disbanded for lack of members in many agricultural neighborhoods because of the Methodist, Freewill Baptist, Christian, and Universalist onslaught. Yet in some areas the Calvinists added churches, especially in small manufacturing villages on inland waterways – villages like South Reading, Perkinsville, and Passumpsic – and in budding commercial and manufacturing centers like St. Johnsbury and Barnet, although they had trouble converting the prominent financiers and entrepreneurs who supported those churches.[46] The Calvinists maintained their broad appeal across all occupational groups through 1830 (Table 2.3). They continued to portray themselves as spokesmen for unity and community within their townships, but in reality they spoke for a diminished, divided community that managed to retain the appearance of inclusiveness while failing badly on nearly every front. They still entertained hopes of ultimate victory and gathered statistics on church membership and ministerial support to chart their progress; but they had mainly to count their losses through 1815, as more and more of the valley's inhabitants embraced genteel and egalitarian alternatives to the covenanted community and pressed their own communal ideals upon the valley.

Political strife

Unlike the advocates of the covenanted community, whose hopes for creating an ideal community had been in trouble in the Connecticut River Valley from the beginning of settlement, the defenders of the standing order, Calvinist and non-Calvinist alike, had achieved a certain success by the late 1780s and early 1790s. Almost every prominent politician and settled minister was included in their ranks; and they had brought political peace and a toned-down version of the standing orders of Connecticut and Massachusetts with them to the Vermont frontier, despite factionalism within the valley's elite and considerable opposition from those who wanted to eliminate state support of religion and public supervision of morals. This early success would prove ephemeral, however. The ideas and social changes that had made it impossible for covenanters to realize their ideal, that had made the valley's inhabitants wayward and ungovernable and had divided them spiritually and socially, would soon disrupt the valley's politics and rekindle hatreds rooted in the Great Awakening and the Revolution.

The political problems began in western Vermont. Loyal followers of Ethan Allen and Thomas Paine, inspired by the French Revolution and upset by the drift of the Arlington Junto away from its radical heritage and by the growing power of Old Lights in the state government, launched a crusade in 1793 for an "uncontaminated" democracy in Vermont. Some were discontent with Vermont's standing order, convinced that its economic policies, which favored developers, harmed the "poor and middling," and that its church–state laws had allowed Congregationalists and Presbyterians to build a de facto establishment. All believed that the democratic spirit of the Revolution was dying, both in Vermont and the nation at large. They considered their adversaries' coolness toward the French Revolution, their willingness to tolerate British depredations of American commerce, and their support of Alexander Hamilton's effort to raise a national elite of financiers, merchants, and manufacturers (by chartering a national bank, funding a national debt, and imposing a protective tariff on imported manufactured goods), to be evidence of a belated Tory conspiracy against revolution and popular government.[47]

The insurgents of western Vermont, who called themselves Republicans and supported the national policies of Thomas Jefferson, won few votes before 1797. But through their newspapers and Democratic–Republican clubs (organized in 1794 to support the French Revolution), they developed a durable and emphatically "progressive" ideology, based on Tom Paine's *Rights of Man*, that proved persuasive throughout Vermont. They interpreted the past as a period of "primeval bondage" from which all men needed to escape, and valued past achievements only insofar as they furthered humanity's emancipation from aristocratic and ecclesiastical tyranny. They called for the creation of a society based on reason rather than tradition, which would facilitate human progress, at whatever cost to traditional institutions.[48]

The Republicans saw many signs that America's escape from the past had been incomplete: Hamilton's policies, the high style of Washington's Federalist administration, the survival of established religion in southern New England, the violent suppression in 1794 of the rebellion by Pennsylvania frontiersmen against a direct tax on whiskey, and the jailing of Matthew Lyon and other Republicans in western Vermont in 1798 for "seditious" criticism of President Adams. In Vermont, where the "aristocratic" institutions upon which Republicans elsewhere focused their attacks had been destroyed long before, Republicans became more radical than their counterparts in the rest of the nation. They extolled pure democracy and a truly popular government. They spread their message in various forms, attempting to appeal to evangelicals, rough-and-ready patriots, and moderate rationalists alike. Republican Titus Hutchinson of Woodstock, a lawyer, spoke to a sedate Fourth of July crowd in 1806; in his speech he traced postrevolutionary evil to the survival of quasi-aristocratic economic privileges that conferred a "monopoly" of wealth upon America's would-be aristocrats. The satirist who styled himself Uriac Faber Republique appealed to Vermont wits. He accused Federalists of complicity in man's original sin against God's "law of equality" (which he nicknamed "Adams' fall," after the president) and of worshipping the Federal trinity, "the King, the Pope, and the unholy Devil...equal in their desire for power and glory." Republican evangelical ministers made the most effective appeal. In sermons and pamphlets they articulated an "afflictive" theory of progress, which held that the path to God's kingdom on earth would grow more difficult the closer God's millennial plans came to realization and that the struggle against tyranny and persecution had just begun. Each form of rhetoric attempted to locate the roots of evil in a past not yet transcended. All encouraged distrust of Vermont's establishment and undermined the deference Vermonters were supposed to owe their leaders.[49]

The ideology formulated by the Republicans of western Vermont terrified Federalists east and west of the Green Mountains. The early Federalists, led by lawyers Isaac Tichenor and Nathaniel Chipman, believed that Republicans only wanted to establish themselves as popular tyrants, and they feared that Republican ideology would destroy respect for authority and bring down Vermont's standing order. They pointed to the "triffling" in Congress against Alexander Hamilton's farsighted policies and the Reign of Terror in France as examples of what could happen when Republican ideologues came to power. Still, they were confident that Americans, including Vermonters, would prove too "industrious," "oeconomical," and clear-sighted to be duped by the Republicans' demagogic appeals.[50]

Vermont's Federalist publishers and politicians answered Republicans with a "conservative" ideology, based on an adaptation of the works of Edmund Burke to American circumstances. Like Burke, they prized tradition and would accept changes in customs and institutions only slowly, if at all. However, their civilization lacked the historical depth of Burke's Britain and its supposed capacity for gradual, organic change. To counter the Republicans' contention that human improvement stemmed from revolutions, peaceful or otherwise, that brought human institutions into conformity with natural law, the Federalists constructed an organic past out of the slim materials offered by Vermont's standing order and by George Washington's first term in office, which they enshrined as a golden time of harmony and disinterestedness.[51]

Like its Republican counterpart, Federalist ideology was original only in its extremity. The Federalists were strongly committed to order, morality, political unity, and deference and were suspicious of "democracy," which Samuel Prentiss, at a Fourth of July celebration in Montpelier, denounced as a delusion, like aristocracy and monarchy, against which republicans had to struggle. Their extremism stemmed from the frailty of their standing order. They were more anxious than conservatives elsewhere for the fate of what conservative institutions remained in Vermont. In their effort to encourage conservatism, they spoke to a diverse assortment of Vermonters, and, like Republicans, used a variety of approaches to attract support. Isaac Tichenor employed legal arguments to persuade voters that the Alien and Sedition Acts, passed by Congress in 1798 to suppress scurrilous attacks on officials in the Federalist administration, were reasonable measures designed to prohibit "trespass" against the reputations of others. Tichenor's private aim was to silence a Republican editor in Vermont, who had "vomated up a part of his venom and spit it upon his GAZETTE," calling Washington a "coward" and Adams a "Tory and a Traitor." Other Federalists satirized their adversaries or denounced them with withering scorn. Samuel Prentiss of Montpelier characterized Republican economic measures as "acts more suited to the capacity of a quack physician, whose genius never wandered beyond the circumference of a pill-box," while an anonymous Federalist writer mocked their egalitarian pretensions by addressing the Republicans as "Gents – Democrats, I mean (Pardon me, I am so used to addressing gentlemen, that I cannot without difficulty recollect that the title does not belong to you)." Federalist ministers drafted their own afflictive theory of the recent progress of society. They denounced postrevolutionary life in Vermont as a "catalogue of sins" and warned that the Revolution's successful defense of traditional values would be sustained only if Vermonters could prevent their newly won liberty from degenerating into license and popular tyranny.[52]

The ideological war between the Federalists and Republicans frightened the valley's leading citizens in the late 1790s, as it spread from western to eastern Vermont. Still, most believed that they could preserve political unity, calm, and moderation in the valley. Unlike their western counterparts, the people of the valley had not faced a Painite insurgency, nor had they been forced to choose sides in sedition trials, for there had been none in eastern Vermont. The valley's ministers and churchgoing men of property denounced uniformly the "unhappy party spirit" that prevailed elsewhere in Vermont and remained loyal to the standing order. Even those who embraced Republicanism before 1800 hoped for compromise on issues about which they disagreed with Federalists. Few wanted to abolish Vermont's nondenominational establishment or bore real malice toward the national administration. They only wanted fuller recognition of the rights of dissenters in Vermont and national policies that dealt evenhandedly with France and Britain, and with agricultural and commercial interests. They had no desire to inflame popular passions, discredit their adversaries, or undermine deference to ministers or men of property. They saw the conflict not as a contest between aristocracy and democracy, but as a debate among leading citizens over specific policies, which they hoped voters would end quickly with a verdict in their favor. They intended to throw off party labels and restore political calm as soon as the verdict was in.[53]

Neither party's leaders could foresee in 1800 that they would soon be locked in a party struggle as bitter and ideologically divisive as any in America. Their first mistake was to believe that they themselves were above partisan behavior. Their anxiety for the future of the republic, which had moved them in previous years to eschew partisanship and to insist on impartial inquiry into every issue, had also given them partisan habits of mind and had made them unyielding on points of principle, suspicious of those who disagreed with them, and quick to take offense when their disinterestedness was questioned. They were not narrow-minded men. They pondered the significance of every national and in-

ternational event, and eagerly discussed the ideas of Paine, Burke, and
other political theorists. They studied Breckenridge's *History of the Whiskey Rebellion* and the transcripts of sedition trials, believing that the
survival of their republic hinged on understanding revolution, on knowing which European nation posed the greatest threat to American principles and security and whether tyranny or anarchy would pose the
greatest danger from within. They were open to ideas, and as a result,
sometimes switched parties in response to national or international
events. James Elliot, for example, an aspiring lawyer and Francophile
Republican from Brattleboro who had fought against the British and
their Indian allies on the northwestern frontier, became a Federalist when
he realized that Napoleon had turned his beloved France into an empire
and that popular tyranny could emerge from America's revolution. Daniel
Buck, a lawyer and Federalist congressman from Chelsea, became a Republican because he was inspired by Jefferson's stand against the British
on the high seas and by his vision of a western empire, the acquisition
of which would prevent the rise of European-style social antagonisms in
America and give America greater legitimacy in the eyes of European
tyrants.[54]

Although ideas and events did sometimes move people to transfer their
allegiance from one party to another, Federalism and Republicanism
generally attracted very different people. The Federalists' conservatism
appealed to those who were afraid of popular upheavals in politics and
religion. According to Donald Smith, roughly three-fourths of the valley's
leading Federalists who had lived through the Awakening had been Old
Lights or Anglicans, and nearly half who had lived in Windham County
during the Revolution had opposed Vermont's independence from New
York.[55] The Republicans' progressivism, on the other hand, appealed to
people who feared political and religious tyranny. Roughly three-fourths
of the valley's leading Republicans who had lived through the Awakening
had been New Lights, and all had favored Vermont's independence from
New York. Federalist and Republican ideologues, by searching for signs
of impending anarchy or tyranny in every event and legislative proposal,
charged all political debate with memories of past battles and made
political soldiers of men with moderation in their hearts.

Both the Federalists and the Republicans also capitalized on contemporary hostility to the workings of Vermont's establishment. Disputes
erupted in many towns beginning in the late 1790s over ownership of
meetinghouses and the apportionment of religious taxes among competing denominations. Conflicts most often arose between Congregationalists and Baptists when the Baptists attained sufficient numbers to
establish independent churches and demanded partial ownership of ex-

isting meetinghouses or compensation for fees paid for the construction and maintenance of those houses. Angry and at times violent conflicts also arose between Congregationalists and non-Calvinists, particularly Methodists and Universalists, whom Congregationalists tried to bar from town meetinghouses to prevent them from wooing away nominal adherents.[56]

Such disputes also drew virtually every Methodist, Freewill Baptist, Christian, and Universalist minister and lay leader into the Republican Party, for they believed the Republicans would defend their spiritual liberties and egalitarian ideals against the machinations of wealthy and powerful Congregationalists. Most Episcopalians, Unitarians, and Old Lights were drawn to Federalism. They sensed that any further recognition of dissenters' rights would destroy the government's power to support worship and maintain order. New Lights moved toward Republicanism, because they believed that Vermont's establishment should be modified, if not abolished, to protect the rights of all dissenters and to guard against the spiritual corruption that religious tyranny brought.

Circumstances peculiar to certain towns or counties sometimes led religious groups to behave in different ways, however. Some leading New Lights embraced Federalism, particularly in towns in the northern valley where Baptists, Separates, and moderate New Lights had formed successful union churches, as in Berlin, or in towns where ministers and prominent laymen embraced the moderate evangelical doctrines of Timothy Dwight, as in Peacham. They felt that further changes in church–state laws would imperil their efforts to unify their towns around Calvinist ideals. At the same time, Old Lights, Episcopalians, and Unitarians embraced Republicanism in towns that were dominated by New Lights, like Rockingham and Guilford in Windham County, both of which were overrun by Baptist migrants after the Revolution. In some instances they did so to free themselves of the obligation to support churches whose congregations were sanctimonious and querulous. In other cases they concluded that the valley's de facto Congregational establishment caused more unrest than it suppressed. Samuel C. Crafts, a lawyer and politician from Craftsbury, wrote a satirical poem called "The Town Meeting" on the subject of the Congregational establishment. In it he revealed how many people were weary of Congregational efforts to support "their" establishment with "the Faggot and the Fire" and two- or three-vote majorities in each town. He had a guarded faith in the ability of plain, pious people like the Baptists and of enlightened latitudinarians like himself to safeguard public morals without a religious establishment.[57]

What had begun as an argument over the specifics of national policy and Vermont's standing order thus turned into a debate over the nature of community life in Vermont and in the valley. By 1808, this debate had divided the valley's ministers and churchgoing men of property. Some became ardent Republicans; others attached themselves firmly to the Federalists. Among this elite, there would no longer be much switching from one party to another. The leading citizens of the valley, both Federalist and Republican, had concluded that they could prevent the rise of permanent parties in the valley only by annihilating their adversaries at the polls. They began to do what they had sworn, as adherents of the standing order, never to do. Rallies were staged, taverns were scoured for voters, dirty tricks were played on opponents, party editors were forced to toe a strict party line and to appeal to popular passions. Candidates treated prospective supporters with whiskey on election day, causing so much disruption that in Cabot the freemen reluctantly voted to lock the whiskey in a closet and to keep the door shut "for the space of one-half hour" so they could vote before returning to revelry. One Windham County Federalist wrote a friend of the "great doings" his party planned for the Fourth of July: "drink punch, get drunk, burn Jefferson, and hang Tom Paine." This was done in fun. However, most electioneering was in dead earnest and was often intended to destroy an opponent's reputation. For Vermont's elite, there was no escaping the new partisanship. "A man may as well burrow like a woodchuck in winter and suck his claws for a licking as attempt a neutral course," future governor Richard Skinner wrote a friend in 1801. People who tried to remain neutral only rendered themselves "suspected by both parties."[58]

The electioneering succeeded in drawing out the valley's voters. Turnout increased from a quarter of the valley's adult males in the congressional and gubernatorial elections of 1800 to 40 percent in the elections between 1804 and 1807. The Republicans won only a tenth of the gubernatorial vote and a quarter of the congressional vote in the election of 1800. Although many voters were already questioning the Federalists' national policies, they were still willing in 1800 to defer to the leadership of incumbents who had proven themselves in the Revolution. The gap between the Republican congressional and gubernatorial vote eroded steadily, however, and disappeared entirely in 1808, as people voted increasingly along party lines and increasingly for Republicans, who were aided by the economic growth and territorial expansion that had occurred under Jefferson's administration.

The valley's voters did not support the same party each year. Town-level returns from 1800 to 1808 reveal that in one-third of the valley's towns the percentage of votes won by the Republicans in a given election deviated sharply – by more than 15 percent – from the percentage of the previous year, once the effects of each town's long-term party preference and of the valley's deviation in each election from its long-term party preference were considered. Some of that volatility reflected differences from year to year in the individuals who voted, but much of it reflected the voters' anxiety about the future of government in the nation and in the valley, which made them watchful, changeable, and increasingly partisan.[59]

By 1808, roughly half of the valley's voters had access to weekly newspapers, and political leaders claimed that their constituents read constantly and pondered national issues as well as local ones. Their political acumen and their concern for the fate of the American Revolution made them quick to dispense with parties or old heroes whose policies no longer served the valley's interests and ideals. One Old Light, for example, was sorry to see President Washington sign Jay's Treaty in 1795 with the hated British and delivered a summary judgment upon him. "He is a great and good man, but I am afraid he has now ... ruined his character forever." John Chamberlain, a New Light, rejected James Madison in 1806, claiming he had "forfeited the confidence of the people" by associating himself with "misterious characters who had been forming dark designs against the peoples rights" and who favored "too strong a government."[60]

Party leaders were exasperated by such behavior on the part of voters, but voter vigilance, once called forth by electioneering, could not be shut off. Most voters remained nonpartisan, were committed to the preservation of political harmony, and were opposed to the creation of permanent parties, yet they deferred only to those to whom they thought deference was due. In the end that meant no deference at all. As John Chamberlain put it, he would give leaders his "respect," but "never [his] worship."[61] Just as postrevolutionary Christians were refusing to submit to church discipline and to defer to the judgment of ministers and congregations, voters were beginning to question the judgment of their political leaders and to assert their right to replace them.

Still, when voters in the valley were persuaded that a particular party represented their interests and values and was capable of reuniting the valley, they became as loyal to that party as any of the valley's elite. Voters appear to have stopped changing parties between elections from 1808 to 1816. Town-level data reveal that in all but Essex County, which was just being settled during these years, the proportion of towns in each election where votes deviated from the previous year by more than 15 percent, fell to 2 percent once long-term effects were considered, far below the one-third that prevailed from 1800 to 1808. The Republicans' median gubernatorial vote in the valley's towns stood at 53 percent over those years and never rose above 59 percent or fell below 51 percent in any election.[62]

The electorate seems to have divided along the same lines as the valley's elite, over conflicts born of the Awakening, Vermont's revolution, denominational conflict, and rivalries among towns and neighborhoods. The median town-level Republican vote over those years stood at 69 percent in Windsor County, the heartland of the New Lights, of popular non-Calvinist dissent, and of Vermont's revolution, whereas the median Republican vote stood at only 42 percent in Windham County, the bastion of the Old Lights, Anglicans, Tories, and Yorkers. There were exceptional towns in each county, but most confirmed the pattern. Guilford, the center of Windham County's Yorker insurgency during the Revolution, went Republican, its Yorker leaders banished from the state in 1783 and their farms and shops taken up by Baptists from just across the border in Massachusetts. Windsor, the center of Windsor County's anti–New York insurgency during the Revolution, went Federalist, after becoming the state's first capital and attracting many lawyers and professionals, who moderated the evangelism of the town's Calvinist churches or supported their Episcopalian rival. The pattern was confused in the valley's northern counties, where all but a handful of the inhabitants had moved to Vermont after 1783 and had missed Vermont's revolution and where the settlers' spiritual beliefs were more heterogeneous. Yet there too the towns with the largest influx of Old Lights and of moderate New Lights of Timothy Dwight's theological and political persuasion, which were concentrated in northwestern Washington County and central Caledonia County, were Federalist, whereas towns inhabited by large numbers of New Light Baptists, Freewill Baptists, and Methodists, like Danville, tended toward Republicanism.[63]

Antagonisms among towns and neighborhoods also divided voters. Vermont's constitution, which required at-large elections for town officials and gave each town two representatives in the state assembly, conferred formal political power on farmers and the inhabitants of less populous communities, but rural people still felt themselves at a disadvantage as geography and trade established hierarchies among communities and neighborhoods, and frustrated expectations of parity. Hill towns and frontier communities voted more heavily Republican than marketing and manufacturing towns, by a median vote of 62 to 51 percent between 1806 and 1817. Rural neighborhoods like West Windsor voted more heavily Republican than commercial villages like Windsor. The separation of West Windsor from the town of Windsor revealed in 1814 that West Windsor's voters were more Republican than Windsor's by a margin of 67 to 6 percent. Of course, poor and frontier communities in Windham County, which were settled predominantly by Old Lights, were predominantly Federalist, whereas market towns away from the Connecticut River (Danville, Montpelier, and Woodstock), which feared being overshadowed by better-positioned rivals, were predominantly Republican.

Once the struggle between Federalists and Republicans had enveloped the electorate as well as the valley's elite, Vermont's standing order was doomed. Partisanship destroyed the spirit of moderation, compromise, and deference upon which that order rested and left Federalist and Republican legislators unable to defend Vermont's establishment, as most had hoped to do by gradual compromise. They had already tried to mollify dissenters in 1797 by granting them a greater proportion of religious tax revenues, and then in 1801 by facilitating the process by which dissenters exempted themselves from paying taxes to support the majority churches in their towns. These reforms, however, satisfied neither the dissenters nor the establishment, which believed the new laws deprived majority churches of the support they deserved. The two forces destroyed the assembly's compromise by making the church–state question a party issue and by manipulating the church–state law to serve their particular purposes in their hometowns. The assembly admitted its failure and quietly separated church and state in 1807. Most Federalist and Republican leaders were unwilling to take credit for its destruction and were afraid of what its loss would mean.[64]

The party struggle reached its height during the eight years that followed the election of 1807. Voters were mobilized by British and French interference with American commerce at sea, by Jefferson's embargo against foreign trade, by the war with Britain, and by economic stagnation. The proportion of adult males who voted jumped to an average of 65 percent between 1808 and 1815 and peaked at a phenomenal 82 percent in 1812, as the war with Britain began. Yet neither the new voters nor the issues raised by international conflict and economic disruption altered the pattern of support for Federalists and Republicans. Neither party had any hope of reuniting the valley politically. Party leaders continued to ask voters to defer to the majority, whenever their own party had just won an election, but such appeals were futile. Correspondence from the period reveals that whether they wanted peace or a just war, whether they hated France or Britain more (most people hated both powers equally by 1808), they rationalized support for the party that shared their deepest political and communal aspirations. Republican peace advocates justified their party's provocative policies, including the embargo and the War of 1812, as measures designed to build a lasting peace, while Federalist advocates of war denounced the Republicans' embargo as ineffectual and the War of 1812 as a foolhardy venture for which the nation had been unprepared.[65]

Some efforts were made to find common ground. Washington's "Farewell Address" and Matthew Carey's *Olive Branch* spoke for nonpartisan ideals and argued, the first from a Federalist perspective and the second from a Republican point of view, for moderate policies they believed all patriots could accept. These tracts proved popular with people who felt that ideologues in both parties were taking freedom for granted and that neither party had yet devised economic or foreign policies that could safeguard the independence and prosperity of the American people. Few people were ready to consider matters in the cool light of reason, however, and the outbreak of war made matters worse. Federalists in the state assembly publicly repudiated the governor's war message and accused the Republicans of trying to "embarrass" commerce. Republicans branded Federalists who sided with the British crown "traitors." Party spirit ran dangerously high. One Windsorite noted that "the neighborly relations between republican and federal citizens, of both sexes, were very much disturbed." They would not mingle at social gatherings or celebrate patriotic holidays together.[66] Even the demise of the national Federalist Party in 1815 did not end the hostility, so deep were the divisions upon which it fed. Both parties still prayed for total victory and counted votes much as rival denominations counted members. The desire for political harmony endured, but the spirit and the institutions that had once sustained it were gone.

The standing order and the covenanted community could not withstand the ideas and social antagonisms engendered by the Revolution and the opportunities of life on the frontier. People had become less willing to submit to discipline, to accept compromise, and to defer to authority. The valley's settlers were not as yet individualists, because they still denied the individual's right to place his or her interests, values, or beliefs above those of the community; but they had moved in the direction of individualism, by becoming more assertive of their rights and more accepting of the independence of others in moral, spiritual, and political matters. The social and political antagonisms that arose on the frontier had also made people less willing to live by a common communal and political ideal. The valley's settlers had not become pluralists or true partisans, but they had also moved in the direction of pluralism and partisanship, by championing particular views of what Christian communities and republican polities should be and by recognizing that denominational and party strife would persist, even though they detested that strife, denied their own contributions to it, and refused to confront the differences in experience, sensibility, and social condition that lay behind it.

The failure of the standing order and the covenanted community had apparently left the valley bereft of unifying institutions and ideals. In 1815, the valley's inhabitants were locked in a bitter struggle. Republicans accused Federalists of destroying tolerance, equality, and popular government, while Federalists blamed Republicans for destroying order, morality, political harmony, and deference toward the valley's political, spiritual, and community leaders. The fact of the matter was that both factions had failed to reconcile conflicting values and neither had been able to put forth an acceptable alternative to the religious and political order they had left behind in southern New England some forty years before.

3

Religion and reform in the shaping of a new order, 1815–1828

With the formal separation of church and state in 1807 and the demise of the national Federalist Party in 1815, many Vermonters, particularly those who were Federalists or devout Calvinists, began to fear that their society might become amoral and politically chaotic. Those fears were unfounded, however, for after the War of 1812 church members and like-minded townspeople of all denominations and political persuasions moved toward common ground in their commitments to their communities and to basic moral precepts. They did not come to that common ground consciously, or all at once. Denominational differences and antagonisms remained. Yet differences seemed to pale in importance before threats of immorality and disorder, especially after a massive crop failure in 1816, and the first signs of economic and demographic congestion in the valley.

Agitated by these concerns, Vermonters flocked to the valley's churches and Masonic lodges between 1815 and 1828, strengthening the institutions that gradually helped church members and like-minded townspeople bring a degree of order to postrevolutionary society. The burgeoning churches and lodges fostered networks of mutual assistance among church members and townspeople who shared their values, and those networks subtly helped them gain control over town resources. That in turn enabled them to draw others into their circle and into their campaign to uphold moral standards within their communities. Leading Federalists and Republicans also undertook interdenominational reform movements to bolster efforts to uphold moral standards, and through these movements they discovered new grounds for unity and won new political prestige. Under these circumstances and with the valley's economy doing well, political calm reigned, and for some thirteen years the leadership of the valley went unchallenged.

Churches, Masonic lodges, and the stabilization of town life

It is difficult to explain fully the spiritual and organizational boom that struck the valley's churches between 1815 and 1828. People seldom spoke of why they or their neighbors participated in it. Many people were unaware of its dimensions because it took shape over fourteen years. Most of those who recognized the boom took it for granted that God's hand lay behind the work, and most people seem to have considered the practical benefits that came from joining and organizing churches too obvious to comment upon.

The boom began with a dramatic awakening in the Congregational and Baptist churches. Massive revivals brought in scores of converts, and many new churches were organized. If the modest revival of 1810 is included, the rate at which members joined Congregational and Baptist churches increased fourfold between 1810 and 1828, from only 3 per year per 1,000 inhabitants aged fifteen and older to 12. The Awakening touched both Old and New Lights and brought about a lasting reconciliation between the two groups, by rallying both Old and New Lights behind moderate evangelical doctrines that reaffirmed their belief in predestination while extending hope of salvation to nearly all who sought it.[1]

The boom took Calvinists by surprise, but contemporary ministers were undoubtedly correct to give some credit to the "Year of No Summer," 1816, when June snows destroyed crops in many areas of the world, and the greatest revival began. There was evidence that a worldwide revival was induced by that phenomenon and the hardship that followed: Revivals broke out that year in every country of the Western world where the crop failure struck people who had evangelical or pietistic traditions, as in southwestern Germany or on Britain's Celtic Fringe. Like Christians in those regions, many of the valley's Calvinists believed that God had sent the disaster to punish their failure to live by the covenant. They crowded into prayer meetings seeking grace and forgiveness.[2]

The crop failure of 1816–17 hit hardest those people who would appear disproportionately in the rolls of the born-again: master craftsmen, and young men and women who were unmarried and propertyless.[3] Cash-short farmers could not purchase the wares of craftsmen, and employers could find no work for young wage earners, who often were forced to donate their savings to their families and to delay their plans to marry or buy land. Since such people were often predisposed to conversion by the circumstances in which they lived, the crop failure could well have helped turn them toward God.

Yet the fact that the Calvinist boom began before and extended beyond 1816–17 suggests that the crop failure may only have intensified existing concerns in the Calvinist community. Also, the revival of 1816–17 won its most enthusiastic converts not among Calvinists placed in precarious economic positions by the crop failure, but among Christians and Freewill Baptists from established farm families. Members of these denominations had long sought to restore the unity that they believed prevailed among Christians in apostolic times. It was their habit to examine every natural disaster and political struggle for signs that the final days foretold in the Book of Revelation had come. They studied every dream and "heresy" with patient interest, because only Christians "free from bias and prejudice" could hope to follow the Bible and God's angels wherever they led. When the revival began, Freewill Baptists and Christians threw themselves into it, praying it might usher in new prophecies, miraculous healings, and eventually, the millennium.[4] They embodied the spiritual passion and hope that the revival inspired in many Christians, including Calvinists, as it progressed, and their reaction to the revival is a reminder that for most Christians the revival represented not a remedy for want, disorder, and sin, but a quest for genuine ways to serve God.

The spiritual boom extended to other non-Calvinists and to nonevangelicals as well, who were not necessarily predisposed to revivalism and may not have believed in a providential interpretation of the summer snow. Church membership among adult males in the agricultural towns studied intensively rose from 12 percent in 1815 to 26 percent by 1828, and from 17 to 37 percent in the marketing and manufacturing town of Windsor. The number of non-Calvinist churches and circuits doubled (from 52 to 114), and the Methodists saw their membership treble, even though the valley's population rose by less than a quarter. In towns and neighborhoods too sparsely populated to support worship for individual denominations, services at village meetinghouses or newly constructed Union meetinghouses (which had increased from 4 in number before 1815 to 19 by 1828) flourished with broad interdenominational support. There was one church or meetinghouse in the valley for every 400 residents by 1828.[5] The vast majority of residents supported churches financially and attended services regularly. More than a crop failure or a Calvinist crisis of confidence lay behind this spiritual boom.

Now that state support for religion had ended, people of every denomination were clearly anxious for the valley's moral and spiritual health, and that anxiety may have fueled the spiritual boom. In addition, the first signs of economic and demographic congestion were manifesting themselves in the valley, and parents and young people were especially concerned by what they saw. For the first time, there was a substantial number of young men coming of age in the valley who had to leave Vermont to seek their fortunes – 16 percent, up from 5 percent in the previous decade. Young women of marriageable age outnumbered young men by 13 percent in 1810, whereas in 1800 young men aged sixteen to twenty-five had outnumbered women by 3 percent. The number of new farms declined, so that proportionately more of those who remained in the valley were forced out of the countryside and into towns and villages, where they entered riskier, more competitive mercantile and manufacturing occupations.[6] Opportunities remained plentiful, but for the first time inhabitants of the valley saw before them a future in which doors that had been wide open were now partly closed.

Churches could be of great use to those inhabitants of the valley who came face to face with these conditions. People could find comfort and guidance there; they could insulate themselves and their loved ones from sins like intemperance, gambling, and premarital pregnancy that dissipated family resources and ruined reputations. They could improve their chances of meeting the right kind of friends and spouses; and they could find business partners and people willing to give them economic help.

In this society of small proprietors, an individual's success depended upon his ability to finance a shop or a farm, and to do that he needed the financial support of family members, patrons, creditors, and customers. The economy had lost its frontier character by 1815. Shops and farms were more specialized in production and were more frequently involved in exchange beyond their immediate neighborhoods.[7] People with sound reputations and connections outside their families and their neighborhoods were more likely to be able to tap sources of support in their townships and market areas, and therefore to succeed, than those who defied community standards and tried to make it alone.

There is little evidence, especially from the early years of the spiritual awakening, that anyone joined a church with these concerns in mind. Most people were drawn to the churches for more immediate reasons (because of the conversion of family, friends, and neighbors or because of the emotional attraction of revival meetings and the millennial expectations they aroused) or for more ill-defined practical reasons (because churches appeared good for them and for society at a time of crisis, when order, piety, and harmony were endangered). Only in the 1830s would many townspeople begin to understand how the churches helped shape a new order in town life by drawing church members together and facilitating alliances among them.

Still, there is much evidence that church membership was economically

Table 3.1. Ownership of Mercantile and Manufacturing Firms,
1815-1830: Marketing and Manufacturing Towns[a]

	Church members[b]	Nonmembers
Single owners	29	51
Partners, same surname	15	8
Partners, different surname	57	41
N =	187	168
Religious status of partners with different surnames		
Partnerships formed with church members	71	46
Partnerships formed with nonmembers	29	54
N[c] =	103	67

[a] The data from marketing and manufacturing are from Windsor and
Woodstock. Data from 1815 to 1820 are not available for Woodstock.
[b] "Church members" are people who had joined churches by the time their
firms organized.
[c] The owners of all firms that existed during each decade are included, even if
the firms they owned were founded in a previous decade. Owners whose firms
were labeled "and Company" are considered persons with partners with
different surnames. These owners are not included in the analysis of the
religious status of partners with different surnames, because their partners
cannot be identified.

advantageous to church members. Data on partnerships reveal that
between 1815 and 1830 church members in major commercial and
manufacturing centers were more likely to form partnerships than non
members, both with relatives and nonrelatives; and that they formed nonfamily partnerships primarily with other church members (Table 3.1),
40 percent of the time with members of different denominations. Church
members were disposed to promote these relationships not simply because
connections with other church members were more readily available, but
because the bonds they formed were of a kind that would prove reliable
in business. Partners who were church members were expected to be
dependable because any instance of impropriety could be brought before
the churches, where actions would be carefully examined (or, in nonevangelical churches, informally discussed), motives probed, and repu-

tations reconsidered. The presence of such sanctions was important in a business environment in which good will and reputation counted for so much.[8]

In agricultural areas, church membership did not offer so many advantages, for there was somewhat less need for strong connections outside the immediate family and neighborhood. Farm owners did not have to attract customers, and they could secure whatever credit they needed with their land. Nor did farm workers always need connections outside their family circles: When wages were high in relation to land prices, as they were from 1815 to 1825, their earnings and whatever they might have inherited from their parents generally sufficed to establish them on a farm somewhere in the valley. There was no tradition of farm workers setting up partnerships with employers outside their families, and at this time there were few openings for young farm workers as tenants on large farms.

Merchants and master craftsmen in the countryside also had less need of connections than their counterparts in towns and larger villages. Each man could rely more on his family's local reputation for customers and credit, and on his own resources for capital. In part, this was because less capital was required to establish businesses that were located in small country villages or at remote crossroads, and because such enterprises served a captive clientele and were not usually in direct competition with other businesses. Rural master craftsmen who engaged in primary manufacturing processes like wool carding, cloth dressing and fulling, and hide dressing had less need of connections and credit than wool manufacturers, clothiers, and shoemakers in large towns, for they were not entrepreneurs seeking large market shares, but intermediaries between farmers or local women who supplied materials and the merchants and other master craftsmen who purchased the materials for further processing. They did not depend on retail customers or need to carry retail inventory.

Church membership still had its advantages in agricultural towns, however. Fewer manufacturing and mercantile firms were organized as partnerships in these towns than in commercial and manufacturing towns between 1811 and 1830 – only a quarter as opposed to over 40 percent – but church members were still more likely to form partnerships, both with relatives and nonrelatives (Table 3.2). As in commercial and manufacturing towns, they formed nonfamily partnerships primarily with other church members, 40 percent of the time with members of different denominations.

Church members also had greater access to mortgage money than nonmembers and favored each other in borrowing and lending. Whether

Table 3.2. Ownership of Mercantile and Manufacturing Firms,
1815-1830: Agricultural Towns[a]

	Church members	Nonmembers
Single owners	48	66
Partners, same surname	12	3
Partners, different surname	40	30
N =	114	264
Religious status of partners with different surnames		
Partnerships formed with church members	59	27
Partnerships formed with nonmembers	41	73
N =	39	77

[a] The data from agricultural towns are from Barnet, Peacham, Pomfret, St. Johnsbury, Weathersfield, rural Windsor, and West Windsor.

Table 3.3. Religious Status of Mortgagees and Mortgagors
with Different Surnames, 1821-1830: Agricultural Towns[a]

	From church members	From nonmembers
To church members	48	23
To nonmembers	52	77
N =	238	262

[a] The data are from Peacham, St. Johnsbury, and Weathersfield.

financiers or private individuals, those who loaned money to people of different surnames did so disproportionately to other church members (Table 3.3). More than three-fifths of those loans in towns with more than one church were made between members of different denominations. Church members, especially those under forty, were also more likely than

Table 3.4. Religious and Occupational Status
of Mortgagors, 1821-1830: Agricultural Towns[a]

	Church members	Nonmembers
Age unknown and under 40[b]		
Farmers	65	55
N =	60	141
Agricultural nonproprietors	44	26
N =	36	147
Unknown persons and new residents in agriculture	68	31
N =	81	220
Nonagricultural proprietors	59	19
N =	17	42
Nonagricultural nonproprietors	58	16
N =	24	146
Unknown persons and new residents not in agriculture	17	6
N =	53	238

[a] The data are from Peacham, St. Johnsbury, and Weathersfield. The data include mortgages concluded both between persons of the same surname and persons of different surnames. Only 7 percent of all mortgages were concluded between persons of the same surname. Church members concluded such mortgages at a slightly higher rate than nonmembers.
[b] The data for persons age forty and over reveal similar trends. Proportionately fewer persons in that age category were mortgagors.

nonmembers of the same occupation to hold mortgages (Table 3.4). That may have reflected in part their greater access as "dependable people" to mortgage money, for the largest difference between church members and nonmembers occurred among nonagricultural proprietors, who represented the greatest risk to lenders, and the smallest difference occurred among farmers, who posed the least, because they sought relatively small loans and secured them fully.

Church membership also offered benefits to farmers and farmhands. Churchgoing hands often won the best jobs because of their reputation as reliable and well-behaved workers, while farmers who hired church-going hands knew that they were getting workers who were accountable to the churches for their misdeeds. Farmhands could be called to account for their conduct even if, as often happened, the offense was committed a long way from home. Noah Martin, a farmer in Peacham, acted as a go-between in a case involving a young man from his home town of Woodbury, Connecticut, who was working on farms in the valley for settlers from that Connecticut town. The young man chose to sow his wild oats while away from home, so his employer sought and secured his expulsion from the church, remanded him to his parents, extracted damages from his pay, and sent the remainder directly to the youth's parents for safekeeping. The farmer in this case did not get a good worker, but he did get full redress.[9]

Church members also had an advantage over nonmembers when it came to the emotional and economic costs of isolation in agricultural areas. This was illustrated by the plight of Charles Fox, a nonmember who had moved from Massachusetts to West Windsor between 1810 and 1815 to settle on a neglected farm. Fox labored diligently for two years, but both his corn crops failed, and he found himself $100 in arrears in his bills for fence repairs, a well, blacksmithing, and taxes, although he and his family had lived "prudently, not even having bought so much as a bit of fresh meat since . . . last summer." As strangers, he said, "we have no company," except for two respected local farmers who admired "the order everything was in" on his farm and offered to buy him out. He wrote, "my pride . . . will not let me take less than the first cost" for the farm (perhaps implying that his shrewd neighbors had offered him less).[10]

By the end of the summer, things were looking better; he had harvested a good corn crop, "when so many other farmers lost so much" to bad weather, and he boasted that he had produced as much as his neighbor, Mr. Cady, a Congregationalist deacon, had on twice the acreage. "If nothing happens, I shall be in a good way for the future," he wrote. But the crop-killing freeze of June 1816 ruined him, and by 1817 he had left Vermont. Perhaps such a hardworking farmer would have succeeded had he been a church member and a respected member of the community like his allegedly less able neighbor, Deacon Cady. He could have counted on church members coming to visit, bringing meat to his family on occasion. Local farmers would have come with aid and advice, as they had come to the Stephen Smith family of South Woodstock in the 1780s, rather than with offers to buy his farm.

The advantages that church members gained from participation in their networks of mutual support worked dramatically in their favor by the 1820s. Those who belonged to churches were more likely to remain in

Table 3.5. Persistence by Age, Occupation, and
Religious Status, 1820-1830: All Towns

	Church members	Nonmembers
Age unknown and under 40		
Nonagricultural proprietors	82	45
N =	38	80
Agricultural proprietors	77	52
N =	137	353
Nonproprietors	56	37
N =	113	605
Age 40 and over		
Nonagricultural proprietors	82	64
N =	38	14
Agricultural proprietors	77	65
N =	199	309
Nonproprietors	58	38
N =	76	252

town during the 1820s, even more so than others of the same age and
with similar assets (Table 3.5). Those who remained in town were also
more likely than nonmembers to be upwardly mobile. The trend was
strongest in commercial and manufacturing centers, where church members were more likely to have risen to proprietorship or to larger enterprises than nonmembers of the same age and occupation (Table 3.6).
Church members under forty were particularly more successful than their
counterparts outside the churches. Church members over forty were still
more successful than nonmembers over forty, but a decline in the magnitude of their advantage suggests that the common health problems of
the middle-aged and their greater family responsibilities (in particular the
provision of dowries and starting capital for their children) were a critical
factor in determining success, with or without church membership.

The advantage of church members was less marked in agricultural

Table 3.6. Social Mobility by Age, Occupation, and
Religious Status, 1820-1830: Marketing and Manufacturing Town

	Church members	Nonmembers
Age unknown and under 40		
Nonagricultural proprietors		
Upwardly mobile	25	0
Downwardly mobile	0	50
Net change	25	-50
N =	16	4
Nonagricultural nonproprietors		
Upwardly mobile	71	25
N =	7	20
Age 40 and over		
Nonagricultural proprietors		
Upwardly mobile	6	0
Downwardly mobile	13	0
Net change	-6	0
N =	16	1
Nonagricultural nonproprietors		
Upwardly mobile	33	0
N =	3	7

towns. Church members there were more persistent (Table 3.5). Those who remained were also more successful than nonmembers of the same age and occupation (Table 3.7), but this advantage was less great among agricultural proprietors and nonproprietors, who depended largely on family resources for success. As in the commercial and manufacturing towns, church members under forty had a greater edge over their non-member peers than did those over forty.

In addition, when church members moved from one town to another, they apparently did so with the assurance that their environment would

Table 3.7. Social Mobility by Age, Occupation,
and Religious Status, 1820-1830: Agricultural Towns

	Church members	Nonmembers
Age unknown and under 40		
Nonagricultural proprietors		
Upwardly mobile	0	0
Downwardly mobile	13	22
Net change	-13	-22
N =	15	32
Nonagricultural nonproprietors		
Upwardly mobile	56	35
N =	9	40
Agricultural proprietors		
Upwardly mobile	19	16
Downwardly mobile	13	21
Net change	6	-6
N =	106	182
Agricultural nonproprietors		
Upwardly mobile	64	43
N =	47	165
Age 40 and over		
Nonagricultural proprietors		
Upwardly mobile	0	0
Downwardly mobile	26	38
Net Change	-26	-38
N =	15	8
Nonagricultural nonproprietors		
Upwardly mobile	22	15
N =	11	26
Agricultural proprietors		
Upwardly mobile	22	11
Downwardly mobile	21	30
Net change	1	-19
N =	153	201
Agricultural nonproprietors		
Upwardly mobile	27	23
N =	30	64

remain stable and supportive. After 1810, residents of the valley moved to other towns within the valley twice as often as they had before, but they did so under the moral auspices of their churches, with letters of recommendation and good standing that enabled them to reconstruct, in their new towns, the network of relationships they had left behind.[11] That church members who appeared on the tax rolls for the first time during the 1820s (that is, new residents and local youths who had passed the age of twenty-one) entered town life with more property and a greater incidence of proprietorship than those of the same age who were not church members suggests that the advantages of church membership began very early and carried over from town to town (Table 3.8).

It is clear from the data that church membership did contribute significantly to persistence and success, but it is not inconceivable that the peculiar persistence and success of church members stemmed in part as well from strong family ties or an ambition on their part to stay in town and succeed, which might have drawn them disproportionately into the churches in the first place. Church members, according to the sparse data available on family partnerships and mortgages, were more likely than nonmembers to form economic alliances with other family members. That suggests that churchgoing families may have worked together more closely to advance the fortunes of their members. It is also clear that in the 1820s some young men began to speak openly of joining the churches of their employers or business associates to get ahead, and that residents who would join churches during the subsequent decade were already more successful in the 1820s than other nonmembers.[12]

It is important to note that those who would eventually join churches in the 1830s were less successful and well-connected in the 1820s than church members. Most were future members of evangelical denominations and betrayed little calculating ambition. Their partial inclusion in the networks of church members was probably based on their standing as regular churchgoers and spiritual apprentices of a kind. Open ambition was peculiar to religious liberals, who were the only church members to view themselves as a temporal as well as a spiritual elite. Such pretensions were censured in other denominations, where people had to await divine election before entering churches, and worldly ambitions and temporal distinctions among men were denounced.

Yet members of nonliberal denominations also outdistanced nonmembers in upward mobility and in the extent of their economic connections, and after 1810 they came subtly closer to drawing definite associations between faith and respectability, just as liberals did. Evangelical sermons and church records after 1810 called less frequently for "love feasts" among the brethren and more often urged that people mind their "P's"

Table 3.8. Proprietorship among New Adult Residents
in 1830: All Towns[a]

	Church members	Nonmembers
Marketing and manufacturing town		
Age unknown and under 40		
Nonagricultural proprietorship	74	16
N =	19	75
Age 40 and over		
Nonagricultural proprietorship	100	14
N =	1	7
Agricultural towns		
Age unknown and under 40		
Nonagricultural proprietorship	41	18
N =	68	392
Agricultural proprietorship	52	37
N =	124	575
Age 40 and over		
Nonagricultural proprietorship	0	5
N =	4	41
Agricultural proprietorship	47	38
N =	15	56

[a] "New Adult Residents" are persons who were on the tax lists or census rolls in 1830 but were not on those lists or rolls in 1820. They include persons who moved to these towns and local youths who became twenty-one during the decade.

and "Q's," a change that offended at least one New Light minister, who charged that "external conduct, and not the heart," had become "the criterion of moral excellency." After 1817 many Universalists embraced Restorationist Universalism, a doctrine articulated in that year by a number of Universalist ministers in the valley and areas adjacent to it. Restorationism proclaimed that sinners would not be "restored" to heaven until they had suffered in purgatory for their crimes.[13] Even believers in universal salvation were interested in giving sinners an incentive to behave. All this suggests that, for evangelicals and Universalists, the commitment to community and to moral standards that brought them together in economic matters increasingly led them to view church membership as a proxy for dependable character.

A new pattern of life had thus emerged in the small towns of the valley by the 1820s. Church members were making use of networks of stable, supportive relationships beyond the bounds of their families and their neighborhoods, networks that insulated them from the disruptive effects of life in postrevolutionary Vermont. By offering entrance into their networks of alliances and friendships to those who shared their standards and communal commitments, they encouraged support for their moral standards without the formal apparatus of the covenanted community. Of course, the bonds among church members were personal and conditional, and the pressures they created toward conformity were generally informal, but the efficacy of these connections in the 1820s – as reflected in the social stability and the continued good fortune of church members during that period and in the matter-of-fact way in which men and women connected church membership, good character, solid connections, and success in their private writings – indicated that they had successfully replaced the formal mechanisms of the covenanted community as a means of preserving Christian dominance within their towns.

Without knowing how it had come about, the valley's Christians recognized that a new order had arisen in the valley. David Watson, editor of the *Woodstock Observer*, wrote in 1820 that people in the valley were "brethren" once again, that they all believed in "one Lord and one faith." Oliver Smith, a Republican orator, tried to put a name to the new order, dubbing it an "Aletheocracy," or reign of truth, brought into being by the passing of the Congregationalists' oppressive "theocracy." Even Christians who lacked such words realized their society had changed. Their communities were more orderly and pious, and the disruptive ideas and social changes that had threatened their way of life in the past seemed to have gone by the board.[14]

No one spoke of networks of support among church members. Nor did anyone question the right of Christians to pressure others into supporting what the churchgoing community wanted. It was not until the 1830s, when adherence to Christian values was no longer truly voluntary, that Christians would invoke "voluntarism" to justify their use of social institutions to pressure the heedless to accept Christian values, and a handful of political insurgents would warn of a conspiracy against the rights of nonmembers.[15] But the ideology of voluntarism arose only after the new order came under stress and church members were prompted to look for new measures to defend their communal values. In this decade the valley's inhabitants did not feel compelled or coerced to become church members.

It is probable that the informality of the church members' system of connections and the lack of conscious pressure on nonmembers was a key factor in the new order's success. Church members were not, under this system, vulnerable to the charges of collusion and oppression that had brought down the covenanted community. Who outside the churches could organize an opposition based on the demand that church members extend their friendship beyond the circle they had chosen of their own accord? Who could behold the legal tolerance of immorality, and the success of some nonmembers, and then assert categorically that the church members' disproportionate prosperity stemmed not from their decency and their commitment to their communities (which in part, of course, it did), but from exclusiveness and collusion? A few such charges were hurled at the Episcopalians, who, by moving closer than other church members toward setting themselves above the people as a business and professional elite, had given credence to local fears that they were conspiring to establish themselves as the local branch of the British aristocracy. However, nonmembers left no evidence prior to 1828 that they suspected church members in general of harboring such designs.[16] By abandoning the disciplinary institutions and the inclusive ambitions of the adherents of the covenanted community and by contenting themselves with marking the boundaries of respectable society in lines drawn closely around their churches, church members effectively robbed those who opposed their leadership and moral authority of any concrete target. From that point, the mere fact of their persistent success enabled them to maintain a moral and economic hold on their towns.

This new pattern of life also helped create two curious phenomena: the expanding appeal of Calvinism in marketing and manufacturing towns and villages where stratification and mobility were destroying the interpersonal bonds on which that communal faith was supposed to be based, and the high rate of church membership among merchants and master craftsmen as opposed to farmers, who have been seen by many historians as defenders of the moral standards that villagers and townspeople were supposedly destroying, but who were in reality less likely to be church members. Proponents of Calvinism in these areas no longer pretended to the encompassment of entire towns and villages, but Calvinism itself had an increasing appeal for certain townspeople. It distinguished them, as the elect, from outsiders and moral reprobates, while alleviating tensions among them by asserting the essential spiritual equality of all church members. With that stark line between the elect and the nonelect, Calvinism drew the boundaries (more rigid, less permeable than in agricultural towns) of the network among church members that was emerging in the towns and villages, and, in effect, linked church members of different social strata in relationships based on trust, support, and mutual obligation.[17]

The material advantages of church membership might explain why merchants and master craftsmen testified to their faith in greater numbers than all but commercial farmers, to whom economic connections were also important (Table 3.9). It might also explain why master craftsmen in agricultural towns involved in primary processing or clothing trades were not more likely than farmers to be church members. It is possible that, associating as closely as they did with farmers and farm families, from whom they bought the raw goods they needed, they perceived themselves and were perceived as members of the same group. Their income levels were much like those of subsistence farmers. Many produced their own food on small acreages. And unlike other master craftsmen, who sold their products directly to the public, these men sold wholesale to distributors in large towns. Connections with anyone save the farmers who sold them raw goods were not crucial.

Although prospects of material advantage could not entirely account for these patterns of church membership, they probably played a part in drawing people into churches at a faster rate in towns than in the countryside. But there were other factors involved. People who lived in towns met their neighbors almost daily and made friendships that often led them into the churches. Newcomers to towns like Windsor spoke of the way the churchgoing community enveloped them upon their arrival. People they wanted to emulate – their employers, friends, and relatives – invited them to church and introduced them to the inner circle of the business community, where spiritual commitment was considered not so much a ground rule as a given. They began attending church regularly and taking an interest in the state of their souls.[18]

In the countryside, where farmers and master craftsmen engaged in primary processing lived, encounters among residents were more infrequent and irregular. Churches often disbanded after short periods of time. Beliefs were more parochial, enthusiasms intense but short-lived. Church membership might depend on the accessibility of a church, the congeniality of its particular doctrines, or the affiliation of near neighbors.

In some isolated rural communities people were closer to each other than townspeople were, particularly because they were of the same class and were often related to one another. In their isolation, these people were apt to become zealous evangelicals. On the other hand, they also

Table 3.9. Religious Status of Proprietors in 1830: All Towns*a*

	Marketing and manufacturing town	Agricultural towns
Proprietors who were church members (percent)		
Merchants	78	42
N =	27	36
Master craftsmen, group A*b*	77	24
N =	13	83
Master craftsmen, group B*b*	61	45
N =	18	31
Millers and taverners		27
N =	-	47
Commercial and family farmers		46
N =	-	403
Subsistence farmers		27
N =	-	541

a The data on millers, taverners, and farmers who lived in Windsor are included with the data from agricultural towns.
b Group A includes wool processors, woolen manufacturers, tailors, hatters, tanners, and shoemakers. All were involved in the clothing trades or in the primary processing of raw materials. Group B includes all other master craftsmen.

seemed more prone to religious indifference and to the hostile rejection of Christian influence.[19]

In general, however, churches gained impressive strength throughout the valley. Only in the fifteen most recently settled, remote, impoverished, "frontier" towns were churches frequently absent, primarily, it seems, because there were not enough people to support churches of separate denominations. None of these towns had more than 400 residents in 1830. Still, they averaged one church for every 600 residents; and they supported numerous neighborhood circuit classes and village meetinghouses, which played an important role alongside more established churches in many small villages and rural neighborhoods.[20]

Churches also gained notable strength among the very poor and the young. Although there is no evidence of hostility among the poor toward churches during these years, and much evidence that they studied the Bible and delighted in hymns, they often felt isolated from the more prosperous, settled world that the churches represented. Orange Scott of Berlin was never taken to church as a child, for he "had not clothes to appear in the House of God," and William Cheney of Danville, a woodsman who moved from town to town in search of logging and clearing work, found himself and his family always on the fringe of society, never having the time, the inclination, or a sufficient sense of belonging to attend services. Yet Scott and Cheney, like many other poor people and nonproprietors, came into the churches in 1820 and 1821, as these feelings were overcome, transcended, or addressed, especially by the Universalists and by non-Calvinist evangelicals.[21]

Young people also began to come into the churches in great numbers at this time. The median age of men at admission to Calvinist churches fell from thirty-two to twenty-five after 1815, and the proportion of those admitted who were under twenty-one quadrupled. The proportion of new female members who were not married more than doubled (Table 2.2). To the churchgoing community, these successes were not grounds for complacency. Full church members were still a minority of the adult population, although together male and female church members made up a majority of the stable population. Also, there were still pockets of indifference in the valley – "moral deserts," as Joseph Tracy, the editor of the *Vermont Chronicle*, termed them – where people's "peculiar opinions, prejudices, and habits cut them off from the approach of any good influence from our churches."[22]

There was one group other than the church members that created a stabilizing web of relations outside their immediate families, and that was the Masons. Masonic lodges in the valley increased between 1815 and 1828 at a faster rate than churches did, from ten in 1810 to thirty-three by 1828. Actual membership may have grown even faster, for each lodge drew members from surrounding communities.

Like church members, Masons were likely to remain in their towns and accumulate property. Masons who were church members and those who were nonmembers formed partnerships in mercantile and manufacturing firms and received mortgage money more frequently overall than did non-Masonic nonmembers. They did not succeed by establishing a network that was at cross-purposes with, or even entirely distinct from, that formed by church members, however. Masonic church members strengthened connections they had already made as church members. Masonic nonmembers won partial access into the society of church members and entered economic relationships both with church members who were not Masons and those who were. Only one loan and one partnership between Masons who were not church members were recorded between 1810 and 1830 in the towns that were studied intensively.[23]

Masons defended Masonry publicly on terms that they believed church members, as the dominant force in town life, could accept, emphasizing that Masonry merely provided an additional route through which civic-minded citizens could disseminate Christian moral standards. As in southern New England, the Masons had their share of freethinkers, rakes, democratic radicals, and latitudinarians, who saw Masonry as a weapon against Calvinism and the standing order. However, Masonry was not as insurgent in the valley as it had been in southern New England, even though its members were primarily Republicans. It included some evangelical Calvinists and Methodists (Table 3.10), as well as Federalists, and it grew most rapidly after the final separation of church and state in 1807 had sealed the fate of the standing order.[24]

Among themselves, the Masons adopted "Christian" patterns of mutual support. They stood "ready to serve and assist each other." They avoided lawsuits, did not demand payment from debt-ridden brothers, offered traveling or poor members free food and lodging, and helped pay a portion of the burial fees for deceased members. Like church members, Masons did not forget that they were "to do good to all," but they believed, in the words of one J. Roberts of Whitingham, that they were "to do it more especially unto the household of the faithfull." They also employed Calvinist-like sanctions against members who had broken oaths or agreements and therefore threatened the Masons' reputation for loyalty and dependability, disciplining some and expelling others, whose names they published in local newspapers. It may be significant that Masons were likely to be nonevangelicals. Because their own religions did not provide them with the kind of fraternal bonds that evangelical religions did, they may have been moved to seek those close connections in Masonry.[25]

Although personal ties among Masons were strong, Masons tended to arrange partnerships and loans with Masons who were fellow church members or with fellow church members who were not Masons, rather than with those Masons who were outside churches. That suggests that Masonry reinforced, but did not replace, the bonds fashioned in churches and that membership in the Masons did not constitute the kind of character reference that church membership did. Furthermore, Masonry was often censured by the churchgoing community. Many people saw the

Table 3.10. Membership in Reform Movements, 1815-1828[a]

		Coloni-zation	Sunday schools	Bible distri-bution	Masonry	Deaf and dumb
Denomination (Percent)						
Congregationalists		52	63	47	8	40
Baptists		4	13	5	7	-
Associate Presbyterians		4	-	13	1	-
Episcopalians		-	13	8	14	60
Unitarians		4	-	-	2	-
Methodists		-	-	-	4	-
Freewill Baptist/Christians		-	-	-	2	-
Universalists		4	-	-	13	-
Nonmembers[b]		35	13	27	50	-
Occupation						
Ministers		13	30	9	1	40
Businessmen/professionals		58	35	26	13	60
Master craftsmen		21	35	4	16	-
Small proprietors		-	-	7	5	-
Millers/taverners		-	-	-	4	-
Clerks		-	-	3	2	-
Journeymen/laborers		-	-	-	15	-
Commercial farmers		8	-	12	4	-
Family farmers		-	-	23	15	-
Subsistence farmers		-	-	10	20	-
Farm tenants		-	-	-	-	-
Farm laborers		-	-	9	5	-
Interrelationships among reform movements						
Colonization	(24)	-	29	88	25	4
Sunday schools	(15)	47	-	60	40	13
Bible distribution	(127)	17	7	-	17	2
Masonry	(289)	2	2	7	-	-
Deaf and dumb	(5)	20	40	60	-	-
Federalists	(38)	17	8	50	18	5
Republicans	(6)	67	17	67	33	-

a Data from Woodstock are included. The Masons of Woodstock are not included in the occupational statistics, because that town's tax lists have not survived. The members of the other movements from Woodstock were so prominent that their occupations can be determined. Dashes indicate that zero percent of the members of a reform organization were members of a particular denomination, occupation, or other reform organization. The N's for each organization appear in parentheses.
b Most nonmembers worshipped at local churches. Sixty-two percent of those who supported colonization would become church members after 1828, 50 percent of those who supported Sunday schools, and 46 percent of those who supported Bible distribution.

evidence of drinking at lodge meetings and heard of the parades and garish ceremonies that in certain ways parodied church rituals, and concluded that the group only maintained secrecy to shield itself from community disapproval. The Masons insisted that their lodges improved the tone of life in the valley and provided a necessary alternative to the society of both taverns and churches. In lodges members could "discover amiable qualities . . . capabilities and abilities, which they could never have ascertained, neither in a sequestered life, nor in a promiscuous crowd."[26]

Many people found the Masonic network of support and mutual encouragement unfair, because it was intentionally exclusive and because prospective members were chosen on the basis of current members' whims rather than on the basis of morality. The Masons argued that, like church members, they were only trying to ensure that people who were committed to their towns and to Christian values would maintain their dominance in community life, but many church members looked upon the Masons' autonomous participation in that effort with disapproval and suspicion. They could not see the need for an extra-ecclesiastical organization with such pastoral pretensions, and they worried that Masonic disciplinary proceedings and vows of mutual aid would usurp power in their towns.

Despite such doubts, members of various denominations and Masonic lodges recognized that they shared a commitment to Christian standards and in many instances attempted to put aside their differences. Church members began to sense an increased commitment to Christian doctrine and morality in the valley between 1810 and 1828. Signs of success were everywhere, both in public life, in great revivals and increased church membership, and in private life. Sales of Bibles and religious tracts increased, whereas the consumption of alcoholic beverages edged down. Young people revealed in their writings more concern for their reputations and those of their friends and prospective spouses. Female church members, eager "to do something for Him who gave his life for lost men," looked aggressively after the souls and morals of husbands, children, and siblings.[27]

The members of the Congregational church of St. Johnsbury rejoiced. Sabbath breaking, gambling, drinking, and profanity, "which were once our disgrace," were "forsaken or driven into a corner." Josiah Dunham, an Episcopalian, Mason, and president of both the Windsor Academy and the Sabbath School Union, claimed in 1819 that the forces of order and morality in the valley stood on the threshold of a "cheering dawn of intellectual and moral light, which announces a new era to mankind."[28] Immorality, youthful intractability, denominational antagonisms, and religious indifference had not disappeared, but church members and like-minded citizens had begun to believe that it was possible to control those forces and assume the leading role in shaping the valley's future.

Reform and the stabilization of politics

The ability of churchgoing men of property to lead their society had been seriously damaged by their failure to preserve the deferential system of politics that had begun to take shape in the mid-1780s and early 1790s. Eventually, however, these men found that through reform movements, they could recover some of the unity, prestige, and political power they had lost. Between 1813 and 1828, leading Federalists and Republicans embarked upon a series of interdenominational movements to reform society and to recover something of their former standing in the valley.

A number of Federalist and Republican party leaders became convinced after the war that their best course of action lay not in political campaigns or appeals, but in spreading sound moral and religious principles throughout society. The Federalists changed tactics primarily because they lost faith in their ability to win elections. Yet leading Federalists, like Charles Marsh of Woodstock, had always understood that the realization of their conservative social vision ultimately depended on their ability to promote "a change in morals and religion," as much as on victory at the polls.[29] The collapse of the national Federalist Party in 1815 made the need for change immediate, however. The valley's Federalists remained strong through 1817; but their party disappeared throughout the South and the middle states, and they entertained no illusions about their ability to resurrect Vermont's nondenominational establishment. New Hampshire and Connecticut had separated church and state completely in 1817 and 1818, and the postwar revival had further strengthened the denominations that opposed established religion.

What was unique about the valley was that victorious Republicans recognized a need for change as much as the defeated Federalists. A few Republicans, like William Czar Bradley, a freethinking, college-educated lawyer and assemblyman from Westminster, set out happily to rid the government of Federalist and clerical influence and to cut its revenues and powers, so that Vermonters could enjoy at last the blessings of economic, spiritual, and political liberty. But a greater number of Republicans were ill at ease with their party's claim that man was by nature tolerably good and that he would remain orderly if government acted within strict constitutional bounds and was periodically purged of corruption. They worried about the party's leveling tendencies. Cornelius P. Van Ness, the most powerful Republican in the assembly, scolded

Republican zealots in 1818 for opposing nonpartisan measures like the bill that discouraged the sale of alcoholic beverages to disorderly persons or the measure that promised to help capitalists revive Vermont's troubled economy. Others revealed a certain distaste for the supporters they had drawn to the polls. Addison Smith, the nephew of former assembly speaker Dudley Chase, complained of being branded aristocratic because he would not "mix with the rabble and become intoxicated." In his opinion, liberty was about to become "synonymous with licentiousness and wild disorder." Smith and Republicans like him hoped to reunify the valley's ministers and churchgoing men of property quickly and to restore moderation to Vermont's politics.[30]

These sentiments prevailed in part because many Republicans feared the loss of Vermont's nondenominational establishment as much as Federalists did, and in part because they faced a volatile, unpredictable electorate agitated by seventeen years of uncommonly bitter party warfare. The peculiar nature of the Republicans' victory in the valley also contributed to their desire for an end to partisan hostility. Unlike their counterparts in southern New England, they were no longer struggling to establish dissenters' rights or adult male suffrage. They could afford to entertain thoughts of rapprochement with Federalist adversaries. They also needed that rapprochement. Unlike their Republican counterparts in most middle and southern states, they had triumphed not on their own merit, but by virtue of Federalist defeats elsewhere, and their rule was precarious.[31]

Leaders of both parties turned to nonpartisan reform to mend fences and to preserve something of the essence of the standing order. It is difficult to connect individual Federalists and Republicans with the various reform movements, for party affiliations are difficult to trace in this era, and membership lists survive for only four reform societies: the Colonization Society, the Sunday School Union Society, the Bible Distribution Society, and the Committee to Aid the Deaf and Dumb.[32] Still, 29 percent of the colonizationists, 20 percent of the Sunday School Union organizers, 16 percent of the Bible distributors, and 40 percent of the Deaf and Dumb benefactors can be identified as Federalists in the towns studied intensively. The most prominent Republicans in the valley, Judge Abner Forbes of Windsor, Judge Titus Hutchinson of Woodstock, William Jarvis of Weathersfield, Thomas Emerson of Norwich, and Israel Dana and William Palmer of Danville, all wealthy financiers, joined every reform movement, as did the leaders of the state's Republican Party, Governor Jonas Galusha (1807–12 and 1815–20) and Lieutenant Governor Paul Brigham. Each movement was led by well-to-do church members and churchgoers (businessmen, professionals, and commercial farmers) – basically the same group that led both the Federalist and Republican parties (Table 3.10).

The memberships of these reform movements overlapped considerably. For example, 47 percent of the Sunday School Union organizers were also colonizationists, 60 percent were Bible distributors, and 40 percent were Deaf and Dumb benefactors. That overlap enabled Federalist and Republican reformers to act in concert, to discover their mutual interests in moral and spiritual reform, and to work informally toward common goals. Eventually they initiated a threefold campaign of evangelical, benevolent, and social reform movements and emerged as the leaders of an effort to rid politics of party labels and to encourage deference once again to churchgoing men of property.

It was evangelicalism that lay at the core of the reformers' campaign. They recoiled from Timothy Dwight's visionary prewar efforts to establish covenanted communities and distanced themselves from millenarian zealots. Yet they recognized the importance of religion to the social order, and the potential of evangelism and its techniques for promoting reform, as did the urban evangelicals in Great Britain and southern New England to whom they looked for inspiration. They supported the postwar revival, but, like their urban counterparts, shunned denominational affiliation as best they could in order to gain more widespread support. Between 1813 and 1825, the reformers worked to encourage temperance and began Sunday schools, Bible distribution, and moral uplift societies all around the valley. It was their intent to spread God's word, improve the valley's moral tone, and, not incidentally, to curb democracy.[33]

Wealthy evangelicals exaggerated their contribution to the growth of the churches, but they did finance and assume leadership of the effort by the churchgoing community to uplift the valley's towns. Men and women of every sect and party joined in the postwar revival, which William Chamberlain, the wealthiest man in Peacham, claimed in a letter to a friend in 1817 had caused politics to subside "almost entirely." The Sunday School and Bible societies gained support from members of many denominations (Table 3.10), particularly Congregationalists and Baptists, who placed the New Light–Old Light conflict behind them as they rose to the defense of community and Christianity. The Methodists supported separate Sunday schools and Bible-distribution programs, however, and the Universalists declined to join either the Sunday School or Bible societies because they believed, in the words of the Universalist minister Robert Bartlett of Hartland, that the evangelical societies wished "to turn the little children's weak and tender minds into the channel of Calvinism." Bartlett was more than willing, however, to "give men all the credit their pious labors deserve in reforming the 'children of disobedience' " and he supported the growing unity of spirit among competing sects and believed their efforts would promote morality.[34]

Reformers from all denominations, Calvinist and non-Calvinist alike, banded together to enlist people in the temperance movement. They believed that the temperance movement had the potential to be the most effective reform vehicle for the campaign against immorality because all religions would benefit from its success. The Republican-dominated state legislature joined the temperance effort in 1817, creating a committee to investigate "the expediency of adopting some measures for discountenancing the too free use of ardent spirits." Chaired by Governor Galusha and comprised of twenty-one prominent clergymen and politicians representing every denomination and party and including many important reformers from the valley, the committee blamed intemperance for every evil from crime to political excesses and "taxes to support the poor." It called upon society to acknowledge that a recognition of proper authority was essential to social survival and exhorted ministers, church members, civil officers, militia officers, physicians, farmers and mechanics, and parents to be temperate and to encourage temperance for the public good, especially among "their guests or their laborers."[35]

The committee refrained from advocating formal state action against intemperance, and the legislature concurred. Apart from stiffening penalties against taverns that allowed patrons to become disorderly and making tavern licenses more difficult to acquire, it refused to move beyond informal pressure and persuasion to check crime, improvidence, vagrancy, and other evils associated with intemperance. Indeed, legislators made the criminal code and the debtors' laws less exacting in the following two years. In 1818, they abolished the whipping and branding of convicted criminals and greatly reduced the number of capital crimes, in favor of imprisonment and larger fines. In 1819, they prohibited the imprisonment of debtors who owed less than fifteen dollars and ended the practice of warning out of town "strangers" who seemed likely candidates for poor relief. These laws, following as closely as they did upon the legislature's declaration in favor of temperance, suggest that lawmakers wished to avoid using the kind of punishment and harassment that built resentment against authority and sympathy for criminals, poor debtors, and wanderers. Temperance, combined with a legal code leavened with charity and dedicated more often than before to rehabilitation, was intended to bring about a wider acceptance of the values promulgated by the bipartisan leadership of the state and greater compliance with the more limited demands now made on citizens.[36]

The evangelical and temperance movements coincided with and helped to foster an expansive humanitarian spirit that found expression in benevolent enterprises to help people who could not help themselves. Benevolent activities gave born-again evangelical reformers, as well as those who were not evangelicals or who had yet to attain grace, the opportunity to fulfill their Christian duty to the less fortunate and to improve the moral tone of the valley through their example of disinterested service. Benevolent activity proved the key to the interdenominational alliance that the reformers sought to forge. Every denomination had a theological and, along with the Masons, a moral commitment to nondenominational benevolent activity.[37]

The benevolent reformers helped both the ailing and the oppressed. They organized local committees to care for the deaf and dumb, like that created in Windsor by Horace Everett, an Episcopalian lawyer and former Federalist politician. They persuaded the Republican-dominated state legislature in 1817 to back their efforts by appropriating an annual fund for the education of deaf and dumb children.[38] A group of them founded the Vermont branch of the American Colonization Society in 1819. The society wanted to transport free blacks to Africa to spread the gospel among their people. Members of the society opposed slavery, but also felt that blacks could never stand on their own in white society, although they disputed whether white prejudice or black inferiority was responsible for that. At least one bold spirit, a son of Republican activist Samuel C. Crafts, wanted freedmen to be sent to the American West, where they could be educated and eventually integrated as equals into American society.[39]

The Colonization Society received strong bipartisan support. It gave former Federalists a nonpartisan vehicle through which to vent their wrath against the "hypocracy" of the Republican South, and it gave Republicans an opportunity to redeem themselves morally (after years of silence for the sake of their party's southern wing) by denouncing every northern "doughface" who made excuses for slavery. Governor Galusha was elected as the first president of the state organization in 1819 and stood behind the legislature's condemnation of the admission of Missouri as a slave state and its insistence on a quick end to slavery through government-assisted colonization. Phineas White, the grand master of Vermont, enlisted Masonry in the cause and solicited contributions personally from each lodge. Men like Isaac Green, a Unitarian and president of the Bank of Windsor, and Richard Ransom, a Universalist and a leading Republican from South Woodstock, perhaps the most prominent lay representatives of their faiths in the valley, joined the Colonization Society because it was founded on moral principles that they shared and that were not connected with any one sect (Table 3.10).

Dozens of reformers also dedicated themselves individually to helping those in need when the crop-killing freeze of the summer of 1816 left many faced with ruin or starvation and raised fears of food riots and insurrections against creditors. No one outshone William Jarvis, a prominent Republican financier, a Unitarian, and the wealthiest gentleman sheep-farmer in the valley, who used his resources to relieve the distress. His daughter wrote that their farm, "being sheltered and warm, suffered but little." Her father, "sympathizing with the people in their sufferings," made his granary "the storehouse for the hill towns," and sold his corn at a reasonable price, offering to wait for payment or to "take it back" in work in haying. He also allowed extensions on mortgage payments on request, and thereby won a considerable reputation for charity.[40]

Although the donors acted consciously out of Christian charity or a sense of noblesse oblige, their benevolent endeavors helped to justify their social order during a period when many people might have been prompted by opportunistic politicians to question its legitimacy. The reformers' actions proved that to some extent they recognized their social obligations to others, especially during difficult times. Their benevolence tended to obscure any injustice or selfishness that hard-pressed citizens might have perceived in day-to-day life by focusing hatred on those wealthy men who refused to contribute to such societies. It was clear who contributed and who did not: Lists of contributors were published for almost every benevolent reform society. That was an innovation. Prior to the war no Christian in the valley could have conceived of publicizing charity, for doing so violated long-standing rural and Calvinist taboos against giving for the sake of reputation and against embarrassing neighbors who received charity.[41]

During the postwar years, social reformers also began to devote their attention to education and poor relief. They concentrated on the larger marketing and manufacturing towns, because their desire to act was stimulated by fear of a specific social group: the poor. The wartime recession and the freeze of 1816 had increased the number of poor and had driven many of them to seek employment in major towns. The political crisis had heightened fears among wealthy men everywhere that there was increased resentment among the wandering poor to which demagogues could appeal.

Unlike their counterparts in Boston and New Haven who set up Lancastrian schools and poor houses modeled after English institutions, the valley's reformers did not create new institutions to reach the poor. They had little money, and poverty in the valley was not as concentrated as it was in the cities of southern New England. With an eye to cutting escalating relief costs, Vermonters created a system of relief that would give the poor work. Successful poor farms were established after the war in the two largest towns of the valley, Windsor and Woodstock.[42]

Reformers also called upon the common schools to provide children, especially those whose parents could not pay for their education, with the habits, morals, and religious beliefs necessary for them to lead useful lives. Josiah Dunham, a grammar school teacher and reformer from Windsor, encouraged his fellow reformers in 1819 to concentrate on helping the children of the poor in order "to snatch . . . the poor miserable vagabonds and outcasts of society from the downhill paths of vice" and "pave the way for both old and young to read the Bible." This would be a "benevolent work, truly, and in perfect accordance with the temper of Christ," Dunham wrote, and he did not hesitate to praise its practicality as well.[43]

The intent of this reform was twofold, reflecting the reformers' dual image of the poor. As they saw it, education and work relief offered the honest poor a chance to lead constructive lives, while restraining the incorrigible who endangered the religious and political life of the community. Opportunity was promised to hard workers, to ensure social justice and to remind the poor that personal failure alone caused their plight, while control was augmented to eliminate radical tendencies and to uplift the shiftless and the sacrilegious.

Initially, Federalist and Republican reformers preferred to portray their efforts simply as conservative or progressive. They believed they were only stimulating the stabilizing mechanisms that every Christian, republican society employed to survive periods of stress. Their Christianity allowed them to believe just that, for as they moved from conservative and progressive ideals toward reform, they were able to invoke the spirit of their faith to characterize each new adjustment or reform as an effort either to preserve endangered Christian traditions or to create the first society to embody Christian ideals. Federalist reformers could set aside concerns over whether they were defending the essence of the old ways they cherished and accept innovations in basic social institutions as giving new meaning to old practices. Republican reformers could set aside concerns over whether they were wavering in their commitment to unfettered democracy and make popular appeals to preserve a hierarchical, deferential society. The ambiguities and inconsistencies of their positions suggest why the entire reform crusade was conceived in moral and religious terms. Christianity was the only element of the reformers' world view with sufficient dynamism, breadth, and variety to allow them to engage in such contradictory behavior.

Only when the reformers came to appreciate the moderate intentions of their former adversaries did they explicitly espouse reform. Federalist and Republican reformers began to call for an "era of good feelings" and for an end to sectarian and party hostilities, because they feared that continued strife would destroy all semblance of piety and republicanism. They asked for interdenominational and nonpartisan support for their movements to help spread a reverence for nonsectarian Christian morality, interdenominational harmony, and republican institutions. Reform societies and the beliefs they stood for would replace the ideal of a standing order as the foundation of the social order. The concern of the reformers was thus no longer the defense or destruction of the old order, but the creation of a new order.

Almost every important Federalist and Republican leader in the valley was numbered among the reformers. Together they brought an end to party conflict. The Federalists endorsed the Republican gubernatorial candidate in 1818, disbanded their party, and left their members to vote and run for office as independents. Leading Republicans denounced the zeal of their own partisans and called for reconciliation. An anonymous Republican poet who had vilified the Federalists during the war captured these sentiments in "An Apology to the Federalists," written around 1816. He expressed the belief that

> Both parties wrong, have taken the extreme,
> Let's quit them both, and take the medium.
> Say one course, we jointly will embrace,
> All party names, from western climes we'll chase.

The author of this exercise in moderation was no stranger to party conflict. He had always been a champion of freethinking, equality, and religious toleration and had vociferously opposed priests and aristocrats. Now, however, he fell in line with Republican reformers and spoke out in favor of religious and political calm.[44]

To quiet the electorate, Republican leaders began to allow former Federalists to participate in government once again. Important ex-Federalist politicians, like Horace Everett of Windsor, a state assemblyman and later congressman, gained Republican support and even campaigned as Republicans, surrendering little except their hope to revive the Federalist Party as an independent force. One-third of Vermont's senators and congressmen between 1815 and 1828 were former Federalists, a figure only slightly below the proportion (40 percent) of actual Federalists who served between 1798 and 1815.

Wealthy churchgoing men of both parties and all denominations worked together to restore the essence of the pre-1798 political system. They tried to resolve their differences amicably and present the voters with a united front, defining and deciding public issues in accord with what they perceived as the will of church members and respectable citizens in the valley. The voters acceded: As the economic crisis and the international tensions of the war years abated, voter turnout dropped from 80 percent in the gubernatorial election of 1812 to 33 percent in the election of 1818. Mobilization fell to its lowest point in 1825, when only 22 percent of the adult male inhabitants cast ballots for Richard Skinner, who ran unopposed for governor.

Between 1815 and 1828, church members, Masons, and men in the uppermost decile of wealth in their towns strengthened their position in local politics. They were more likely to become selectmen than they had been between 1808 and 1815, while the proportion of terms held by selectmen who were nonmembers declined slightly from 53 to 46 percent. Members of every denomination, including Calvinists, who had been widely despised during the party battle, found sufficient support to win seats. The proportion of terms held by Masons rose from 9 to 20 percent, and the percentage held by selectmen in the upper decile of wealth rose from 24 to 56 percent.[45]

Stability had been attained in the valley. There would be but one party, and if many sects, only one religion. The belief in republican institutions and in the separation of church and state remained to ensure a measure of liberty, and the emphasis on evangelicalism, benevolence, and social reform tended to curb selfishness, irreligion, and popular resentment of the powerful and the well-to-do. Interpretations of the immediate postrevolutionary period that provoked political intransigence or insurgency were anathema. Rationalists worked to transcend the conflict between Burke and Paine; satirists denounced the "Tom Grumbles" who were "ever wishing the return of times that are past, and clamorous for some change"; evangelicals depicted the Federalist–Republican era evenhandedly as a time when the forces of darkness loosed both anarchy and tyranny on the world to test the mettle of Christian republicans. The conservative Federalist view, which portrayed the postrevolutionary era as a time of decline into disorder and impiety, and the progressive Republican view, which interpreted those decades as a period of struggle against aristocracy and priestcraft, both disappeared – suppressed or forgotten. The advocates of reform insisted that they, and not the few remaining Federalist and Republican partisans, were the true heirs of the American Revolution, which they interpreted in both a conservative and a progressive sense, as a time of Christian unity, and as an effort to realize revolutionary ideals through political and institutional change. They agreed to safeguard the Revolution by creating a society loyal to their interpretation of its traditions and designed in accord with transcendant norms – a Christian, reformed society.[46]

This settlement was far from reactionary or static. It represented an attempt to define the meaning of the revolutionary heritage and the New England way in the United States, to shape a political system without an aristocracy or an established church. With a truly republican government and a moral citizenry to make it work, the leaders of the valley could, for a short while, absorb conflicts among themselves and transcend the dilemmas of democratic life. They created a society that was pious, orderly, and politically harmonious, and committed to equality, tolerance, and popular government. They combined the New England heritage of a religiously purified society with the revolutionary quest for a secularly just order, merging the forces that made the nation's civilization an advance over Europe's in the tradition of reform.[47]

The leading citizens of the valley celebrated their achievement openly in the 1820s, rejoicing in the "Era of Good Feelings" that spread across the nation during Monroe's presidency. The self-congratulation peaked in 1826, when they participated enthusiastically in the nation's commemoration of the Federalist and Republican heroes, John Adams and Thomas Jefferson, both of whom died on the Fourth of July that year. That miraculous coincidence gave orators and editors an opportunity to rewrite the history of the Federalist–Republican controversy around the assumption that Americans never disagreed on fundamentals and would never again allow their passions to divide them into hostile factions. They did not ignore the differences between Jefferson and Adams. They often portrayed the two as living embodiments of the principles of freedom and order that were so perfectly balanced in America's institutions (an image popular with those who campaigned to replace Vermont's unicameral assembly with a bicameral legislature in order to ensure that the same balance would be struck in Vermont). Most eulogies emphasized Adams and Jefferson's similarities, however, and ignored each man's denunciations of various trends in postrevolutionary life.[48]

Vermonters were content to enjoy peace and freedom in the 1820s, while Europe was caught in the throes of the post-Napoleonic reaction, its aristocrats and established churches restored by force to power in the wake of the failures of its democratic revolutions. They took heart in the knowledge that their revolutionary example had inspired Mexicans and Greeks to strike out against despotism in 1821 and 1823 and that their missionary societies were spreading God's truth throughout the world. Amariah Chandler, a New Light minister from Waitsfield, spoke for all reformers in his election sermon of 1824, when he expressed a hope that Vermont's period of affliction was past and declared that God had brought "his glorious plan of beneficence and grace" to fruition in Vermont "in a gradual manner." "Regular progress" would come as God imparted "wisdom" to mankind through churches and reform societies. This, too, was a stabilizing vision, suggesting that Christians and republicans had completed their most difficult work at home, and that none need fear a return to the extremism of the Federalist–Republican era.[49]

Despite its successes, reform did not reassert the hegemony of wealthy churchmen to the extent anticipated, especially where the poor and outsiders were concerned. By the 1820s the drive for social reform had all but disappeared, without reaching the people it sought to aid and discipline. School reform made little progress. Although elementary school texts, grammars, and mathematical primers sold briskly, and although the assembly created a small state fund in 1822 to aid education, reformers could not persuade voters to improve their local schools, and many parents still refused to send their children to school on a regular basis. There was no hint of an increase in school attendance, and there was no real pressure brought to bear on poor parents to send their children to school if they preferred to have them work. The first formal survey of school attendance, conducted in 1846, suggests that attendance had remained low throughout the period. In that year, an average of only 51 percent of all children between the ages of four and eighteen attended common schools or private academies during the winter term; attendance fell even lower during the summer term. In 1827 the state legislature established a Board of Commissioners for Common Schools, staffed by reformers, to remedy the problem of irregular attendance and poor instruction, but the legislators abolished the board after it delivered its first report in 1828. The board had made grand plans to instill in the students "an early discipline of the mind and heart, for successful discharge of the duties incident to their respective situations in life." But most inhabitants of the valley were unwilling to allow their children to be prepared for life according to the board's plan, and the state legislature did not want to override popular opposition to the board's demands for certification of teachers, text selection by instructors rather than by local school boards, and courses in civics, patriotism, and patriotic singing. Legislators capitulated quietly to those who feared that state involvement in education would lead to the indoctrination of children by one faction or to compulsory attendance. Opponents of the board might not have objected to reform itself, but when reform became mandatory or spoke with the authority of the state, they feared it.[50]

Programs directed toward helping the poor also fell far short of the mark. Towns failed in their efforts to employ poor relief and poor farms to rehabilitate and discipline the wandering poor and the idle. Only Windsor and Woodstock established farms, and even they did not extend relief to anyone other than resident orphans, widows, and elderly people who had no families to support them. Under no circumstances was aid given to newcomers or to the able-bodied.[51]

In short, the common schools served the children of parents who wanted or could afford to have their children attend school (although most very young children did attend school, and even older boys who were farmhands went occasionally), and poor relief served the dependents of deceased taxpayers. There was an increased assurance that those who desired and were eligible for schooling and relief would receive it, but there was little impetus to impose either upon the poor, once stability had returned in the early 1820s.

Charity and benevolence could not wholly revive the spirit of deference toward those with wealth and power. As always, there were many people who resented the rich because they were rich and because they represented a kind of aristocracy. One man who was saved from ruin by William Jarvis during the year with no summer wrote a ballad about his benefactor, ostensibly to bring his kindness to the attention of fellow townspeople. While commemorating Jarvis's benevolence, however, the balladeer slyly tweaked his nose, comparing him to "Egypt's lord" (Moses or Pharaoh?) and thanking him because he had "agreed to take his pay/ In stout days' work in making hay," adding gaily, "God speed his plough and bless his store,/Then when we want we can have more."[52]

Egalitarian Christians clearly were not reconciled to social inequities, although as a group they were politically quiescent in the early 1820s. Despite their belief that social wrongs would be rectified in the next world, for example, the Methodists nursed a grudge against the rich. In their hymns, they portrayed the rich as a necessary evil, and took a dim view of the "benevolence" of the worldly:

> When the Lord's people have need,
> His goodness can find out a way . . .
> By ravens he sends them their food.
> Thus worldlings, tho' ravens indeed;
> Tho' greedy and selfish in their mind,
> If God have a servant to feed,
> Against their own will must be kind.

Still, rather than rail against what they could not change, Methodists and other egalitarian Christians often joined benevolent, educational, and moral improvement societies, expressing their desire to be a part of respectable society rather than to overturn it. Yet their doing so did not mean that they were reconciled to their station in life or guarantee that in time of crisis they would support the policies of the valley's leaders.[53]

The successes of the crusades for moral and spiritual improvement were also limited. The temperance movement declined almost as soon as it began. The report of the legislature's Committee on the Use of Ardent Spirits in 1817 marked both the rise and fall of organized state-level activity in the postwar period. Reformers tried to discourage alcohol abuse in their towns and churches, and it appears that the consumption of alcoholic beverages did drop between 10 and 15 percent after 1815, as church membership and a heightened concern for reputation inhibited excessive drinking; but few temperance societies were formed at this time, and no one went so far as to call for total abstinence.[54] The proportion of new members dropped or expelled from Calvinist churches rose for men from 10 to 24 percent during revivals, and for women from 6 to 9 percent. Soul-searing evangelism, whatever its power to terrify or inspire young men and women, could not bring everyone into the fold, even though the majority of conversions proved lasting.[55] The informal pressures exerted by churchgoing men and women and by concerned parents made a more lasting impression on behavior than did revivals or temperance crusades.

The reform campaign also suffered from its failure to draw significant female support, even though women were largely sympathetic to its ideals. A small band of women, primarily wives of evangelical reformers, enrolled in Bible society registers beneath the names of their husbands. Some taught Sunday school, and in several instances, as in Barnet and Windsor, women organized independent, interdenominational missionary societies to save the souls of Indians or children. Neither Indians nor children were of primary concern to male evangelical reformers, and women believed they could treat them as dependents in need of their spiritual guidance. A few women took up the cause of poor relief. The women of St. James' Episcopal Church in Woodstock made decorative objects for sale at a church bazaar and donated the proceeds to a relief fund.[56]

Such efforts were few, however, and did not become in any way regularized. The problem was not simply that women were not encouraged by men to join the reform effort, but that so many of the young women who were fervently caught up in the spirit of the awakening married and found themselves absorbed in ministering to the needs of their families. Lucy Gibbs, who believed on the eve of her marriage to a local farmer that she had at last discovered her Christian "duty" in service to her prospective husband and family, put aside her spiritual diary on her marriage day and did not resume it for many years. Lois Leverett no longer spoke of spiritual matters in her letters in the 1820s but instead rehearsed the difficulties of raising seven children and lamented that "my grey hair and loss of teeth make me look very old." Such women would form the core of female activism in the 1830s, when their youngest children had passed infancy and when their older children had begun to face difficult social circumstances. At this time, female activism was still largely confined to the larger market and river towns, like Windsor and Woodstock, where women had fewer children on average and were less absorbed than women in the countryside in textile production and farm chores. Like women in contemporary northeastern cities, they had more time to watch over the moral and spiritual development of their families and communities, and may also have had a greater incentive to do so, given the generally greater fear of disorder in more densely settled communities.[57]

The reform effort was also hampered by the limited ability – and desire – of wealthy church members to persuade or coerce others into accepting their programs. They had entered reform movements at a time of economic and political crisis, when their prestige, their political power, and the stability of their society were threatened. With citizens jealous of their prerogatives, men of property did not want to create political controversies; nor could they exert an inordinate amount of control over the electorate or society in general, as long as work was generally available to those who sought it. By the mid-1820s, as the economy improved and voter turnout declined, they moved with less urgency in their reform efforts and increasingly distanced themselves from those reformers who continued to crusade fervently against the evils of the world or sought to impose one view of right conduct upon society.

The valley's inhabitants had made a conscious effort during the Revolution to create a tolerant and equitable yet orderly and pious society. That effort had failed, but their less calculated attempts to shape such a society after the War of 1812 brought no small degree of success. They created a new order in town life and politics that carried them closer to the realization of their ideals and away from a liberal society. Despite the fact that this order imposed fewer formal sanctions upon people who refused to abide by community standards or to recognize society's claims upon them, there were now fewer violations of community expectations: less public drunkenness, less rowdiness, less Sabbath breaking. The sheer number of observing Christians exerted pressure upon the unchurched community. That pressure did not threaten, however, but held out promises of advantage, and was all the more powerful for its subtlety. Thus the assertiveness that had characterized Vermonters during and just after the Revolution was diffused and absorbed. Political and denominational rivals became less combative and less distinctive. The valley's inhabitants did not merely halt or slow the trend toward individualism, pluralism, and partisanship; they reversed it.

The political and social order that the valley's inhabitants had created did not restore the fortunes of political conservatives, but neither did it give progressives free rein. It helped communities accommodate new ideas and new freedoms while maintaining unity and stability. Church members and Masons had no formal mechanisms to protect their towns against immorality and disorder; ministers and churchgoing men of property had no laws or political vehicles to institutionalize their leadership and rule. Yet through their commitment to nondenominational Christianity and nonpartisan reform, the valley's church members, Masons, and leading citizens expanded their influence and enhanced their prestige, drew others to their standards, and for a time brought peace to the valley.

4

From an era of promise to pressing times, 1815–1843

Economic development in the valley and the nation had been constrained by international hostilities and trade embargoes since 1807. The economy was expected to rally when the War of 1812 ended, but the crop failure of 1816, the return of inexpensive British manufactured goods to American markets, and the scarcity of lending capital during the financial panic of 1819, hampered economic growth throughout the country as late as the early 1820s. Still, both the national and the local economies grew steadily from the early 1820s through the 1830s. The annual rise in per capita income was not large by standards of modern industrial societies – only 1 percent nationally – but by previous standards it was dramatic. Certainly it was large enough for the valley's politicians to proclaim blithely that "old king 'Hard Times' had been knocked in the head once and for all."[1]

By the late 1820s and early 1830s that optimism appeared to some to be mistaken, and by 1834–5, people had begun to complain of "the pressures of the times" and to look "with melancholy forbodings to the future."[2] The problem was that growth had reneged on what people thought of as its most important promises: the promise that family and community life would go on undisturbed, that every citizen and every town would share in the prosperity with rough equality, and, most important, that opportunity would increase for those who wished someday to operate their own farms and shops. The failure of growth to fulfill these promises had a pronounced impact on individual ambitions and on the social fabric and led people in the valley to believe that, despite their greater average wealth, a novel kind of crisis was afoot. This was not a crisis of the sort associated with war, depression, or crop failure. Times were "pressing," but there was no sense of despair. It was only that so many people found themselves increasingly frustrated in their pursuit of long-cherished goals. Still, the intensifying social pressures were in some respects more disruptive than a true crisis, for everyone did not feel their effects equally, and there was no assurance they would end.

Thus after one brief decade of respite, there was again a widespread belief among the inhabitants of the valley that their way of life was endangered.

From growth to a decline in proprietorship

The valley's economy grew in the 1820s and 1830s primarily because improvements in transportation and marketing enabled farmers and manufacturers to profit from the growing demand in southern New England for the cheese, butter, maple sugar, meat, wool, leather, lumber, and manufactured goods that the valley's farms, woodlots, and workshops produced. The costs and methods of producing most agricultural and manufactured goods changed little, but the improved quality of land and river transport enabled Vermonters to capitalize on their proximity to southern New England and to market their goods at lower cost, which increased profits for producers and shippers. Vermonters fixed their attention on dramatic developments like the appearance of steamboats on the Connecticut River in 1829 and the construction of a butchering facility near the boat company's wharves in Windsor, which would slaughter thirty to forty hogs and cattle each day and open a "permanent and profitable market" for Vermont beef and pork along the length of the Connecticut River. That would add, by one estimate, $100,000 annually to the local economy. More important were the patient efforts of the valley's merchants and financiers to improve roads and bridges and clear the Connecticut River of navigational hazards, so that drovers, teamsters, and flatboatmen could move goods efficiently within the valley and to markets in Boston, Springfield, and Hartford. Their efforts had been under way since the 1790s, but war, embargoes, and a weak national economy had stood in the way. In the 1820s they were greatly aided by a state law that put a stop to haphazard maintenance of important thoroughfares, by assigning control over major routes to the county courts and by giving the county the power to force local governments to make improvements and repairs.[3]

The valley profited greatly from improvements in transportation and marketing, because its natural resources fit the needs of New England's expanding economy. Dense forests, rough terrain, and difficult soils did not prove a liability in these years, when timber and wool were in demand and there was plenty of wooded and improvable land left in Vermont. The acreage being tilled, mowed, and grazed in the valley rose 45 percent between 1820 and 1840. Rocky land in the valley's northern reaches, previously deemed useless, yielded the nation's largest potato crop; potatoes, starch, and liquor were profitable commodities.[4]

The valley's farmers were able to make the most of what they had by changing their crops and practices in response to market conditions and technological advances. The wealthiest farmers bred sheep and cattle according to the latest scientific advice, using both American and imported stock, and sought higher yields of corn and oats through crop rotation and fertilization. They subscribed to journals like *The New England Farmer*, and in Windsor County they founded an agricultural society. Farmers of moderate income, themselves unusually literate and well-informed, kept up with the latest agricultural information in the valley's newspapers. They too adopted new practices, shifting quickly from the wooden to the iron plow, and halting wheat production when rust and competition from wheat producers in western New York made other crops more profitable, particularly wool. By 1836, half the valley's towns had over 5,000 sheep, and only towns with the roughest terrain had fewer than 1,000.[5]

The valley responded with similar success to the growing demand in New England for manufactured goods. At a time when wool, leather, and wood provided the raw materials for most manufactured goods, and when swift-moving water was the preferred source of power for mills, the valley had ideal natural resources for manufacturing. The number of master tailors, hatters, fullers, carders, wool manufacturers, tanners, shoemakers, sawyers, and carpenters grew by 60 percent between 1820 and 1830 in the towns studied in depth.[6] There was a particular increase in new jobs for young women. They worked as seamstresses in the expanding clothing trades or as operatives in newly constructed woolen mills, where they tended the latest power-driven looms and spindles, constructed by mechanics from southern New England.

Outside the woolen industry, there was as yet no concentration of the manufacturing, processing, and construction industries in large towns or factories. Vermont had an unusually high number of inventors, however, as it had had since the 1790s, when Samuel Hopkins received the first United States patent for a new method of making potash, and Cyrus Gates invented an apple corer—quarterer to speed cider production. Inventor-entrepreneurs like Erastus Fairbanks (scales and plows), Lemuel Hubbard (pumps), and Nicanor Kendall (guns), won great renown for their creativity and by the 1840s had begun to build the enterprises that would make the valley, and in particular Windsor and St. Johnsbury, an important manufacturing center for machined goods. Inventiveness was also common among the valley's craftsmen. Like their urban counterparts, they were frequently adept at several trades and quick to master new techniques, and they were generally better acquainted with the latest technical and scientific literature than their urban peers. Not all were as well-positioned as gunsmiths, plowmakers, and toolmakers, who could take full advantage of the opportunities opening in the local and national economy. But men like globemaker James Wilson of Bradford and engraver George White of Weathersfield gained renown in traditional crafts, and their success inspired others to turn their hands to such trades.[7]

The growing number of artisans in the valley meant that the population increased in villages and major towns. That increase stimulated the local economy. The presence of village artisans and merchants encouraged farmers and rural craftsmen to bring crops and processed raw materials to town to trade for manufactured goods and services. Farmers and rural craftsmen remained rooted in the neighborhood economy, but improved terms of trade with the valley's marketing and manufacturing centers drew rural people increasingly into broader markets in their townships and in the valley. Some households were too poor or isolated to participate in this economy, and some neighborhoods were self-sufficient, but by the 1830s, according to William Gilmore's study of the valley's commercial life, three-fourths of the valley's households traded with a village merchant at least once each year. Many rural families attained a modest prosperity – had varied diets, store-bought clothes, some fine furniture, and pumps for their wells. Stronger markets within the valley contributed as much to its prosperity as exchange with the cities of southern New England did.[8]

The valley's economic resurgence rested to a lesser but still important degree on improved access to capital. People in the valley had always been willing to lend or borrow money, to pool their resources in mercantile and manufacturing partnerships, and to take calculated economic risks in the interest of profit. That enabled local farmers, craftsmen, shopkeepers, and entrepreneurs to make the most of the financial stability of the 1820s and early 1830s, although few people were yet willing to commit themselves to notes or projects that carried more than five years into the future. Individual efforts to improve the use of capital were augmented after 1817 by the state assembly's modest campaign to increase the availability of capital and to encourage investors to undertake high-risk industrial ventures. The assembly granted limited-liability charters to banks and other private enterprises that promised to spur economic growth.

The assembly had previously granted corporate charters only for public institutions, such as county grammar schools and fire societies, and for projects that would benefit the public directly, such as a marble quarry to provide stone for the state buildings under construction in Montpelier, iron and textile firms to prepare for industrial self-sufficiency in the event of war or embargoes, and transportation projects that reverted to the people once investors recouped their original investments. Before 1817, the assembly had refused to charter private banks and industrial firms whose products were not directly related to national defense. It supported the incorporation of community projects, but it opposed limited-liability charters for profit-making private enterprises.[9]

Entrepreneurs and financiers in both parties had long favored state-chartered banks and private corporations. Prior to 1817 few people agreed with them. The struggle between the parties and the failure of development to maintain parity among townships and neighborhoods had stirred class feeling and sparked antagonism between town and countryside. Voters of both parties were wary of granting state charters to capitalists who would have the power to destabilize prices and interest rates to the detriment of farmers, to push small manufacturers with less capital and more liabilities out of the market, and to practice favoritism in granting loans and setting interest rates.

That wariness survived the party conflict. Regardless of their party affiliation, the vast majority of the valley's inhabitants believed in commerce and development. Few bore malice toward entrepreneurs or financiers. But they did not want their society to become materialistic, impersonal, and unequal. Although people who could afford luxury goods bought them, even prosperous families spent the preponderance of their income on their shops and farms, and on schools and churches, and expected the society at large to share their material priorities and reflect their values. They treasured the intimacy of their economy and still traded goods and labor almost exclusively with people they knew well. They did not want to see control over production and exchange fall into the hands of an alien minority. In 1806, the voters of Vermont had approved the chartering of a nonprofit state bank designed to increase the supply of negotiable commercial paper, because they were committed to improving commerce. But they rejected efforts to repeal usury laws and to grant limited-liability charters to private banks and corporations, because they feared the greed and irresponsibility of entrepreneurs and financiers. Governor Jonas Galusha spoke for most Vermonters when he expressed his mistrust of private banks and corporations in 1818. He warned that private charters would lead entrepreneurs to ignore the welfare of their fellow citizens, and that private banks and "unlimited credit" would lead to the purchase of superfluities, to lawsuits against debtors, and to "the ruin of too many valuable citizens."[10]

The reconciliation of leading Federalists and Republicans and the appearance of chartered private corporations in neighboring states gave the valley's entrepreneurs and financiers an opportunity to present their case in a new light. They discovered a rationale for development that would restore the power and prestige they had enjoyed in the early 1790s as leaders of the town-building campaign. They embraced the cause of "growth," arguing that private banks and corporations would help the economy produce more goods and services without transforming the character of the society or concentrating economic power in the hands of a few wealthy individuals or towns. Former Federalists and former Republicans, united behind the leadership of future governors Richard Skinner (1820–23) and Cornelius Van Ness (1823–26), now argued together that private charters would not generate inequality or corruption, but would merely help enterpreneurs and financiers pool capital so that it might be used more effectively on behalf of economic growth.[11]

The campaign for economic growth helped reconcile the valley's capitalists and noncapitalists in the postwar years, much as Christianity and reform helped reconcile denominational and political adversaries. It enhanced the prestige of prominent investors, who portrayed themselves as leaders who risked their capital so that all might prosper. Only a handful of stiff-necked Republicans challenged the claim that private corporations would benefit capitalists and small proprietors equally and would pose no threat to self-employment, good government, Christian values, or equal rights. Only fifteen private firms received public charters in the valley between 1815 and 1828, and those charters were limited to no more than twenty years, with the assembly reserving the right not to renew the charter of any bank or corporation that threatened the public interest. The first bank charters restricted profit and risk. But private incorporation had gained legitimacy after years of partisan argument about its propriety in a Christian republic. Every proposed charter received a hearing in the assembly, and by the mid-1820s those that the legislature deemed viable and important could expect to pass by a wide margin, despite opposition from rival towns and investors. The assembly's pro-development posture itself stimulated growth by fostering a booster spirit.[12]

The economic changes in the valley were not without consequence for the social order. Between 1815 and 1825, before growth-related problems became apparent, the promise of prosperity allayed tensions in ways that facilitated the stabilization of town life and politics. According to data from Weathersfield and Peacham, land prices were reasonable in 1820 in relation to the wage of farm laborers, so rural workers could anticipate outright ownership of a viable seventy-five-acre farm in the southern half of the valley if they could save the equivalent of six years of farm labor wages, less room and board, or four years of wages in the northern half of the valley. Mortgages, legacies, and dowries made ownership still more accessible for many (Table 4.1). The growth of certain trades also stim-

Table 4.1. Land Prices, Wages, and the Purchasing Power
of Farm Labor

	Wages per month, with board[a]	Index of purchasing power of farm labor in goods and services, not including land or buildings (1.00 = 1914)
1820-1	9.90	0.54
1825-6	9.00	0.60
1830-1	9.50	0.63
1835-6	11.40	0.65
1840-1	12.67	0.71
1845-6	10.19	0.71
1850-1	12.10	0.79

	Dollars per acre, including buildings[b]		Acres per wage-month of farm labor	
	Peacham	*Weathersfield*	*Peacham*	*Weathersfield*
1820-1	6	10	1.57	0.99
1825-6	9	10	0.99	0.90
1830-1	10	17	0.93	0.57
1835-6	11	17	1.01	0.67
1840-1	12	21	1.04	0.60
1845-6	11	17	0.93	0.60
1850-1	11	20	1.10	0.61

a Wage rates and index of purchasing power are from Thurston M. Adams, Prices Paid by Vermont Farmers for Goods and Services and Received by Them for Farm Products, 1790-1871 (Burlington: Vermont Agricultural Experiment Station, 1939).
b The data on land prices are from the land records of Peacham and Weathersfield. Data on the prices of waste land and timber lots are not included.

ulated the hopes of journeymen. Opportunities to become masters seemed plentiful. The net exodus of youths from the valley – as yet only 16 percent for young men in the decade after 1810 – indicates that in the war years, when citizens from elsewhere in New England were migrating in great numbers to western New York and beyond, most of the valley's youths could still find satisfactory places in society.

Expectations of independent proprietorship helped to spread the conviction that the line between employer and employee in the valley was drawn by age and experience, and that the stratification of wealth stemmed from the benefits that naturally accrued from hard work and sound morals. The existence of opportunity made it easier for church members and Masons to hold sway in their communities, not only because it compounded the resources they had to help one another, but because their success did not seem to preclude the success of others. As long as most responsible, industrious adults succeeded to their own satisfaction or felt themselves and their families to be in the process of doing so, the advantages of those engaged in networks of mutual support were obscured and went unchallenged. The success of church members in particular only served to reinforce the general feeling in society that success was born of virtue.

The prevailing attitude toward prosperous investors was approbatory, too. Most of the trustees of the new banks, insurance companies, and transportation or manufacturing firms were deeply involved in churches and reform societies, and their prosperity was interpreted as an affirmation of the moral values of their devout fellow townspeople. Between 1815 and 1828, 85 percent of the fifty-nine corporate trusteeships held by men from the towns studied intensively were held by church members, 36 percent by Masons, 25 percent by Colonizationists, and 37 percent by Bible distributors.[13] Little notice was taken of the speculative nature of their enterprises; nor did anyone object at this time to their using incorporation not only to pool capital, but to limit their own liability.

The hope that growth would continue to create new opportunities for proprietorship soon faded. The decline began in the countryside, because the great increase in farm acreage between 1820 and 1830 did not give rise to an increase in the number of farms or farm owners, although it did enable those with farms to reap handsome profits in the growing market for agricultural produce. The continued growth of the rural population left an ever-expanding pool of Vermonters competing for ownership of a fixed number of farms. Farmers and landlords did not divide newly improved acres among heirs or sell them in separate parcels, but kept them intact, taking advantage of recent increases in farm income and productivity. The proportion of farms involved in subsistence farming in the towns studied intensively fell from two-thirds to a half, and the proportion of farms run for commercial profit doubled to 12 percent. The actual number of farms remained static, as existing farms were improved and oriented toward new markets (Tables 4.2 and 4.3).

These developments left farm laborers who aspired to own farms in an increasingly difficult position. Between 1820 and 1830, their wages rose 17 percent in terms of real goods and services other than land, and the clearing of new acres and the improvement of farm buildings demanded more of their labor. In the long run, however, the demand for farm labor did not increase substantially. More important still for the farm laborer intent on ownership, the price of farm land went up at a far faster rate than did wages. In Peacham and Weathersfield, land prices

Table 4.2. Size of Farms

	1820	1830	1840
Improved acreage of farms owned by farmers[a]			
Farms over 89 acres (percent)	5	12	18
Farms 45 to 89 acres	30	40	44
Farms 10 to 44 acres	65	49	38
Improved acreage of farms owned by rentiers and nonfarmers			
Farms over 89 acres (percent)	7	15	8
Farms 45 to 89 acres	27	32	29
Farms 10 to 44 acres	67	53	63
Mean improved acreage of farms			
Owned by farmers (acres)	37	52	61
Owned by rentiers and nonfarmers	40	50	43
All farms	37	52	59

[a] Improved acreage includes all acres tilled, mowed, or used as pasture. It does not include acres that were not cleared or used. Pomfret is not included because its 1820 tax list has been lost.

rose 40 percent in terms of farm wages, reflecting in part increases in farm income and improvements in land and buildings, and in part increased competition for land. By 1830, farmhands needed not four (as in 1820) but seven wage-years to buy a viable seventy-five-acre farm in the north of the valley (that being the total, and not the improved acreage), and not six but eleven wage-years to buy a similar farm in the south (Table 4.1). Even if a laborer kept his consumption of goods at 1820 levels and saved his increase in real wages, he faced a discouragingly long period of itinerant labor, especially if he had a family and had to spend a large proportion of his wages each year. In addition, there were fewer unimproved farms for sale that would serve as stepping-stones to larger purchases.

The expansion of trades dealing in processing and manufacturing goods from wool, leather, and lumber could not entirely counter the decline of opportunity for farm ownership in the countryside. Although small shops sprang up in the agricultural towns to meet the demand for textiles, shoes, hats, clothing, and construction work, these shops were poor and undercapitalized, so turnover was rapid and advancement to larger establishments difficult. They provided a living, albeit a meager one, for some, and a path to farm ownership for a fortunate few. For young

Table 4.3. Ownership and Occupancy of Farms

	1820	1830	1840
Ownership of farms (percent)			
Owned by individual farmers	88	85	82
Owned by farmer-partners	3	5	7
Owned by nonfarmers	9	8	7
Owned by rentiers[a]	0	2	3
N =	826	814	835
Occupancy of farms[b]			
Individual farmers	93	86	80
Farmer-partners	6	10	15
Tenants	1	4	6
N =	780	805	864
Partnerships			
Partners, same surname	91	86	85
Partners, different surname	9	14	15
N =	22	42	62
Tenancies			
Tenants, same surname as landlord	10	13	24
Tenants, surname different from landlord's	90	87	76
N =	10	30	50

[a] Rentiers let their lands to tenants and had no ascertainable source of income other than rent.
[b] Nonfarmers are not included as farm occupants.

women especially they were a mixed blessing. Those who could not find work in woolen mills or as out-workers for clothing shops found themselves bereft of their source of income – the production of homemade cloth and clothing – as more people bought ready-made goods at steadily falling prices.[14]

There was no relief elsewhere in the countryside from the decline in opportunity for proprietorship. The trades that provided services, household goods, and luxury items did not grow; they merely emerged from underemployment. Existing shops met what increases in demand occurred, and they expanded only in the northern towns of St. Johnsbury and Barnet, which were slowly losing their agricultural character and displacing Danville, the nearby market town, as centers of commerce and manufacturing in that part of the valley. Meanwhile, rural merchants and storekeepers were hard hit by changes in marketing and transportation. These changes undoubtedly benefited rural customers who found themselves able to purchase a wider range of goods at affordable prices, but they did not help rural merchants, who could not buy merchandise at bargain prices or market produce in large quantities as effectively as the merchants in the important river towns. They found themselves virtually excluded from the profitable river trade, and forced, as was one Weathersfield grocer and dry goods merchant, to advertise wares "at Windsor prices" to compete against merchants in river towns. Each town lost two or three stores between 1820 and 1830.[15]

The decline in proprietorship had a definite impact on the social structure of the agricultural towns. The proportion of all farms occupied by tenants rose from a negligible level in 1820 to 6 percent by 1840; and the proportion of adult males who were not proprietors edged upward from under 40 percent in 1800 to 55 percent by 1840. Only the persistent rise in the net exodus of young men from the agricultural towns, from one-sixth in the decade after 1810 to over one-third in the 1830s, kept the crisis from becoming much worse. Young women also moved away at a greater rate, although there were still fewer places for women to go for jobs than for men. Their net exodus rate rose from 6 percent in the 1810s to 30 percent in the 1830s.[16]

Migrants from agricultural towns flooded into the flourishing river towns of Windsor and Brattleboro, hoping that these towns, gaining in size, wealth, and power, would offer better prospects than the countryside. The growth of these towns did not bring enough new opportunities to the valley to help in real terms, however. The number of merchants and financiers, most of them quite prosperous, doubled in the 1820s, as marketing and finance came to center in these towns. Yet the towns' growing business sectors did not actually add to the number of merchants and financiers in the valley, because they displaced a greater number of rural entrepreneurs who could not compete successfully against firms from these towns that sought more direct access to rural markets.[17]

In the river towns, as in the countryside, there was strong growth in tailoring, shoemaking, hatmaking, and carpentry. The growth of these trades did not stem from a proliferation of small shops, as it did in rural areas, but from the rise of large firms that employed great numbers of journeymen, apprentices, and pieceworkers. In consequence, opportunity in the river towns was reduced as the proportion of master craftsmen per adult male worker decreased. There were several reasons for that reduction in opportunity. First, the capital requirements for opening firms in the river towns rose faster than wages. As the demand for apparel from these towns grew, as a result of their greater marketing reach, tailors, hatmakers, and shoemakers had more customers who bought in large lots for rural distribution or who wished to buy ready-made goods during a day's visit to town and were unwilling to wait or return for made-to-order goods. Thus larger inventories of ready-made clothing had to be kept in stock. Similarly, because the construction of wharves, warehouses, merchants' rows, and mansions increased, master carpenters and masons needed more equipment, greater resources, and better credit if they were to land and fill major contracts. The advantage in these trades went to men with greater capital.[18]

Large firms also restricted opportunity by lowering prices to levels that undercut competition from smaller firms. Small firms had to rely on masters and skilled workers to perform almost every task; they could maintain only a few apprentices to do less difficult jobs at lower cost. In contrast, heavily capitalized firms could divide production into a series of discrete tasks and could hire cheap, unskilled labor to perform them. Master carpenters and masons likewise hired day or month laborers to excavate, haul, and lift, doing the planning and supervising themselves and letting their journeymen do the sawing, nailing, and mortaring.

The same was true in the apparel business. Jesse Cochran, a merchant-tailor in Windsor who was supplied with "the latest New York fashions," set patterns, cut cloth, and altered clothing himself, and left all the time-consuming sewing and trimming to the ten young men and women who worked for him. He taught them each certain advanced skills from time to time, but kept a basically unskilled work force that included at most one or two journeymen.[19]

Women who worked at such jobs received roughly two-fifths of what men did for the same work.[20] Indeed, the women who flocked to Windsor and Brattleboro in search of employment ironically undercut the economic fortunes of the very men they would marry, for they bid down the price of their labor and earned too little themselves to save much toward setting up households. Many women never got beyond piecework. For apparel firms, the use of pieceworkers ensured efficiency at low cost. By paying the worker a set fee for completed work of acceptable quality, firms could avoid having to pay for time wasted in talking or resting or turning out pieces of poorly done work.

There was no increase in opportunities for proprietorship in other trades in the valley. Most did not undergo the period of rapid growth that carpentry and tailoring did. Existing firms could meet increases in demand by expanding production and putting on extra hands at peak periods. Overall, the proportion of nonproprietors in Windsor rose from 56 percent in 1810 to 68 percent in 1830. The proportion of men without property rose by half to over 40 percent, and the percentage of wealth held by the wealthiest tenth of adult males rose from 53 to 70 percent. Men who moved to the river towns in search of opportunities seldom found any niche at all. They were more transient than nonproprietors in the agricultural towns and were thirty times more likely not to leave even a trace of their passing on the tax rolls or on lists of eligible voters.[21]

Women had an equally difficult time in the major towns. They did get more jobs in the apparel trades and as servants in boarding houses or prospering households, but their wages were niggardly and working conditions difficult, and they still outnumbered young men. Their lives were epitomized by those of Martha and Sarah Norton, who moved to Windsor around 1829 to look after their grandfather, a deacon in the Congregational Church. They kept from three to six boarders in their grandfather's house and made shoes on the side, but could "barely make a living." Their days were an endless round of cooking, washing, and sewing, all for so little profit that they could afford no new clothing and depended on gifts from their brother, a Congregationalist missionary, to survive. Marriage was their only hope.[22]

Life was no better in marketing towns that were located away from the major new routes of trade. Although the tax lists for these towns have not survived, so that a detailed appraisal cannot be made, it appears that they suffered stagnation or stunted growth. Usually shire towns (Montpelier, Woodstock, and Danville) or would-be shire towns (Norwich and Chester hoped to fashion new counties around themselves) located inland from the river, these towns had once controlled most of the trade in the valley. In the 1820s, they had been major population centers with large concentrations of craftsmen. They were not well positioned to attract new, less localized trade, however, and so entered a period of relative or absolute decline. Still, they were not spared the influx of workers from the countryside looking for jobs and advancement.

Even the valley's most sparsely settled hill towns offered few new opportunities for self-employment. Land remained fairly inexpensive in Essex County, central Orange County, and along the spine of the Green Mountains, but by the mid-1830s all that was left was of poor quality and was isolated from main transportation routes. The number of farms in the hill towns did not increase. These towns also offered little opportunity for merchants, manufacturers, or professionals. Their economies revolved around the export of lumber, maple sugar, and some wool to the nearest market, generally in a village or hamlet some miles away (often small county seats like Chelsea, Guildhall, or Newfane). Hill people also had to travel to these towns for most of their loans and store-bought goods. Since there were relatively few buyers and sellers in such towns, hill people fared relatively poorly in those exchanges, yet they still diverted enough business from their own towns to prevent the rise of local merchants and craftsmen. Unless hill towns had good sites for woolen mills, they remained home almost exclusively to hardscrabble, near-subsistence farm families.[23]

Young women found little to hold them in such towns. In 1839 Sally Rice resisted her parents' pleas for her to return home to their farm in Somerset, a poor hill town in Windham County. Rice had just found steady work in Union Village, New York, as a domestic servant. For the first time in her life she was enjoying herself, living in "good society" and saving money for the family she hoped someday to have. She saw no future for herself or her parents in Somerset. "What can we get off that rocky farm?" she asked her parents. "It would be another thing if you kept 9 or 10 cows and could raise corn to sell." If they were desperate for help they could hire a servant girl "that would be contented to stay in the desert." She didn't want her parents to think her unkind, however, and tried to encourage them to leave Somerset. "Do come away dont lay your bones in that place I beg of you." Rice's view of her family's prospects in that mountain community was reasonably realistic. Such towns offered people no way out of poverty.[24]

The valley was not the only region in the nation that found growth a mixed blessing. The opening of the Champlain and Erie canals brought great prosperity and optimism to the Champlain Valley and the Genesee Valley of western New York, but it also drove up land prices, increased tenancy, undermined domestic textile and clothing production, and forced many young men and women to leave the region or seek work in boomtowns like Rochester, Utica, and Burlington, which were soon flooded with poor young people. The decline in proprietorship was at work everywhere in the burned-over districts. It had not issued from any shattering social transformation, and it did not result in a wholesale reduction of the inhabitants into a propertyless, late-marrying people. Still, it frustrated ambitions and would create severe problems that defied all the initial efforts of the inhabitants of the valley to solve them.[25]

The impact of pressing times on the family

The growth of the economy and the population affected the families of the valley deeply. Most parents felt it to be their responsibility to see their children safely established in life. There were undoubtedly parents who felt that their responsibilities ended when their children came of age, and still others so fatalistic about their own lives that making provisions for the lives of their children was beyond them, but most parents felt a duty to try to assist their children through the decline in opportunity for proprietorship and moved quickly to husband what resources they had.

The Merrills of Peacham, a substantial farm family active in the Congregational church, responded in ways typical of strong families. Jesse Merrill, the family patriarch, found himself hard put to provide for his eight children (seven of them sons), who ranged in age from twenty to forty. Two sons, David and James, had graduated from Dartmouth College and left farm life, and his daughter, Betsey, had married and set up a household with the aid of a substantial dowry that the Merrills could ill afford, but that they believed, like most families, was her due. Those children still needed help, but the other five needed more. To meet the challenge, Jesse, instead of dividing his profitable commercial farm among his children (and thereby undermining its profitability), kept it intact and brought his son Hazen into the operation as a full partner and permanent hand. He then mortgaged the farm for several thousand dollars and gave the money to his sons Samuel and Franklin, who went to Indiana to become partners in a mercantile venture. The responsibility for repaying the mortgage loans remained with Hazen, to compensate his brothers for his retention of the family home. Later, an outlying farm was given outright to another son, Schyler, with the same managing arrangement.[26]

The Merrills had also been careful to provide for their daughter's future in the event she did not marry. She had been trained in a female academy and probably could have found a position as a teacher. Female teachers received poor wages, roughly $5 per month plus room and board, compared with the $11–12 male teachers could expect, but because of this difference, the teaching profession was opened to women in these years, and families were given a way to establish their daughters in a respected occupation. Families with fewer resources than the Merrills encouraged daughters who could not find suitable employment at home to take jobs in marketing towns or in the cities of southern New England, as seamstresses, textile operatives, or domestics. Such jobs were limited in number, but they did give a substantial number of young women an opportunity to earn money.[27]

There were many families like the Merrills that attempted to evade the effects of the decline through mortgages on consolidated farms, formation of family partnerships, and western migration. The number of family partnerships, created to pool capital, spread proprietorships, and ease the transfer of ownership from one generation to the next, increased steadily as the decline intensified. They never became a dominant feature of the economy, however, and were dissolved as soon as children could be established independently. The proportion of all farms and of mercantile and manufacturing firms owned by partners of the same surname rose from 2 percent in 1820 to 6 percent in 1840. Mortgages arranged between persons of the same surname rose from 7 percent of all mortgages in the 1820s to 13 percent in the 1830s.

The mortgaging of consolidated farms became so common that it drew public attack for exacerbating – some said causing – the hardship and forced emigration it was intended to relieve. The Reverend J. Todd, a Congregationalist minister, blamed the decline in opportunity for proprietorship on a vicious cycle in which a farmer would bestow his farm on one son and force him to mortgage it, giving four-fifths of its value to other sons, who had no alternative but to go west to try their luck. The son left in Vermont would then spend the rest of his life trying to repurchase the farm so that his children could repeat the cycle when they came of age. In the name of family and community, Todd called upon farmers to cease coveting so much land, so they might "be surrounded by [their] own sons, instead of large land-holders, and a floating population who hire themselves out to cultivate it, and own no land."[28]

Although Todd was correct in his contention that large farms forced many young men to leave the valley, it was not simply covetousness that prompted farmers to preserve large farms and unimproved tracts.[29] They could have divided their farms among their sons, but how could the resulting noncommercial farms sustain the mortgage burdens necessary to establish their remaining children and their children's children? It was clear to them that the family farmer's lot was to be but a generation away from disaster.

Awareness of decreasing opportunity had also led families to try to limit the number of children they had. Delayed marriage and rudimentary family planning, common not only in the valley but in other burned-over districts and in most regions in the United States that were experiencing crowding, had brought about a steady decline in the white female birth ratio (crudely estimated as the number of children under age ten for each female of child-bearing age) in the valley since 1800 (Table 4.4). The ratio was always lowest in the towns in the southern half of the valley with the best land; those towns had been settled first and had the highest land prices. The ratio was lower still in the commercial and manufacturing towns, but the greater number of single working women in these towns might have been as important as the intense competition for proprietorship in causing the ratio to fall.[30] In any event, family limitation and delayed marriage did not cut deep enough to avert the crisis or eliminate the need for better cooperation and resource management within families.

Even cooperation and careful management were not enough to keep the Merrills, and many other families whose resources were slim, afloat

Table 4.4. White Birth Ratios
in the Connecticut River Valley of Vermont, 1800-1840ᵃ

	1800	1810	1820	1830	1840
Windham, Windsor, and Orange counties					
Marketing and manufacturing towns	2.0	1.5	1.3	1.1	1.1
Agricultural towns, good land	2.0	1.6	1.4	1.2	1.2
Agricultural towns, fair land	2.2	1.8	1.4	1.3	1.3
Agricultural towns, poor land	2.2	2.0	1.6	1.3	1.4
Washington, Caledonia, and Essex counties					
Marketing and manufacturing towns	2.0	1.7	1.4	1.2	1.1
Agricultural towns, good land	2.2	1.9	1.5	1.5	1.2
Agricultural towns, fair land	2.1	1.8	1.5	1.5	1.3
Agricultural towns, poor land	2.2	2.0	1.7	1.6	1.4

ᵃ The birth ratios are computed by the following formula:

$$WBR = \frac{\text{no. white males (0-9) + no. white females (0-9)}}{\text{no. white females (16-44)}}$$

The ratios express the number of young children in the population for each female of childbearing age. The censuses after 1820 grouped women of childbearing age in the age categories of 15-19, 20-29, 30-39, and 40-49, rather than 16-25 and 26-44. The number of females 16-44 is therefore estimated for census years after 1820 according to the method employed in Colin Forster, G. S. L. Tucker, and Helen Bridge, Economic Opportunity and White American Fertility Rates, 1800-1860 (New Haven: Yale Univ. Press, 1972). The censuses assigned Afro-Americans to age categories that are too broad to permit calculation of black birth ratios.

during the decline. For all Jesse's planning, his children were not safely established by the time of his death at age seventy-eight in 1840. Two of his sons, Franklin and James, had failed completely. His children regrouped upon his death to try to help those who had fallen victim to the times. Hazen, Samuel, and Jesse, Jr., relinquished their claims to their father's estate in order to prevent costly litigation and to leave more for Franklin, James, and David. Their resources of capital and goodwill had begun to fail, however. Hazen needed repayment to protect his farm. David, who was an impoverished Congregationalist minister, cast aside his scruples about defaulting on debts and advised Franklin to take advantage of a new bankruptcy law. "Why not [you] as well as thousands of others?" The brothers did not want to go on paying off Franklin's and James's debts. Upon the urging of their mother, they continued to do so, but neither Franklin nor James ever stood on his own, and the ill will created by the burden of supporting them divided the family permanently.[31]

Poorer families, like the Townsends of Reading, faced greater hardships. They often had no alternative but to pack their male children off to the city to seek their fortunes. Elmer Townsend, as we have seen, did well in Boston and his prosperity made life easier for most of his younger siblings. With the money he gave them for education, dowries, and business ventures, some of them did very well in the valley. However, the boys from the Reading area who had accompanied Elmer to Boston found only dead-end jobs or no jobs at all. Joel Turner had to go back home poorer by one summer's wages. Amasa Parker and Daniel Stearns found no jobs, either, and left Boston to try another big city. Elmer never heard from them again.[32]

Other poor boys tried their luck at sea, in the gold fields of Georgia, or as traders with Indians and frontiersmen in the backwoods of Mississippi and Alabama. Judging by the letters they wrote to their relatives back home in the valley, few of them ever managed to do more than scrape by.[33]

More prosperous families had an option denied the poor. They could sell out at high prices and move west. Homesteading was expensive. The cost of moving, clearing land, raising buildings, carrying crops to more distant markets, and securing mortgage money where cash was scarce was only partly offset by the lower cost of raw land. Families had to endure a lower standard of living during their first years in the West. However, the owner of a median-sized farm of roughly seventy-five acres could accumulate the $500 to $1,000 needed for homesteading simply by selling out.[34]

Those who ventured to Ohio, Illinois, and Wisconsin often boasted, as did George Petrie, who had migrated from Hartland to Illinois, that they could make "a good living here with one quarter of the labour" and that yields surpassed anything known in Vermont. But relatively few of their friends and relatives who owned shops or farms took their advice to go west. Migration was costly, stretching resources and family ties to the breaking point. Farmers especially resisted: Their rate of persistence remained above 70 percent from the 1820s through the 1840s, despite the decline of opportunity. They heeded the advice of other pioneers, like Timothy and Sabrine Humphrey, formerly of St. Johnsbury, who complained from Ohio that pioneer life, while perhaps easier for a man, was "harder for a woman," and that there was "such a lack of society [we] had rather live [in Vermont] with one acre of land than two here."[35]

Like their counterparts in rural areas throughout the Northeast, most families in the valley sought to combat the economic decline by some combination of skillful resource management, family limitation, and migration. People in the valley were not satisfied with those alternatives, however. Parents began looking for new ways to provide for their children and their own security. In the 1830s, concerned families would provide the backing for political movements that promised to increase opportunity and for moral crusades that they hoped would ensure a safer environment for young people who were at loose ends for increasingly long periods of time.

The impact of pressing times on household government, labor relations, and politics

In the decade following the War of 1812, successful labor management and government of those who lived or boarded with families unrelated to them had been dependent on watchfulness, a certain amount of tolerance, and the guarded use of incentives to encourage boarders and employees to participate more fully in town life. However, growth began to create problems for household government and labor relations, just as it had for the family. By sharply increasing the amount of work employers could ask of their employees and the number of residents in need of governance at a time when prospects for all were depressed, growth made it difficult for employers to maintain harmonious relationships with employees, and undermined the ability of established household heads to oversee their boarders.

Household government decayed most severely in market towns like Windsor, where hard-pressed newcomers were simply too numerous for the town to accommodate. The proportion of adult males in Windsor who were not household heads rose from 39 to 55 percent between 1820 and 1830, with the result that there were more people boarding, not only in private homes, but in taverns, hotels, and boarding houses, some of which were erected at that time specifically to accommodate the overflow. The proportion of household heads owning homes fell from 54 percent in 1820 to 36 percent in 1830. There were various reasons for this decline (housing, for example, was in short supply), but its effects were obvious: With proportionately more renters and tenants in town, household heads were less well established than they had been. In addition, the proportion of the male work force fifteen and older that lived unsupervised in boarding houses and hotels rose from one-tenth in 1820 to one-fifth in 1830, and the households that tried to absorb the newcomers, some of them taking in ten or more boarders, became de facto boarding houses with little control over their residents.[36] People in market towns who rallied around the flag of law and order, particularly church members, began to fear that less established household heads would prove incapable of governing the people they took in, and that the ungoverned boys and men in their midst would introduce vice into their towns. They were no longer confident that unruly boarders would eventually be assimilated into society, that they would set aside childish ways and settle down to the serious business of life.

As the quality of household government deteriorated, church members and other advocates of order lost patience with freewheeling public celebrations and amusements, especially those at which alcohol was available. Such activities had become occasions of riot and disorder, where the wildness and corruption that were breeding beyond the reach of the respectable community visited themselves upon the town. At a public meeting in Windsor, the Reverend Hale pointed to the number of rum-soaked raisings, horse races, and elections there were in the valley, and wondered aloud if "the Republick is safe." People worried that on militia training days young, unchurched militiamen, full of revolutionary fervor and liquor and anxious to impress the young women who gathered to watch them drill on the parade grounds, might forget themselves and jeopardize the safety of the townspeople. Some even feared that the young men might stage an uprising for "love of military glory" in support of some glorious new world Napoleon – Andrew Jackson, perhaps.[37]

The fear of disorder never became as great in the countryside as in the towns, for residential patterns did not alter quickly enough there to have an adverse effect on the ability of respectable citizens to supervise the young, the transient, and the poor. A few complained that the "constant growth of the population" in the immediate vicinity of rural woolen mills had in association with "a combination of causes...painfully reversed" the moral timbre of several neighborhoods – a reference to unsavory conduct on the part of mill operatives who lived in boarding houses or in rude company shacks in those communities. Mill workers moved frequently and apparently seldom considered themselves part of the surrounding community.[38]

Living arrangements changed little in most rural neighborhoods. The proportion of adult males who were household heads held steady at roughly 70 percent between 1820 and 1830, and the proportion of household heads who owned homes remained at just under 60 percent; that is to say, the number of males fifteen and older per household rose only slightly during these years, and the stability of the households themselves was essentially unchanged. The proportion of males fifteen and older living in households headed by nonproprietors remained slightly above one-third, and there were no males living in boarding houses or hotels in 1820 or 1830.[39] Rural residential patterns proved more conducive to household government than patterns in the marketing towns; as a result, there was less fear of riot and rebellion.

Nevertheless, disorder and mischief were drawing unprecedented censure in rural areas by the 1830s, especially from church members. Where those concerned with public order had once seen nothing but youthful exuberance in the escapades of Henry Stevens and Joel Winch, they now saw concerted efforts to disturb the peace and destroy morals. A letter to the *Weekly Messenger* in 1832 complained that a band of young men from a neighboring town had recently alarmed the people of St. Johnsbury by parading through the streets in a wagon after midnight and uttering "the most horrified and fiendlike yells." The correspondent demanded that the names of the "drunken rioters" who had carried out these "scandalous transactions" be published. What in earlier years would have been looked upon as just another prank in an ongoing rivalry between youths from bordering towns was now considered a great threat to order and decency. Most denunciations of such escapades stemmed not from a fear of general disorder, however, as in the largest towns, but from a fear that the young would do injury to the community and its morals. People were increasingly afraid that young people, even if boarded in respectable homes, would not allow themselves to be guided by the good citizens of the town.[40]

Thus it was, too, that the hired man became the most feared person in the agricultural towns of the valley. His prospects of owning a farm had greatly diminished in the decline of opportunity; growth had increased both the number of hired hands and the number of commercial farmers who had to hire and board them. That made for an explosive situation. The hired hand, who had always stood in an uncertain relationship to the farmer and his family and to the community at large, was now perceived increasingly as a threat to both, as a man with nothing to lose and no reason to identify with the farmer who employed him. The greatest danger was to the farmer's daughter, of course, whose prospects of marriage were growing slimmer and who as a result was especially vulnerable to the blandishments of a young man living in such close proximity to her. In 1834, Harriet Strong of Hardwick wrote to a cousin from Peacham of shocking developments at home: Their friend Mary had eloped with her father's hired man, "a poor, drinking, profane man twenty two years of age." Strong reported that the news "almost killed" Mary's family. "Who would have thought it of her? Mother said that she knew young girls needed watching but she shall give up in despair if they do such things at thirty."[41]

Families with hired help lived in constant fear of such disasters. It was not merely coincidence that the most notorious criminal case of the era in the Connecticut River Valley involved a hired man. William Comings's history was common enough. He had failed miserably at business and had been forced to hire on as a farmhand with the Moses Abbott family. He and his wife quarreled. Urged on by her family, who thought young Comings was no good, she left him, going back to her parents, evidently hoping that in her absence William might work a little harder. In her absence, however, William sought solace in Sarah Abbott, Moses' young daughter. The news of this affair spread quickly. William continued to meet Sarah Abbott even after his wife had come back to him, even after he signed on to work at another farm, even after the birth of his first child. Then one morning his wife was discovered dead, hanging by a sheet from the bedpost. Most of the evidence indicated that the young woman had committed suicide, but suspicion and strong feelings against Comings in the neighborhood led to a charge of murder. The trial held the valley spellbound. The story of William's seduction of Sarah Abbott, and the ruin visited upon the Abbott household, must have appalled many parents, who knew that they harbored in their own homes young men whose circumstances were very like those of William Comings.[42]

Employers in other occupations also encountered difficulties in their relationships with employees. Master craftsmen, who employed the bulk of the work force in market towns, faced the greatest problems. Their profits indicate that they did not lose control over the production process, even though more pieceworkers and part-time laborers were used. Labor under those terms enforced its own rough discipline. Nor did masters shirk the responsibility of overseeing their workers. The average number of males fifteen and older living in the households of master tailors, hatters, shoemakers, carpenters, and masons rose from three to six between 1820 and 1830, and in the households of other masters from two to four. Unlike their counterparts in America's large cities, where workers lived increasingly in separate households and neighborhoods, masters in the valley maintained a strong presence in the lives of their workers.[43] There were pressures on masters to remain competitive, however, to further their family fortunes and to fulfill the promise of greater income and profits for their firms, and those pressures led them to demand steadier, faster work at a time when greater numbers of workers made complete supervision impossible. They asked workers to be more industrious and more frugal at a time when many of these workers were growing anxious about their chances of becoming proprietors.

This predicament manifested itself in the increased frequency with which newspapers and other publications put forth encouragement and advice for young workers. The "Rules for Young Tradesmen" appeared in the *Vermont Journal* in Windsor in 1828. The "Rules" promised journeymen and laborers that success lay ahead, but to attain it they had to spend less, work harder for their masters, and avoid sin and despair. Workers were warned against paying too high a rent for stylish lodging and reminded that those who wanted success ought not to be ashamed to eat "brown bread first": That was the best way to provide for "your future family." Those who fell into vice, visited taverns, or married too soon, stood little chance of prospering. The "Rules" allowed one ray of hope to shine through the darkness of the immediate future. "As you advance in life and succeed, it will be expected you should give yourself greater indulgence, and you may be allowed to do it both reasonably and safely." Commercial farmers wrote articles for the valley's newspapers to give their workers the same advice. With opportunities for advancement decreasing, it was thought that workers needed reassurance that they could still succeed, even if it took a little longer than before, and that the poverty in which they found themselves was nothing more than the first stage on the journey to success.[44]

Yet another casualty of the economic and demographic pressures of the period was unity among the well-to-do. Beginning in 1826 and 1827, the apparent prosperity of the river towns in the southern part of the valley gave leading citizens in towns that were situated away from the river reason to feel that the pressures they were experiencing stemmed not entirely from impersonal social processes, but in part at least from a concerted effort by prominent men in the major marketing towns to use their political influence to prevent other towns from sharing in the valley's prosperity. These dissatisfied leaders, who lived either in the countryside or in would-be market towns like Norwich, Danville, and Chester, were, prior to 1828, few in number. Nevertheless, they undertook to fight every public initiative and every government practice that seemed to favor more prosperous towns, and tried to split voters along economic and geographical lines – something the Federalists and Republicans, despite their frequent appeals to class prejudice, to self-interest, and to the rivalry between villagers and the inhabitants of the countryside, had largely failed to do.

The first major split among the valley's most prosperous citizens occurred in 1826 over the petition by investors from Bellows Falls, Brattleboro, Windsor, and other important river towns, to incorporate a steamboat company to serve the upper Connecticut. A group of prominent men from Norwich, a beleaguered river town excluded from the list of proposed steamboat stops, campaigned under the leadership of Captain Alden Partridge, a hero of the War of 1812 and founder of the Norwich Military Academy, to prevent the incorporation, in favor of construction of a state canal to facilitate flatboat travel. They argued on practical grounds that canals were cheaper and that flatboats could carry more freight by running continuously day and night and for a longer season than steamboats, but they were more concerned that steamboat travel would drive local market towns into stagnation and prevent all but a few individuals and towns from sharing in the valley's prosperity. They believed a canal would harmonize better with the "desultory complexion" of the valley's commerce, which required that cargo be handled at nearly every point along the river, and would bestow "its benefits and its blessings, like descending showers, on every member of the community whether he be rich or poor." To be sure, steamboat opponents did not go so far as to denounce the campaign for economic growth, or incorporation itself, but they did assert that in this case the "river gentlemen" were "influenced by principles which honourable men would be unwilling to avow." In short, they accused men in the river towns of using the valley development project to corner the market.[45]

In the same year, battles commenced over representation in the state legislature. Several editors and legislators from prosperous towns in the southern half of the valley suggested that representation in both houses be based on population, so that prosperous towns might have greater political influence. Attacks on that suggestion followed swiftly. Ebenezer and William Eaton, editors of the influential *North Star* of Danville, claimed that the proposal was yet another plot by the downriver towns to cheat Danville and its environs of their share of power and wealth. Only small towns could be trusted to guard the people's rights and welfare "from that spirit of monied, aristocratical, monopolizing corporation mania, which so often discovers itself in populous, speculating, commercial towns."[46] Impatient with the decline of their town, the Eatons questioned the wisdom of continued political unity with men from towns that seemed bent on political and economic suzerainty over them.

Political disputes arose over county government as well. Towns that felt themselves ill-served by distant county governments and overtaxed for roads that helped other parts of their counties prosper sought redress in a drive for independent counties. The leading citizens of the suffering market towns of Chester and Norwich, along with people from surrounding towns, believed that having more local county seats would help resuscitate local commerce, and they demanded to be allowed to secede from Windsor County.[47]

These political disputes did not result in any deep or widespread divisions among wealthy men through 1828. The steamboat company was incorporated, no new counties appeared, and marketing and manufacturing towns increased their political power. Although these towns did not succeed in getting reapportionment, their inhabitants filled more than half of all gubernatorial, senatorial, and congressional seats between 1815 and 1828, up from only one-third between 1798 and 1815. The nominations and popular votes for state officials in 1827 and 1828 were nearly unanimous. There was one short-lived effort in 1826 by former Federalists in Windham County to replace Ezra Butler, a Baptist from Waterbury, with a gubernatorial candidate more to their liking, because Butler had a reputation for spiritual and partisan zealotry. That effort subsided once Butler was elected and proved his dedication to nonpartisan, nonsectarian ideals. Sizable, persistent opposition to incumbents came only from Norwich, Chester, and an occasional hill town. Yet the sense that there were political causes as well as cures for their towns' plights haunted many substantial citizens, who recognized that the prevailing political order could not meet their needs and who realized that political and economic power had tilted away from the countryside toward the valley's largest towns. They would soon launch new political crusades and reform movements to right the wrongs they felt had been done them.

The stability of town life and politics had been undermined by diverse social pressures. Despite its obvious benefits, growth had frustrated old ambitions at the same time that it had satisfied new needs and desires. The expanding economy and population had caused a decline in opportunity for proprietorship, a rise in inequality among citizens and towns, and a host of other social problems. These problems, which plagued the other burned-over districts as well, disrupted the lives of the valley's inhabitants, revived old difficulties with young people, with discipline, with geographical antagonisms and factionalism, and in the end induced citizens to join new political, reform, and religious movements.

5

A clamor for reform,
1828–1835

During the winter of 1834, when concern over the decline of proprie-torship and public morals had reached a desperate peak, a committee from Woodstock called a meeting of the freemen of the county to discover what "extraordinary cause" had brought about "the unusual pressure" of the times. The committeemen believed, as did people throughout the burned-over districts, that the circumstances in which they found them-selves were as threatening to the freedom and happiness of the citizenry as George III's plot against American liberty. In language that echoed the dramatic rhetoric of the revolutionary era, they described a political conspiracy against their rights and property and a moral declension that had caused people to neglect their duty to defend the public good and had disposed some men to place their private interests over that good. Although they could not reach a consensus on the cause of their predic-ament, there was general agreement that the young republic, which had seemed so stable in the postwar years, was in real danger of coming undone.[1]

To preserve the republic and encourage people to rededicate themselves to the ideals of nondenominational Christianity and nonpartisan repub-licanism, the valley's inhabitants embraced a flurry of reform movements between 1828 and 1835. The movements originated outside the valley, but Vermonters took them up, particularly Antimasonry, antislavery, and temperance, with a fury and intensity unknown outside the burned-over districts. Unlike postwar reform movements, which were organized as voluntary societies, most of these movements were organized as political parties or as petition campaigns against specific government policies. Reformers believed they had to get rid of the political leaders and the policies that were undermining the republic. In their minds, the postwar order of the early 1820s marked the only time the country had come close to being an ideal republic. To preserve the harmony and stability of that period, they would encourage the valley's inhabitants to engage in political insurgency and counterinsurgency and to pressure others into conformity on moral issues. The principles of the new order would not be well served by their activities. They would be testing the bounds of nonpartisanship and voluntarism and reopening divisive moral, spiritual, and political issues that the new order had closed.

The rise of political insurgency

In 1828, the Jacksonian Party, the Antimasonic Party, and the Workingmen's Party began to attract the support of people who felt themselves at a disadvantage in the postwar scramble for wealth and power and who believed their Christian and republican values to be endangered. Support for these insurgent movements came only gradually, for it was some time before a majority of people could be persuaded to consider their problems in a political light. That lag was reflected in private letters and diaries, which prior to 1835 remained largely silent on politics, and in the slow but steady rise in voter turnout in gubernatorial elections, from one-quarter of the electorate in 1827 to three-fifths in 1835. Party organizers and party-affiliated newspapers, which by 1835 reached roughly four-fifths of all households each week, were the instruments of change. They broadcast the idea, couched in the dramatic language of the era, that the most powerful and prosperous citizens in the valley and the nation, men who professed loyalty to Christianity, reform, nonpartisanship, and prosperity, had smuggled themselves or their minions into office as the first step of a plot to enrich themselves and to corrupt and subjugate a once free people.

The Jacksonians, the first insurgents to organize in the valley, had no quarrel with the professed ideals of the postwar settlement. Yet they felt strongly that they had been denied their share of political offices and prosperity and that the egalitarian, benevolent spirit that had heretofore inspired and sustained their republic had withered. Jacksonians blamed this situation on the resurrection in town life and politics of the would-be aristocrats who had earlier endorsed the standing order and its political arm, Federalism. It was their contention that these men were masquerading as reformers and nonpartisan republicans and that their hero, John Quincy Adams, was a charlatan whose belated conversion to Republicanism during the war masked a virulent contempt for the people. The editor of the *Vermont Phoenix* of Chester claimed that Adams, "with his high rank in life, and the clergy and village aristocrats in his service, with the whole host of officers and all the government in his hands," was bent on establishing "an order of nobility, a standing clergy, and the full exercise of civil and religious power." Only the election of sincere republicans like Andrew Jackson could stop the Federalist plot before it destroyed the republic.[2]

The Jacksonians' appeal was simple, but it spoke to important realities. Former Federalists held nearly as many offices in state and national government as they had before the War of 1812. Many were wealthy, erstwhile proponents of established religion, who proclaimed themselves "Republicans" only after their party had been repudiated at the polls. The major towns in the valley, and the wealthy men who lived in them, had a greater share of political power now, and the revival of deferential politics had allowed many important decisions, especially those concerning which investors would receive corporate charters, to be made behind closed doors. Calvinists and religious liberals, many of whom had been sympathetic to Federalism and established religion, had gained strength and influence in town life since the war. It was not difficult for Jacksonian orators and editors to blame these people for the rise in inequality and immorality that was perceived in the valley or to paint fearsome pictures of what would happen to the republic if the conspiracy was not stopped.

Jacksonianism was not Republicanism reborn, however. It was not a progressive insurgency fighting for equality, tolerance, and popular government, but a reformist insurgency, equally concerned in its public pronouncements for the preservation of order, morality, harmony, and deference toward Christian men of property, and unwilling to entertain the possibility that the valley's problems were deeply rooted. Leading Jacksonians wanted to preserve the balanced achievement of the new order and believed wholeheartedly in its central premise: that the valley's and the nation's institutions were sound and that the republic would be safe if it were governed by Christian reformers like Andrew Jackson.

That is why the Jacksonians made the dedication of the valley's political leaders to Christian and egalitarian ideals the central issue of their campaign, and why "reform" was for them a simple matter of throwing Adams's "dynasty" out of office. Jacksonian editors and orators seized upon evidence that Adams and his associates had betrayed the values of the new order. The *Vermont Enquirer* of Norwich accused Adams's supporters of gouging the poor and of suing cash-short farmers and tradesmen to collect small debts – acts unbefitting prosperous Christians – and they claimed that their participation in benevolent reform movements was only a way of deceiving people into thinking them selfless humanitarians who acted from the highest motives. William Jarvis, the wealthy Weathersfield financier and landowner who took a prominent part in many postwar reform efforts, topped every Jacksonian's list as the valley's most dangerous conspirator, because he had "betrayed" his

Republican principles for the sake of a customs post in the Adams administration. Why, asked the Jacksonians, was such a wealthy man so frantic
to fatten himself at the public table, if not because such fattening had
been critical to the establishment of his wealth in the first place? How,
if Jarvis was really a hard-working, egalitarian fellow, had he acquired
a taste for powdered wigs, imported wines, and large parties catered by
a retinue of some twenty servants? The Jacksonians hoped that Jackson's
victory in 1828 and his removal of Jarvis and other neo-Federalist conspirators from office would lay the matter to rest and tried to forestall
further political combat by warning that "none but traitors to freedom,
would lift up the voice of resistance," now that the people had spoken.[3]

The Jacksonians soon discovered that their crusade to save the new
order was saddled with two liabilities: Andrew Jackson and his policies.
As a slaveowner, Indian fighter, duelist, gambler, and whiskey drinker
who attended church irregularly and courted rough-and-ready voters on
their own terms, Jackson did not epitomize the values of the new order.
Nor did his old-fashioned Republican suspicion of the national bank,
protective tariffs, and unlimited federal financing of internal improvements accord with the policies of the valley's leading Jacksonians.

The task of improving Jackson's image and selling his policies fell
primarily to newspaper editors like G. W. Hill, who edited the *Vermont
Patriot* in Montpelier. Hill promised that Jackson would not tamper with
the tariff on wool or restrict the supply of paper currency and endorsed
local efforts to build railroads and extend bank charters to more towns.
He and other Jacksonian editors had declared themselves antislavery and
pro-Indian by 1829, and claimed that Jackson's subsequent attacks on
abolitionists and his efforts to remove Indians across the Mississippi
were consistent with reformers' plans to free the slaves gradually through
colonization and to assimilate Indians through religious missions. Like
Jackson himself, they appealed to voters on the issues of equality of
opportunity and condition, but had no desire to level proper distinctions
among men. Hill, for example, denied charges that Jackson was a rabble-
rouser, and characterized Jackson's opponents as the real demagogues
in the valley, "low born" individuals eager to seize power at the expense
of Christian men of property.[4]

The Jacksonians' portrait of Jackson as a defender of the new order
evaded certain truths and at times was little more than a cynical way of
selling Southern policies and moral sensibilities in Vermont for the sake
of the party. Defensive and confused, their efforts reflected the difficulty
of turning a heterogeneous national movement to local purposes. They
whittled away at the Republican legacy until nothing was left but its
prestige and insurgent spirit, and worked to prevent Jacksonianism from

becoming a progressive rebellion against the valley's churches, reformers, and capitalists. Most leading Jacksonians wanted to save, not destroy, the new order, and believed that their version of Jacksonianism would provide the means.

Jackson's support came from three groups that had suffered in distinctive ways under the new order and that had reason to find the idea of a Federalist conspiracy compelling. The elite architects of the Jacksonian movement in Vermont were state politicians allied with former Governor Cornelius Van Ness. Van Ness had supported Adams warmly through 1825 and seemed an unlikely insurgent, but he and his associates, including government workers in Montpelier dependent on his patronage and Old Light Republican lawyers from Windham County who enjoyed rehashing the days when they fought openly with their Federalist neighbors, differed from other Vermont politicians. They enjoyed politics, which they perceived largely as a struggle among competing interests over patronage. Van Ness had first entered politics as an anti-Clintonian in eastern New York, where he learned, alongside his friend Martin Van Buren, to use conflicts among various cliques, economic interests, and ethnic groups to his advantage.[5]

Having retired from the governorship in 1826, Van Ness bid for a seat in the U.S. Senate, but lost to Horatio Seymour, a lawyer from Middlebury. The legislature selected Seymour because he was closer in policy to President Adams and in temperament to other Vermont politicians, most of whom had enjoyed youth to the fullest before ripening into men of rigid principle. Stunned at his defeat, Van Ness turned on Adams, seizing upon the fact that a friend of Adams from Massachusetts had written a friend of Seymour in the legislature to venture his opinion that Adams would rather work with Seymour. It did not make for much of a Federalist conspiracy – everyone involved had long been Republican – but Van Ness and the politicians who had tied their fortunes to his were furious. They quickly forged a political alliance with Andrew Jackson through Van Buren and launched a scurrilous campaign against Adams.

That campaign drew immediate support from local elites who were disappointed by the economic progress of their towns under the new order. Leading citizens in Chester and Norwich, hoping that the Jacksonians would bring county seats, banks, and internal improvements to their towns, launched Jackson papers in 1828–9. Captain Alden Partridge, the head of Norwich's flourishing military academy, increased local support for Jackson by accusing Adams of military weakness. Benjamin Fellows, editor of the *Phoenix*, enlisted Chester's clamorous Universalist minority under Jackson's banner; they chafed under Calvinist dominance in that town. Tiny pro-Jackson committees were organized

Table 5.1. Social and Religious Status
of Political Activists, 1828-1834: Windsor County Towns

	Jacksonians	Antimasons[a]	Workingmen[b]	National Republicans[c]
Political activists who were (percent)[d]				
Ministers	0	3	5	0
Businessmen/professionals	25	4	5	29
Master craftsmen	25	4	47	15
Nonagricultural nonproprietors	31	11	10	12
Agricultural proprietors[e]	12	26	-	31
Agricultural nonproprietors[e]	0	8	-	2
Agriculturalists (Woodstock)[e]	6	18	26	8
Unknown	0	24	5	2
Upper decile of wealth[f]	33	15	-	41
Congregationalists	13	4	0	17
Baptists	0	7	0	5
Episcopalians/Unitarians	50	4	16	46
Methodists/Freewill Baptists/Christians	0	10	21	2
Universalists	6	21	32	8
Nonmembers	31	55	32	21
Masons	44	7	11	29
N =	16	121	19	86

[a] Only thirty-four of the activists represented here were Antimasonic leaders; the other eighty-seven were rank-and-file Antimasons who signed an Antimasonic petition from South Woodstock and West Windsor. Only the thirty-four leaders should be compared directly with the leaders of the other movements. Twenty-four percent were nonmembers, two were of unknown occupation, and 43 percent were in the upper decile of wealth. Like the Antimasons overall, they were disproportionately farmers, Universalists, and egalitarian evangelicals.
[b] Workingmen can be identified only in Woodstock. The loss of that town's tax lists make it impossible to determine whether Workingmen engaged in agriculture were proprietors or nonproprietors and whether they were in the upper decile of wealth holders.
[c] The totals include "Young Republican" leaders as well as general party leaders. Their inclusion does not alter the proportions substantially.
[d] Small proprietors are included with businessmen and professionals, and millers and taverners with agricultural proprietors, in Tables 5.1, 5.2, 5.5, and 5.6.
[e] Persons in Woodstock who were engaged in agriculture are entered separately, because the loss of the town's tax lists makes it impossible to separate agricultural proprietors from nonproprietors in that town.
[f] Activists from Woodstock are not included in this category.

in Weathersfield and Woodstock by wealthy Episcopalians (Table 5.1). Episcopalians were underrepresented in town government and political life, because they were considered troublemakers by the Congregationalists, who lost members and revenue when the Episcopalians founded liberal churches in 1824 and 1826. A small Jackson organization also appeared in Windsor, led not by long-term residents but by professional men who had come from small towns in the valley hoping to increase

Table 5.2. Social and Religious Status
of Political Activists, 1828-1834: Caledonia County Towns[a]

	Antimasons	National Republicans
Political activists who were (percent)[b]		
Ministers	2	0
Businessmen/professionals	10	70
Master craftsmen	3	15
Nonagricultural nonproprietors	3	0
Agricultural proprietors	73	10
Agricultural nonproprietors	7	5
Unknown	2	0
Upper decile of wealth	31	40
Congregationalists	36	45
Baptists	3	5
Associate Presbyterians	3	5
Reformed Presbyterians	5	0
Methodists	2	5
Universalists	15	0
Nonmembers	36	40
Masons	8	30
N =	59	20

[a] Lists of Jacksonian leaders are not available for these towns. The Jacksonians gained some support in these towns, but never developed strong organizations.
[b] Activists from Ryegate are not included in the occupation or wealth categories, because the town's tax lists have been lost.

their fortunes in the boom town. Thomas Emerson, the wealthiest man in the valley, who moved from Norwich in 1829 to head the Windsor Bank, and Jabez Sargeant, a lawyer from Chester who came to assume the postmastership when Jackson removed the pro-Adams incumbent, brought their politics to town with them. The others may have acquired theirs when they found the town's elite hard to penetrate (the "Small Potatoes Aristocracy" of Windsor remained a favorite target of Jacksonians throughout the 1830s). Of course, Jacksonian leaders claimed it was not jealousy, old grudges, hero worship, or economic self-interest that stimulated their demands. They wanted the benefits of their society to be shared fairly and wanted to see members of all faiths treated equally.[6]

Despite that stirring appeal and their party's national success, the Jacksonians never won more than a fifth of the votes cast in any election in the valley through 1835. Unlike their counterparts in western New Hampshire, who reassembled the prewar Republican coalition and rode it to victory, the Jacksonians of eastern Vermont remained a minority party and suffered their worst defeat in Windsor County, the heartland of prewar Republicanism in Vermont. Jacksonian charges of a conspiracy to revive aristocracy and established religion proved more compelling in western New Hampshire, where the standing order – complete with a Congregational establishment, enforcement of morals laws, a restricted franchise, and an entrenched Federal elite – had survived the war, and where the separation of church and state in 1817 had not ended the Federalist–Republican conflict. The refusal of Dartmouth's trustees in 1819 to allow the state legislature to transform the college from a private Congregational institution into a nondenominational state school, together with the suffering caused by the New Hampshire bank panic of 1828, triggered in part by fraud and bad loans at the Portsmouth branch of the Bank of the United States, convinced most Republicans and even many Federalists that a conspiracy threatened their rights and interests. That fear gave the Jacksonians the support of many New Light Calvinists, Universalists, and egalitarian evangelicals in western New Hampshire, enabling them to remain strong in formerly Republican towns and to capture many former Federalist strongholds outside Cheshire County, the last bastion of Old Light Federalism in the valley (Table 5.3).[7]

Vermont's Jacksonians could not match that achievement, because the new order and the early demise of Vermont's standing order had rendered conflict between Federalists and Republicans, Old Lights and New Lights, obsolete. The new order had also diminished hard feelings between Calvinists and non-Calvinists, and between church members and nonmembers throughout most of the valley. The new order, not the old, was the issue in Vermont, and Jacksonians simply could not persuade many Vermonters that Jackson, with all his moral and economic liabilities, could save it. The Jacksonians did not attract many religious liberals or Calvinists and won over no more than a fifth of all egalitarian evangelicals and Universalists, and no more than 15 percent of all nonmembers in the areas settled initially by New Lights, which included Windsor County, the northwest corner of Windham County, and the southern tier of Orange and Washington counties. The Jacksonians appealed with some success to economically disadvantaged towns, winning perhaps 5 percent more votes from each religious group in poor towns than in wealthy towns. They won substantial support only among nonmembers in areas settled originally by Old Light and moderate Calvinists (except in Caledonia County, the birthplace in the valley of Antimasonry). Only in those areas did the Jacksonians do well in former Republican strongholds (Tables 5.3 and 5.4).

These nonmembers left no record of their political feelings. It is likely that Jacksonianism appealed to them because they had not found a place in the new order in town life, and because they were less willing than nonmembers in towns founded by New Lights to concede the right of

Table 5.3. Geography of Party Vote, 1806-1844[a]

	Median percentage Federalist, 1806-17	Median percentage Republican, New Light area, 1806-17	Median percentage Republican, moderate and Old Light area, 1806-17[b]		R[2]
Connecticut River Valley of Vermont					
Jacksonian, 1834	.18 (.05)	.11 (.05)	.67 (.05)		.46
Antimasonic, 1834	.50 (.05)	.60 (.05)	.21 (.06)		.43
National Republican, 1834	.32 (.04)	.29 (.04)	.11 (.05)		.24
Median percentage Whig, 1836-44[c]	.65 (.03)	.70 (.04)	.31 (.03)		.44

	Federalist, Cheshire County, 1813	Federalist, Sullivan County, 1813	Federalist, Grafton and Coos counties, 1813	Republican, 1813	R[2]
Connecticut River Valley of New Hampshire					
Whig, 1840	.79 (.05)	.66 (.06)	.46 (.04)	.16 (.04)	.59

[a] Standard errors of the coefficients are in parentheses. On statistical methods, see Appendix D.
[b] The towns of Caledonia County are excluded from the calculations on the election of 1834 because over three-fourths of the voters in both Federalist and Republican areas voted Antimasonic.
[c] The slightly positive correlation between National Republican votes and Whig votes and per capita taxation and the proportion of males age sixteen and older engaged in commerce and manufacturing indicates that voters in the 1830s and 1840s may have tended to differ along economic lines more than voters in the 1800s and 1810s did. The inclusion of these variables in the equations, however, does not increase the precision of the estimates substantially or alter the patterns of party strength.

church members to dominate town life and politics. They lived in the areas of greatest Federalist strength, where fears of the resurrection of Vermont's standing order, however ill-founded, were most intense. They were often found in towns whose settlers had detested Congregationalism, towns on poor land in northcentral Orange, northeastern Washington, and northern Essex counties that had been settled late. These voters had reason to question the legitimacy of the postwar rapprochement between Republican and Federalist leaders, for it was all too obvious that their communities had been bypassed by postwar economic growth.

Table 5.4. Social and Religious Status of Party Voters, 1834[a]

	Liberals, Calvinists[b]	Non-Calvinist evangelicals	New Light area nonmembers, Universalists[c]	Moderate and Old Light area nonmembers, Universalists	Per capita taxation[d]	R^2
Jacksonians, 1834	.02 (.11)	.20 (.12)	.16 (.06)	.41 (.06)	-.008 (.009)	.37
Antimasons, 1834	.58 (.11)	.68 (.12)	.54 (.06)	.29 (.05)	-.025 (.008)	.36
National Republicans, 1834	.06 (.08)	-.06 (.09)	.00 (.04)	-.01 (.04)	.019 (.006)	.09

	Non-Calvinist evangelicals	Other church members and nonmembers[e]	Per capita taxation[d]	R^2
Nonvoters, 1834	.31 (.06)	.17 (.12)	.015 (.008)	.02

[a] Standard errors of the coefficients are in parentheses. On statistical methods. see Appendix D.
[b] Separate estimates of the proportions for religious liberals and Universalists are unstable because few towns had liberal churches and because the proportion of Universalists in each town must be estimated by a step variable. The inclusion of these denominations in the categories above causes the least instability in the estimates and does not alter other proportions substantially. The unstable estimates for religious liberals are close to those for Calvinists. The unstable estimates for Universalists are close to those for non-Calvinist evangelicals.
[c] Caledonia County is included in the New Light area in 1834 because of its high Antimasonic vote, which caused it to behave more like a New Light than a moderate county.
[d] Per capita taxation ranged from $3.61 to $9.79, with a median of $6.56.
[e] The estimates suggest that voters who were not non-Calvinist evangelicals voted in roughly the same proportions regardless of their religious affiliation. Liberals, Calvinists, Universalists, and nonmembers in New Light, Old Light, and moderate areas are included in this category.

Nonmembers who lived in communities settled by Old Lights, moderates, and foes of Congregationalism may also have been attracted to Andrew Jackson himself. Jackson's suspicion of tariffs, banks, and internal improvements was appealing to people who did not stand to benefit from state-assisted, corporate-directed growth. His willingness to deny the right of churches to supervise public policy and morals struck at evangelical presumption, and his concern for the domestic and international rights of his countrymen contrasted with the solicitousness of the valley's reformers for the rights of slaves and Indians. Fear that Jacksonians like these might launch an attack on reformers, churches, banks, and private corporations, prompted some party leaders, including half the members of Jackson's organizing committees in Woodstock and Weathersfield, to quit the party by 1832. State politicians at the head of the party felt it necessary to distance themselves from Jackson in 1833 to improve the party's electoral performance. It is doubtful, however, that rank-and-file Jacksonians would have supported a truly insurgent movement. There is no evidence before 1835 that they wanted to do anything other than ensure that the new order worked properly.[8]

It was clear that most Vermonters disagreed with the Jacksonians over the causes of the new order's problems. Many of them looked for explanations and solutions to the Antimasonic party, which had become the majority party in the valley by 1833. The Antimasons' appeal was strikingly similar to that of the Jacksonians. They too were obsessed by a conspiracy against equality and spiritual liberty. According to the *Vermont Luminary* of Randolph, the valley's first Antimasonic paper, Masonry was the source of all evil in the valley. It sought to destroy "all principles of equality, by bestowing its favors on its own to the exclusion of others equally meritorious and deserving." The partiality of Masons toward each other in politics endangered democracy, and in business Masonic favoritism threatened equal opportunity and the livelihoods of hardworking non-Masons. Worse still, Masonry sought to subvert Christianity. Why would Masons hold garish ceremonies, swear profane oaths, forbid dissent on penalty of death, and keep the mysteries of their faith a secret, unless they wished to restore a kind of priestcraft to society and undermine the "bland and reforming influence" of Christianity? The Antimasons warned that a people dedicated to "equal rights and privileges" could not look with indifference upon an attempt to supplant the wholesome bonds of mutual respect and free association in business, politics, and religion with those of uncritical partiality and blind loyalty, to replace bonds strengthened by mutual interest or liking or faith with those enforced by threats of persecution and death.[9]

Antimasonry superseded Jacksonianism in part because it drew strength from the Antimasonic hysteria that gripped New England and upstate New York. In the fall of 1826, Masons from Batavia, New York, kidnapped and apparently murdered William Morgan, a former Mason, because Morgan had broken his Masonic vow of silence and had arranged to publish an exposé of Masonry. The incident and subsequent attempts by Masonic sheriffs, judges, jurors, and witnesses to exonerate Masons of all wrongdoing, caused a sensation in the valley. Morgan's tract (published after his disappearance) sold briskly, and Masons, according to the *North Star* of Danville, were "indiscriminately excluded from even the lowest office" in several towns. Leading editors denounced the whole affair as a publicity stunt designed to sell books, but Antimasons soon uncovered a Masonic plot in the valley itself. Several wandering laborers from the Windsor area returned from New York in 1829 with reports that Joseph Burnham, a former Mason and convicted rapist who had allegedly died in the state penitentiary in Windsor, was alive in New York. Antimasons pointed out that the attending physician at the prison, the warden, and several of the guards and staff were Masons and charged that Masonic officials had conspired to help their fellow Mason, Burnham, escape justice. It was alleged that they had buried an unknown prisoner (perhaps after murdering him) under Burnham's name and smuggled Burnham himself out of the prison under cover of darkness in a load of cloth woven on the prison looms. The state spent $1,000 investigating the case but could not identify the decomposed body in Burnham's grave, locate Burnham in New York, or confirm the testimony of key witnesses on either side of the controversy.[10]

Fear and ill will toward Masons spread rapidly. Rumors reverberated through Hartland when Josiah Brown, a Royal Archmason, "made a hasty visit out west," came home, took an overdose of opium, and died. People speculated that he had been murdered, perhaps because he had some knowledge of the Morgan affair, and that suspicion was supported by the fact that those who found him dead in his home were Masons themselves. At a Danville funeral in 1830, Masonic and Antimasonic mourners refused to speak to each other. They sat apart at the service, and stood apart at the burial. In Barnet, vandals knocked the Masonic emblem off the gravestone of Adam Duncan, who had been the town sheriff. Dr. Ira Davis of Barnet complained that the Antimasons had stirred passions to violent levels. At the end of a training day, several militiamen, "in the full exercise of the true antimasonic spirit," patrolled the streets "declaring that they would shoot the Masons! – and did actually fire upon some of them but without injury." The Antimasonic *North Star* accused Davis of being a Mason who only acted the part of a concerned citizen. The paper did not deny the incident had occurred, but claimed that it had all been in fun.[11]

Hatred of the Masons and fear of conspiracies only partly explain why Antimasonry prevailed over Jacksonianism. Antimasonry spoke to the problems of the new order rather than to fears of a largely forgotten standing order. Even in their attacks on Antimasonry, Jacksonians could not disengage themselves from antiaristocratic and anticlerical rhetoric. More important, Antimasonry was not saddled with Andrew Jackson himself and did not have to prevaricate on the questions of slavery and Indian rights. Nor did Antimasons have to explain attacks by allies in other states on protective tariffs, which wool growers needed, or on the national bank, which Vermonters looked to for stable prices, a plentiful supply of negotiable paper currency, and easier access to credit. They warned of the danger that a corrupt national bank and spendthrift government could pose to independent proprietorship and called for reform of each, but they did so in the name of active government, internal improvements, and strong banks.[12]

Like the Jacksonians, the Antimasons charged their adversaries with promoting immorality, but whereas the Jacksonians meant primarily to underline the moral hypocrisy of their self-righteous adversaries, the Antimasons wanted to alert people to the broader dangers that society risked when it allowed bands of indolent, cigar-smoking, supposedly mature louts to set a poor example for weaker spirits under the protection of lodges that were removed, in a way that taverns were not, from public scrutiny and regulation. Women, who were drawn to Antimasonry as to no other movement, were especially troubled by the threat that these men's clubs posed to their families. Through their churches women worked to convince Christians to give up membership in the Masons, and along with male Antimasons they warned that such activities on the part of adults who pretended to moral leadership would not be tolerated by respectable citizens.[13]

The Antimasons also echoed the Jacksonians in questioning their adversaries' commitment to benevolence. They believed that Masonic "charity" was a scheme to assist fellow Masons under the cover of benevolent activities that purported to help all the needy and were suspicious of the Masons' circumvention of existing charitable organizations and their vows to stand by each other in times of need. They demanded that all charitable activities be conducted in the open, so that the springs of generosity would not be poisoned by partiality. The Antimasons' assault on violations of benevolent ideals did not stop with the Masons, however. They pointed to an ominous erosion of the sense of neighborhood and community in the valley, and declared that people no longer believed in the fundamental equality of all men. Relationships among neighbors had soured. They sued one another over minor problems like stray animals and small debts. The rich looked down on the poor, and the poor resented the rich.[14]

The Antimasons pressed benevolence to its egalitarian and communitarian limits, limits that had gone untested since the War of 1812. They were deeply troubled by false benevolence, particularly on the part of the wealthy, in whom they sensed an increasing reluctance to "extend the hand of fellowship" to those "a little lower down" on the economic scale. Benevolence was a deadly serious matter to them, and they demanded that their leaders give proof that their hearts were filled with true benevolence and a sense of the equality of all men. The Masons obviously failed that test, but so did many non-Masons, particularly those who pretended to leadership in town life and politics after the war.[15]

Antimasonry was thus to its supporters not a monomaniacal chase after conspirators, but a multifaceted movement that directly addressed the concerns of a wide range of people who embraced the ideals of the new order, who felt the pressures of the times and worried about their own well-being and that of their dependents and their towns. Antimasonry identified for them the awesome forces that were blighting their lives. Masonry had not been a significant force in the valley before the war; it had grown powerful only in the 1820s, at the time the valley's problems first appeared. It lacked the prestige it had garnered elsewhere in New England as a predominantly Republican organization that championed liberty against the standing order. It had also attracted bipartisan support in the valley, and that made it a perfect target for a nonpartisan insurgency on behalf of the new order and meant that the valley's Masons could not seek political shelter in the Jacksonians' neo-Republican crusade, as had their counterparts in western New Hampshire. The Antimasons made accusations that the Masons could not easily turn aside. It was true that Masons were more successful than non-Masons in business and politics, and Masonry did appear to foster practices at variance with Christianity and republicanism.

The Antimasons drew their leadership from smaller communities in the valley. Initially, at least, established state politicians ignored them. A few, like William Palmer, a former U. S. senator who became a political pariah by voting for the Missouri Compromise in 1820, signed on with the Antimasons because they could not pursue their ambitions within the nationally powerful Adams or Jackson parties, but the majority of Antimasonic leaders in the valley were new to elite politics. Among them were small-town politicians who felt that since the war they had lost power to politicians from marketing and manufacturing centers, and ministers from all but the liberal denominations. These ministers, like Samuel Loveland, the editor of the *Universalist Watchman* and pastor of a church in Reading, saw Antimasonry as a communitarian crusade that would lead people to embrace true Christianity and egalitarianism. They provided the party with its foremost pamphleteers, orators, and editors and ensured that thousands would attend the first mass political meetings in the history of the valley in 1829. At those meetings, in Weston, Danville, Randolph, and West Windsor, the Antimasons organized their party and publicized its intent: to force Masons to disband their lodges and relinquish whatever offices they held.[16]

At times the Antimasons rallied entire communities to their cause. In Danville, they attracted a broad coalition of professional men, master craftsmen, and commercial farmers, including the leading lay officers of every church in town. Danville was fast losing ground to St. Johnsbury, which was then on its way to becoming a major marketing and manufacturing center and would eventually reduce Danville's central village to a tiny cluster of shops and churches. The town would not go down without a fight, however. Both its leading citizens and its craftsmen were quick to band together in the face of economic trouble. Danville's master craftsmen and their employees who lived in the village center were proud and politically assertive people. They believed that they, and not the more recently arrived financiers, entrepreneurs, and internal improvers, had made their town what it was, and they were not about to let prosperity slip through their fingers. When the professional men of the town, led by William Palmer and by the Eaton brothers, editors of the *North Star*, began a campaign to bring down the men they thought were injuring Danville, they joined them immediately.[17]

Two Masons, Israel Dana, the wealthiest man in town, and William Mattocks, heir to the most powerful legal family in the county, had been the major promoters of banks, insurance companies, and general economic growth in Danville, and were thus particularly vulnerable to the charge that they acted as agents of outside forces bent on the ruin of the town. Virtually the entire population of Danville joined the crusade to crush these men, including wealthy citizens who had invested in their promising enterprises and claimed to have been unwitting accomplices of their conspiracy against Danville. The Congregational church demanded that Dana and Mattocks humble themselves before the congregation and renounce Masonry as inconsistent with Christianity and morality. When they refused, they were excommunicated. The Antimasons thought it significant when the two sought refuge in the Congregational church on St. Johnsbury Plain, for Masonry flourished there and St. Johnsbury was growing steadily stronger at Danville's expense.

Despite their success in Danville, the Antimasons on the whole did poorly in marketing and manufacturing centers. They did better in secondary villages and in the countryside. There they were led not by the most powerful local leaders of the postwar period, but by substantial farmers, clergymen, and young professionals who had supported postwar religious and reform movements but had seldom delved into politics beyond the local level or undertaken new financial or corporate ventures. They looked with suspicion upon the new economic developments and the men who oversaw them, upon growing marketing and manufacturing villages, and upon the important role Masons played in those villages.

Antimasonic leaders in West Windsor and South Woodstock, for example, resented the prosperity and political dominance of Windsor and Woodstock proper, which they perceived as seats of privilege and corruption. Those sentiments were reflected in their spiritual commitment to Methodism, Freewill Baptism, and Universalism (Table 5.1). The situation was similar in Peacham, Ryegate, and the agricultural hinterlands of Barnet and St. Johnsbury, except that the Antimasons there were led by Scottish Presbyterians and rural Congregationalists, who clung tenaciously to the Calvinist vision of the closely knit community, a vision reawakened when the postwar revival restored the Calvinists' theological solidarity and evangelical optimism (Table 5.2). They believed that the lawyers, merchants, and financiers in the small but growing manufacturing villages in St. Johnsbury and Barnet spoke for an antithetical vision of community based on privilege, selfishness, and mistrust.[18]

These leading Antimasons did not see themselves as dissidents, or as people asserting a new place for themselves in society. They believed they were guardians of society, and they were attracted by Antimasonry because they cared as much about order and community as about prosperity and power, although they acknowledged that those things were interdependent. They supported the new order, but when their frustrations increased in the 1820s, they condemned the people they believed to be the primary beneficiaries of postwar economic growth and political calm: the leading citizens of prospering marketing and manufacturing centers. Even non-Masons came under attack. John Clark, the major financier on the St. Johnsbury Plain, and Henry Stevens, the woolen manufacturing king of Barnet, were both asked to furnish proof of their loyalty to the Antimasons' vision of community and their independence of the Masonic plot by denouncing Masonry. Neither complied.

Prominent men in the valley's prosperous manufacturing communities could seldom be persuaded to join the Antimasons. In those villages, where Calvinists had largely relinquished the idea of an intimate community and religious liberals saw Antimasonry as little more than a highhanded effort to destroy the reputations of the valley's finest citizens, people did not question the right of Masons to forge bonds among men made of better stuff than their neighbors. They offered sanctuary in their churches to members of churches in neighboring communities who were excommunicated for refusing to renounce Masonry. Most church members in Windsor, Woodstock, and the manufacturing villages in St. Johnsbury and Barnet who were not Masons stood with their Masonic neighbors in opposition to Antimasonry, just as many Masons in the surrounding countryside renounced Masonry and stood with their neighbors.[19]

The Antimasons' communitarian and egalitarian ideals thus did not appeal to all communities. Nevertheless the party had won over a majority of the valley's voters by 1833. The Antimasons could not appeal as well as their pro-Adams adversaries to religious and economic insiders. They did poorly among religious liberals, won roughly 15 percent fewer votes from each religious group in the valley's wealthiest towns than they did in the valley's poorest towns, and were overwhelmed in prospering river towns like Windsor and Brattleboro. Nor could the Antimasons match the Jacksonians' appeal to nonmembers in areas settled by moderates and Old Lights. Those people were frightened by the moral intolerance and quasi-religious oratory of Antimasonic leaders. The Antimasons prevailed, however, because they appealed at once to outsiders and to Calvinists in rural areas who felt their dominance in town life and politics to be slipping away. The party carried over half the votes of all egalitarian evangelicals, Universalists, and rural Calvinists, as well as over 40 percent of the votes of nonmembers in Windsor, northern Windham, and southern Washington counties (Table 5.4). These people still had a vision of a well-ordered, egalitarian community that was similar to the communal ideal of the New Light revolutionaries who first settled their communities. The Antimasons did particularly well in the struggling internal marketing towns of Danville and Randolph, whose Antimasonic newspapers also carried the surrounding communities in Caledonia and southern Orange counties. They did well in former Federalist and Republican strongholds. They did not get as many votes as the Jacksonians in former Republican strongholds where fear of the standing order endured, but they made up for that failure by doing equally well in former Federalist and Republican areas in Caledonia County, and by bettering the Jacksonians' performance in former Republican areas in Windsor County and adjacent communities once dominated by New Lights. By transcending old party conflicts and portraying themselves as the defenders of the new nonpartisan order, they came to victory and in doing so revealed how completely prewar political loyalties had been scrambled by the new order (Table 5.3).

The last insurgent movement to arise during these years was the Workingmen's Party. It was the smallest of all the movements, and seemed out of place in the valley. Big cities were generally the only places where artisans, steeped in a tradition of solidarity and independent organization, were numerous enough to strike out against privileged urban elites on behalf of labor. There was no such self-conscious artisanry in the valley, no such inequity, and consequently not much support for the Workingmen's movement, which lacked the strength to run independent candidates for office. The movement was important, however, because it tested the bounds of insurgency, and revealed the unwillingness of the valley's inhabitants to move beyond reform to a progressive attack on the postwar order.[20]

The movement originated at a meeting of self-styled "workingmen" in Woodstock in September 1830. They had gathered to discuss the decline in opportunity for self-employment and the increasing economic inequality in the valley. They blamed these trends on "nonlaborers" – doctors, lawyers, merchants, and financiers – who used their professional expertise and control over the exchange of goods and services to subjugate laborers and expropriate their wealth, and they agreed that the credit system, which encouraged laborers to buy "more than is necessary" at inflated prices, was the foundation of the nonlaborers' power. It led to poverty and bankruptcy, to "servile, obsequious" behavior, to dependency and degradation, and to intimidation at the polls, where it was "impossible to conceal from the prying eyes of our noblesse, or of their minions, the political complexion of every vote thrown into the ballot box." Preferential government policies secured the privileged position of nonlaborers, by favoring merchants, financiers, and lawyers in the taxation of property, by distributing aid for internal improvements unfairly within both the state and the nation, by freeing nonlaborers of liability for poorly done work, and by limiting the liability of corporate investors, which allowed them to "swallow up" the firms of independent artisans and the savings of independent farmers.[21]

Nonlaborers, dangerous as they were, were not the only people in the valley who were of concern to the Workingmen. Some of them believed that the sponsors of the religious and reform movements of the 1820s were bent on preserving established religion. Nahum Haskell, editor of the *Workingman's Gazette* and an avid reader of the radical journals of Boston and New York City, and Thomas Powers, an eccentric physician who acted as gadfly to the Woodstock elite, had begun their attack on the postwar order a year and a half before on just those grounds. Haskell, Powers, and twenty-five "respectable young men" of "good moral character" had met at Cutting's tavern in Woodstock on a frigid night in January 1829. Their ostensible purpose was to celebrate the memory of Thomas Paine. Their actual purpose was to found the Woodstock Free Reading Society and inquire into the possibility that "orthodox" zealots and hypocrites – including not only Calvinists, but members of every denomination – were using evangelism and evangelical reform societies to reunite church and state. It was the Free Readers' hope that the "Worshippers of the Lamb" would "never pull the wool over the eyes" of the Sons of the Green Mountains.[22]

Haskell and his colleagues believed that the organizers of the religious and reform movements sweeping the valley were out to destroy people who, like the Free Readers, believed that the sole purpose of religion was to promote "good conduct and mutual happiness" on earth. Haskell accused the supporters of Sunday school unification, tract and Bible distribution, and missionary training of stealing the savings of destitute widows and robbing credulous children of their gingerbread money on the pretext of furthering Christ's cause, when their real purpose was "universal empire." The Free Readers questioned the need for charitable organizations with equal zeal. They had kind words only for temperance and educational reform; but even then, they deplored the slow pace of improvement and questioned whether leading reformers sought to free the growing mass of respectable, hardworking poor from want and degradation, or only to control them.[23]

The Free Readers believed that the valley's problems were more deeply rooted than the Jacksonians or Antimasons thought. They ascribed the decline of equality and public morals in the valley to the failure of the Revolution and the Republican Party to rid the nation of aristocracy and established religion and claimed that many foes of privilege and orthodoxy were being "injured in their respective callings" by economic persecution.[24] They suspected that talk of order and respect for wealth and office served only to perpetuate clerico–aristocratic rule and that the Revolution would be complete only if the valley's freemen renewed their forbears' single-minded struggle for democracy. It was true that the Republicans' triumph in 1817 had not diminished the economic and political power of wealthy citizens, or increased self-employment, or loosened the grip of "orthodoxy" on community life. The Free Readers recognized this and concluded that new leaders and redirected policies and institutions would not suffice, that reforming the postwar order would not help. A progressive assault on that order was necessary.

The Free Readers' newspaper failed in February of 1830, and shortly afterward the society itself was subsumed in the Workingmen. The Workingmen designed an agenda that differed slightly from that of the Free Readers. They continued the Free Readers' attacks on individual reformers, but dropped their campaign against evangelical and benevolent societies, as well as their criticism of orthodoxy, out of regard for the Christians and reformers who joined the Workingmen when they organized in September. The Workingmen sustained their rhetorical campaign against nonlaborers, but they never embraced the radical measures that their urban counterparts believed were necessary to crush the power of nonlaborers. Instead they lobbied for work–study programs to open the state's academies and colleges to the poor and called for an end to imprisonment and seizure of tools for debt and for laws that would curb lawsuits against debtors. They demanded that corporate charters hold investors personally liable for their collective debts and that doctors and lawyers be held legally accountable for malpractice. They never devised an alternative to the credit system, however. They supported the creation of new banks and only called for "united exertion" to limit purchases on credit. Nor did they call for limits on professional fees; they asked only that citizens refuse to pay exorbitant fees. The Workingmen's economic proposals and condemnations of Christian hypocrisy were more specific than those of the Jacksonians and the Antimasons, but most were compatible with the policies of political reformers and had surfaced frequently in gubernatorial addresses and legislative debates since 1817.[25]

With its strident (albeit moderated) attack on the postwar order, the Workingmen's movement spoke to the aspirations and interests of numerous artisans who lived in internal marketing towns that had declined in economic importance since the war. The *Workingmen's Gazette* reported active interest in the party in Norwich, Montpelier, and Woodstock, where half the party's committee members were master craftsmen (Table 5.1). These artisans looked back on the prewar period with nostalgia as a time when men prospered according to their virtue and opportunities for proprietorship were plentiful, when masters shared the blessings of prosperity with their employees, and there was a greater spirit of cooperation and solidarity among working people. They were not solely concerned with economics, however. There were no strikes or wage disputes in the valley. Nor were they much interested in changing the role that religion played in the community. Two-thirds of the leaders of the Workingmen in Woodstock were church members – a higher percentage than in any other insurgent movement – and they profited from the connections church membership brought them. Unlike many of their urban counterparts, the Workingmen did not support free thought, women's rights, unions, cooperatives, land reform, or the ten-hour day. Their main concern was to preserve a more equitable way of life in the valley.[26]

The Workingmen's movement subsided within a year. It died out not because of the controversial nature of its social vision, but because its agenda and proposals were too close to those of defenders and reformers of the postwar order. Members from Montpelier, Norwich, and Calais were the first to fall away. Disgruntled elites in these towns persuaded discontented artisans and farmers that their chances of countering the decline of their towns and the assault on their values would be improved if they became Jacksonians. Only in Woodstock, the sole internal market town in which the elite refused with near unanimity to admit that there were any serious problems in the valley, did the Workingmen last out the year. They signed their death warrant, however, when they let themselves be seduced into joining the Woodstock elite to create a lyceum that would give adults the opportunity to continue their education in economics, political thought, and other subjects. The Workingmen had hoped that the lyceum would provide a forum in which the Workingmen and the Woodstock elite could debate social problems on an equal footing. However, the lyceum's lectures were delivered almost exclusively by the town's businessmen and professionals, who used them to extol the virtues of postwar economic policies and to persuade the Workingmen that their lack of education disqualified them from speaking on important issues. Nearly half of the Workingmen's committeemen would sign petitions circulated by Woodstock's elite in 1832 and 1834 that blamed their plight on the lack of credit produced by Andrew Jackson's anti-bank policies. By 1835, most of the Woodstock Workingmen had joined the elite's counterinsurgent political crusade to save the valley from yet another conspiracy: insurgency itself.[27]

It had been the decline of proprietorship and morality and the uneven development of the valley that drove the Jacksonians, the Antimasons, and the Workingmen to insurgency. Their discontent struck some as unwarranted, and their attacks were often construed as self-interested efforts to blame those more fortunate than themselves for their personal problems. But the insurgents were not idle souls jockeying to improve their social position by tearing down those they envied, or hypocrites waving the flag of morality in order to impugn the reputations of honest men. They did not understand as clearly as they thought how and why life in the valley had changed since 1815, but their charges were rooted in fact. They perceived that new leaders had come to power in politics, that men no longer prospered on the basis of good character and hard work alone, that religious and civic institutions had been venturing into new territory, and that times were pressing. They were wrong to think that these changes stemmed from a conspiracy or a body of people who set themselves up as an aristocracy. These changes were the largely unforeseen fruit of religious and reform movements, of economic development and population growth, which they themselves had applauded and which many of them had actively furthered. Indeed, their complicity in so many of the movements that had altered society blinded the insurgents to the sources of their troubles and led them to accuse others of complicity in fouler schemes in order to find a plausible explanation for their plight. Perhaps because of their social position, however, the insurgents were acutely sensible of the fact that those who sought wealth and power often knew how to make economic policies, personal connections, and a well-groomed reputation for piety and decency work for them; and they realized more quickly than other people in the valley that the postwar order was not working equally well on behalf of all towns or all citizens.

Part of the insurgents' problem was that they tried to reform the postwar political order according to the political theories that had been initially set forth by the creators of that order, many of whom were again among their own number. The Jacksonians and Antimasons believed wholeheartedly that periodic purges of those who had become morally corrupt and who conspired to subvert the liberties of the people could effectively cleanse society and preserve their way of life in the valley. The Workingmen went a little farther and momentarily revived the progressive political vision of their revolutionary and Republican forebears. They still respected honest church members, sincere reformers, and worthy men of property, but they felt that the moral corruption and conspiracies threatening the valley ran deeper than the Jacksonians and Antimasons guessed and that more than a purge was necessary to protect the working man from oppression. Still, their program boiled down to little more than a call for a moral reawakening and for renewed respect of all men regardless of occupation, and they only echoed the Jacksonians' and the Antimasons' call for a purge of those officeholders who were morally corrupt or who had set themselves up as superior to the common man. In the end, all three movements were unable to devise proposals that would alter society drastically enough to solve the problems in the valley.

Alternatives to political insurgency

Joining the Jacksonians, the Antimasons, or the Workingmen was not the only recourse for people who wanted to fashion solutions to the valley's problems. Many people turned to benevolent and moral reform movements to attack moral decay and disorder directly and to try to recreate a moral consensus in the valley by persuading others to rededicate themselves to equality and Christian ideals. Some people turned to the National Republican Party, which was organized in an attempt to revitalize the political center of valley life. The center was now diminished by the departure of the insurgents and tarnished by its association with the failure of the postwar economy to increase proprietorship and equality. As a political alternative to insurgency, National Republicanism did not have so widespread an appeal as the reform movements, but it shared many of the same general concerns and goals and lent support to many of the reform movements while focusing on ways to improve the valley's economy and fulfill the promise of prosperity for all. It too was an attempt to restore the unity and order that had been lost in the valley.

The first noninsurgent movements to appear in the valley were petition campaigns aimed at ending the federal government's complicity in the oppression of human beings. The campaign to exclude slavery from the District of Columbia was organized in 1828–9 by William Lloyd Garrison, editor of the *Journal of the Times* of Bennington (on the other side of the Green Mountains). Garrison complained of a lack of progress toward emancipation and asked Vermonters to do everything within constitutional limits to end slavery, which meant expelling it from every locale in which the federal government was sovereign. The petitions that circulated throughout the valley during this campaign eloquently expressed the outrage Vermonters felt at the idea that a manacled slave could be "driven to market by the doors of our Capitol, and sold like a beast in the very place where are assembled the representatives of a free and Christian people."[28]

A second petition drive, organized in 1830–1 by anti-Jacksonians in southern New England, condemned the attempts by President Andrew Jackson and the state of Georgia to force the Cherokee, a people who had settled into a productive, peaceful way of life under the tutelage of Christian missionaries, to sell their lands to white settlers and speculators and move beyond the Mississippi. There they would be "protected forever" against the violence and corrupting influence of the white man. The petitioners were angered by what they perceived as a violation of the public faith, and they hoped not only to change federal policies, but to affirm the nation's detestation of all violations of God's laws and the rights of man.[29]

The petition campaigns seemed to have little to do with the direct concerns of the valley during these difficult years. But the petitioners, especially those who had rejected political insurgency, believed that these campaigns were truly the first step in the quest for moral renewal in the valley. They claimed, for example, that the republic's willingness to victimize "weak and defenseless" citizens "in whom no offense is found" had undermined efforts to reclaim the poor, the ignorant, and the irreligious in Vermont. They also believed that the covetous spirit that led Southern land speculators and slaveowners to claim ownership of what did not belong to them had inspired greedy Vermonters to conspire in subtler ways against the shops and farms of their neighbors.[30]

The petition campaigns were of special importance to ministers and churchgoing men of property who opposed political insurgency, many of whom would later join the National Republican Party. Indeed, over a third of the future leaders of that party in the towns studied intensively signed the petitions that passed through their towns (Tables 5.5 to 5.8). J. H. Hubbard, an Episcopalian judge, and the Reverend Joseph Tracy, a Congregationalist publisher, were leaders of the anti-removal campaign in Windsor and had been deeply involved in religious, reform, and economic initiatives after the war, as had Levi Parks, a Baptist deacon and merchant, who led both an anti-removal and an antislavery campaign in

Table 5.5. Social and Religious Status
of Reformers, 1828-1834: Windsor County Towns[a]

	Anti-removal	Sabba-tarian	Temper-ance	Anti-Sab-batarian	Aboli-tionist[b]
Reformers who were (percent)					
Ministers	1	10	18	1	5
Businessmen/professionals	7	41	36	2	11
Master craftsmen	10	14	16	9	0
Nonagricultural nonproprietors	26	10	7	22	16
Agricultural proprietors	25	0	4	-	37
Agricultural nonproprietors	17	0	2	-	5
Agriculturalists (Woodstock)	-	10	11	17	16
Unknown	14	14	5	49	11
Congregationalists	20	72	32	2	11
Baptists	9	3	14	1	21
Episcopalians/Unitarians	15	14	25	5	5
Methodist/Freewill Baptists/Christians	4	0	2	4	16
Universalists	5	0	14	9	11
Nonmembers	48	10	14	79	37
Masons	9	17	20	5	5
N =	307	29	44	365	19

[a] There were no antislavery petitions from these towns. There was no anti-removal petition from Pomfret or Woodstock, no Sabbatarian petition from Pomfret, Weathersfield, or West Windsor, no temperance organization in Pomfret or West Windsor before 1835, and no anti-Sabbatarian movement outside Woodstock. The loss of Woodstock's tax lists make it impossible to separate agricultural proprietors from nonproprietors in that town.
[b] Those abolitionists who joined the movement between 1835 and 1843 are included. There is no evidence that the nature of support for abolitionism changed markedly after 1834.

Barnet, and Josiah Shedd, a Congregationalist merchant and financier, who did likewise in Peacham. The same was true of Sewall Kinney, an Episcopalian woolen manufacturer, and William Jarvis, the landowner, financier, and sheep-raiser, who led the anti-removal forces in Weathersfield. Because of their determination to defend the postwar order against what they perceived as ill-conceived reforms and unprincipled reformers, these men had been widely suspected, in the late 1820s and early 1830s, of having aristocratic ambitions. The petition drives offered them an opportunity to put the Jacksonians on the defensive, to steal the Antimasons' egalitarian thunder, and to press their own claims to leadership.

Unlike postwar benevolent reformers, the anti-insurgents who led these campaigns drew an explicit connection between their commitment to reform and their right to political power. As one anti-removal campaigner wrote, in praise of the campaign's leaders, it was an "encouraging" sign

Table 5.6. Social and Religious Status
of Reformers, 1828-1834: Caledonia County Towns[a]

	Anti-slavery	Anti-removal	Sabba-tarian	Temper-ance	Aboli-tionist[b]
Reformers who were (percent)					
Ministers	0	0	2	4	9
Businessmen/professionals	7	3	10	15	9
Master craftsmen	9	8	11	12	4
Nonagricultural nonproprietors	10	19	11	25	7
Agricultural proprietors	31	31	38	13	52
Agricultural nonproprietors	18	19	18	14	9
Unknown	24	19	9	19	11
Congregationalists	32	42	18	53	52
Baptists	5	1	4	3	2
Associate Presbyterians	1	0	22	0	4
Reformed Presbyterians	0	0	16	0	8
Methodists	1	2	0	3	6
Universalists	11	9	1	7	2
Nonmembers	49	46	39	36	25
Masons	4	5	2	5	4
N =	202	260	165	76	48

[a] There was no antislavery or anti-removal petition from Ryegate, or Sabbatarian petition from Peacham.
[b] Those abolitionists who joined the movement between 1835 and 1843 are included. There is no evidence that the nature of support for abolitionism changed markedly after 1834.

that "publick men [were] made to feel their accountability to the publick, and their obligation to bring...measures of state within the rules of private morality." Men who were willing to be held accountable to moral laws in their dealings with the helpless and who could identify with the downtrodden and feel their sufferings, were worthy to be trusted in their dealings with Vermont freemen. Men who wavered on slavery or Indian rights were considered suspect.[31]

The linking of a commitment to reform with suitability for leadership reveals that the relationship between civic and religious leaders on the one hand and townspeople on the other had grown less trusting. In the eyes of prominent anti-insurgents, the social order was threatened by this distrust, and they were moved by that realization to seek more active support for their leadership and to make more formal promises about their behavior in office. This they accomplished through the petition campaigns. In addition, where there had been a hint of condescension on the part of postwar reformers toward those they aided in their benevolent campaigns and toward the electorate (which was supposed, after all, only to assent quietly to their judgments on most matters), there was

Table 5.7. Affiliations of Reformers
and Political Activists, 1828-1834: Windsor County Towns[a]

	1	2	3	4	5	6	7	8	9
Reformers and activists who were (percent)									
1. Abolitionist[b]	-	1	0	7	0	0	2	0	3
2. Anti-removal[c]	21	-	7	25	-	13	5	-	34
3. Sabbatarian	0	1	-	16	0	6	1	0	6
4. Temperance	16	4	24	-	1	13	6	11	9
5. Anti-Sabbatarian[c]	5	-	0	9	-	19	16	32	7
6. Jacksonian[d]	0	1	3	5	1	-	0	5	8
7. Antimasonic	11	2	3	16	5	0	-	21	4
8. Workingmen[c]	0	-	0	5	2	6	3	-	3
9. National Republican	16	9	17	18	2	44	3	16	-
N =	19	307	29	44	365	16	121	19	86

[a] The overlaps in political affiliation among groups 6 through 9 indicate changes in political affiliation. The proportions for group 8 show the political choices Workingmen made after the demise of their movement in 1831. (There is no record of any individual leaving another movement to join the Workingmen.) The proportions of groups 6 and 7 that were in group 9 describe persons who left the Jacksonian or Antimasonic movements by 1834 to join the National Republicans. The proportions of group 9 involved in groups 6 through 8 thus indicate the proportions of National Republicans who had been Jacksonians, Antimasons, or Workingmen before joining the National Republicans.
[b] The overlap between abolitionism and other movements is understated, because the abolitionist data extend to 1843 and include individuals too young to have participated in other movements before 1835.
[c] Dashes appear at the intersections between group 2 and groups 5 and 8, because there was no anti-removal petition from Woodstock, the only town in which anti-Sabbatarians and Workingmen organized.
[d] The proportions of Jacksonians involved in the various reform movements are deceptive, because they represent the data for the seven Jacksonians who quit the movement by 1834 as well as for the nine who remained in it. None of the nine who remained loyal to Jackson opposed Indian Removal and three favored Sunday mail service. Only one of the nine, a financier from Woodstock, supported temperance or Sabbatarianism. Those who remained Jacksonians were thus more closely affiliated with the anti-reform forces than those who did not.

no condescension now toward either, at least in public. Like Jacksonian and Antimasonic leaders, the men who led the petition campaigns embraced more egalitarian notions of benevolence and leadership.

The campaigns had real power in the valley. They reinforced the legitimacy of and increased public trust in the anti-insurgents who led them. Leading Jacksonians were left to defend as best they could their president's unpopular policies, and leading Antimasons could only latch onto the campaigns as followers. The petition campaigns enabled some anti-insurgents to build a strong political base. Whereas the wealthy men

Table 5.8. Affiliations of Reformers
and Political Activists, 1828-1834: Caledonia County Towns

	1	2	3	4	5	6	7
Reformers and activists who were (percent)							
1. Antislavery	-	31	21	16	33	21	40
2. Abolitionist	7	-	6	4	9	17	5
3. Anti-removal	27	31	-	10	30	30	30
4. Sabbatarian	12	13	7	-	21	10	35
5. Temperance	12	15	9	10	-	7	45
6. Antimasonic	7	25	8	4	7	-	0
7. National Republican	6	2	2	4	12	0	-
N =	202	48	260	165	76	59	20

who led the early colonization movement and committees to aid the deaf and dumb had not offered membership to the public at large, the leaders of the antislavery and anti-removal campaigns sought to persuade massive numbers of townspeople to commit themselves to their view of equality, benevolence, and public policy. Their campaigns yielded forty-four petitions from all corners of the valley. Most bore the signatures of from one-fifth to one-third of the adult male inhabitants in the forwarding towns. The signers were from all occupations, and the petitions attracted far more nonproprietors (about one-third) and untaxed residents (one-fifth) than had previous benevolent enterprises (Tables 5.5 and 5.6). Every denomination was represented, along with nonmembers as well, although the strongest support came from the Congregationalists, as it had in earlier interdenominational reform movements. Only Jacksonian leaders and towns were poorly represented. Clearly, the campaigns tapped the kind of nonpartisan, interdenominational support that anti-insurgents needed to reassert their leadership.[32]

These years also saw the rise of other movements that attempted to combat simpler kinds of moral decline. The first such movement was a petition campaign in 1829–30 to plead for an end to the transportation or delivery of mail on Sundays. The supporters of this campaign believed that Sunday mail service was a form of approbation for Sabbath-breaking activities. They insisted that the government recognize that there were "no acts of human beings with which religion had no concern" and that allowing the mail to be delivered on Sunday damaged the character and conduct of every man and woman. But the Sunday mails were not only a "profanation of the Lord's day." On a practical level, they were a public nuisance, because people who were not churchgoers would gather in front of the post office on Sunday mornings and idle away the day drinking, gambling, smoking, wrestling, racing horses, debating, and fighting. These Sunday rowdies disturbed churchgoers who attended services nearby.[33]

The second movement was a teetotal temperance campaign, which began in the valley in 1827 and encouraged people to abstain "totally" from alcoholic beverages, except for medicinal purposes. Advocates of total temperance blamed alcohol for every manner of evil, from increasing numbers of foreclosures, mortgages, and attachments and the abuse of wives and children to poor citizenship, because drunken partisans carried on at political rallies and on election day and voted not "in faith to the Constitution, but under the bias of whiskey." Teetotal temperance societies tried to persuade local militia companies to remain dry on training days (the Hardwick Society did so successfully in 1828) and to raise public buildings without the benefit of alcoholic bonuses (the people of Cabot and North Danville abstained from alcohol when they raised a Freewill Baptist church and meetinghouse in 1829). They tried their utmost to curb drinking through persuasion, by forswearing the use of alcohol themselves and by asking not only houschold heads and their wives, but boarders and children above the age of twelve to take the "tee-total" pledge and join teetotal societies. The men and women who promoted temperance sought support among people of every class, age, denomination, and neighborhood. They wanted to create a phalanx of such strength and magnitude that it would be clear that the respectable community would no longer tolerate drunkenness.[34]

The Sabbatarian and temperance crusades, like the antislavery and anti-removal movements, were led by wealthy church members, many of them anti-insurgents and future National Republican leaders (roughly two-fifths of whom joined these crusades in Barnet, Peacham, Ryegate, and St. Johnsbury; see Tables 5.5 to 5.8). These people blamed the pressure of the times on a postwar moral declension. Like their counterparts elsewhere in the nation, they worried about the example President Jackson set for others by neglecting church and supporting Sunday mail service, and about the nationwide boom in the production of corn, wheat, and potato liquor that occurred after 1790, a boom that may have trebled per capita consumption of alcohol in the nation. Their primary concern, however, remained the disorder and economic hardship threatening the valley.[35]

Clearly, these reformers had lost confidence in the ability of churches to deal with the dangers they faced. No one wanted a return to direct coercion through the enforcement of moral laws. Reformers did not insist on arrests for drunkenness or disruption of Sunday services, or request legal bans on public drinking. However, they felt that the churchgoing public needed to do more than set a good example to save the valley. Churchgoers had to try to eliminate the occasions of sin and, through explicit social pressure and ostracism, end the use of stimulants whose evil influence poisoned life in the social sphere outside the churches.

Critics of Sabbatarians and temperance reformers soon surfaced. It was charged that the Sabbatarians wanted to revive the standing order and employ government power to dictate religious and moral standards. Sabbath breakers could still break the Sabbath without the Sunday mails, of course, but the Sabbatarians clearly wished to use the government to eliminate the rowdies' reason for gathering on Sunday. That was a subterfuge that marked a definite departure from the spirit of the postwar order.

Temperance reformers were accused of persecuting those who drank. Most were quick to deny it. One reformer pointedly and publicly condemned a statement by a fellow reformer in 1830 that the "division line is to be drawn, and all who don't join our societies must be ranked with the drunkard." He claimed that the line was "not about to be drawn, because we have no disposition to draw it" and because it would be "unjust and imprudent" to deny temperate men who had not yet joined an opportunity to "study and weigh" the subject on their own.[36] Such denials could not hide the fact that there were temperance advocates who did want to transform their societies into extralegal and explicitly proscriptive agencies, aimed not only at drunkards but at all who drank. Still, the vast majority of temperance reformers insisted that persuasion and informal influence would remain the sole means of encouraging proper behavior. The feeling that they needed special organizations beside the churches to foster such behavior, however, indicates that they had grown impatient with the laissez-faire attitude of their society toward immorality and that they were looking for new ways to put pressure on the wayward, without resorting to the enforcement of the hated moral laws.

The Sabbatarians and the temperance reformers anticipated the same broad support won by the antislavery and anti-removal campaigners, but they did not get it. The Sabbatarian campaign elicited fewer petitions and signatories than those campaigns, and encountered considerable resistance. Its fourteen petitions seldom received the support of even a tenth of the adult males in petitioning towns and won broad support only in Barnet and Ryegate, where Scots Calvinists still hoped to preserve the covenant ideal. The campaigns did win a few fervent supporters in marketing and manufacturing towns like Rockingham, Norwich, Windsor, and Woodstock. In those towns there had been a great influx of young laborers; and ministers, master craftsmen, businessmen, and professionals signed up in great numbers because they were afraid of social disorder. Elsewhere petitions were few, especially in areas removed from the Connecticut River where the mail did not arrive on Sundays anyway.[37]

The Sabbatarians' effort to unite the respectable community on new grounds won the support only of people who had either lost confidence completely in informal methods or decided that the perilousness of the times was great enough to warrant risking new measures that would intensify conflict in their towns. Except for the strong support of Episcopalians in Windsor and Woodstock, the Sabbatarians found their appeal limited almost exclusively to Congregationalists and Presbyterians, some of whom did not fear state action on religious matters of interdenominational concern. The campaign won the support of few political insurgents, who had already proposed alternate means of improving public morals. Jacksonians denounced Sabbatarianism as the first salvo of a campaign to reunite church and state, while leading Antimasons dodged the issue, fearful of alienating either the Calvinists or the anti-Calvinists in their party (Tables 5.5 to 5.8).[38]

The Sabbatarian campaign provoked the very forces it was meant to suppress into organizing a powerful, militant countercampaign in defense of the Sunday mails. Woodstock's Free Readers proposed a toast to the Sabbatarians at one of their meetings, expressing the hope that these opponents of Sunday travel would "secure a passage to heaven in the Sunday mail," and circulated an anti-Sabbatarian petition that protested "the persevering and untiring efforts of a widespread religious party" to adjust government policies to fit the demands of religious zealots. The petition received the signatures of roughly half the adult male inhabitants of the town. Four-fifths were nonproprietors and nonmembers – precisely the people the Sabbatarians did not want politicized (Table 5.5). The fact that the church members who signed were primarily Universalists and Episcopalians discredited the Sabbatarians' portrayal of themselves as more than simply a Calvinist movement. A similar petition came from Windham County. It was signed by Jacksonian operatives who seized upon Sabbatarianism as proof of their charge that neo-Federalists intended to reunite church and state. Instead of rallying the respectable community around firm moral standards, the Sabbatarians had divided church members and alienated many nonmembers from the churchgoing community.[39]

The temperance movement was far more successful, in part because it did not call for a change in church–state relations and because its proponents spoke as often of the practical as of the religious benefits of temperance. Support was firmly interdenominational. The core of support for temperance consisted primarily of nonagricultural proprietors in mercantile and manufacturing centers, as it did for Sabbatarianism, but the temperance movement spoke more directly to the concerns of rural residents about public disorder and wayward youths and to the desire of many nonproprietors to steel themselves against temptation and assert a claim to respectability. The movement again had a particular appeal for anti-insurgents, but it won the support of a number of leading Antimasons and Jacksonians (Tables 5.5 to 5.8). Insurgent presses spoke warmly of temperance, even though they remained silent on the need for temperance societies for fear of alienating supporters who drank in moderation.[40]

Whereas Sabbatarianism was virtually dead by mid-1831, temperance reform grew steadily through 1833 and succeeded to some degree in curbing both the production and consumption of alcohol. Reports of the glorious successes of the temperance crusade came from nearly every corner of the valley. There were dry harvests, workshops, militia trainings, and quilting bees. Attitudes toward the use and sale of liquor were changing. According to local societies, consumption often was cut in half and in some towns was reduced to one-sixth of its previous level. Temperance was credited with everything from improving the health and productivity of workers to curbing spitting and immodesty in dress.[41]

The movement reached the limits of easy growth in 1833. The reformers found that they had managed to curb liquor consumption primarily among those who had not been much of a problem in the first place: respectable citizens, moderate drinkers, women, and children. They had nearly succeeded in unifying the valley behind temperate principles, but they had failed to convince most citizens that intemperance was the major evil in valley life or that total abstinence was needed to combat it.

It was in part the perception that temperance and other moral reform movements could not deal with the problems of postwar society that led leading anti-insurgents to organize a political movement, the National Republican Party, to combat the social disorder, economic problems, and political insurgency that plagued the postwar order. Like their Antimasonic and Jacksonian adversaries, they believed that the valley suffered not only from a moral declension, but from a conspiracy against the rights and property of the people. They laid that conspiracy not at the feet of Masons or neo-Federalists, however, but at the feet of leading Jacksonians and Antimasons, who they believed had been driven by envy and greed to defame the postwar order and its defenders and to destroy the economic success and social harmony the valley had until recently enjoyed. To Samuel Elliot of Brattleboro, Antimasonry was a "witch persecution" instigated by ambitious men who wished to set themselves atop the valley's political and economic hierarchy at the expense of civic-minded Masons. And according to Ephraim Brown of Bloomfield, Jacksonianism was nothing more than a plot by "aspirants to office" to ride into power on the coattails of a popular "military chieftain" guilty of "murder – of adultery – of swindling and of lying." By stirring the worst fears and passions of the people and by attacking faithful politicians and businessmen, these traitors had already insinuated themselves into office, looting the public treasury and encouraging discord and immorality. They now threatened to put an end to prosperity in the valley and the nation by overturning the economic policies that had created that prosperity in the first place.[42]

The National Republicans blamed the valley's problems, including public immorality and insurgent conspiracies, primarily on inadequate economic growth, which had frustrated and demoralized hard-working people and had driven men into the clutches of political demagogues. Under the prodding of William Jarvis, Congressman Horace Everett of Windsor, and J. H. Harris, a merchant from Strafford, they set about studying economic theory and lectured one another privately and publicly on the best way to deal with the economy. Much of their formal advice to the public consisted of old homilies. Luther Jewett, a physician, Mason, and editor of the *St. Johnsbury Farmer's Herald*, lectured readers on the need to scrimp and save when times were hard and to simplify dress and diet. The party platform was more substantial. It dealt with the need for more banks, factories, and markets and called for implementation of the American System designed by Henry Clay and supported by Adams. The American System required the federal government to support local economic interests through aid to internal improvements, tariffs to protect domestic industries from foreign competition, a national bank to help stabilize the currency, and sales of public lands at prices high enough to provide funds for further improvement projects. The National Republicans favored a similar program on the state level, one that would commit the state to intensify the efforts already under way in the 1820s to stimulate the local economy. Here they had departed to some extent from the methods and goals of postwar political leaders. They were preoccupied with economic solutions to the valley's problems. They were no longer promising modest economic gains, but substantial prosperity for everyone. Economic concerns were no longer too vulgar a subject to be publicly discussed, but occupied a position at the forefront of their campaign.[43]

The National Republicans did not forget the problems of immorality and social disorder in their quest to restore economic prosperity, but they found themselves less unified in their approach to these issues. They paraded their opposition to slavery and Indian removal before the voters as proof of their egalitarianism and benevolence, but they remained divided on the proper means of promoting temperance and respect for the Sabbath. Many, like Simeon Ide, editor of the *Vermont Journal*, had already embraced both Sabbatarianism and temperance reform. Others, like editor Luther Jewett, believed the Sabbatarian campaign actually encouraged disorder, by fueling resentment on the part of those who did not want to observe the Sabbath, and feared that the party would alienate moderate drinkers if it endorsed teetotal temperance. This created a conflict in the party, which party leaders attempted to resolve by representing party candidates in terms that everyone in the party could approve and by promising that immorality would disappear when the economy improved. Ardent reformers were disappointed by the party's decision not to endorse their programs as strongly as it endorsed economic measures. Nevertheless the party leadership generally presented a united front, at least until 1835.[44]

The final goal of the National Republicans was to end political insurgency. Like their adversaries, they hoped to reunite the valley politically and to return political power to good men. To advance their cause, National Republican businessmen and politicians organized nonpartisan "public improvement" meetings on railroads, river improvements, and tariffs. They used those meetings to inform voters of the soundness of National Republican policies and of the propriety of corporate enterprises that "risked the rich man's money for the poor man's benefit." William Jarvis and Simeon Ide went so far as to pack a rival Jacksonian improvement meeting in 1829 to prevent Norwich's Captain Alden Partridge from claiming widespread support for his anti-steamboat, pro-canal initiative. A National Republican editor in Woodstock, B. F. Kendall, wrote a popular parody on the Antimasonic movement called *The Doleful Tragedy of the Raising of Jo. Burnham*. The play, which was performed several times in the Woodstock area before large crowds, gave life to National Republican charges that the Antimasons had invented a Masonic conspiracy, by recounting the details of Antimasonic efforts to seize control of the government. Antimasons from the valley were parodied under pseudonyms like Parson Rawlimbs (for Edward Rollins of Randolph, editor of the Antimasonic *Vermont Luminary*), Sir Roderick Makefuss (for Richard Makepeace Ransom, a South Woodstock attorney), and Squire Deal-He-Knows (for Jabez Delano, a commercial farmer from West Windsor); their characters were made to swear loyalty "to the death" to their conspiracy and perform comical pseudo-Masonic rituals.[45]

Party editors also made it clear that they understood the discontent of the common man. The *Vermont Journal* published militant letters from "mechanics" denouncing the taxation and militia systems as unfair and complaining of the contempt with which they were treated by college-educated neighbors who considered them "dangerous." Simeon Ide, the *Journal*'s editor, did not endorse such militant egalitarianism, but he assured the authors of these letters that National Republican policies would end economic hardship and eliminate class feeling. National Republican editors believed that they could attract the support of mechanics and others who were unhappy with life in the valley, and the party's economic "realism" and its egalitarian electioneering did give it some new ties to the discontented, ties that the rump supporters of the postwar order badly needed to fend off the attacks of insurgents.[46]

The National Republicans had the advantage of the support of the great majority of experienced state politicians, including Governor Samuel Crafts, Senators Horatio Seymour and Dudley Chase, four of the state's six congressmen, and most state legislators and federal appointees. These politicians, who had tied their political fortunes to Adams, Clay, and the American System, were vexed because Jacksonian and Antimasonic triumphs cost them offices and patronage. Most accepted personal setbacks philosophically, as did J. W. Vail, postmaster of Montpelier until his ouster by President Jackson in 1829, who joked about having been made "a subject of the great *work of reform*!!!" They all bristled, however, at Jacksonian and Antimasonic charges that they had conspired against the liberty, property, and moral values of Vermonters. They were proud of the postwar order, which many of them had helped to found, and were quick to deny that they were unprincipled self-promoters eager, in the words of the Jacksonian *Freedom's Banner*, to "nurse on treasury pap." They believed that Vermonters would support them if they knew the truth and were not misled by demagogues with specious solutions to the valley's problems. That is why they placed such faith in their party's effort to get hard economic facts to the voters.[47]

The party was led locally by men who had done very well under the postwar order. In contrast to Jacksonian and Antimasonic leaders, National Republican activists were more likely to be in the uppermost decile of wealth holders in their towns and to be Masons and corporate trustees (Tables 5.1 and 5.2). They were more likely to live in towns that had prospered in the 1820s, particularly river towns like Brattleboro and Windsor, and growing manufacturing villages like those in St. Johnsbury and Barnet. They were members of many denominations, yet they were more strongly tied to religious liberalism and Calvinism than to the Methodists, Freewill Baptists, Christians, and Universalists. Often they were proprietors of burgeoning factories, like Erastus Fairbanks of St. Johnsbury (the scale manufacturer), or prominent lawyers, like Charles Marsh of Woodstock, or financiers and commercial farmers, like William Jarvis of Weathersfield. They were people who felt that the well-being of the valley depended on their continued leadership in politics and commerce and on the preservation of a united front among men of property and respectable citizens.[48]

It was ironic that these National Republican leaders won the debate on economic policy and gained prestige through the struggle against slavery and Indian removal, but saw their party's support in state elections dwindle from nearly 100 percent of the two-party vote in 1828 to only a quarter in 1834. The National Republicans' senatorial and congressional candidates, most of whom had more distinguished records of public service than their insurgent adversaries, garnered enough Antimasonic and Jacksonian votes to win three-fourths of Vermont's seats in Congress between 1828 and 1835. Yet voters did not trust the National Republicans to rule at home. They won the support of almost a fifth of the valley's religious liberals and Calvinists in 1834, but lost heavily among egalitarian evangelicals, Universalists, and nonmembers everywhere. In areas settled by Old Light and moderate Calvinists, they did far better in former Federalist strongholds than they did in former Republican strongholds, where National Republicanism, because of its association with Sabbatarianism, was thought by many former Republicans to be attempting to revive the standing order. Elsewhere the National Republicans' failure was nearly as great in areas of prewar Federalist strength as in areas of Republican strength (Tables 5.3 and 5.4). The National Republicans won enough votes to deny the Antimasons a clear majority in all but two elections, but they could not win. They could only stalemate and thereby perpetuate the party contest that they believed was destroying the postwar order.

The National Republicans lost in part because they were too closely associated in the eyes of many voters with Masonry, with "coercive" moral reforms like Sabbatarianism and temperance, and with the economic failures of the postwar order. That meant, of course, that the National Republicans were also associated with the successes of the postwar order; therefore they got roughly 12 percent more votes among the members of each religious group in the valley's wealthiest towns than in its poorest towns. Party members could not deny, however, that there were a disproportionate number of Masons, pietists, and very successful capitalists in their midst, as well as Federalists from Old Light areas. The party's spokesmen tried to play down such connections, but there was too much feeling in the valley against certain party members. The *Vermont Journal* was at one point forced to print a notice denying that there was any truth to the rumor that William Jarvis had said privately that the "rich man's money was a fair offset for the poor man's blood." Such denials were fruitless, of course: They only revealed that such men were indeed in the National Republican camp and that the party sought to advance their interests and protect their names.[49]

Between 1833 and 1835 the National Republicans were also confounded by the failure of antislavery and temperance reformers to sustain the kind of unifying reform movements that might save the social order through moral regeneration instead of insurgency. The unity of the temperance movement shattered in 1834, when a number of reformers, many of them from marketing and manufacturing communities, tried to push beyond suasion to proscription and coercion. As the limits of the movement's success became apparent, many supporters were persuaded that "there [was] no such thing as neutral ground." They began to deny the claim of moderate drinkers to "a respectable rank in society" and to denounce merchants who continued to sell liquor as "enemies" of temperance.[50]

In 1834 temperance advocates in Woodstock tried to force the town council to use its powers to discourage drinking. The leading citizens of the town – Charles Marsh, Titus Hutchinson, Dr. J. A. Gallup, Judge Gilbert Dennison, and others – testified before the council that the times required drastic measures. Titus Hutchinson was blunt: For him, the question was whether Woodstock "would be a community of drunkards or of sober citizens." The council was won over by Marsh's testimony. He persuaded them that some legal restraint of liquor traffic was not only practical and moral, but benevolent, when he confessed the horrible guilt he suffered "because he had sold spirits to a person who under its influence had abused his family, and in consequence had been imprisoned."

The council voted to raise the license fees for selling liquor, first to fifty and then to one hundred dollars, feeling that "those who made money by making paupers should pay for the privilege." In explaining its decision the council neatly sidestepped the charge of using the law to impose moral standards by invoking the principle established upon settlement of the valley, that the law was to be used against sinners only if their actions harmed others or cost the taxpayers money. The council's intent was to shame drinkers, to persuade retailers to stop selling liquor, and to drive the liquor trade into neighboring Bridgewater, a hill town with a bad reputation. They did express hope, however, that even Bridgewater would someday follow Woodstock's lead.[51]

When a minority of valley temperance advocates pushed for complete prohibition at the state convention in Woodstock in 1834, divisions grew worse. Name-calling occurred, and there was a floor battle between voluntarists and prohibitionists that nearly destroyed the state society. National Republican leaders debated which position the party should assume (they would not formally endorse any position in 1834 or 1835) and fretted that they would lose temperance reformers to another party. Still, they did not want to be hamstrung by an association with a movement that might prove to be as short-lived and controversial as Sabbatarianism. For the sake of moderate votes, they spoke of temperance, but not of teetotalism or prohibition.[52]

For those who sought reformist and political alternatives to insurgency, the course of the antislavery movement between 1833 and 1835 was even less encouraging. The widespread support for the abolition of slavery in the District of Columbia and for the Vermont Colonization Society, which increased its receipts and trebled the number of contributing churches and lodges between 1828 and 1832, had led many reformers to believe that the valley was united behind the antislavery cause. Unity among antislavery reformers faltered in 1833, however, when many reformers broke with the colonization campaign and called for immediate abolition.[53]

Inspired by the activities of former Vermonter William Lloyd Garrison and his fellow abolitionists in southern New England, these reformers established an antislavery society similar to those then arising in Massachusetts. The Vermont Anti-Slavery Society made no bones about its disillusionment with moderate measures. Its charter stated that "no scheme for the abolition of slavery in the United States, which offers any prospect of success has ever been proposed but that of Immediate Emancipation," and went on to declare war against slavery. "Our weapon is truth – our basis, Justice – our incentive, Humanity – our force, Moral Power – our watchword, Onward – our hope of success – in God."[54]

Few of the society's members perceived themselves as radicals. Like most rank-and-file abolitionists in southern New England, the valley's abolitionists eschewed, with rare exceptions, the "come-outerism" of the Garrisonians. They did not sever their ties with the Constitution, the federal government, or the valley's churches, because they did not believe that institutions forfeited their claim to loyalty simply because they were tainted with sin or were neutral in the war against slavery. Nor did they fear that the nation was irredeemably corrupt because of its association with slavery. They were distressed by the slow progress of emancipation since the war and irritated by the colonizationists' reluctance to embrace slaves as fellow citizens. Indeed, the valley's abolitionists were more concerned with the evils of colonization than with the evils of slavery itself. The Montpelier branch of the Anti-Slavery Society accused the Colonization Society and its mouthpiece, the *Vermont Chronicle*, of being "insidious and subtle" enemies of freedom. Their "worldly expediency," their silence on racism and Southern intransigence, and their willingness to turn "the cause of equal and universal freedom" into a transportation problem had blunted the antislavery argument and stalled the drive for emancipation. Only the destruction of the Colonization Society and the displacement of its unprincipled leaders could ensure the ultimate extinction of slavery.[55]

The abolitionist movement, the extremism of which shocked most antislavery reformers, won solid minority support in the valley. Societies were organized in over one-third of the valley's towns between 1833 and 1838. None of these societies ever galvanized a majority of the local population, but their members spoke out with an enthusiasm that made up for their small numbers. Dr. Josiah Shedd of Peacham, a member of his town's Congregational church and the organizer of its anti-removal and antislavery campaigns, gave all his spare time to the abolitionist cause. He helped found an abolitionist library society, kept himself and others informed of the actual facts and evils of slavery, and made a practice of telling his young daughters bedtime stories about wicked masters and noble slaves yearning for freedom.[56]

Unlike the early campaign against slavery in the District of Columbia, the abolitionist movement encouraged women to participate, both to forge a stronger movement and to create one that was more clearly and inclusively Christian and above politics. Female abolitionists brought scores of new members to the movement. Ruth Buckman, a Universalist from South Woodstock, recorded in her letters that she had pressed antislavery tracts on her father, urging him to become involved in the crusade. Nancy Barnard, the young daughter of a taverner from Peru, tried to make her slaveowning uncle from the South see the light. Women were never leaders in the valley's abolitionist movement, as they were in some cities in the northeast, but the cause did inspire them to act independently. In 1834 the women of Jamaica (the birthplace of abolition in the valley) took the unprecedented step of petitioning the federal government on their own to demand an end to slavery in the District of Columbia.[57]

Abolitionists took up the cause with a single-minded, thoroughgoing resolve once common only among valley youths who had found themselves called to be ministers or missionaries. For them conversion to the cause was a spiritual rebirth, a conscription into the legions of truth. They invoked the Bible for authority for their mission and imitated its language when they urged others to enlist. As might be expected from the character of their commitment to the cause, they were primarily evangelical Christians (Tables 5.5 and 5.6). The proportion of abolitionists who were church members was higher than for any other reform movement in the 1830s (conversely, the movement's appeal to nonevangelicals and those who were not church members was relatively weak). Yet abolitionism was not an inevitable concomitant of evangelical faith or of the peculiar, world-reforming zeal that sudden, revival-induced conversions produced. A majority of evangelicals and a larger majority of all church members opposed immediate abolition in favor of colonization or other moderate antislavery programs.

In the towns studied intensively, abolition appealed most strongly to rural Calvinists – Congregationalists, Baptists, and Reformed Presbyterians. Only one of the movement's leaders came from a Calvinist church in the marketing and manufacturing centers in Woodstock, Windsor, and St. Johnsbury townships. One-fifth of all the abolitionists identified were also leading Antimasons (Tables 5.7 and 5.8). It was in areas strongly supportive of Antimasonry, areas away from the Connecticut River, that abolitionist societies formed. Of the towns that voted over 60 percent Antimasonic in 1834, a quarter had abolitionist societies by the end of 1835, versus only 8 percent of those towns that voted under 60 percent. The proportions grew somewhat closer by 1838 (40 percent versus 30 percent), when organizations spread to all corners of the valley, but the geographical association was still strong.

Abolitionism thus was not only a function of religious commitment or evangelical zeal; it was a politicized expression of that zeal. The abolitionists challenged, as did the Antimasons generally, the benevolence and the right to leadership of all who had anything to do with sin or the oppression of human beings. Commitment to abolition became a symbol for them, as opposition to Masonry had for Antimasons, of a truly benevolent, egalitarian spirit – the kind of spirit on which the revitalized sense of community that Calvinist Antimasons sought would have to rest. Acceptance of and rigid adherence to the Antimasonic understanding of benevolence, equality, and morality may thus have provided the impetus for abolitionist commitment, among both men and women. That would also help to explain why the valley's abolitionists spent so much time attacking the leading colonizationists in the valley (many of whom were National Republicans, Jacksonians, and Masons). Plainly, they wanted to bring to account all prominent citizens who were trying to salvage their leading roles in society by committing themselves to moderate antislavery programs.

The antislavery cause was thus embroiled in a tremendous struggle between the abolitionists, some of whom were wealthy men who had been among the founders of the original Colonization Society, like Dr. Shedd, and those still loyal to colonization. The latter comprised the bulk of churchgoing men of property who opposed Antimasonry and included even some wealthy Antimasons. These men saw clearly that the abolitionists were taking the antislavery initiative away from them and casting suspicions upon their motives for taking the more moderate course.

Erastus Fairbanks wrote a friend in 1837 that "the friends of religion and good order" had much to fear from the abolitionists, determined as they were "to bring upon all those who will not go all lengths with [them] ... the stigma of being pro-slavery." He recognized that his own commitment to egalitarianism and benevolence was being questioned and that his right to exercise his influence upon society and government was at stake. He was also worried about the fate of the national political party that he and his fellow National Republicans were trying to form, and for which they needed support in slave states. The abolitionists both angered and frightened him, and it was with some desperation that he insisted to his friend that "public sentiment ought to be guided by those who are better informed & have the means of forming more correct judgments. Such men *must* be induced to take the lead in this cause, or we must consent to see our State overrun with this wild fire."[58]

The abolitionists did question whether men like Fairbanks, who condoned by their ineffectual opposition the oppression of blacks, could be truly concerned about the oppression of whites. Were they fit to govern? Could they be trusted in positions of power? William Porter, a student at Dartmouth, felt that "a majority" of the college's colonizationists "care no more about the blacks here or in Africa than they do about so many dogs," and listed by name colonizationists he felt unworthy of trust on any account. Those reformers who remained loyal to colonization saw their hopes for a renewed consensus evaporating in the face of such antagonism and were unable to fashion a satisfactory response to the abolitionist challenge. At times they vilified the abolitionists for exaggerating the evils of slavery. They believed that Congress would remedy those evils peacefully and with respect for the rights of property owners, if the abolitionists would stop fomenting sectional hatred and suspicion. They also occasionally accused abolitionists of Garrisonian radicalism. Charles Paine, a woolen manufacturer from Northfield and president of the Vermont Colonization Society, was angered by Garrison's refusal to be bound by the federal Constitution's promise to protect slavery in states where it already existed. That view, according to Paine, made abolitionists enemies of decency and of enterprise itself, "false to all obligations, deliberate repudiators of contracts, who renounce the vows made for them by their fathers."[59]

For the most part, however, those who sought reformist and political alternatives to insurgency tried to ignore the abolitionist threat. They trumpeted the successes of colonization, dismissed their differences with the abolitionists as unimportant, and sponsored their own petitions (both men's and women's) against slavery in the District of Columbia in 1837–8 to prove their solidarity with abolitionists on practical questions. When the opportunity arose in 1837, they did support efforts to form a moderate antislavery organization that would act as a foil to the more extreme voice of abolitionism and "obtain the confidence of community to such an extent no misrepresentation would shake it."[60]

The consensus behind moderate antislavery was difficult to maintain, however. No churches or reform societies had actually split over abolition before 1835, but support for colonization among such organizations fell precipitously, out of a regard for the divisions that requests for donations might create. Contributions to the Vermont Colonization Society fell from a high of $1,421 in 1832 to only $271 in 1837. Only the campaign against slavery in the District of Columbia drew general support, now from both sexes and from nearly every town in the valley.[61]

A number of the valley's commercial and manufacturing centers were shaken by divisive antiabolitionist protests in 1835. Some of the protests were relatively peaceful, like those in Windsor and Woodstock centers, where the trustees of the major churches – Congregational, Baptist, and Episcopalian – refused the abolitionists permission to hold public meetings in their churches. The trustees of these churches were wealthy colonizationists and National Republicans and were understandably reluctant to lend their churches to an organization bent on undermining their antislavery program, disrupting their party, and tearing down their personal reputations. The abolitionists as a result could find no place to meet in Windsor and retired to the county court house in Woodstock (where it was reported that the hall was only half filled), even though they were welcome at the meetinghouse in South Woodstock, where the town's leading Antimasons worshipped.

In Montpelier, the confrontation between abolitionists and their enemies was more direct. Forty civic leaders protested against the use of the State House and the town's Old Brick Meetinghouse to hold lectures on abolition that endangered the unity of the nation and the tranquility of the town. When the lecture began, Colonel Timothy Hubbard, the president of the Bank of Montpelier, arose to denounce the speaker's "un-gospel and anti-union harrangue." His charges were accompanied by cheers from the audience. The lecturer was pelted with eggs and hooted off the stage. Serious violence was prevented only by his speedy withdrawal from the platform and by the willingness of a handful of townspeople to defend him. There were similar incidents in Newbury and in Randolph Center. As in Montpelier, prominent citizens encouraged others to mob speakers who had been permitted to talk at a local church. Each incident resulted in the silencing of the speaker and, in Newbury, the arrest and conviction of several people for disturbing the peace.[62]

The motives of the protesters can be construed only from the sparse data on their identity and from the few comments attributed to them in newspaper reports of these incidents. The protests followed a pattern. They occurred exclusively in commercial and manufacturing towns, where the village elite was strongly supportive of colonization and the National Republican or Jacksonian Party. (The same pattern pertained in the one additional antiabolitionist disturbance that occurred in Brattleboro in 1837.) The protesters were members of the local elite who stood to lose power and prestige if Antimasonry and abolitionism triumphed. They incited protests only when outside agitators threatened to stir up new support for abolition, and claimed they were not trying to halt abolitionist activity, which had its local partisans, but only to prevent outsiders from influencing townspeople. Coming from citizens who supported lecture campaigns for their own reforms and party programs, that was a feeble excuse.[63]

Clearly, the antiabolitionists felt that abolitionism was a serious threat to their interests, their way of life, and their vision of a peaceful Union. Their efforts to stop abolitionist activities were in vain, however. Abolitionist support only increased throughout 1835, and protesters discredited themselves by behaving just as the abolitionists had predicted they would, shedding their benevolent disguises and attempting to deny others' rights.

With the antislavery movement permanently divided into two warring camps, reformers' hopes of reunifying the valley began to fade. Those who had cheered the "mighty work of renovation" in 1833 showed signs of flagging optimism by 1835.[64] The critical problem of unifying the society in service of Christian ideals, of rallying its members behind more rigorous codes of behavior and benevolence, was all but forgotten. The reformers could not remedy the social problems underlying the valley's difficulties by appealing to a moral consensus, nor could they inject moral resolve into the midst of social and political antagonisms. Each party attempted to twist the Christian message to suit its own ends; each party's commitment to reform became the sole standard of decency and respectability. It was only natural that so many members of the churchgoing community, who had profound confidence in reform societies and were utterly convinced that moral decline lay at the heart of the valley's problems, should have tried to revive the reform drive to save their way of life. They could not have foreseen how badly their efforts would fare.

With the abolitionists baying at their heels and many people in the valley persuaded that their economic policies were both unworkable and unjust, the National Republicans also failed in their effort to construct a powerful political alternative to insurgency and to restore political unity in the valley. Political vilification reached levels that had not been seen since the War of 1812, and esteem for public men fell to a new low. The electorate grew more and more agitated. The one party that stood on the verge of complete victory in the valley, the Antimasons, had seen its affiliates in other states collapse before the National Republicans or the Jacksonians, leaving the party without appeal on the national level. Its rivals could not oust it from power in the valley, however, even in 1833, when in desperation they joined forces to support Ezra Meech, a Jacksonian, for governor as the Jacksonian–National Republican candidate against Antimasonic Governor William Palmer (1831–5). The move further alienated anti-insurgent reformers from the National Republican Party and gave the Antimasons their greatest victory.[65]

What had happened? Obviously, the leading citizens of the valley had split over fundamental issues. Anxious in various ways about social disorder, economic difficulties, and political life, and aware of the discontent among ordinary citizens, they returned to reform movements in search of solutions. Churchgoing men of property were generally successful in keeping a grip on town office (three-fifths of all terms were served by men in the upper decile of wealth and only one-fifth by those who were not church members), but their partisan bickering undermined the ability of any one officeholder to convince the community that he would act on behalf of the community as a whole. The average length of service dropped from 2.5 to 2 years from 1816–28 to 1829–35, and the percentage of single-term selectmen doubled, as representatives of different parties continually dislodged each other from office. Thus, although collectively churchgoing men of property retained leadership, no one party was victorious, and the unchallenged legitimacy of the valley's leaders was not restored.[66]

The opponents and proponents of insurgency had much in common, however. The various political parties and reform movements that spread through the valley from 1828 to 1835 were generally dedicated to the familiar, shopworn ideals of the postwar order. All wanted a society dominated by Christians and Christian values. All wanted leadership by principled, substantial citizens who stood above faction and interest, and rapid economic growth that benefited everyone. With the exception of a handful of Workingmen and radical abolitionists, the insurgents and anti-insurgents also shared a reformist vision of history. They believed that their society was fundamentally sound. It had eliminated deep-seated evils or doomed them to destruction, as in the case of slavery. People were free to realize their ideals. Whether they were evangelicals or rationalists, however, the reformers believed in an afflictive vision of progress, which warned that the valley's and the nation's dedication to Christian, republican ideals would wane as each new plateau was reached and that time-honored laws and institutions could lose their efficacy over time and impede progress. To keep progress in force, reformers would need to purge their society of corruption from time to time and to modify its laws and institutions.

That vision of history transformed the valley's republican quest into a process, an ongoing struggle between the forces of reform and the forces of decay. Although it augured a difficult future in which reformers would have to exercise both vigilance and restraint, it gave them confidence that the dangers they confronted would in time be surmounted. Nathan Haswell, a Jacksonian editor whose cries for reform were as urgent as any, wrote that he was not "alarmed at excitements. We have had them in some form or other ever since our government was formed." He was confident that parties, conspiracies, and other evils would eventually disappear, just as "the Sun rises and the Sun sets." The nation would again be calm and purified, and the various religious, moral, and political movements remembered "only for the violence and self-destroying materials" that prompted or composed them.[67]

The valley's reformers tacitly renounced the historical visions of previous Vermonters. They no longer believed in the gradualism of the Era of Good Feelings, the conservatism or progressivism of the Federalist–Republican Era, or the immediatism of Vermont's Founding Fathers, who believed they could establish an enduring, near-perfect republic by laying down proper laws and institutions. Reformers simultaneously altered their understanding of Vermont's past to conform to their vision of the republican quest. They purged the Revolution and the Republican Party of all taint of progressive insurgency, transforming them into reform movements that had saved Vermont from Tories, Yorkers, and Federalists, who in turn were transformed from Royalist aristocrats into mere conspirators. They remembered the struggles of the revolutionary and postrevolutionary eras as less dangerous than they had been, forgetting that the future of liberty in America and the valley once hung by a thread. In their minds, the valley had avoided progressive–conservative conflicts at home because Vermonters had enjoyed equality, democracy, and toleration from the first years of settlement. Reformers had recast the past after their image of the present, and the successes of the past gave them confidence that reform would work again, as they embarked upon what they saw as the third cycle of reform in the valley.

6

The great revival,
1827–1843

A man who called himself Plain Dealer wrote to the *North Star* of Danville in 1830 to point out ominous parallels between the spiritual condition of Vermont and that of Israel at the time of the prophet Ezekiel. He saw a "great declension of religion" behind the manifold threats to the "peace and prosperity" of the valley. The causes of that declension were not clear to him, but he was certain of the cure: a revival of religion. That alone, he wrote, could heal "the contentions and divisions among us."[1]

Most Christians shared Plain Dealer's belief that the political and social discord in the valley had its roots in a widespread indifference to God. They had faith in the restorative power of religion and had begun to think the only hope for the valley lay in a revival. But if a revival came, would it be genuine? Would it regenerate the souls of those it touched, sanctify their behavior, and restore the valley to God's grace? Would it restore prosperity, political unity, and sound morals?

To the delight of most Christians, what appeared to be a genuine revival began, albeit modestly, in 1827. It produced dramatic effects. By its end in 1843, at least 43 percent of adult men and women in the valley were full church members, and the vast majority attended church regularly. In the valley's principal marketing and manufacturing towns, 55 percent of the inhabitants over fifteen years of age were members; in secondary marketing and manufacturing centers and more prosperous agricultural towns, 44 percent; and in towns that had poorer land and were less involved in the market economy, 38 percent. That was a sizable increase. The proportion of adult males who were church members had risen in the agricultural towns studied intensively from 26 percent in 1827 to 38 percent by 1843, and in Windsor from 37 to 56 percent. The annual rate at which new members entered Calvinist churches almost doubled (from twelve per thousand inhabitants age fifteen and older to twenty). Membership in Methodist churches doubled as well, as did the number of non-Calvinist churches and Union meetinghouses, although the valley's population increased by only 5 percent. By 1843, there was one church or meetinghouse for every 325 people in the valley.[2]

Christians realized, however, that numbers alone could not prove the revival genuine. The serenity of early revival meetings, the stability of the first converts, and the enthusiasm of the churchgoing community made the revival seem at first a genuine work of grace. But by 1831 the churchgoing community had injected the revival with a variety of temporal and denominational concerns, and that led to conflict among Christians and with nonchurchgoers. Converts entered churches for diverse reasons, and some did not find their hopes fulfilled. Many fell away into sin or indifference, others gave up on the temporal world and prayed for the advent of Christ's kingdom on earth. Still, the number of church members and sincere Christians mounted steadily. By 1835, however, there were so many signs that the revival was touching many converts only fleetingly and missing some people altogether, and that it was dividing communities and churches and stirring passions as well as souls, that its genuineness came to be questioned and its ability to solve the valley's problems generally doubted.

The course of the revival

The great revival began in the northern reaches of the valley. It received no widespread public attention at the time, for there were no signs that the tiny, seemingly spontaneous local revivals signified that an extraordinary work was at hand. News of the revivals spread by word of mouth or by letter and was usually passed on by Christians who wanted to further the revivals' progress and draw friends and relations into them. Ann Carter, who lived in the rugged Caledonia County hill town of Groton, wrote about them to her brother, Willard Stevens, who lived in nearby St. Johnsbury. She prayed that God's work would continue until her town might "appear like one united family" and hoped "to see converts multiplied like the drops of the morning." Every day brought a new manifestation of God's power, every church meeting the addition of a new member or the return of a backslider. As of April, when Ann Carter wrote to her brother, there were already twenty-one or twenty-two people who had applied for admission to the Congregational church. All had had what they felt were conversion experiences.[3]

The revival did not tarry long in the remote backcountry towns of Caledonia and Washington counties. In 1828 and 1829, it spread to market towns and manufacturing villages, especially along the Connecticut River. It reached Newbury, the largest town in Orange County, in the fall of 1828. The decorum with which the revival was conducted convinced the Reverend Clark Perry of the Congregational church that it was genuine. "There has been no crying out, or swooning, or very loud rejoicing. But there have been solemn countenances – feelings of deep anxiety – tears of penitence, and earnest prayers for mercy."[4]

From the church members themselves, the revival spread to their families, particularly from "pious wives" to their "unbelieving husbands," and then to the town at large. In Newbury, conversions were most numerous along the river road (the most densely populated and developed area in the town) and among people who attended services at the Congregational church, but Perry noted that "several cases of hopeful conversion have occurred in parts of the town remote from the river" and in rival denominations as well. People of all ages and all walks of life were involved.

In 1831 the revival assumed the character of a great revival. Thousands of souls were saved in that year, in every corner of the valley. Reports of simultaneous revivals in western Vermont, western New York, and northeastern Ohio convinced church members of every denomination that an extraordinary work of grace was under way. Hazen Merrill of Peacham marveled at the productivity of the revival in a letter to his brother in Indianapolis. Every special religious service "seemed to produce wonders." Almost two hundred and fifty people joined Peacham's two churches (Congregational and Methodist), and Merrill reported that even "careless professors and men of the world" were tending to their souls. The revival also delivered the townspeople from some of the problems their own efforts had failed to solve. "This church and people have for a long time tried other things and made divisions among us which in a few months have vanished in thin air," Merrill wrote, noting with particular glee (as an Antimason) that the townspeople had forsaken Masonry. In fact, they had also rejected Antimasonic bigotry, in a "permanent" agreement to entrust their fate to Christ alone.[5]

The Peacham revival was not unusual in its scope and power. Individual churches commonly won a hundred or more new members that year. For a while it seemed that the hopes of the Plain Dealer that God Himself would save the valley might be fulfilled. As its pace quickened, however, the revival took a self-conscious turn. The revivals of 1831 were not as spontaneous as those of 1827–30, because the churchgoing community increasingly worked to instigate them. The devout flooded religious and political presses throughout the burned-over districts with demands for a religious awakening, and employed specific mechanisms to increase spiritual enthusiasm. These mechanisms were not new; evangelicals and nonevangelicals alike had previously used hell-fire preaching, weekly prayer meetings, special youth societies and Sunday schools, protracted meetings (multiweek series of daily revival meetings in a single town), and camp meetings (continuous two- to four-day revival meetings that gathered participants from a wide area in camps on open fields) to win souls and improve morals. It was the extent to which these mechanisms were employed by Congregationalists, Baptists, and Methodists and accepted by members of nonevangelical denominations that was unprecedented.

The churchgoing community was not entirely in agreement about specific means of furthering piety. The *Universalist Watchman* condemned four-day revival meetings, claiming they produced "moral desolation, and aweful consequences" and promoted a frenzied, superstitious orthodoxy. The *Watchman* also asserted that "intemperate preaching" had caused more deaths in the past year than "intemperate drinking," because it had driven weak, credulous people to lose all hope of salvation. Still, there was no evidence of widespread support for the *Watchman*'s criticism of revival meetings in 1831. Even though they generally did not believe in the conversion process, Episcopalians, Universalists, and Unitarians often participated in protracted meetings, simply because they too felt an urgent need for religious awakening and a desire for an intensely religious experience. Many long-settled ministers of relatively staid parishes, like Peacham's Leonard Worcester and Weathersfield's James Converse, were not above using these newly popular methods to attract new converts. Hazen Merrill preferred to attribute Worcester's success in 1831 to his long, persistent labors on behalf of God. "Our old minister sees a day which he dared not hope for but he has labored faithfully," Merrill wrote, "and it very much animates him to see so much success even at this late day." Actually, the venerable Worcester had gotten up some new, extraordinarily fiery sermons and had sponsored protracted meetings to supplement his humbler efforts.[6]

Most church members did not have difficulty justifying such methods. Although religious liberals and Universalists did not believe conversion experiences necessary for salvation and did not themselves move beyond special prayer meetings and intense proselytization in pursuit of the revival, for the most part they accepted the idea that God could grant men grace through conversion experiences and that well-conducted revival services could legitimately further God's work. They credited man with the ability to approach God – indeed, they thought it his responsibility to do so.[7]

Most Congregationalists, Baptists, and Presbyterians in the valley relied upon the teachings of predestinarian evangelicals to legitimize their crusades. By 1843, some members of these denominations had come to reject the "disheartening" doctrines of predestination and innate depravity. They claimed the power to accept God's grace of their own free will, to hasten the onset of the millennium by speeding the harvest of souls through revivals, and to achieve victory with the help of God's grace over sin, temptation, and, in the case of Ann Niles of West Fairlee, over the desire for sleep and food. Although the vast majority did not abandon their belief in man's inability to achieve grace through his own efforts, in practice they moved farther toward Arminianism and perfectionism than predestinarian evangelical theologians had intended. The valley's Calvinists were confident that human efforts could further revivals and that God's grace would enable them to build a Christian commonwealth on earth. This evangelical theology enabled them to join non-Calvinist evangelicals in the pursuit of an ever greater revival.[8]

Supporters of the revival became self-conscious not only about the means they used to further their cause but about the pursuit of specific ends. They wanted to use the revival to wipe out the evils that they believed most endangered the valley: political contentiousness, greed, and disorderly conduct. The revival's proponents spent much of their time trying to convert male sinners (it was thought that women, in their somewhat more restricted sphere of life, posed fewer problems for society than men, and were in any event generally more pious and sober). They drew a bead on people who frequented taverns and workshops; they traveled to poor backwoods areas where strangers were infrequently seen and people put up a grim resistance to the civilizing influence of ministers and churches. Nor were they blind to the evil that existed in higher places: Revival sermons, religious tracts, and periodicals also focused on high-society parlors and on the selfishness of the well-to-do.[9]

The bulk of the churchgoing community resolved consciously in 1831 to press for new members. Not even the Calvinists among them had previously been willing to bring forceful pressure to bear upon the unchurched. Now, in the face of what they thought were great perils, and with the great promise that the revival seemed to extend to them, the churchgoing community grew militant, particularly at its Calvinist core. In an election sermon in 1833, the Reverend Tobias Spicer asserted that Christianity was "the only source of national prosperity" and happiness, and the only hope of mitigating the evils Vermonters faced. Failure to join a church was not only a sign of spiritual failure, it was unpatriotic. As full church membership blossomed in the minds of many Christians into a requirement for good citizenship, the voluntary principles invoked by the new order were severely undermined.[10]

Few Christians believed that the millennium was at hand. They felt, as did Horace Greeley, then a printer's apprentice in western Vermont, that they were not wise enough "to say where and when the deliverance of our race from evil and suffering shall be consummated." They saw spiritual progress just as the valley's reformers viewed moral progress: as a struggle whose end was not yet in sight. They believed that every revival except that which preceded the millennium would be followed by a declension, as the forces of darkness redoubled their efforts to capture the world; and they had no way of knowing whether their efforts to stem the current declension would be blessed. They believed, however, as did Greeley, that suffering was "disciplinary and transitional," that it represented both a test of their spiritual mettle and an opportunity to carry the world closer to "universal holiness and consequent happiness." They took heart in the success of past revivals and in the signs of the present work, and were confident that they were taking yet another step forward in the valley's and the nation's spiritual improvement.[11]

This vision of history, shared by virtually all evangelicals and non-evangelicals alike, was the spiritual counterpart of the reformist vision of history. Christians, like reformers, had lost faith in the gradualism of the new order. They began to look upon revivals in the way that reformers looked upon reform movements: as vehicles through which they could address the continuing disappointments of democratic life and defend their varied and often contrary interests, aspirations, and ideals. Christians and reformers were reassured by the complementary nature of these visions of history and heartened to think that they could work toward the same ends in different ways. The Christian vision of history subsumed the reformist vision of history, giving divine sanction and a promise of ultimate victory to the reformist quest for moral progress, and the reformist vision of history gave Christians confidence that spiritual improvement was a manageable process, a struggle against periodic conspiracies and declensions.

The revival subsided temporarily in 1832–3, but in 1834–5, revival activists stepped up their efforts to increase the number of conversions. In a number of towns, churches cooperated with one another to stage interdenominational crusades to resurrect the revival. These crusades necessitated tremendous financial outlay, months of preparation and publicity, cooperation with Christians in neighboring communities, and assistance from expert revivalists from outside the valley, but church members and ministers had grown desperate for further works of grace and were willing to try almost anything. The period of preparation lasted up to a full year, during which local churches held special services to stimulate piety and conviction. Missionary activity was increased, and churches banded together informally to collect funds for three- to four-week protracted meetings that would attract a thousand or more participants from their towns and surrounding areas. The preparations came to a head in 1834 with an interdenominational call to Jedidiah Burchard, the renowned revivalist, to preside in the fall and winter of 1834–5 over crusades in Chester, Weathersfield, Windsor, Woodstock, Springfield, Norwich, Royalton, Strafford, and Montpelier in Vermont, and in Claremont, Charlestown, Hanover, and five other towns in New Hampshire. Burchard would prove to be the most important revivalist to visit the valley, and the one most able to draw interdenominational support. His wife was an Episcopalian and played an important part in the revivals, working with youthful converts. Her presence served to convince religious liberals that revivals were not for evangelicals alone. Burchard himself was an orthodox Calvinist, but he embraced the millennial optimism of his Arminian mentor, Charles Grandison Finney of upstate New York, and spoke eloquently to the concerns of both Calvinist and non-Calvinist evangelicals.[12]

Ministers publicized the impending events and vowed that nearly everyone in their area would be touched by the crusade. Christians expected great things. According to Richard Streeter, a Universalist minister in Woodstock, "the name of 'Burchard' was upon every lip." Marvelous stories of mass conversions at Burchard's first stops in Springfield and Windsor stirred the expectant and roused up the guilty. "Every nerve was put upon the stretch – every eye wide open, and the populace on tiptoe."[13]

Crusade organizers helped stir excitement by pressuring everyone to attend Burchard's revivals. In most towns, businesses were closed during services. Streeter wrote that in Woodstock "they ransacked the village, the town, and other places, and almost dragged people, especially the young and the diffident, from their homes and their business, to the scene of mental slaughter." Organizers scoured "streets, work-shops, and public houses" in search of "poor, hell-deserving" souls they could save. "Every un-Burchardized heretic... from 'Sambo to his illustrious master' " was collared; every "kitchen and corner" invaded.

Targets of the crusades were various. The Reverend James Converse of the Weathersfield Congregational Church frankly admitted that his town's crusade aimed at capturing the souls of those who worked at the woolen mills in the fast-growing manufacturing village of Perkinsville, situated on the Black River in the southwestern corner of the township. However, crusaders also took aim at well-to-do churchgoing men who had not experienced conversion. Burchard mocked the unwillingness of such men to humble themselves and to allow the spirit to move them. He likened them to the man who complained to the person who saved his son from drowning, that he should have taken him "under the arms, and saved his life genteely!" Austin Chase reported that when Burchard came to Dartmouth, he lit into the unconverted genteel with particular fervor. "He seems to fear nobody here and often reprimands the inhabitants fearlessly . . . for their stiffness, formality and aristocracy. . . . Some of the most obdurate, both on the plain and in college are among the converts." Even the faculty "in some measure" threw aside formality and entered the work "as much as could be expected." The Reverend Russell Streeter observed that in Woodstock Burchard roused the crowd by humiliating the high and mighty, pointedly questioning the well-to-do about their values, and forcing them to perform menial tasks in front of the assembled throng during revival services. Such attempts to humble the proud obviously served the interests of the Calvinist denominations, which had lost ground to the Unitarians and Episcopalians among businessmen and professionals, and which had been accused by ministers of egalitarian denominations of catering to the rich.[14]

With some exceptions, the crusades of 1834–5 succeeded in increasing church membership and in rousing people from spiritual torpor, but they marked the high point rather than the rebirth of the revival. The crusades divided the revival's proponents in unforeseen ways, undermining the unity so vital to the progress of their spiritual enterprise. Many wealthy churchgoers and nonevangelical church members were driven into opposition to the revival, and evangelical churches were split over the genuineness and reliability of revivals and revival-induced conversions. Still, the indisputable successes of the revival and its inspiring legacy drove many to continue to promote it and to see hope in its progress. The valley never again shared as generally in a specific revival as it did in 1831 and 1834–5, but numerous revivals occurred in various towns until 1843, and there were general upswings in conversions and church membership in 1839 and 1843, especially in the countryside.

Those later revivals were not orchestrated or fomented by crusades as earlier revivals had been. They touched certain towns in a sporadic, seemingly spontaneous fashion reminiscent of the earliest days of the revival. They occurred more often in rural areas than in villages, excited emotions to a still more feverish pitch than before, and were more often led by ill-lettered preachers from the more popular denominations. Yet their promoters and participants had the same conscious concerns and hopes that their counterparts had during the revivals of 1831 and 1834–5. Their desire to promote a great revival had become even stronger in some ways, since the problems that had initially inspired the revivals had become more serious, especially with the advent of a depression in 1837.[15] There were no more ringing pronouncements that the revival would soon save the valley, however. These late revivals enabled the churchgoing community only to maintain the position it had achieved in the mid-1830s, and confirmed the suspicions of critics who believed the revivals had done little more than excite people temporarily into an irrational frenzy.

The causes of the revival

The most important questions about the revival – who joined the churches, and why? – have not as yet been answered. Most accounts of the revival described its success as "general," as spread through every region and denomination, as successful among people of every age, sex, and occupation. No one drew any systematic profile of the new church members. Few observers or new church members offered any insights into the motives of those touched by the revival. Participants usually spoke only of the joys that flowed from their final commitment to God, rather than of the paths that brought them to that commitment. The identity of the new church members must be derived from church and other records, and the reasons they entered the churches deduced from sources that only indirectly shed light on their motives.

Those who claimed that the revival's appeal was general were not wholly in error, nor were they wrong when they claimed that many Christians were drawn toward conversion and church membership by a powerful desire to share in God's work. The revival enveloped the valley's inhabitants in an atmosphere of expectation so powerful that all things seemed possible, including personal revelations from God and the coming of the millennium. People from all walks of life joyously surrendered to God's power and joined the struggle to spread the gospel to all humanity. In 1831, Abel Adams of West Windsor was yearning to join in the work. He rose at one Sunday meeting "to give vent" to his feelings and share the "agony" of his soul with the congregation. At first "it seemed impossible to utter a word! But I commenced by repeating the words of the Lamentation of Jeremiah, 1:12...I said a few words in heaviness, then sudden and unexpectedly the glory of God burst into my soul like a mighty fountain! My countenance changed, my soul expanded and I mounted up with wings as Eagles. I talked until my voice failed.... This was the beginning of days to my soul!" Spiritual rapture like Adams's was common. If such people had any motive in experiencing conversion and joining churches other than to serve the Lord, any coarser aim than to win salvation for themselves and their loved ones, or any impetus other than the revival itself, they did not betray it.[16]

Yet surviving records reveal that the revival did have a definite shape, and that it moved some people more deeply and more often than others. The revival attracted a disproportionate number of young men and

Table 6.1. Occupations of New Church Members, 1810-1843:
Marketing and Manufacturing Town[a]

	1810-28, except revivals	1810-28, revivals	1829-43
Professionals	8	0	6
Businessmen	15	0	3
Master craftsmen -- group A	8	13	6
Master craftsmen -- group B	10	13	8
Small proprietors	8	0	1
Clerks	10	0	8
Journeymen/laborers	18	33	27
Unknown[b]	23	40	42
N =	39	15	130
Proprietors	49	27	24
Nonproprietors	51	73	76

[a] Those who joined the Unitarian church, which was founded in 1836, are not included in the table, because the dates of their commitment to Unitarianism cannot be determined.
[b] Unknown persons were listed on neither census rolls nor tax lists. Nearly all, therefore, were under the age of twenty-one, although some males over twenty-one may be included with them, because some adult males were transient enough to miss inclusion on such lists.

women. The few revivals that had occurred prior to 1827 had brought large numbers of young men and women into the churches, but the great revival surpassed their appeal to these groups. The median age at which males entered Congregational and Baptist churches fell precipitously. Prior to 1827, the median age at entry had been in the late twenties; during revivals, it had been twenty-five. During the great revival, the median age at entry dropped to twenty-two (Table 2.2).[17] The proportion of men who were not proprietors entering all churches thus also rose, as did the proportion who were not married or heads of households, to levels somewhat above even those of previous revivals, which had always drawn them disproportionately into the churches (Tables 6.1 and 6.2). The proportion of female admittants who were married stood at just above a third throughout the revival. During previous revivals that rate had been the same, whereas in spiritually calm times two-thirds of women admitted were married.

Why did young people join churches in such great numbers during this revival? It may have been that the ideals set forth during the revival were particularly compelling to the young. Revivalists condemned the mercenary character of humanity unredeemed and promised that those who eschewed the things of this world would be first in heaven. Young people

Table 6.2. Occupations of New Church Members, 1810-1843:
Agricultural Towns[a]

	1810-28, except revivals	1810-28, revivals	1829-43
Professionals	1	0	1
Businessmen	1	0	1
Master craftsmen -- group A	1	2	3
Master craftsmen -- group B	0	1	2
Small proprietors	3	1	1
Millers/taverners	3	1	0
Clerks	0	1	1
Journeymen/laborers	9	11	11
Unknown	32	41	43
Commercial farmers	2	4	2
Family farmers	11	9	10
Subsistence farmers	24	13	9
Farm tenants/farm laborers	14	16	16
N =	115	258	647
Proprietors	46	31	28
Nonproprietors	54	69	72

[a] Those who joined Universalist or Unitarian churches are not included in the table because the records of those churches do not indicate the dates that members joined. Also not included are people who could be identified from partial lists as joining new Methodist societies in Peacham, Pomfret, and Weathersfield during the Great Revival. The partial lists understate the number of nonproprietors who joined these churches, because they record society rather than church membership.

may also have been won over by the ability of revivalists like Burchard to humble their elders, and nonproprietors were undoubtedly delighted when they saw their "betters" brought low. Probably more significant, however, was the effect of the pressures of the times upon the balance of power between young and old. Because the decline in opportunity had left them more dependent on adults for help in finding a niche in the valley, young men and women may have been more vulnerable to pressure or persuasion from parents, employers, prospective in-laws, and ministers. Furthermore, churchgoing adults were far more united across denominational lines than before and more willing to employ their full powers to win young souls. The young were not powerless. They could still defect politically or morally from the causes of their elders, as they had on occasion before the War of 1812, and they could always pack up and leave. Nevertheless, their horizons were more constrained, and if they envisioned futures in the valley, they had to safeguard their reputations at home. They had, in short, to toe the line.

Table 6.3. Household Composition
and Entry into Churches among Proprietors, 1827-1843[a]

	Proprietors without persons 0-19 in household	Proprietors with persons 0-14 and without persons 15-19 in household	Proprietors with persons 15-19 in household
Farmers			
Church members, 1827-43	12	20	27
N =	324	333	362
Master craftsmen			
Church members, 1827-43	22	30	49
N =	73	64	57

[a] Household composition is determined from the censuses of 1830 and 1840. All persons who were church members prior to the revival or who joined churches prior to becoming proprietors during the revival are excluded from the table. All proprietors who did not join churches during the revival or who joined churches prior to 1835 are assigned the household structure they had in 1830, even if they remained in town and were still proprietors in 1840, when additional household data are available. Persons who became proprietors after 1830 or who joined churches after 1835 are assigned the household structure they had in 1840.

There was also, of course, considerable satisfaction, prestige, and advantage to be derived from standing among the holy. Young people could assume prominent places in the revival and the moral crusades associated with it, and the benefits that stemmed from inclusion in the Christian network of mutual support promised them an edge in the ever more frantic struggle for place in the valley. A large number of young people may have been drawn for such reasons toward the nonevangelical churches in particular, for those churches did not require "changes of heart" from new members or question the righteousness of those whose Christian convictions were intertwined with practical concerns.

The problem remains, however, to discover precisely how circumstances heightened the peculiar problems and concerns of youth in ways that provoked spiritual crises. There is little evidence that young church members, especially evangelicals, resolved to find Christ only upon determining that the benefits of church membership outweighed the costs. The key may have been that the prolongation of their journeys suddenly eroded their hopes for success and exposed them for longer periods of time to wayward company, temptation, and self-doubt. They may have been as anxious as their parents about their prospects and reputations. These anxieties would have heightened their awareness of their sinfulness and immaturity, or of their superfluousness and unworthiness, an awareness that young people like Henry Stevens, Joel Winch, and Lucy Gibbs had been hard put to deal with at an earlier period. Many found it more difficult than ever to live poised between social spheres, dwelling on the fringes of adult society, fearful of falling into waywardness or of leading a useless life, and yearning after the kind of respectability, economic success, and good family life that lay beyond their grasp. They grew to despair of human remedies. Once they turned to God, however, they found themselves welcomed into the adult world and fortified against sin by the loving approbation of the religious community.

In 1833, at the age of eighteen, William Townsend found himself poised between two worlds in just such a way. He was as much at ease in that position as it was possible to be. From Boston, where he was trying to make his way in the mercantile business, he wrote home to his family. In his letters to his sister he was himself: good-humored, frankly irreverent, even ribald. In his letters to his parents, he was all discipline, severity, and devotion. The division William made between the adult sphere and the sphere of his contemporaries began to break down, however, as he grew increasingly uncertain about his future and increasingly embarrassed about his crude, rural ways. He began to express in all his letters (not only those to his parents) a yearning to make something of himself – a yearning that displaced the old carefree, ribald spirit, and that was fed by a fear of failure. He worried about his inability to discipline himself: He still wavered before temptation.[18]

It was at this time that William first expressed a hope that he might be granted grace. He became intent on spiritual matters, and tried to steel himself against sin and launch himself forcefully toward maturity. He began to avoid the company of fun-loving friends and wrote his parents that he had resolved to keep his mind on "better objects." At about the same time he startled his younger brother Dennis with a scathing attack on Dennis's plans to learn to play the fiddle. In a letter intended to be read by the entire family (and with which he sent along, for Dennis's benefit, a copy of *The Young Man's Guide*, a tract on the temptations youth too often succumbed to), William warned him that he was wasting valuable time. "It is true a fiddle makes a very pretty little squeaking noys and is a good instrument for Negroes.... If you wish to be a real fine White Nigger practice fiddling and when you get learnt you can go and play for Dancing parties." William told Dennis flatly that he would never become rich or great if he fiddled "like them black ones." "To learn a knowledge of the world, the ways and manners of people, study human nature, &c. These I think are far beyond fiddling. Dennis I hope you feel an anxiety to go ahead in the world. I am sure I do for you." His anxiety for his brother reflected his anxiety for himself and his own future. He was nearly frantic to cut himself off from sinful social circles, which despite his resolve continued to fascinate him far more than the business world.[19]

For two years, William languished in the sense of his own sinfulness and fretted over his uncertain standing in life. Finally, in 1836, at the age of twenty-one, he was released from his anxiety. His conversion experience brought him to the realization that "without God, I can do nothing." No longer did he straddle the fence between the two social spheres: "I find that there is no such way as holding religion in one hand and the world in the other ... we must forsake all the worldly pleasures if we wish to grow in wisdom."[20]

William Townsend's spiritual journey could not be called typical. His conversion experience led him to enter the ministry and allowed him to put a good face on his decision to give up a mercantile career he hated. The anxieties that drove William into spiritual crisis, however, were not uncommon. William's brother Dennis shared them completely. At first he had responded to William's warnings by saying that he sensed no danger in "a little innocent sport once in a while." Already, however, he was worried about his future. He tried to deal with his growing anxiety by lowering his sights, but by the middle of the following year he too had changed his tone, fiercely renouncing any attachment to youthful pleasure. Ambition had awakened in him, and with it anxiety over his susceptibility to temptation.[21] The result was a conscious decision to seek God. Such anxieties, and the decisions that resulted from them, were being experienced by young men and women in Vermont at an extraordinarily early age. Where before the majority of young people did not begin to think about getting religion until they were past their mid-twenties, now it was common for them to renounce youthful ways at the ripe old age of eighteen.

Occasionally the anxiety among young people produced casualties. In 1828, Enoch Ide of Coventry, a town just eight miles to the west of the Essex County border, committed suicide by drowning himself. He was twenty years old, a clerk in a grocery and dry goods firm. He left this note: "I now take leave of you all. I have spent many happy hours in my life, and I have spent many hours in my life which were a burden to me – therefore I consider my life as useless, as I am master of no business on account of my own negligence. Water is my bed."[22]

Undoubtedly Ide was a disturbed youth. That he focused in his agitation upon the fact that he had not yet established himself in business, however, is a sign that there was an unusual degree of anxiety among young people in the valley over success and their diminished chances of attaining it. Before the late 1820s it had been extremely rare for such a young man to be overly concerned about proprietorship. With the decline in opportunity there had come increased pressure for the young to begin the business of being adults at an earlier age.

Young women experienced a parallel crisis, as pressing times heightened their fears of never finding happiness. Before she left the valley for better opportunities in New York, Sally Rice of Somerset was despondent about her life. She lamented that she had nothing of her own – no savings, no children, no home – even though she was "most 19 years old." She resolved to make her way by saving all her wages, by trying to meet the right people, and by severing her ties with "the profane Sabbath breaking set" in Somerset. To strengthen that resolve she spent her free hours praying and meditating, both at church and at home, and eventually she turned to God. Martha Norton of Windsor, who shared Rice's fears and ambitions, was almost at the point of despair when she experienced conversion in her early twenties. Her younger sister had more than one suitor and was likely to marry and leave Martha alone to care for her troublesome grandfather and six boarders. Feeling trapped and fearful of the future, she embraced religion with a new seriousness.[23]

Anxiety for the future could also produce a sense of inadequacy and worthlessness. Such feelings were acute in Nancy Taft of Barre, a teacher who at age twenty-nine in 1838 was prone to despondency over her prospects, her physical ailments, and her feelings of superfluousness. Convinced that she was too selfish and undeserving to merit a better fate, Taft surrendered herself to religion and found strength in serving God selflessly and satisfaction in the company of other church members.[24]

It would be wrong to portray all young converts as surrendering themselves to God out of a sense of hopelessness. Aurelia Townsend had all the advantages her brother Elmer's wealth could afford her, including an expensive academy education. She also had all the suitors she could handle. Austin Chase, scion of a leading Norwich family, was a promising undergraduate at Dartmouth with the whole world before him. Both young people recognized their good fortune, and enjoyed the pleasures of everyday life. Both also converted, and joined evangelical churches. Had the evangelical spirit of the revival not been so strong in the 1830s, they might well have been too proud to do what they did.[25]

Why they converted is not altogether certain, for neither ever described what drew them to Christ. Their spiritual commitment may well have flowed not from an inspired ambition to stand in the ranks of the godly, but from a desire to wage war against all forms of sin, from spiritual lassitude to intemperance and slavery. Both were eager to lead where their elders had failed. Chase criticized the Dartmouth faculty for its reluctance to allow itself to be swept up by religious enthusiasm. Townsend expressed a yearning for influence over her siblings and students (she eventually married another teacher and set up a select school). That is not to say that they forced their conversions so that they might be promoted to the vanguard of the evangelical ranks, for Chase and Townsend were neither arrogant nor insincere. However, when they asked themselves earnestly whether they were humble enough or blessed enough to consider themselves saved, they were eager to say yes and anxious to interpret their good fortune and good character as signs of God's blessing upon them.

It is difficult to draw a more detailed picture of young converts. There are no longer many letters or narratives in existence. Little is known about the large numbers of very young people who joined churches, many at the age of twelve or thirteen. It is doubtful that they were as anxious as the Townsends about getting religion, although the Joel Winches and Elias Smiths of earlier years had not been placid converts. Many of them were at an age when pressure from adults would produce conversions or prompt them to go through the motions of conversion. Such conversions had not generally been accepted, of course, in earlier times, because adults like Joel Winch's parents suspected spiritual precocity to be the result of imitation. Such restraint was abandoned in the 1830s. Adults began to press young people to join churches even at the onset of their journey years, and tried to strike the fear of God into children of all ages.

The only exception to the trend toward more and younger conversions seems to have occurred among the Presbyterians of Barnet and Ryegate. The average age at conversion barely dropped at all at the Associated Presbyterian churches in those towns (Table 2.2). The church members in Barnet and Ryegate refused to press for younger conversions, which they felt threatened to erode the seriousness of heart and mind with which people were meant to enter the covenant. Also, Scots youths had less to fear from the future than other young people, for their parents were more willing to divide their farms into smaller units or to form partnerships with their children to keep their ethnic enclave intact. Thus there were more proprietors on farms in these towns in the late 1820s and the 1830s, although they occupied smaller farms or jointly owned farms. Whether this was done out of a disregard for the consequences of such actions for future generations, when the farms could not be subdivided any more without becoming too small to carry the burden of debt necessary to secure funds to establish children, or whether the Scots had not yet learned the Yankee practice of semipartible inheritance is unclear. What was clear was a strong desire to remain together as a people. Scots youths were ensured of safe havens, too, even if they did leave town, for Barnet and Ryegate Scots had founded other Scots settlements, first in the valley, at Topsham, then just to the northwest in southern Orleans County, and, finally, in various places out west.[26]

Proprietors and married women did not stampede into the churches in the way young men and women and nonproprietors did. The reason may have been the obvious one. They did not face the same anxieties over sin, immaturity, and unworthiness that younger people did. Most had safely overcome those difficulties while traversing the path to proprietorship and independent households. Like earlier revivals, the great revival had its greatest impact among proprietors on master craftsmen, who, as was noted in the discussion of denominational affiliations, were as youths more likely to be trapped in cycles of sin and repentance than merchants, professionals, and farmers, and thus probably found greater meaning in the dire warnings to incorrigible sinners put forth by revivalists. Even that trend was not strong, however.[27]

There were certain groups among proprietors that were more likely to join churches during the revival. Farmers and master craftsmen who presided over households with children under the age of twenty, especially those with youths in their households between the ages of fifteen and nineteen, joined churches more often than those who did not preside over households or had no one under twenty in their homes (Table 6.3). Although it is impossible to tell whether the wives of these proprietors were also more likely to join churches if they presided over households or had older children, it is likely that a similar pattern held for married women, since church membership tended to run in families. Unfortunately, it is impossible to tell whether the youths aged fifteen to nineteen in these households were the children of the household heads themselves or simply employees or boarders.[28] Many of the fifteen- to nineteen-year-olds living with commercial farmers or Windsor master craftsmen were undoubtedly employees. The relationship between them and their employers obviously had some bearing on the employers' spiritual lives. Still, the connection between conversion and the presence of children, especially those fifteen to nineteen years old, was just as strong among family farmers, subsistence farmers, and rural master craftsmen, all of whom were less likely to hire wage workers and more likely to rely exclusively on the labor of their own children.[29]

Like the young, proprietors and married women with teenaged dependents in their households would have had practical reasons for joining churches. Any demand for greater industry or better behavior from their dependents would have carried greater weight if proprietors and their wives spoke with the authority of the churches behind them. Husbands and wives with children to care for and establish would have had all the more reason to seek the advantages in business that accrued to those in the Christian networks of mutual support. In addition, husbands and wives who joined churches together were more likely to be able to keep their children near them; children of church members stayed in town more than children of nonmembers. Parents who feared losing their children in the exodus from the valley looked to church membership with hope.

Consider the despair of the Sheldon family of Caledonia County when they learned in 1829 of a serious indiscretion (it remained unspecified in their letters) that son Charles and several of his friends had committed in Windsor, where Charles had moved to work alongside his brother in the shoe trade. Charles's sister wrote him that he had wounded his parents by what he had done and had made them terribly anxious about his reputation and his future. After a period of bewilderment and sorrow, the Sheldons turned to God. They had been stricken by the realization that they could not always watch over and protect Charles, and they looked to the church for help. Charles's sister Sophia reported that "the news almost overcame us at first but the affect was, it drove us to the thrown of grace where I trust we found comfort."[30]

Most parents, household heads, and employers did not encounter such setbacks in their efforts to provide for their dependents. Successful couples like Daniel and Mary Thompson of Montpelier, whose children were still young and whose financial prospects looked bright, converted during Burchard-led revivals, not out of despair, but because they were eager to serve God and to set the best possible example for their children.[31] Nevertheless, like many other parents, the Thompsons had suffered increased anxiety about the future and felt greater uncertainty about the methods they used to discipline their children.

Allen Hazen, a Congregationalist commercial farmer and corporate investor from Hartland, received letters in 1836 and 1838 from two fathers who were worried about their sons (aged twelve and thirteen) and hopeful that a few years under Hazen's care would turn them around. Both fathers invoked the traditional reasons for placing their children in households away from home – among them the hope that bad habits would be broken once the children were away from familiar surroundings. One man's son needed "looking after" to ensure that his work would be "uniformly done." The other's required "good management ... till he acquires habits of diligent attention to business.... He is a boy of kind affections, active and susceptible, but volitile & needs a steady, firm hand to keep him steady in the harnass."[32]

Both fathers made novel demands on Hazen as a master. They philosophized in their letters about the proper methods of child rearing, in the process revealing their uneasiness with the putting-out system and their uncertainty about the way to raise children in a dangerous period. Both fathers asked that their sons be kept out of the company of hired hands or "village boys" whose influence might prove harmful. This may have been a sign of growing class prejudice within the valley. Farm laborers on commercial farms were increasingly perceived as men of questionable character, men with no future, and parents were willing to embrace antiegalitarian sentiments and bar their children from intercourse with certain wage earners to insulate them from danger. One father told Hazen that his son was "a boy of domestic habits" who had not been "permitted at all to acquire the vicious habits of village boys" and expressed a wish that he remain that way, even if it required Hazen to keep his farm hands out of his own domestic circle.

The other father wrote that he hoped above all for a religious conversion in his son. That would of itself solve most of the boy's problems. He asked Hazen to keep "an eye after him in regard to the Sabbath" and to encourage his religious feelings, which had already "at times been much excited; & I should hope his absence from boys and from home might have a good influence in that respect." He wished too that Hazen refrain from any disciplinary acts that his son might regard as unjust or oppressive, out of a fear of driving the boy into rebelliousness. His son's inquisitiveness sometimes proved "troublesome," he admitted, but advised it was "better guided than repressed." He demanded that Hazen distinguish in disciplinary proceedings between "accidents and carelessness, & that which was either wrong in itself, or yielding to temptation."

The extraordinary solicitousness these men showed for their sons' moral and spiritual development and their suggestions to Hazen give some indication of the seriousness of the problems parents were confronting at this time, of the depth of their anxiety, and of the kinds of remedies parents, guardians, and employers were applying. While the putting-out of juveniles was still a common practice, the anxiety it engendered in parents had become intense. In 1831, Mary Williams of Woodstock sent her eldest son Henry away to high school in Bellows Falls and began to put out his siblings to live and work with masters or relatives. She hated having to send her children away and felt guilty about it, even though she considered it a time-honored custom of unquestionable value. Henry was homesick, and Edward, who would be put out in the Woodstock area for some three years (1832–35) while his mother helped relatives in Montreal, quickly became a discipline problem. In 1835 she returned home despite not having completed her tasks in Montreal, because Edward was growing more and more estranged from her and from his father. Mary was glad to be back in charge and in league with Mr. Peek, the local teacher, who had begun to inspire her son with "a little wholesome terror."³³

Mary and her husband Norman (whose letters often revealed similar concerns) would have liked to keep all their children under their care until they reached maturity, but like most parents, they retained a commitment to sending the children away and worried constantly while they were gone. Whether the conversions of both Mary and Norman in 1831 stemmed directly from these concerns cannot be determined. They never spoke of their own spiritual lives in their letters. Yet it was during Henry's first trying year away from home that they joined the church, and thenceforth they continually turned to God for assistance in guiding their children. It was not unusual, even in circumstances where there was no sudden awakening to the dangers that surrounded their children, as there had been for the Sheldons, for parents' solicitousness to turn back upon itself, leading them to examine their own spiritual lives more closely and to seek solace and security for themselves, and by extension for their children, in the churches.

Last on the list of those people who were more likely than others to join churches were trustees of chartered banks, insurance companies, and industries like textile mills and iron works. These men joined more frequently than did people of the same occupations who were not trustees. Nine of the twenty trustees from agricultural towns who were not church members prior to the great revival joined during the revival, and fifteen of the nineteen from the marketing and manufacturing towns of Windsor and Woodstock also did so. Even when classed by their occupations and household composition, corporate directors were much more likely to join churches than the average members of their occupational groups – even those members who had young people between the ages of fifteen and nineteen living in their households.³⁴ This trend was not unexpected. Trustees were associated disproportionately with churches even prior to the revival. They were men who were deeply involved in the organizational lives of their communities and who stood to gain a great deal from religious ties.

Yet the outpouring of faith among trustees of chartered enterprises during the great revival was unprecedented in two ways. First, the great revival brought a larger body of professionals into the churches than any previous spiritual movement in the valley. Among their number were the eleven attorneys and physicians in the towns studied intensively who were trustees during the 1830s and who had not joined churches prior to the great revival. Second, trustees from the manufacturing and marketing towns who joined churches during the great revival turned decisively toward evangelical religion. Only five of the thirty-one trustees from Windsor and Woodstock who had joined churches prior to the revival had experienced conversion, but ten of the fifteen who joined during the revival did so. That shift was evident not only among trustees in those towns, but among all trustees.

The reasons for this remain obscure. Not one of these men left any personal record of his spiritual experiences. Some of their motives may be inferred from circumstance: Norman Williams of Woodstock appears to have been upset about his sons, while Edward Forbes and George B. Green of Windsor were both apparently alcoholics and were under great pressure from the churchgoing community to change their intemperate ways. Generally speaking, however, as men deeply involved in the market economy, trustees had the greatest need for the connections church membership could bring. Also, in the face of public hostility toward nonproducers and profiteers, they undoubtedly would have found comfort in any legitimacy that the churches could lend their enterprises, and in any bonds that might ensure them at least of the loyalty of the churchgoing community in the political struggle over corporate and professional privilege. Again, however, the reasons they committed themselves to the churches cannot be inferred from the benefits that accrued to them from that commitment, especially when we consider that most of these established citizens, well connected and in the prime of life (most were in their thirties or forties), entered the churches on their knees, professing unworthiness and eschewing all taint of self-interest. It may have been that, faced with a decline in the economy they had helped to build and personally pressured by citizens who thought them at least partly responsible for the decline, they were overcome by feelings of guilt, self-doubt, powerlessness, and impending ruin and thereby were driven to humble themselves before God and the churchgoing community, as revivalists like Jedidiah Burchard commanded they do.

The fruits of the revival

The early years of the great revival were a time of joy for Christians. The revival seemed to sweep away guilt and animosity, division, and weakness of spirit. It was not merely wishful thinking on Hazen Merrill's part when he claimed that the revival had banished partisan rancor over Masonry from Peacham, or when Ruth Buckman, a Universalist from

South Woodstock, observed that it had ended neighborly bickering. Throughout the valley people began to hope that they might really be able to create a Christian commonwealth in Vermont.[35]

The revival sparked new moral passion in the valley's Christians and inspired them to think seriously about the ideals of "brotherhood." Many Christians took up the fight against slavery and intemperance with renewed commitment, confident they could lift downtrodden blacks and drunkards into their holy band, where they would embrace them as equals in Christ. The Freewill Baptists of Corinth listened attentively one Sunday to sermons by Charles Bowles, a black minister from across the Green Mountains, and by Clarissa Danforth, a lay preacher. "Neither color nor sex was regarded with prejudice by the people of Corinth," wrote one auditor, "for the last condition of the wicked, and the fulness of the atonement, engaged their whole attention." The male members of the Congregational church at Weathersfield Bow even voted to allow women and minors to vote in church affairs, in recognition of their equality in things spiritual. Herein lay signs for many Christians that the revival was not only genuine, but that it might usher in the millennium.[36]

The revival was flawed from the beginning, however, and even before it began to fade, Christians had come to doubt its ability to transform their society. There was no decisive move by Christians to break through the barriers to equality posed by sex, age, and race. The members of the Weathersfield church who missed the meeting at which women and minors were enfranchised were incensed by the church's decision. They defeated the measure at three subsequent meetings, until its proponents at last conceded defeat. Throughout Vermont, many white Christians failed to live up to the image with which popular history has endowed the freedom-loving Vermonter. Racist stereotypes of profane "black fiddlers" and amorous "negro wenches" were invoked all too frequently as countersymbols of the true Christian (ironically, these stereotypes seemed to be most popular among well-to-do young white men who hired black musicians to entertain at their private parties and who yearned to satisfy their sexual appetites with black servant girls). Christians did not support temperance or abolition unanimously, and those who did often had little sympathy for drunkards or blacks. And as we shall see, partisan and neighborhood squabbling was not permanently silenced.[37]

These and other failings did not mean that the revival was bereft of blessings. After 1834, however, the issue of the revival placed its genuineness increasingly in doubt. The valley's churches found that revival conversions had failed to improve the behavior of many new members. The disciplinary records of the Calvinist churches reveal that an extraordinary proportion of revival converts were dropped for sinful behavior (especially intemperance) or neglect of religious duty. The great revival did well from 1827 to 1833, losing only a slightly higher proportion of converts than had been lost over the thirty-seven years from 1790 through 1826. When the great revival began to press more earnestly for converts, however, the expulsion rate jumped. During the final ten years of the revival, from 1834 through 1843, the Calvinist churches sacked roughly three out of every ten male converts and three of every twenty female converts – a rate roughly double that which had previously prevailed.[38]

The Reverend Perry of Newbury had worried from the onset of the revival that conversions of children, youths, and chronic drinkers – prime targets of the revival – were prone to be short-lived. They could not distinguish as well as others "between conviction of sin and the excitement of animal feelings." Joseph Tracy, editor of the *Vermont Chronicle*, remarked that young converts were "in special danger," because of their spiritual arrogance and backsliding. "They need particular watchfulness ... to remember as they ought, *their own personal need of God's grace.*"[39] Writing as they did before 1834, however, both Clark and Tracy were convinced that these problems could be remedied simply by looking out more carefully for false conversions and by reminding new church members of their dependence on God.

By the mid-1830s, the debate over the desirability and acceptability of young converts grew heated. Could the churches rely on such weak supporters? Even strong advocates of the revival, like the Reverend Morton of Springfield, were aware of the problems young converts posed and recognized a "diversity of opinion" among church members respecting their admission. He passed "no censure upon our respected brethren who may think and act differently than us" and acknowledged that "it is possible that we have been premature in the early reception of these dear lambs," even though scripture encouraged "the reception of persons into the church, as soon as they give satisfactory evidence that they have been 'born again.'"[40]

Several churches simply opened their communions to all who showed evidence of spiritual rebirth, but they usually suffered. The Baptist church of Windsor found itself casting out many new members and was wracked with disciplinary controversy. Other evangelical churches responded more cautiously, by placing suspect applicants for church membership on probation for one year, putting them under the watch and care of the church, yet denying them communion and full membership until they sharpened their understanding of scripture and proved their conversions lasting. They saw no alternative to adopting this innovation in light of the excesses the revival fostered after 1834.[41]

The probation system won praise from a number of evangelicals for its fairness and its usefulness in protecting both the churches and the individual from false hope, but some assailed it as unscriptural and insisted on admitting all those who exhibited the biblical signs of regeneration.[42] Still, even churches that did employ the probation system, like those in Windsor and West Windsor, found themselves compelled to drop many of the converts they accepted. No solution proved ideal. Church members increasingly doubted the efficacy of revival-induced conversions in altering sinful habits, but remained mired in disputes over how sinful people found their way into the churches, and why conversion and church membership had proved less powerful than anticipated in bringing an end to sinfulness.

The revival also failed because the spirit of moral seriousness that it cultivated was marred by intolerance. At the height of the churchgoing community's campaign to rid the valley of disorder and immorality, many churches insisted that members abstain totally from alcohol of any kind on penalty of excommunication. That aspect of the campaign for morality seemed a genuine enough concomitant of the revival, but the price of such moral seriousness was high. It altered the meaning of Christianity in subtle ways, especially in Calvinist churches, by encouraging a harsher attitude toward sinners and by defining sin in more narrowly personal terms. Intemperance, adultery, Sabbath breaking, and swearing were looked on with much greater disfavor than were the interpersonal sins of gossip, slander, and bringing lawsuits against fellow church members. The proportion of disciplinary cases concerned with personal sins, as opposed to interpersonal sins, rose from half just prior to the revival to three-fourths (Table 2.1). The valley's churches were led farther away from their vision of Christian fellowship and unity when they began to scorn and abuse those who fell into personal sin.

During the revival, those who committed personal sins were quickly expelled from churches. There were no long labors over cut-and-dried infractions, as there had been before 1827. Sinners proved guilty received a single opportunity to find fault with themselves, and if they refused or were unable to do so satisfactorily on their first try, they were excommunicated. Those who afterwards sought reconciliation with their churches were forced not only to admit their guilt and exhibit sorrow, but to reapply for admission and persuade church members once again of the genuineness of their spiritual commitment. Although none of the churches in the valley, Calvinist or non-Calvinist, believed in the perfectability of man, all of them increasingly expected "genuine" members to be capable of near-perfect behavior and held members accountable for their failings in an unprecedentedly inflexible, legalistic manner.

The preoccupation with personal sin often led church members into another sin — that of malicious gossip. The vilification of those who sinned, particularly those who were intemperate, permitted church members to engage without fear of punishment in what earlier would have been held up as sinful gossip and slander. Martha and Sarah Norton of Windsor carried tales in 1833 to their brother Reuben (a missionary to the Cherokee in Georgia) of the latest doings of respectable citizens who had fallen into error. They wrote him that George Green, a druggist who had joined the Nortons' church that year during a Burchard revival, had "been intoxicated for 3 weeks past," and that Edward Forbes, a merchant who had converted later during the same revival, had recently been discovered "so intoxicated" that townspeople had been obliged to douse him with cold water to bring him to his senses. Charles Sheldon, a suitor of Sarah Norton and a church member himself, carried the same "intemperate news" to Reuben Norton, writing that "George B. Green is making a beast of himself," and "E. Forbes is a sot."[43]

Like the Norton sisters, Sheldon undoubtedly thought he was merely reporting local news. But in years past it had been thought that such news was best left untold, or reserved for relation to the sinner himself, who might thereby be persuaded to quit his despicable activities. When Lois Leverett of Windsor gossiped in 1806 in a letter to a friend, she knew she was engaging in a forbidden pastime. Lois wrote that she detested the Reverend Samuel Shuttlesworth, who delighted in hurting his wife's feelings in public, but she knew such gossip to be wrong, and considered the poor impression it might make on her friend. "Do you think that I have been doing a wicked thing to write so much slander?" she asked.[44] Her question, even if disingenuous, was one neither Charles Sheldon nor the Norton sisters would have thought to pose. This seems especially remarkable in Sheldon's case. He was corresponding with a potential brother-in-law and wooing the granddaughter of a deacon in his church.

Of course, Sheldon's gossiping may have only been an indication of a flawed character, but a gossipy tone was prevalent in other letters of this period as well. It would appear that the untoward behavior of neighbors had become a proper subject for conversation among the valley's church members. Gossip fit nicely, in any event, into the churches' campaign to impose strict standards of personal conduct on people. Those who did not meet certain standards were publicly ostracized and privately ridiculed.

The targets of gossip were not selected randomly. Far from being people hostile toward or distant from the churchgoing community, they were usually church members or people on the fringes of the churches seeking entrance into them (like Forbes and Green in Windsor). They were targets not only because the details of their private lives were better known to the churchgoing community, but because gossip was meant to work primarily on people who had already accepted that community's stated norms, not on those who challenged them. Furthermore, gossip primarily influenced those who heard it and passed it, not its targets, who often did not hear it or complained bitterly when they did. Those who engaged in it were reinforced in their commitment to the community's values and placed renewed emphasis on the importance of strict adherence to those values.

Gossip was particularly rife in the 1830s, because it was being employed by its purveyors not only to reinforce old standards, but to persuade the community to establish new, stricter standards, often at the expense of some people who were already formally members of the community but could not or would not live up to them. Gossip, however, sapped the churchgoing community of unity, goodwill, and strength, both by creating ill will and by leading people to dwell on the striking failings of a few symbolic wrongdoers. It represented a fall, especially on the part of the Calvinists, into a less rich understanding of sin. Increasingly, Calvinists identified righteousness with unblemished personal conduct, and the result was that church members showed a tendency to exhibit pride in their own conduct, uncharitableness toward the fallen, and blindness to other, interpersonal sins.[45]

As many church members became content to gather themselves around standards like temperance and proper Sabbath observance, standards that excluded just the right people, the revival suffered. Christians were diverted from the questions of motive and purity of heart; the outward show was more important than the truth within. With increasing frequency, revivals and even religion itself became the butt of satire from skeptics and town wits who laughed at church members for their sanctimonious posturing and public displays of righteousness. Thomas Emerson, president of the Bank of Windsor and a prominent Jacksonian whose pleasure it was to contribute generously to religion while remaining, himself, deliberately uncommitted, took aim at such posturing in an 1834 letter to his friend Henry Coles of Detroit. The purpose of the letter was to ask Coles to press Thomas Palmer, a Detroit fur dealer, for the interest overdue on a bond.

> My Dear Hal: — I am rejoiced to say to you that the Lord hath been among us here in Windsor; that a day of Pentacost is here, and that there has been an outpouring of the Holy Ghost, and I have been snatched as a brand from the burning.... Oh, Hal! how I wish you and our old friend, Tom Palmer, might see the error of your ways .... now I learn that the "pestilence is stalking at noon-day among

you [cholera]," and we know not how soon you may go.... You, and he too, ought to prepare for death, and he ought certainly to settle that bond at once. Oh, Hal, if God would only open your eyes, and Mr. Palmer, surely he will pay the interest on that bond now. I pray nightly and daily for you and Mr. Palmer; and trust he will pay the interest on the bond.... I will take fur, shingles, lumber, apples, fish, or anything else he has. God bless and preserve you both; but please do not let Mr. Palmer forget to pay the interest on the bond.[46]

Yet another consequence of the revival was the exacerbation of the social tensions that underlay denominational differences. The Burchard crusades of 1834–5 undermined the interdenominational alliance in the valley upon which the revival (and indeed, the new order) relied for success. They divided nonevangelicals and evangelicals over the proper place of emotion and conversion in the revival and alienated a number of important people. Universalists believed increasingly that the revival had become purely Calvinist, and saw their worst fears realized when revivalists like Burchard began to lambaste Universalists for their non-evangelical doctrines. Universalist writers took to denouncing the evangelical enterprise; one produced an article entitled "Recipe for Making a Religious Fanatic."

Take equal parts of total depravity and free agency, of election and reprobation, each half a pound, one ounce of the works of the creature, put them into the mortar of deception and pulverize them with the pestal of envy, put this into the bottle of self-righteousness, and còrk it with inconsistency, shake it well together, then sweeten it with infant damnation, let it stand in the desk through a protracted meeting and heating often in the fire of vindictive wrath, and stir it with the stick of misconstruction, and it will be fit for use.[47]

More frequent and more dangerous to the spirit of unity in the valley were signs that some genteel people, disinclined to take life or faith as seriously as the ardent evangelicals, were scoffing at the revival. Jeremiah Walcott of Newport, New Hampshire, chided his friend William Sabin of nearby Windsor for his spiritual seriousness in July of 1834. He fretted that Sabin, who prior to 1834 had been an easygoing and witty fellow, was becoming too much of a sobersides under the influence of the revival. He poked fun at him and refused to take his new-found religiosity seriously. "Sabin, why do you dissemble so much hypocrisy," he wrote. "You need not pretend to be so strenuous in religious affairs."[48]

In addition to arousing such affable antagonism in individuals, the crusades of 1834 and 1835 also provoked serious and significant organized opposition, especially in Woodstock. Burchard himself was partly to blame, because his ridicule of baptism by immersion, free-will doctrines, and universal salvation enraged nearly every sect in that town of few Congregationalists.

None were angered more than the Universalists, who rallied behind William Bell, editor of the *Universalist Watchman*, and applauded his scorching denunciations of the "Calvinist" revival. Bell and other Universalist clergymen undermined the crusade by standing up to Burchard at meetings and demanding retractions of statements that attacked Universalists and other decent citizens who had not been "born again." They were convinced that the valley's revival had seen its day and believed that Burchard "was not sent to this village, of God."[49]

They did not stand alone. A body of local citizens circulated a petition demanding that the town authorities prevent Burchard from preaching again in Woodstock, branding him a "nuisance" that a "candid and intelligent community" could not countenance. They alleged that his "insidious arts" had driven at least one young man caught up in spiritual turmoil insane (a charge confirmed by a physician from Claremont, New Hampshire) and that his jokes about denominations other than his own pandered to the baser emotions of his audience and were calculated to stir religious bigotry. Their petition received nearly one hundred signatures, and they managed to pass a resolution at the next town meeting that barred Burchard from setting foot in the town again.[50]

Half the leaders of the petition movement had been associated with the Jacksonians or with the campaign against "orthodoxy" in Woodstock. Half had been Workingmen. Three had signed the anti-Sabbatarian petition, and all were either Universalists or not church members at all. They included such ardent foes of the existing order as William Bell, Nahum Haskell, and Dr. Thomas E. Powers, secretary of the Free Readers' Society. They were joined by the leaders of Woodstock's black community, the largest in the valley. Like nearly all the valley's black men, they did not belong to churches and may well have harbored resentment against professed Christians who they believed kept them and the question of prejudice in Vermont at arm's length.

Proponents of the revival denigrated the resolution as a shameless plot by an unrepresentative minority to subvert the will of the majority. One editor accused the protesters of pressuring at least one black citizen into siding with them, who "on reflection . . . declared himself ashamed of his company and his vote, and wished to have his name erased." Yet the resolution was never overturned. Certainly the town's National Republicans, who had just recently recruited three of the petition leaders into the town's "young Republicans" by persuading them that the party stood for a sound economy, and not for orthodoxy, did not want the controversy brought up again.[51]

The revival aroused resentment elsewhere as well. It seemed to a growing number of citizens that church members, especially evangelicals, had
gone beyond spreading their power and influence by informal means and
were now "endeavoring to be a kind of aristocracy over them." In Bradford and Whitingham, Free Readers' societies organized to combat the
"orthodox" onslaught. In Wilmington, a band of men who were referred
to by the Reverend Emerson Andrews, a Baptist revivalist, as "universalists and rummies" were enraged by the town's protracted meeting.
They "upset and tore in pieces the pastor's carriage, [and] assailed the
Baptist house with eggs, stones, and otherwise." They also "besmired
the pastor's wagon seat with filth, and did other mean things in defense
of their wounded cause."[52]

Matters did not get so far out of hand in Strafford, but Abel Rich, the
town's tithingman and "droll wit," intimated that he would not have
minded if they had. Indignant at the news that Burchard was coming to
preach, Rich observed "I have heard there is talk of a mob-b-b. If Burchard should be mobbed and I was the only witness, I would forget it
before morning-g-g, that I would-d-d." As it was, he marred the occasion
only by answering, when asked by a revivalist whether he had got religion,
"Not any to boast of, I tell ye-e-e." Like the opponents of abolitionism,
the opponents of revivalism were not challenging the right of their neighbors to further spiritual enthusiasm, but the right of itinerant outsiders
to come and do so, especially if they questioned the character and piety
of those who were not "born again."[53]

Individual opponents of the revival continued to make themselves
heard throughout the valley. A student in Hanover, New Hampshire,
apparently requested at a public meeting that Burchard pray for the devil.
Burchard announced that "a young man in the gallery requests prayers
for his Father." Other Dartmouth students banded together in a secret
society to poke fun at preachers and drink, smoke, and hold parties as
long as the revival lasted. An observer in Norwich reasoned that the
crusade there failed to achieve greater heights because a man had established a dancing academy during the revival. "It was probably done to
counteract seriousness," the writer surmised, calling the dancing master
"an infidel."[54]

It was doubtful that such outright opposition, or, for that matter, the
reawakening of denominational bigotry, posed a deadly threat to the
revival. Individuals outside or on the fringes of the churchgoing community organized themselves into a powerful lobby only in Woodstock
(already renowned for its antiorthodox movement), and a number of
revivalists took pains to avoid offending members of all denominations.
Still, the opposition that did arise was an indication that the revival faced

greater and greater difficulties as it grew. It provoked anger as it moved beyond the former boundaries of the churchgoing community to impose its will on more people, and its backers fell to bickering over the best methods to increase their harvest of souls.

The revival encountered opposition in 1834 and 1835 that could not be overcome, however. Many wealthy churchgoing men, both evangelical and nonevangelical, who had supported the revival became alienated from it. If the Reverend Streeter's account was accurate, their doubts about it had arisen even before Burchard's crusade reached their towns, as reports of his methods filtered in. Charles Marsh stated publicly, a few weeks before Burchard's arrival, that "out of seven hundred converts made by Mr. B in the western part of New York, there were but thirty of them that kept any where within the bounds of decency." Norman Williams also opposed "these high pressure measures for making christians, and suddenly introducing them into the church."[55] Streeter reported that many important Congregationalists were "not desirous of having Mr. Burchard visit this village," although they eventually relented and endorsed his coming when they were faced with widespread support for him among younger, more recent converts in their churches.

Streeter noted too that many clergymen would "not consent to have [Burchard] go on here" in the valley "and fill up the Church with young converts, before they have had time to see whether the conversions are genuine or not." The point at issue was not simply the proper way of conducting a revival, but who would control it, and what ends it would serve. Streeter knew that it was "the younger and more zealous of the flock, who by the way, 'rule both parson and people,' who insisted on having a visit" from Burchard. The threat of domination by the Joel Winches of the valley, by overzealous young converts who attacked their elders for their cool-headedness, now loomed. Who would be guiding whom?

As the revival increasingly ran afoul of preachers, the well-to-do, and prominent individuals who had yet to convert, leaders in the churchgoing community were put on the defensive. Their prestige in their communities was at stake. The emotionalism and lenient admission policies revival meetings fostered did not seem to be good "for the dissemination of religious truth and the promotion of morality and good order," and what had appeared to be the savior of the valley now seemed to these people to pose a threat to it. Yet those who called for a halt to Burchardism faced the danger that they "would be reckoned by the Burchardites as enemies of all religion, and be classed with such as boyishly 'cracked their jokes' upon Burchardism, and laughingly turned the whole concern into merriment and burlesque."[56]

Not all religious leaders or men of property opposed Burchard or his methods, of course. The Reverend Streeter claimed that the Reverend Benjamin C. C. Parker of the Episcopalian church in Woodstock had become second only to Burchard in scouring the town for souls. Parker's church had gained more than any other from the revival, both in terms of warmth of piety and numbers. Many of its members experienced conversion, participation in communion went up, and it became almost an evangelical church, much to the delight of Parker, who was predisposed to low church practices anyway. The president of Dartmouth College, Nathan Lord, liked to emphasize Burchard's power in "developing the resources and drawing out the power of Christians," although he granted that Burchard had "great defects of character" and that he would "in some circumstances ... break down more than he would build up." That assessment did not satisfy George Marsh, son of the prominent Woodstock lawyer, Charles Marsh, who thought it tantamount to saying "that we may do evil in order that good may abound."[57]

The fears of many citizens were compounded in the later stages of the revival by the spread of "fanatick" movements through the countryside. Most notorious were the Mormons and the Noyesian perfectionists. The New Lights of Hardwick, a short-lived holiness sect that appeared in 1837, were less well known. According to one unfriendly observer, those who would eventually become members of New Light had initially distinguished themselves by interrupting regular religious services, "occasionally uttering in a tremendous sing-song scream or yell, passages or parts of passages of scripture, pretending to act under the influence and guidance of the Holy Spirit." Soon, however, they gathered their own "motly and multitudinous assemblage" at a meetinghouse in South Hardwick. Their services consisted of "frightful yellings, barking in imitation of dogs, foxes and cuckoos, jumping, swinging the arms and rolling on the floor. From this last circumstance they were sometimes called 'holy rollers.'" Members also received revelations from God, one of which commanded them never to shave, whereupon they became known as the "long beards."[58]

More popular, and much more influential, were the Millerites, an Adventist group that followed the teachings of William Miller. Miller was a Baptist preacher from Low Hampton, on the Vermont–New York border, who believed the world would end with Christ's coming on March 21, 1843. He rejected the vision of history that nearly all the valley's Christians held in the early 1830s. He did not believe that the current revival was one of an ongoing series of revivals that by fits and starts would draw mankind toward the millennium. He believed that hope of spiritual progress was vain, that human history would end in the Apocalypse, and that Christ would launch his thousand-year reign on earth without human help, once he had judged the quick and the dead. Miller also believed that prophecy foretold the day of the Apocalypse, which meant, if he had interpreted the prophecies correctly, that the current revival marked the last gathering of saints.

In 1837, rural evangelical churches everywhere opened their pulpits to Miller, who told his listeners to prepare themselves and their loved ones for the Last Judgment. Many people took his injunction literally. They left their fences and fields untended as the day approached and sat waiting on hillsides on March 21 to prove their faith in Christ's coming. A few even gave their property away, believing Christ would look more favorably on the poor, and some fashioned paper or cloth wings, so they might fly directly to heaven when the moment came.[59]

The Millerites left few records or personal writings. Like the members of other "fanatick" groups, most of them came from poorer agricultural towns and poor sections of more prosperous towns. Most came from the families of farmers and rural craftsmen; if not actually poor, their families certainly lacked the resources to establish their children near home. The surviving evidence suggests that the Millerites had been members of all evangelical churches, but primarily Methodist, Freewill Baptist, and Christian – all of which appealed to outsiders. Miller portrayed the world much as these denominations did, as a place of suffering, and he offered eternal happiness to all who would accept God's freely given grace. In his study of the *Evidence from Scripture and History of the Second Coming of Christ*, Miller wrote of the unhappiness man experienced in life. He believed that the present was a particularly bad time for God's children. Churches and missions had spread everywhere, but lust, ignorance, and selfishness still ruled. Rich men laid up unprecedented treasures in abundance, through monopolies, corporations, banks, and insurance companies, while they ground down the poor. But the wicked acted only to "fulfill the text." Salvation was at hand.[60]

Certainly Miller's calculations convinced only a tiny minority of the valley's evangelicals, but why he gained the respectful attention of so many people was no mystery. The dominance of respectable religion after 1815 had not wholly extinguished the millennial hope that had fired many evangelicals during and just after the Revolution. They had seen God's providential hand in every event, had copied down every extraordinary occurrence that might contain a message from God (from hurricanes to giant figs and pictures in the clouds). Most expected the millennium to come about through divinely assisted human efforts to improve mankind, but Miller said such talk of "the agency of man" was presumptuous. Only the Apocalypse and the divine institution of a new order could inaugurate it. That came as a message of hope to those who believed that pressing times, immorality, and selfishness had made it impossible to protect themselves or their loved ones in this world, who saw the end of the entire world in the crisis of their own. "I have nothing from this world to hope I have nothing from it to fear – my hope, my confidence, my all is in God," said one Millerite.[61]

By the end of 1835, many religious leaders had come to doubt the spiritual and practical efficacy of revival crusades. This crisis of confidence offered Universalists like the Reverend Streeter and the Reverend Bell an important opening, for they could now criticize the revival and be sure of an audience. Bell claimed the revival was creating just those effects its supporters hoped it would help suppress: intemperance in politics, recreation, and religion. Its language and theology were "familiar" and "revolting," its emotional displays unseemly, and its spirit persecuting. Could this fanaticism set a proper example for conduct in politics and in society in general?[62]

Streeter pursued the enemy along the same lines. He published verbatim Burchard's attacks on the "genteel," and criticized his promotion of irrational, emotional, and intolerant sentiments. The tide was turning: After 1835, both the Unitarians and the Episcopalians would be mute on the subject of revivals, and calmer spirits among the Congregationalists became more circumspect about promoting them. The revival had alienated too many religious liberals and lukewarm evangelicals to retain the firm support it needed to press on to new heights. It had revived dangerous social tensions between young and old church members, between the churchgoing community and those outside it, between the social groups that found their differences reflected in denominational rivalries, and between the wealthy and those with less. In short, the revival's campaign to reunite the inhabitants of the valley proved counterproductive, and that was increasingly interpreted as a sign of its weakness as a spiritual work.

The revival was not wholly a failure, of course. It was the most powerful spiritual work the valley had ever seen, and it touched an unequaled number with its spiritual enthusiasm, moral earnestness, and hope. As its shortcomings were magnified, however, and as members of the churchgoing community lost faith in it, it flagged. Although it remained strong through 1843 (drawing sparingly on outside revivalists), it reached primarily the very young children of church members. It solidified its hold on those already within the bounds of the churchgoing community, but its mission to society at large slowed to a stop, the victim of strong resistance, dissension within the churches, and the desire of certain citizens to bank the fires of spiritual enthusiasm for the sake of social peace and spiritual purity.

7

A modified order in town life and politics, 1835–1850

Adding to the difficulties posed by the political impasse in the valley, the sharp divisions among reformers, and the crisis of confidence in the revival, a serious recession struck Vermont in 1837 and did not abate until 1843. Financiers and entrepreneurs were stymied. Financial institutions struggled to stay afloat. The largest bank in the valley, the Bank of Windsor, went into bankruptcy in 1838; the smallest, the Bank of Guildhall, followed suit in 1839. Incorporation petitions dropped off drastically for want of capital and ready markets for manufactured goods. Thirty-five woolen mills had incorporated in the valley between 1834 and 1836, but none incorporated between 1837 and 1843. No machinery firms were incorporated either, and plans drawn up at a rail convention in Windsor in 1836 to crisscross the valley with railroads were set aside. All types of construction lagged, and carpenters and day laborers were thrown out of work.[1]

In the countryside, mechanics and farmers felt the pinch of a drop in urban demand for their goods and produce. Faltering demand for woolen goods and ready-made apparel drove a number of rural master craftsmen engaged in wool processing, tanning, shoemaking, hat making, and tailoring out of business. Women and children employed by woolen mills or on the putting-out system in these crafts found fewer opportunities to add to the family income. The drop in demand hurt farmers, who lost almost a quarter of their purchasing power between 1839 and 1843 because their wool and hides were no longer wanted, and rural mechanics, who could find few farmers willing to buy their furniture, wagons, and plows.[2]

Many people lost confidence in the valley's future. In 1843 Francis Upham of Waitsfield wrote to a friend who had already left Vermont for the Wisconsin prairie, to tell him of his decision "to move somewhere in that section in the course of the present year." Although his land in Waitsfield was "a good country for the state of Vermont," he had been considerably in debt when he bought it and had taken on more than he should have "considering the hardness of the times." He was determined to sell out and seek his fortune "somewhere in the far west."[3]

Upham was more fortunate than James Vaughn of Pomfret, who could not afford to leave because he was so deep in debt. His land was of poor quality and although he worked desperately hard, he could not get ahead. He cursed Vermont, and swore that he would leave or die. "We will go somewhere else if it is even Hell or Texas," he wrote. "We will not stop where God has never ironed or even took his rolling pin acrost the mountains to smooth them." As the recession descended upon him, Vaughn felt increasingly injured and angry. In his diary he began to cast about for someone to blame for the economic crisis, settling in the end on the valley's mechanics and professional men.[4]

In Windsor and surrounding towns, it was the bankers and the Democrats who were accused of being responsible for hard times. The Windsor bank had collapsed in 1838, and, although most of the bank's directors were Whigs, the predominantly Whig population of the area chose to blame the bank's Democratic president, Thomas Emerson, and his Democratic attorney, Jabez Sargeant, for the failure. Emerson, Sargeant, and other Democratic leaders were sued by their neighbors, while the Whig directors of the bank escaped all blame. Emerson, whose house was mobbed by angry townspeople, landed in debtors' prison, while Sargeant endured the indignity of a disciplinary trial at St. Paul's Episcopal Church for allegedly defrauding the widow of a late director of the bank. It was the only instance of discipline in the history of that church.[5]

Partisan feelings ran high in the area. Mutual regard and support, even among church members, shattered along party lines. In 1840 the wealthy landowner William Jarvis called in a $200 loan from a Democratic rival in Hartland, D. H. Sumner. Singling out Sumner for the recall, Jarvis curtly told his debtor that he was responsible for the Jackson and Van Buren administrations' "destructive measures" against banks and the local economy and that if Sumner had temporary difficulties it was his own fault because he was a Democrat.[6]

The recession did not, of course, make enemies of everyone. Rural people in many communities established joint-stock cooperative stores between 1839 and 1843 to ensure, in the words of the constitution of Peacham's Farmers and Mechanics' Store, "the management of Trade ... for our common benefit." The stores were designed to provide goods at lower cost in rural areas poorly served by the mercantile community and to extend greater credit to hard-pressed customers. They transported produce and finished goods at frequent intervals to market towns along the Connecticut River.[7]

These stores were most popular in the heavily Antimasonic towns in the northern reaches of the valley, especially in Caledonia and Orange counties. Antimasons were not their only supporters, however. In Peacham and St. Johnsbury, store trustees represented all major denominations – Congregationalist, Methodist, and Universalist – and there was an above-average incidence of church membership among stockholders in Peacham. Support for temperance was also strong among stockholders and trustees. No store could be located that sold alcohol for other than medicinal purposes.[8]

The cooperative movement rested primarily on the formalization of relationships within the churchgoing community in agricultural towns with strong communal traditions. Here the bonds of church membership evidently outweighed partisan divisions and drew inhabitants together in the face of their common economic plight. The stores did not last long, however. The West Fairlee store closed in 1842, because its hard-pressed members could not settle their debts at the end of the year. The Peacham store dissolved after three years of profitable operation. It would appear that the farmers and mechanics who supported that store had come to respect and trust the store's hardworking agent, Isaac Watts, whose astute decisions had been largely responsible for the store's success. It was undoubtedly difficult to continue to deny proprietorship to such a deserving young man, who had worked so hard for the store and for the local Congregational church. They sold the store to Watts, and he conducted it successfully for some years thereafter.

The cooperationism that dawned briefly in Caledonia and Orange counties and the partisan persecution that infected the neighborhood of Windsor were both signs that the valley was in deep trouble. The great majority of the inhabitants of the valley responded to their difficulties in other ways, however. To counter the instability and conflict that wracked their society, they began to adjust their economic aspirations to the "realities" of high land prices, population pressure, and competitive national markets.

A modified order in town life

Henry Stevens was a prominent Barnet entrepreneur in 1835, his youthful escapades firmly behind him. Late in that year he became concerned about the failure of the revival to restore moral order. In a draft of a temperance address, he condemned public officials for lacking "virtue or moral courage enough" to enforce laws "connected with the morals of society," laws that they "in the presence of the people have solemnly sworn to perform." This was a remarkable stand for a man who as a justice of the peace in the 1820s had not prosecuted a single person for a morals infraction. Clearly, Stevens, like many other members of the churchgoing community, had come to believe that persuasion, informal pressure, and revivals could not bring moral order to the valley.[9]

The churchgoing community realized, of course, as did Stevens, that a return to the formal, coercive methods identified with the standing order was impossible, but they still wanted some means of insulating their towns from evil, some way to build and judge the character of townspeople and to defend the prestige and the economic position of "respectable" citizens. The revival had proved undependable. It excited unreliable emotions, unleashed charges of religious tyranny and fanaticism, and raised questions about a Christian's duty toward others. Informal bonds among church members were not sufficiently far-reaching in their effects. The churchgoing community discovered in 1835, however, that it could fight directly for its ideals and interests through the teetotal temperance movement and a variety of adjunct movements that were created in the ensuing years.[10]

Although it could not eradicate sinfulness, the temperance movement could go a long way – farther than revivals – toward checking the evil consequences of sin. It protected men and women from temptation, set a standard of conduct that all could be asked and expected to meet, and could enlist more members than the churches, which in the best of times could claim fewer than half the valley's adult citizens as full members. Both church members and nonmembers could be persuaded, as Henry Stevens argued, that temperance was inextricably bound up with "the interest the happiness and the prosperity of people in this life." Revivals had their place, but Stevens, like many temperance reformers, was a practical man who wanted a practical solution to the valley's problems. Temperance was for the time being the better weapon against disorder.

Temperance advocates appealed to the fears of young people and their parents. They were the same fears that had fueled the revival: fears for futures and reputations, fears of exclusion and ostracism. In his address to the newly formed Caledonia County Young Men's Temperance Society on January 1, 1836, Henry Stevens spoke directly to mothers, and through them to their families and the entire valley. He warned them that he could determine their character from the kind of beverages their husbands and children drank, or from the contents of their pockets or dinner satchels. Any observer could tell from such evidence whether mothers were "kind" to their husbands, "neat and economical" in domestic affairs, whether the family had "a barnyard gate or whether the pigs geese & turkeys are in the entry." From such superficial signs he could read "your faults, your natural disposition, better than a phrenologist can by feeling the lumps upon your head." Stevens warned mothers that if they had any regard for their reputations or those of their husbands and children they had best stop their families from drinking.

No speech could have affected the inhabitants of the valley more deeply. Citizens had been warned that everywhere there were telltale signs of "character" that men like Henry Stevens, the major employer in his hometown, could read in a flash. When such men looked for evidence upon which to base their judgments of others, they had only to look at the surface: Bad character would show. Stevens was telling them, more bluntly than a revivalist could, that what they needed was a badge of good character that every employer or creditor would recognize. Membership in a temperance society was such a badge.[11]

Stevens was also hinting that men like himself would use their powers in the cause of morality by favoring those who committed themselves to temperance and proscribing those who refused to do so. Stevens's friend Erastus Fairbanks, the St. Johnsbury scale manufacturer who was president of the state temperance society, spoke about his own hiring policies in a letter written some years later to P. H. White, a financier from Brattleboro. Fairbanks had been upset by an article in the *Claremont* (New Hampshire) *Eagle* that claimed that the Fairbanks Scale Works enforced "certain arbitrary rules . . . in regard to 'loud talking' – 'signing the temperance pledge' – 'Attending church' &c." The article commended these policies, but Fairbanks was afraid that the article would give credence to the protests of those who accused temperance advocates of trying to abridge freedom of conscience and revive the oppressive measures of the standing order. In a disavowal that was as damning as the accusations of protestors, Fairbanks claimed that he only tried "to select such men as choose to respect themselves and always give a preference, in hiring, to such as entertain correct views on all great moral subjects, and if we get others into our employ we try to hold out inducements for them to improve – and if any are found to be profane or Sabbath breakers or immoral and continue so we feel bound to exchange them for others for the good of the whole." He denied that these measures compromised the independence of his employees: "In doing this we do no more than what the great majority of our men expect of us and would probably require as the condition of remaining themselves."[12]

Strictly speaking, there were no actual rules or enforcement mechanisms in Fairbanks's company and no required pledges. There was only the clear expectation of temperate behavior and proper conduct. Although church attendance was expected, church membership was not, and thus Fairbanks could say with a clear conscience that his policies did not infringe on religious freedom or encourage men to feign spiritual commitment while punishing sincere Christians still awaiting conversion.

It was his contention that when expectations were made plain, as they were in his factory, both employer and employee benefited, for employees knew that if they behaved well they would be preferred.

Stevens and Fairbanks were among those who defined and implemented a modified order in town life, an order in which respectable citizens would band together self-consciously to support one another and to discriminate against those who refused to meet their standards: people who drank, missed church, had poor manners, were slovenly, failed to maintain homes and yards, were habitually late, or behaved publicly in any way that betrayed "bad" character. They offered churchgoers an effective way of protecting their families, reputations, enterprises, and communities.[13]

The creators of this modified order did not intend to harm religion, nor did they advocate a wholesale shift of energies away from the churches into nonreligious movements like temperance. Despite the failings of many converts, church membership was still the ultimate sign of commitment to respectable society. Stevens and Fairbanks were religious men who regretted that the churches had been unable to instill in every resident of the valley a wholehearted desire to abide by the strictest moral standards. They recognized their debt to the revival, which despite its failures had given the churchgoing community a broad base of support that did not exist before 1835–6. They also hoped that the measures they took to persuade people to abide by their standards would in the end strengthen the churches, providing them with sounder converts and a purer environment in which to grow. There was ample room in their campaign for people who remained enthusiastic about the revival and saw movements like temperance as extensions of the evangelical crusade through which they could bear witness to God.

Nonreligious movements like temperance could also unite evangelicals and nonevangelicals, church members and nonmembers, in a common cause without offending particular religious principles. By making people think of their reputations rather than their souls, they could spread more quickly a compulsive concern for personal rectitude, and they could demand some token of commitment to respectability from everyone, even those who felt no call to membership in a church. They made respectability, not church membership, society's password; they fostered a profound concern for reputation and appearance to give respectability meaning; and they offered powerful new means to defend it.

With entrepreneurs and financiers in the lead, the temperance crusade at times took on the appearance of a capitalist initiative to impose new discipline on workers, which in part it was. But it was also a new way to defend old interests and aspirations. The teetotal temperance move-

Table 7.1. Social and Religious Status
of Reformers, 1835-1850: All Towns

	Agricultural Society	Anti-Texas	Temperance	Pro-license[a]
Reformers who were (percent)				
Ministers	3	1	2	0
Businessmen/professionals[b]	25	5	8	4
Master craftsmen	5	6	8	9
Millers/taverners	3	1	1	12
Nonagricultural nonproprietors	7	14	17	11
Agricultural proprietors	42	25	30	25
Agricultural nonproprietors	0	17	11	12
Agriculturalists (Woodstock)	8	1	1	5
Unknown	7	30	22	23
Congregationalists	31	22	31	6
Baptists	3	5	6	2
Associate Presbyterians	3	7	0	-
Reformed Presbyterians	2	5	0	-
Episcopalians/Unitarians	16	1	2	13
Methodists/Freewill Baptists/Christians	3	4	10	5
Universalists	16	5	7	5
Nonmembers	26	51	43	68
Masons	15	2	5	9
Anti-removal	10	12	17	1
Sabbatarians	8	7	4	0
Anti-Sabbatarians	8	1	2	4
Antislavery	5	8	10	-
Abolitionists	5	5	5	0
Agricultural society	-	1	4	3
Anti-Texas	11	-	28	3
Temperance	40	28	-	12
Pro-license	5	1	2	-
N =	62	590	576	93

a Pro-license organizations formed only in the Windsor County towns of Pomfret, Weathersfield, West Windsor, Windsor, and Woodstock. Those towns did not forward antislavery petitions to Congress, and none of their inhabitants were Associate or Reformed Presbyterians.
b Small proprietors are included with businessmen and professionals.

ment won widespread support in the churchgoing community and among the various denominations (Table 7.1) by appealing to people's eagerness to protect their families and to their increased willingness to impose stricter discipline upon church members. Individual churches, like the First Baptist Church of Windsor, wrote the temperance pledge right into their church covenants. So did state church conferences: The Congregationalists and the Baptists declared drinking or selling alcoholic beverages an excommunicable offense, in 1835 and 1837, respectively. The Methodists, who generally refrained from taking such stands on public issues, did not erect a similar provision until 1848; and the Universalists, Unitarians, and Episcopalians, who did not usually engage in disciplinary proceedings, never did; yet by 1837 the trustees of the churches of these denominations in Peacham, Pomfret, St. Johnsbury, West Windsor, Windsor, and Woodstock had already assumed leading roles in the temperance crusade.[14]

Women were as active as men in the movement. Some may have become involved because their husbands or fathers were trying to broaden the base of support for the temperance drive, just as in the early 1830s men of property had tried to enlist all male citizens in their reform crusades. Some temperance petitions, like those from rural areas in Barnet and West Windsor in 1837, were clearly passed from house to house, with women and children signing after the male household head. In far more cases, however, it was obvious that women acted upon their own initiative. Adding to the powers they had assumed during the great revival, they moved beyond home and church into secular temperance societies and public petition drives. They attended temperance meetings alongside men and passed their own petitions at temperance rallies in many towns. They staged parades on behalf of the cause. Some seventy West Windsor women marched on the town's merchants in 1845 to ask them to stop selling liquor.[15]

The temperance crusade spawned movements that strove with similarly unprecedented vigor to impose the standards of the respectable community on the valley. Temperance and militia reformers fought to eliminate forms of recreation that provided occasions for immoral conduct. They sought laws that would allow the freemen of each town to decide annually by majority vote whether their towns would permit the retail sale of liquor during the ensuing year. They pressed for legislation that would exempt all males from compulsory military service during peacetime. Like the Sabbatarians before them, these reformers wanted to use government power indirectly to discourage activities they disliked. Unlike the Sabbatarians, they succeeded with a state referendum on liquor licenses in 1845 and a legislative act on militia service in 1844.

Although moral reformers had gained strength since the late 1820s, they succeeded in this instance because they argued their case on practical rather than scriptural grounds. Samuel Chipman, a lecturer for the state temperance society, wrote in 1839 that the "no-license" law would "prevent or repress crimes against individual rights and social order" and would decrease public expenditures on jails and poor farms, which were tenanted "in a great degree by those whose first impulse to crime came

from the distillery & the dram shop." The *Vermont Chronicle* objected
to the unfair burden the militia system placed on the poor and on young
family men, who lost wages, had to bear equipment costs, and risked
injury because they could not afford to pay ten dollars each year to
exempt themselves from service. The paper objected above all to the
threat the militia system posed to youths. Young men needed to be "taken
under parental guardianship" at that "perilous time of life," and youths
who served in training camps were "almost sure to be ruined."[16]

By 1835 these had become powerful arguments. Reformers aided their
cause by making no attempt to suppress drinking by force and by being
careful not to compromise the nation's security. The "no-license" referendum curbed "tippling" at stores and taverns, but did not outlaw the
production, consumption, or wholesale distribution of alcoholic beverages. The militia act allowed towns to organize voluntary companies and
required all able-bodied men between the ages of eighteen and forty-five
to register for service. The strategy worked. Since the Mexican War was
unpopular in Vermont and there was peace along the Canadian border,
most Vermonters were willing to forgo the risks and expense of militia
service. By 1849, only Norwich, home to Alden Partridge's prestigious
military academy, supported a large company and regular training days,
which gave the cadets an opportunity to perform precision drills before
appreciative and orderly crowds. By that same year, all but 23 of the
valley's 116 towns had voted to prohibit the retail sale of alcohol. Two-
thirds of all voters (and three-fourths of all church members who went
to the polls) voted against licenses for taverns and stores (Table 7.2). In
the principal marketing and manufacturing towns, where there was an
increased willingness to pressure the recalcitrant into behaving well because of a fear of disorder, a median of three-fourths of all voters supported temperance. However, median support remained at a high level
in prosperous agricultural communities and in poor, well-settled agricultural towns, where concerns about disorder were less pressing.[17]

These attacks on the sale of alcohol and on militia training days were
accompanied by efforts to provide constructive alternatives. Dry Fourth
of July celebrations became commonplace. Planning committees provided
food and festive decorations and saw to it that young people had the
opportunity to mix with members of the opposite sex so that there would
be no incentive to resort to alcohol or to private parties for amusement.
Agricultural fairs also gained enormous popularity at this time. Sponsored
by the county agricultural societies that sprang up in the late 1830s and
early 1840s, the fairs were intended not only to disseminate scientific
information about agricultural improvements and stimulate competition
among farmers, but to provide young people with a salutary diversion

Table 7.2. Social, Religious, and Political Status of No-License Voters, 1849[a]

	Liberals, Calvinists[b]	Non-Calvinist evangelicals	Nonmembers and others[c]	Percentage in commerce and manufacturing[d]	Percentage change in population[e]	R^2
No-license, 1849	.45 (.07)	.44 (.08)	.26 (.02)	.09 (.12)	-.06 (.04)	.12
Pro-license, 1849	.19 (.08)	.10 (.09)	.32 (.03)	-.43 (.13)	.06 (.04)	.22
Nonvoters, 1849	.36 (.09)	.46 (.10)	.42 (.03)	.35 (.15)	.00 (.05)	.02

	Median percentage Whig, 1836-44	Median percentage Democratic, 1836-44	Median percentage nonvoter, 1836-44	Percentage in commerce and manufacturing[d]	Percentage change in population[e]	R^2
No-license, 1849	.37 (.06)	.28 (.05)	.21 (.09)	.20 (.12)	-.09 (.04)	.07
Pro-license, 1849	.31 (.07)	.31 (.06)	.21 (.10)	-.53 (.13)	.08 (.04)	.18
Nonvoters, 1849	.32 (.08)	.41 (.06)	.58 (.12)	.32 (.14)	.03 (.05)	.03

[a] Standard errors of the coefficients are in parentheses. On statistical methods, see Appendix D.
[b] Separate estimates of the proportions for religious liberals and Calvinists suggests that religious liberals were less likely to vote against liquor licenses than were other church members. The estimates, however, are unstable.
[c] Separate estimates of the proportions for Universalists and for other members and nonmembers suggests that Universalists were as likely to vote against liquor licenses as were Calvinists and non-Calvinist evangelicals. The estimates, however, are unstable. The differences between nonmembers in Old Light, New Light, and moderate areas were negligible. Temperance did not divide these voters as did church-state issues.
[d] The proportion of males age sixteen and older engaged in commerce and manufacturing ranged from 0.00 to 0.43, with a median of 0.12.
[e] The proportional change in population between 1830 and 1840 ranged from -0.32 to 2.00, with a median of 0.03.

during the troublesome harvest months. Many of the organizers of the agricultural societies were also leaders in the temperance movement (Table 7.1). They wanted to give young people an incentive to use their idle moments to work on domestic and agricultural projects to be exhibited at county fairs. Some of them even believed that once the evil influence of alcohol was banished from the countryside, a rural utopia might evolve there.[18]

Stimulated by many of the same concerns that fueled the temperance movement, interest in educational reform also arose in the 1840s. Enthusiasm for state efforts to remedy the "objective" problems of the schools — inadequate textbooks and buildings, spotty attendance by older children — was limited in rural areas, but was high in the twenty-four principal and secondary market centers in the valley. Residents of those towns forwarded nine of the twenty-one petitions on behalf of school reform that reached the state legislature in 1845. Most enthusiastic were the businessmen and professionals who dominated the local educational committees that arose in most of the valley's towns that same year.[19] They dreamed of making the schools "good enough for the wealthiest" and wanted to offer all children a preparatory education in the public schools that would obviate the need for expensive private boarding academies. Anxious parents like Norman and Mary Williams of Woodstock would not have to send their young children away for schooling. Leaders of the movement were also committed to the idea that every child should have the opportunity to move up the valley's mercantile and professional ladders. They wanted to enlighten the countryside, to give it access to the latest spiritual, moral, and practical knowledge, and to further the spread of values and skills vital to the valley's progress.[20]

These visions were not realized, because the majority of people who supported educational reform did not believe that improved schools or colleges were critical to the success of their children. They did not think their children needed more education than they themselves possessed, and they did not want to incur the costs associated with improving the schools and taking their older children out of employment. "High Schools" and "theoretical" training were irrelevant to them; all they wanted, as the Methodist convention made clear in 1848, was an education that would improve the moral character and the prospects of the average citizen's children.[21]

State Superintendent Horace Eaton concurred. A good common school ought, he wrote, to "awaken a feeling of self-respect and regard for reputation" at an early age "by disclosing the perils and pains incident to every deviation from the path of rectitude ... which gradually impairs the energy, and stills the voice of that 'monitor in the human breast.' " Education could protect the prospects of children by giving them basic skills and by penetrating and destroying the moral deserts that lingered in the valley. According to Windsor County Superintendent James Taft, there were places in the valley where children indulged in profanity, dallied with members of the opposite sex, and treated teachers not with "the affection of children" but "the familiarity and rudeness of street loafers and rowdies." By teaching these ruffians "morals and manners," "bows and courtesies," education could secure what Governor William Slade called in 1845 the children's "right to protection" against "vice and immorality" and imbue them with a proper regard for cleanliness and decency. Education would thus serve alongside temperance in the practical campaign for respectability and, like it, foster sentiments from which self-discipline and success would emerge.[22]

The schools did not need advanced courses, longer terms, or more textbooks to accomplish these goals: They needed experienced and talented teachers whose efforts were supported and supervised by the citizenry. In 1845 a legislative act helped fill these needs by requiring all teachers to be certified and by establishing town, county, and state commissioners to oversee the common schools and report on conditions in them. That act was supplemented by the efforts of local citizens, especially ministers, to visit the schools frequently to assure they were well run and by a self-conscious turn to female teachers. It was believed that women would set a more inspiring example of conduct to the young and would rule by that example rather than by force. Women generally kept their positions longer than their male counterparts and were paid between half and two-thirds what men were.[23]

It is difficult to judge how successful the advocates of these reform efforts were in imposing their standards on the valley's inhabitants. Retail sales of liquor had plunged by 1850, but it is not clear whether production and consumption had fallen far. Nor is there any way to prove statistically that people discriminated more than before against those who offended respectable sensibilities in their manner, dress, or behavior, even though most citizens who accounted themselves respectable spoke openly and explicitly about doing so in public addresses and in private correspondence.[24] It is also difficult to determine precisely how association with the temperance movement affected people's fortunes, for in marketing and manufacturing towns the temperance movement was too closely intertwined with the churches to admit of independent study. The lists of temperance reformers in Windsor and Woodstock in the 1830s, for example, included the names of few adult male taxpayers or household heads who were not also church members.[25]

The evidence does make it clear that church members in Windsor drew together in business more closely in the 1830s and 1840s than they had in the 1820s. That enabled them to protect their economic position at the expense of nonmembers, who bore the brunt of the decline of opportunity in that town. At the same time, those who were temperate but who were not church members entered the existing networks of mutual support among church members in agricultural towns. These were networks that were still not as pervasive or strong as those in commercial centers and that did not choke off opportunities for nonmembers to the same degree. They still functioned more openly and effectively than they had in the 1820s, however, enabling church members and temperate nonmembers to attain a preeminent position in those towns.

Data on the organization of mercantile and manufacturing firms in Windsor between 1831 and 1850 indicate that church members who had joined churches both before and during the revival (excepting those who

Table 7.3. Ownership of Mercantile and Manufacturing
Firms, 1831-1850: Marketing and Manufacturing Town[a]

	Church members, by 1829	Church members, 1829-43	Nonmembers
Single owners	30	35	52
Partners, same surname	17	17	11
Partners, different surname	53	48	37
N =	87	48	83
Religious status of partners with different surnames			
Partnerships formed with church members by 1829	53	65	26
Partnerships formed with church members, 1829-43	30	26	7
Partnerships formed with nonmembers	16	9	67
N =	43	23	27

[a] The data are from Windsor.

had been excluded through disciplinary action) clung together more closely than nonmembers and more closely than they themselves had in the 1820s. Church members were more likely than nonmembers to enter business with the aid of partners. The vast majority of the church members who formed partnerships with people of different surnames found their partners in the churches, and by the 1830s, two-thirds of these partnerships linked members of different denominations. The most typical pattern, which prevailed in a majority of the cases in which church members came together, saw a member who had joined a church during the revival move into partnership with an established church member who had joined a church prior to the revival. The revival thus appears to have advanced to proprietorship a number of those in Windsor who shared in its spiritual blessings, in addition to having strengthened the interdenominational bonds among church members (Table 7.3).

These networks of support clearly helped church members, both those

Table 7.4. Ownership of Mercantile and Manufacturing Firms, 1831-1850: Agricultural Towns

	Church members by 1827	Church members 1827-43	Temperate non-members	Non-members outside Barnet[a]	Non-members in Barnet[a]
Single owners	43	51	42	76	60
Partners, same surname	15	9	11	5	4
Partners, different surname	42	40	47	20	36
N =	95	116	55	176	80
Religious status of partners with different surnames					
Partnerships formed with church members by 1827	55	15	16	23	7
Partnerships formed with church members, 1827-1843	15	57	24	13	10
Partnerships formed with temperate nonmembers	10	13	16	17	21
Partnerships formed with nonmembers outside Barnet	15	9	20	47	-
Partnerships formed with nonmembers in Barnet	5	7	24	-	62
N =	40	46	25	30	29

[a] Nonmembers who did not live in Barnet did not form any partnerships with nonmembers who lived in Barnet.

who had joined before and after the revival, to stay in town longer and advance further economically than nonmembers of the same age and occupation. Indeed, their edge was as great as or greater than it had been in the 1820s, especially among nonproprietors (Tables 7.5, 7.6, and 7 8). Church members had become a commanding presence in town life by 1840, for whereas only half of the adult taxpayers and household heads in 1830 were either already church members or would soon join during the revival, fully 70 percent of those who remained in town over the decade of the 1830s were church members. That pattern continued

Table 7.5. Persistence by Age, Occupation,
and Religious Status, 1830-1840: All Towns

	Church members by 1827	Church members, 1827-43	Temperate nonmembers	Nonmembers
Age unknown and under 40				
Nonagricultural proprietors	58	71	78	44
N =	52	35	9	66
Agricultural proprietors	81	74	94	52
N =	90	70	18	236
Nonproprietors	59	68	68	35
N =	94	90	28	662
Age 40 and over				
Nonagricultural proprietors	67	69	100	83
N =	43	16	3	18
Agricultural proprietors	70	76	88	59
N =	220	54	17	286
Nonproprietors	42	71	70	36
N =	92	35	10	311

through the 1840s. The people who prospered and did not leave town, who comprised the ongoing community of Windsor, were overwhelmingly church members.[26]

The situation was more complex in most of the agricultural towns, where temperance and church membership were not so closely associated. Distinctive towns like Barnet and Ryegate, where the predominantly Scottish population banded together on the basis of ethnicity rather than church membership and where nonmembers in general were viewed with greater tolerance, developed different patterns of social life in the 1830s. On the whole, however, agricultural towns moved toward greater closure in the 1830s and 1840s, although they would remain less closed to nonmembers and would offer fewer advantages to church members than commercial centers.

Table 7.6. Social Mobility by Age, Occupation,
and Religious Status, 1830-1840: Marketing and Manufacturing Town

	Church members by 1829	Church members, 1829-43	Nonmembers
Age unknown and under 40			
Nonagricultural proprietors			
Upwardly mobile	7	0	0
Downwardly mobile	14	14	100
Net change	-7	-14	-100
N =	14	7	1
Nonagricultural nonproprietors			
Upwardly mobile	0	89	14
N =	2	9	14
Age 40 and over			
Nonagricultural proprietors			
Upwardly mobile	7	0	0
Downwardly mobile	7	0	50
Net change	0	0	-50
N =	15	4	2
Nonagricultural nonproprietors			
Upwardly mobile	50	100	13
N =	2	4	8

Outside Barnet, data on the organization of mercantile and manufacturing firms suggest that church members and temperance society members who were not church members were more likely to become involved in partnerships than merchants and manufacturers who were neither church nor temperance society members. Church members, both pre-revival and post-revival entrants, and nonmembers identified with temperance were more often engaged in partnerships than nonmembers who were not temperance society members (Table 7.4). Furthermore, when

Table 7.7. Social Mobility by Age, Occupation,
and Religious Status, 1830-1840: Agricultural Towns

	Church members by 1827	Church members, 1827-43	Temperate nonmembers	Nonmembers
Age unknown and under 40				
Nonagricultural proprietors				
Upwardly mobile	19	22	14	4
Downwardly mobile	31	17	0	21
Net change	-13	6	14	-18
N =	16	18	7	28
Nonagricultural nonproprietors				
Upwardly mobile	50	44	40	24
N =	10	9	5	41
Agricultural proprietors				
Upwardly mobile	25	21	29	22
Downwardly mobile	16	10	6	17
Net change	8	12	24	5
N =	73	52	17	123
Agricultural nonproprietors				
Upwardly mobile	58	79	57	43
N =	43	43	14	174
Age 40 and over				
Nonagricultural proprietors				
Upwardly mobile	7	0	0	0
Downwardly mobile	14	14	0	46
Net change	-7	-14	0	-46
N =	14	7	3	13
Nonagricultural nonproprietors				
Upwardly mobile	11	13	25	4
N =	9	8	4	23
Agricultural proprietors				
Upwardly mobile	13	10	20	15
Downwardly mobile	26	24	0	27
Net change	-14	-15	20	-12
N =	155	41	15	169
Agricultural nonproprietors				
Upwardly mobile	32	36	67	22
N =	28	13	3	80

Table 7.8. Proprietorship among New Adult Residents
in 1840: All Towns

	Church members by 1827	Church members, 1827-43	Temperate non-members	Non-members
Marketing and manufacturing town				
Age unknown and under 40				
Nonagricultural proprietorship	50	56	-	27
N =	4	18	0	63
Age 40 and over				
Nonagricultural proprietorship	-	100	-	0
N =	0	2	0	6
Agricultural towns				
Age unknown and under 40				
Nonagricultural proprietorship	28	34	44	13
N =	36	44	41	395
Agricultural proprietorship	47	51	50	35
N =	59	86	30	626
Age 40 and over				
Nonagricultural proprietorship	33	0	0	0
N =	3	1	2	17
Agricultural proprietorship	54	30	50	20
N =	13	10	6	115

church members founded those partnerships with people of different surnames, they did so more often with other church members than they had in the 1820s. Just as in Windsor, two-thirds of partnerships among church members linked members of different denominations by the

Table 7.9. Religious and Occupational Status
of Mortgagors, 1831-1840: Agricultural Towns[a]

	Church members by 1827	Church members, 1827-43	Temperate non-members	Non-members
Age unknown and under 40[b]				
Farmers	47	74	140	32
N =	47	38	10	213
Agricultural nonproprietors	67	145	42	34
N =	33	22	12	135
Unknown persons and new residents in agriculture	62	73	75	42
N =	42	44	24	237
Nonagricultural proprietors	43	158	33	37
N =	14	19	6	19
Nonagricultural nonproprietors	62	63	13	13
N =	31	27	8	185
Unknown persons and new residents not in agriculture	24	72	28	3
N =	29	32	29	240

[a] The data are from Peacham, St. Johnsbury, and Weathersfield.
[b] The data for persons age forty and over reveal similar trends.
Proportionately fewer persons in that age category were mortgagors.

1830s. Church and temperance society members also had greater access
to mortgage money than nonmembers and concluded a disproportionate
number of mortgage agreements with other church and temperance society members. Church and temperance society members increasingly
wrote mortgages for other members and received them from other members, and half of all mortgages contracted among church members were
between members of different denominations (Tables 7.9 and 7.10).

Table 7.10. Religious Status of Mortgagees and Mortgagors
with Different Surnames, 1831-1840: Agricultural Towns[a]

	From church members by 1827	From church members, 1827-43	From temperate nonmembers	From nonmembers
To church members by 1827	35	16	8	17
To church members, 1827-43	24	33	33	21
To temperate nonmembers	6	9	8	4
To nonmembers	35	41	50	58
N =	213	148	24	184

[a] The data are from Peacham, St. Johnsbury, and Weathersfield.

These connections helped church members and temperance reformers stay in town longer and prosper more than nonmembers (Tables 7.5, 7.7, and 7.8), although their position was not generally as strong as it was in Windsor. Their advantages were not as great in agricultural occupations as in manufacturing and commerce, and among manufacturers in Barnet, church members and temperance advocates had very little edge at all. Still, church members generally managed to preserve or extend the advantages they had enjoyed in the 1820s. Half of the adult male taxpayers and household heads who managed to persist through the 1830s were members of churches or temperance societies, and those who remained were generally more successful than nonmembers who remained, by margins greater than in the 1820s. These patterns persisted through the 1840s.[27]

The situation in Barnet was unique. There nonmembers formed partnerships at the same rate that church members did, and those who organized them with partners of different surnames did so an astonishing four-fifths of the time with other nonmembers. In other towns nonmembers tended to try to brave the business world alone in the 1830s. Again, it seems that shared ethnicity was sufficient assurance of trustworthiness for the Scots of Barnet and Ryegate. Also, because of their distinctive patterns of inheritance and migration, the Scots were less anxious for the future and for their reputations than their Yankee neighbors. As a result, their towns did not move as quickly as other valley towns to try to impose a stricter code of behavior upon residents. Nor would the effort to impose such a code have been well received by the Scots. They were an earthy lot, who prided themselves on their rustic manners and their ribald humor (Ryegate's "Tickle Naked Pond" remains the only physical feature of the valley with a salacious official name). Nearly all of them, church members and nonmembers alike, were still in the habit of drinking occasionally in the 1830s, and enjoyed the custom of drinking with friends at stores and shops. They respected temperance reformers, just as they did church members, but only as long as they restricted to Sundays their efforts to make others follow their example. Many temperance advocates, like the members of the Reformed and Associate Presbyterian churches, simply adjusted their notions of temperance to suit the Scots character. Drinking would not harm a Scot, they reasoned, for Scots were by nature too thrifty and prudent to drink to excess.[28]

The Scots' habits troubled their Yankee neighbors. George Cowles, a young Yankee who opened a store in Ryegate in the mid-1830s, complained to his fiancée in Peacham that the Scots were "a different kind of people to deal with from the Yankee." He could not get rid of bands of Scots who chattered away at his shop until half past midnight, nor could he afford to discontinue the sale of rum for fear of losing customers, who made it clear they would not trade with people who tried "to put down something" they had "no business with." Cowles knew that people in Peacham would censure him for selling rum, but there was nothing he could do. It was "no use to contradict Scots." That would be "too much like spitting in the wind."[29]

The fear that Cowles felt about the consequences of selling rum was not unreasoning. The modified order that came into being in the mid-1830s, with its increased emphasis on temperance and personal morality, was hard on people who contravened its standards. Isaac Ewell, a miller from Peacham who had been excluded from the Congregational church at the beginning of the revival for intemperance, readmitted in 1843 when he experienced a second spiritual renewal, only to be sacked again for drinking in 1845, offered a glimpse into life on the outside in a letter he wrote that year to Hazen Merrill, a Congregational deacon, temperance leader, and the most important citizen in the neighborhood. Merrill had earlier been of some help to Ewell, apparently when Ewell was still in the church, but later he had decided not to do business with him. To Ewell this seemed unfair. He was too proud to beg Merrill to bring his grain to him once again, but he wrote to him to point out that Merrill had no good reason to shun him. "I observe that you do not come here to mill. I think I grind as well as ever. I sometimes have more to do than I know how . . . but not withstanding I still invite you." He realized that

Merrill differed with him "respecting theological opinions," but he did not believe Merrill had any accusation against him "relating to toll or mony matters." He did not mean to discourage him from using other millers, and he hoped they were "faithful," but it was his "business to grind for all [and] to invite all." He promised to do Merrill's work "in good stile."[30]

Ewell was a frightened man. People who trusted Merrill would take their grain elsewhere, and when Merrill left he took away the protection that the patronage of an important man could give to a poor one. People had begun to write Ewell abusive letters, denouncing him because of his intemperance. With the economy still in decline and the attitude toward intemperance what it was, Ewell needed Merrill to stand by him. Merrill would not.

By the mid-1830s, most people had come to assume that if a man drank at all, he could be neither successful nor honest. Intemperance was identified more closely than ever with coarse habits, wage work, failure in business, and criminality. William Jarvis and his son-in-law Henry Cutts, a commercial farmer in Hartland, spent more time denouncing three men who stole a wagon from them for their intemperance than for their actual crime. They had expected such behavior from two of the men, who "were both intoxicated when here" and were known to be unreliable. They were surprised, however, that the other, "a farmer in Norwich who has had some property and still retains a portion of it," had been embroiled in the scheme. Cutts noted by way of explanation that the fellow had "for a year or two been much given to intemperance."[31]

Harsh attitudes toward drinkers followed them even to the grave. In 1844 Arthur Bennett of Woodstock attended the funeral of Otis Cox. In his diary he wrote that Cox "died with a cancer on his neck occasioned by drinking rum. No tears were shed over his remains but was hurried to his grave as fast as convenience and decency would admit of and in a very few days he will be forgotten." He noted by way of contrast the funeral the very next day of E. H. Billings, prominent attorney, church member, and temperance advocate. "Yesterday scarce a tribute was paid or a tear shed or one act performed to call [Cox] to memory," but for Billings a "throng" came to pay their respects and "mingle their sympathys with the friends of the deceased." Sober citizens like Bennett had come to believe that drunkards, with their continual and apparently willful trespassings against the dictates of respectable society, were as bad as or worse than criminals and were undeserving of human sympathy.[32]

Some people questioned the churchgoing community's standards of behavior and clung to the belief that the informal ministrations of parents, teachers, and churches could best serve the cause of morality, as they had in the 1820s. Sarah Hill of Randolph doubted the efficacy of censorious laws and societies. She believed that there was "more sin at home" than reformers could prevent by their efforts abroad and that reformers could accomplish more by instilling their doctrines in their children. Bishop John H. Hopkins of the Vermont diocese of the Episcopal church refused in 1836 to commit his denomination to the temperance movement and commanded local parishes to avoid official commitment as well. He approved of the cause, but he criticized temperance reformers for invading the church's territory and trying to make "improvements" on the Gospel. By overemphasizing personal morality and making total abstinence the "Eleventh commandment," they encouraged pride in people who were temperate. He called for charity toward the fallen and for faith in God and God's instruments: revivals and conversions. His stand encouraged resistance within the churchgoing community to the campaign for respectability, not only among religious liberals who defended the practice of social drinking, but among all Christians who believed that moral reformations could not be brought about by other than spiritual means.[33]

Respectable citizens were thus not equally or always bent on discriminating against those who behaved in undesirable ways. Christian sympathy still softened spirits, as did reluctance to part with the more modest standards and patient methods of the postwar order; and concerns other than respectability, such as family, neighborhood, and politics, still had power to draw people together or to divide them. Most social and economic alliances among townspeople were still concluded unthinkingly, through churches rather than extra-religious organizations. Support for temperance increased steadily, but support for temperance laws varied widely from year to year and remained far weaker on state referendums that would have prohibited the sale of alcoholic beverages throughout the state than on those that granted towns the option to prohibit such sales. Even the most respectable citizens hesitated at the thought of outlawing moderate drinking and imposing their views not only on their neighbors but on the state at large.[34]

The campaign for respectability also inspired intense, organized opposition. Friends of the military academy at Norwich founded an independent newpaper in 1840, the *Citizen Soldier*, to defend the militia system and the integrity of militiamen.[35] Anti-teetotal temperance committees sprang up in many towns. They favored a "judicious" license system, in which taverners and merchants would be held responsible for limiting alcoholic consumption to safe amounts. The committees included a disproportionate number of taverners and unchurched young men, but among their number there were also church members and proprietors who saw no danger in moderate drinking, but did see a threat to liberty in morals laws (Table 7.1).[36] Raucous revelers occasionally staged defiant harvest and Independence Day celebrations in full public view. None of these counterattacks diminished the power of the crusade for respectability, but they signaled that its success in the valley would never be total.

The march toward a modified order in town life seems to have bypassed the remote hill towns of the valley. These towns, fifteen in all, were isolated along the spine of the Green Mountains and in the granite expanse of the Northeast Kingdom and had grown estranged from the rest of the valley. Even after the great revival churches remained weak in these towns; average adult membership stood at only 10 percent in 1843. They did not have enough people to support many churches (in 1840 only 3 percent of the valley's population lived in the hill towns), and isolated families always relied more on their own moral and material resources anyway. These frontier people may well have supported strong village societies or circuit classes that left no membership records, and, like other Vermonters, they did have their share of family Bibles and hymnals. Yet their low median support for local prohibition (37 percent) and their failure to forward any petitions favoring educational improvement suggest that people in these towns may have had different ideas about bettering themselves than people in the rest of the valley.

Although parents in these hill towns had the fewest resources per capita with which to provide for their children and had little good land near home, they continued to have more children than people in other towns (Table 4.4), even in the 1830s when their towns were producing as large an exodus of young people as any town in the valley. Yet they showed little interest in reform movements that promised to help their children, choosing instead to entrust their hopes for the future to their own labor. The hill towns offered cheap, unimproved land in the 1820s and 1830s that poor people could buy on credit or work on shares. Speculators were happy to offer land in these communities on easy terms or on shares (over a fifth of all farms in these communities were occupied by tenants, four times the rate that prevailed in communities on good land), because they knew that improvements by the occupants would enable them to command high prices for foreclosed or rented farms. People who farmed these lands rested their hopes of independence and of moving beyond subsistence farming and establishing their children on their ability to wring wealth from poor land.[37]

Hill people, like the rural poor throughout northern New England, understood the magnitude of the task they faced. They charted prices, expenses, and income carefully, but usually fell short of their financial goals each year. A poor harvest, a greedy landlord who provided poor seed or tools and did not pay fairly for improvements, or bad luck could ruin them. One family in North Danville fell hopelessly into debt when they rented out a $50 pot that they themselves had rented from a wealthy neighbor, only to have a penniless potash maker crack the pot. Parents needed cheap young laborers in their households to plant seeds, clear brush, ride plowhorses, tend charcoal pits, work maple stands, care for infants, and weave cloth they could ill afford to buy; and they needed heirs to support them when they were old or to take their place in case of illness or death.[38]

In such circumstances education or moral reputation mattered less than industry. Steady woodsmen made the most money, and hardworking neighbors received help in time of illness, although Nancy Batchelder of Peru admitted that people "sometimes even helped the lazy ones." God was called on for help primarily during times of physical danger (a common theme in folk songs about hunting and logging) and personal crisis rather than on a regular, weekly basis. Mothers taught their children about life, history, and morality as much through ballads and tales as through the Bible and other books, and parents taught practical skills through demonstration. Drinking – like games, sports, pranks, and festive occasions such as huskings and bees – was expressly prized for its ability to lift fatigued spirits and break the monotony of dull routines.[39]

The poor did all they could for their children. They counseled moderation in all things, taught frugality by example, read the Bible at home, attended services by itinerant preachers, and sometimes sacrificed time and labor to send their children to school, determined, like Horace Greeley's father, to "give their children the best education they could afford." Sometimes they dreamed of sending them to academies and giving them legacies.[40] Most of their children would leave town when they were old enough, however, and would have to succeed in the city or on the frontier through gumption and fight. Therefore their parents believed they were better off exposed to the rough-and-tumble of life at an early age.

The willingness of many poor parents to allow their children to drink, to fight, and to sing bawdy folk songs frustrated many reform-minded teachers. Male teachers often had to establish authority over older students by thrashing them in fist fights or by besting them at practical jokes, as did one teacher who retrieved his barricaded schoolhouse from rowdies in midwinter by boarding up the chimney and smoking them out. The efforts of female teachers to appeal to the better nature of their students were often frustrated. Adeline Reed, a teacher in "the wilds of Roxbury," a hill town in Washington County, was forced to invent "numberless strange punishments" to keep one willful student in line. On one occasion she made him balance a heavy basket on the end of a ruler; on another she tied his hands behind his back, put a string around his neck and tied it to a nail on the wall. When she wrote to school friends she tried to make them understand the necessity for what she did.[41]

There were other reasons for the hill people's estrangement from churches and reform. Exhaustion and disappointment caused Horace Greeley's parents to retreat from society in their early fifties. Calvin Hulbert's father eventually resigned himself to poverty and accepted that people born in frame houses would always be "smarter" than people born in log cabins. Women in hill towns were more isolated from each other than women in other parts of the valley. Their work load was heavier, and their households were often more paternally dominated. They could on occasion rebel against their circumstances, as did a band of women in western Vermont who were angered by their husbands' refusal to vote for construction of a new schoolhouse. When the men were away on a winter wolf hunt they took up axes and built their own school. But most were unable to find the time or opportunity to organize on behalf of causes that concerned them.[42]

It is also likely that some hill people may have been different from the beginning of settlement, outsiders who chose that life not only because they were poor, but because they disliked churches, nosy neighbors, pressures toward conformity, and the need to compete for economic success. Some hill people had an understandable antipathy to the campaign for respectability, too, because college-educated reformers often slandered them, calling on the rest of the valley to shower enlightenment and civilization upon these allegedly uncivilized and feckless backwoods people.[43] The citizens of these communities may have persisted defiantly in the way of life that had dominated the valley prior to 1815, a way of life in which the majority of the citizenry enjoyed popular amusements, a laissez-faire attitude prevailed toward the young, and efforts to draw invidious distinctions among people were strongly resisted.

These pockets of resistance were not the only stumbling block in the way of the campaign for a modified order in town life. There were many church members and temperance activists who agreed with some of the campaign's aims but opposed the move toward proscription and greater closure in town life and felt that distinctions made openly on the basis of respectability were unchristian and unrepublican. The trend toward greater closure was thus only partial and hotly debated. It did not result in a closed society or in complete acceptance among respected citizens of the need for more systematic (albeit still informal) sanctions against the impious. Ties among church members and temperance reformers were still informal and conditional. Many church members and temperance activists met with failure in business or farming, while some nonmembers and temperance foes succeeded, especially in the agricultural towns where success had always been less dependent on connections. Thus, although the inhabitants of the valley were generally willing to move toward greater closure when opportunity was curtailed and their values were threatened, the pattern of life in their towns remained substantially unchanged. Neither closed nor open, life in the valley was designed to help respectable citizens reach proprietorship and uphold Christian values primarily in informal and noncoercive ways.

A modified order in politics

By 1835 the valley's political leaders were as frustrated by their inability to settle the conflict among themselves as the churchgoing community was by the failure of the revival. The conflict intensified that year, because no party's gubernatorial candidate won a sufficient plurality of votes to carry the election. After dozens of roll call votes, the legislature could not declare a winner, and the successful candidate for lieutenant governor, Silas Jennison, was asked to serve as acting governor for a term.

That stalemate and the collapse of the Antimasonic Party outside Vermont encouraged state politicians in each party to believe that they could bring about a second "era of good feelings" on their own terms through the destruction of the Antimasonic Party. The primary architects of Antimasonry's demise were Antimasonic leaders like William Slade of Middlebury and Ebenezer Eaton of Danville, both newspaper editors. They hoped to stack the party's 1836 convention in favor of one or the other of the two national parties, which had changed their names to the Whig Party (formerly National Republican) and the Democratic Party (formerly Jacksonian) in order to distance themselves from Adams and Jackson. These leading Antimasons, who had once denounced all organizations that compelled men to compromise their principles, now spoke in their private correspondence of the need to keep rivals "hemmed in and hedged up" and of the need to find stratagems that would make it difficult for politicians and editors "to get out of the traces" in case they were "disposed to go astray." Leading Whigs and Democrats wrote letters of their own to dozens of Antimasonic leaders in 1835–6, declaring their parties fervently Antimasonic and warning either that the protective tariff and the national bank would go by the board or that the cause of true equality would perish if Antimasons did not stand by their principles and join them.[44]

Their efforts met with some success. The state politicians destroyed

Antimasonry, a movement that Vermont's voters had never repudiated, by preventing the 1836 convention from fielding a slate of independent candidates. Most former Antimasons had enlisted in one party or the other by 1837. The valley was not reunified politically, however. Neither Whigs nor Democrats could win a clear majority. Both parties were riven by internal conflict, for the economy, the revival, and reform movements had begun to divide the parties' long-standing supporters, and new support came from people who were really neither Whigs nor Democrats, but former Antimasons who distrusted both national parties. The struggle among the leaders of the surviving parties eventually produced a temporary solution to the state's political problems, but that solution made it necessary for people to learn how to live in an atmosphere of distrust and discontent. Vermont took on the appearance of a two-party state whose inhabitants had accepted partisanship as a fact of life.

The struggles for control that broke out in both parties were for the most part obscured because neither the Whigs nor the Democrats made many changes in their leadership, policies, or rhetoric. The Whigs still favored economic growth and moral improvement through the American System, even though a growing body of Whigs considered that position weak and evasive. A small band of influential Whigs, primarily wealthy entrepreneurs, lawyers, and financiers from the larger towns, led by Erastus Fairbanks of St. Johnsbury and Joseph Tracy, who was now editor of the Windsor-based *School Journal and Vermont Agriculturalist*, tried in the mid-1840s to push the Whig party toward a frank commitment to capitalism. These men, the founders of the National Republican Party, had been shaken by the depression of 1837, by Vermont's economic stagnation, and by the ineffectuality of the economic measures they themselves had supported. They looked with envy upon the prosperity and prestige of Massachusetts (and beyond that, of England) and wondered why Vermont, "with a soil far more fertile, with a climate of unrivaled salubrity, and a population equally vigorous," could not likewise support a large population "unsurpassed on the face of the globe" for its "energy, activity, and judicious enterprise." They came to the conclusion that if an area not peculiarly blessed by nature hoped to progress even as its population increased, it would have to take action. The key was to encourage innovators and risk-takers, to facilitate the flow of capital into financial and industrial enterprises by repealing laws that set ceilings on interest rates, by forgiving bankrupts their debts, and by allowing any firm to incorporate upon application. Above all, the pursuit of knowledge that had the potential for economic application had to be subsidized. To that end they wanted greater funding for the University of Vermont, more preparatory and scientific education in the common schools, and a new style of teaching that would encourage the critical and creative habits of thought that led to productive innovation in agriculture and industry and would instill in students the moral probity and intellectual depth that had always prompted the citizens of Massachusetts to "act their part manfully" in every important cause and bring their "influence for good ...to bear, not only on the rest of the United States, but upon the world."[45]

The proponents of capitalism dominated the inner circles of the Whig Party. They provided the party with gubernatorial candidates like Charles Paine, a woolen manufacturer from Northfield, and Carlos Coolidge, a Windsor business attorney. From their ranks also came the party's leading political operatives, like William Jarvis, the commercial farmer from Weathersfield. They believed that their ambitious schemes would receive an increasingly sympathetic hearing from Whigs in the 1840s, as the populace became more desperate to promote economic growth and as capitalists more frequently got worldwide attention for their achievements. In 1849, Governor Coolidge asked the legislature to endorse the capitalists' proposals and heaped special praise upon railroads, whose growth had charged Vermonters with a new economic optimism and had created greater economic unity among the various sections of the state. Yet none of the Whigs' proposals became law before 1850.

The bulk of Whig voters, both former National Republicans and Antimasons, were shopkeepers and farmers interested in realizing older aspirations. Like Paul and Olivia Flinn, who ran a farm and a mill in Bethel with the help of their four young children, most Whig families believed in "the golden mean." They lived "contentedly between the little and the great," seeking to minimize their debts and risks, to avoid both "the pressing ills" of poverty and "the dangerous temptations" of wealth.[46] They did not have much use for higher education and did not feel secure ceding all public power over chartered enterprises or banks. They took pride in Vermont because, unlike Massachusetts and England, it was a land of independent small proprietors in a rural and small-town setting. That did not make them hostile to capitalists, but it made them wary of capitalism. They did not wish to vest tremendous power in an educated, monied elite, nor would they support an ideology that spoke only occasionally in defense of widespread proprietorship, that extolled the virtues of equality of opportunity almost to the exclusion of the virtues of equality of condition, that considered the accumulation of wealth the source of prestige and happiness, and that implicitly conceded the superiority of urban life and civilization.

Whig politicians were forced to reckon with such views. The Whig editor of the *St. Johnsbury Caledonian*, A. G. Chadwick, recognized the party's need to attract the support of former Antimasons and never ventured into capitalist waters in his editorials. He favored frugal government, portrayed the Whigs as champions of the common man, and attacked the greed of Democratic entrepreneurs like Robert Harvey, a wool grower from Barnet, who was known as "a pretty close shearer" by "many an honest farmer." Carlos Coolidge feared privately that the "ultra spirit" of Antimasonry would ruin the party, but as speaker of the Vermont assembly he worked for "harmony" because he believed the Whigs could not "accomplish anything" without their support. Erastus Fairbanks and Joseph Tracy had no choice but to publish the *School Journal and Vermont Agriculturalist* as an independent newspaper and give it a name that had nothing to do with capitalism or industry, because its ideas were as yet too bold for most voters.[47]

The Whig-dominated legislature became attentive to the needs of indebted small proprietors. It exempted property worth up to $500 from attachment, including a homestead, ten sheep, one hog, one cow, three swarms of bees, and a supply of seed grain and potatoes. (The legislature did not act to forgive bankrupts their debts or exempt property of the kind that the valley's businessmen and professionals were most likely to own.)[48] In their public pronouncements, most Whigs still tried to appeal to everyone at once, using a modified version of the National Republican platform. They touted economic measures that would encourage general economic growth and called for state support to agricultural improvement societies, a state geological survey to locate untapped resources, and rapid chartering and granting of rights-of-way for railroads. On the issues of education, business, and the meaning of equality, the Whigs were divided and so spoke publicly about those matters in a deliberately indeterminate way.

The issue of reform was to divide the Whigs as deeply as the economy. Many reformers wanted to make the Whig Party the political arm of the respectable community, to employ it as a weapon in their campaigns against sin and ignorance. Governor William Slade, a former Antimason who was an abolitionist and a faithful reader of William Lloyd Garrison's *Liberator*, urged the party to abandon colonization. Whig colonizationists denounced abolitionism vehemently and demanded that the party endorse their antislavery program. Erastus Fairbanks asked the Whigs to pass no-license resolutions at their annual conventions. Local temperance societies encouraged politicians like former governor Silas Jennison to "stand publicly" behind temperance, militia reform, and education reform. The militance of these reformers antagonized many Whigs, however. Governor Charles Paine had no complaint with the reformers' ideals, but he had little patience with people who would deny slaveholders and drinkers their constitutional rights. Paine had suffered personally from the accusations of sanctimonious reformers. Not only did he enjoy his glass of Madeira, he had a common-law wife (formerly a worker in his factory) and three children whom he was unable to acknowledge because his family threatened to disinherit him if he did. He was not about to hand over the reins of the Whig Party to reformers. There were many other Whigs who resented the pressures reformers brought to bear on them. Nahum Haskell, who became editor of the Whig *Vermont Mercury* in 1837, was inundated by threats from Whigs who promised to cancel their subscriptions if he continued to use the paper as a forum against liquor licenses. Seventeen of the twenty-two political activists who led the campaign to uphold the sale of liquor licenses in Windsor County were Whigs, who feared the anti-license crusaders more than they feared intemperance.[49]

Most Whig leaders fell back on the National Republican policy of supporting reform in general terms. They encouraged individual Whigs to join reform crusades and tried to keep reform "above" politics. At times they worked actively to channel reform into politically safe avenues, as did Erastus Fairbanks, who sounded out his friends in 1839 about founding a moderate antislavery organization that might reunify colonizationists and abolitionists and make it easier for the Whigs to profit from the antislavery movement. They made a special effort to enlist pro-temperance and antislavery women in their cause, praising their involvement in the petition campaigns against liquor licenses and slavery in the District of Columbia and inviting them as observers to party rallies. Leading Whigs had little difficulty portraying the national Democratic Party as more pro-slavery and more tolerant of intemperance than the Whigs, or branding Vermont Democrats as less concerned about the state of the common schools or about militia training days. The Whigs could boast of a deep involvement on the part of party activists in reform organizations and of substantial support for no-license legislation among the party's rank-and-file members (Table 7.2), but as an organization, the party left the broad sweep of high principles and great causes to reformers and remained primarily a source of carefully moderated support.[50]

This policy did not satisfy everyone. For a time Ruth Buckman and her husband Isaiah, devout Universalists, abolitionists, and Antimasons from South Woodstock, conducted their personal correspondence on official "log cabin and hard cider" stationery and endorsed a presidential candidate, William Henry Harrison, who had once favored the introduction of slavery in the Old Northwest; but they renounced Whiggery quickly when in 1841 the Liberty Party offered them an alternative free of all taint of drink and slavery.[51]

The Democrats were even more deeply divided than the Whigs. As in the past, they were led by wealthy Christians who were concerned that their towns were not receiving a fair share of the valley's prosperity. These Democrats did not question the American System or capitalist institutions; they questioned the conduct of the men who controlled them. They accused leading Whigs, particularly the proponents of capitalism, of using these institutions, in the words of the *North Star*, "to enrich themselves at the expense of the many" and "to abridge the just and equal rights and privileges of community." The entrepreneurs and financiers who financed the Democratic Party still wanted railroads, banks, factories, and colleges in their neighborhoods, and most of them conceded that they could attract investment only with guarantees of liability limits and with protective tariffs on imported wool and woolens. As Windsor lawyer Samuel Price declared, they only wanted to ensure that charters and other benefits would be granted "on fair terms." That meant lower tariffs on products Vermonters could not produce locally, more equitable distribution of grants for education and internal improvements, charters of limited duration subject to legislative renewal, greater personal liability for stockholders, more Democratic trustees to protect local interests, and fewer or no charters for manufacturing firms that would compete against smaller, unlimited-liability partnerships in the production of woolens, machinery, or other items.[52]

The responsibility for promoting these measures fell to the party's key editors: the Eatons of Danville, recent converts from Antimasonry, and Charles Eastman of Woodstock, an erstwhile Jacksonian. They spoke directly to people like themselves, ambitious men of modest origins who had not had as much success as they believed they deserved. They blamed wealthy Whigs for using banks, corporations, and universities to grind so many young men of the region "to dust" and to fashion them into "stirrup-holders and lick-spittles." The proponents of capitalism in the Whig Party were singled out for special scorn, as men who had done violence to the ideals of freedom and equality. Both Eastman and the Eatons attacked the paternalism of "Daddy Fairbanks." Eastman satirically accused William Jarvis of having made "Jarvis Collars" to prevent a "mutiny" among his political "slaves." Drawing on the ideas of the Jacksonians, the Antimasons, and the Workingmen, they accused the well-to-do Whigs of Woodstock, Windsor, and Brattleboro of encouraging speculators to build "a petty woolen factory on every waterfall among the Green Mountains," to the detriment of smaller firms run as common-law partnerships, and of giving railroads unlimited powers that could be used to monopolize commerce or stifle competition. Whigs were accused of loaning bank funds outside the valley, sending profits to out-of-state stockholders, denying credit to political opponents, and discounting notes from other banks – that is, paying those who deposited them only a certain fraction of their face value in specie, on the premise that it cost them money to return the notes to the issuing bank and that it was always possible that the issuing bank would default. Their aim, according to Eastman's *Spirit of the Age*, was to build a monopoly as high as "Huge Olympus," over which young men could never climb.[53]

In the *North Star*, the Eatons made it clear that they had no intention of supporting "the prostrating spirit of radicalism" or of "pandering to the appetites and passions of the poor." Even during the depression, party editors balked at radical measures that would have jeopardized the interests of the wealthy Democrats who backed them. They vowed they would not stand by while "the great *middle class*" was "broken into pieces"; nor would they allow the valley's independent proprietors to "degenerate into serfs and groveling dependents of haughty and purse-proud lords." They tried to appeal to the common man with Jacksonian attacks on privilege and promises of a more modest and equitable American System and rapid territorial expansion and western settlement.[54]

The Democrats spoke powerfully to the frustration and jealousy that had intensfied among ordinary Democrats by the late 1830s. Like the vast majority of the valley's residents, most Democrats had no desire to "level all to a common condition." They only wanted to ensure that the postwar order worked fairly. Gilbert Grant of Windsor, a struggling young lawyer from New Hampshire who had seen firsthand the ways in which Windsor's elite had driven the town's leading Democrats into bankruptcy and had watched a friend conceal his Democratic convictions in order that he might seek the hand of William Jarvis's daughter, believed that the party would give poor, freedom-loving youths like himself an opportunity to stand atop the town's hierarchy someday. Lester Johnson, formerly of Peacham, whence he had departed in haste to avoid bill collectors, denied that he felt any hostility to those more successful than he and claimed that he had curtailed his ambitions after failing at farming. Letters to his Whig creditor reveal, however, that ambition and envy plagued him still. He looked to the Democratic Party to bolster his self-esteem, and dreamed of prostrating the high and mighty Whigs.[55]

Leading Democrats soon realized that their rhetoric had created a whirlwind of discontent among poor and middle-income Vermonters. The continuing pressure of the times and the economic collapse of 1839–42 had led many of the valley's inhabitants, particularly in the countryside, to distrust politicians, colleges, capitalists, and capitalist institutions. Rural people were often suspicious of higher education. Many Democrats believed that colleges dealt in useless knowledge and existed only to confer social status on their graduates. Harriet Hutchinson, the young daughter of a farmer in the rural village of East Braintree, complained in 1844 that some of her neighbors felt "big" or "smart" whenever they received "visits from a college educated person." The prosperous factories scattered in villages throughout the valley, and the families that owned them, were another focal point of popular antipathy. Charles Paine owned a woolen mill in the factory village of Northfield. In 1845, President Polk transferred the post office from the factory village to a store owned by a Democrat in the Center Village, and it fell to Paine's nephew to make the ride to the Center Village to pick up the mail. The people of the Center Village delighted in the Paines' humiliation and mocked young Paine when he rode by. Years later, the memory of their heckling still rankled. "I had to bear the jeers and sneers of the meanest sort of Loco-focos, elated by their triumph over the respectable people by whom they lived, for the factory supported them indirectly." He condemned the villagers for their "petty jealousy of the prosperity at the Factory."[6]

Rank-and-file Democrats seized every opportunity to cut the mighty down to size with humor. In Calais, a Democratic hill town, revelers on Independence Day cheered Joshua M. Dana, a local minstrel, as he recited poems roasting the valley's great politicians and celebrating the egalitarianism, common sense, and decency of ordinary people. That contrasted starkly with sedate Whig celebrations, in which row upon row of successful lawyers, businessmen, and politicians were presented to audiences to bear witness to their collective success. Yet few of these Democratic levelers endorsed the policies of the valley's radical Democrats, who found inspiration in the Workingmen's movement and in the radical Locofoco movement among Democrats in New York, and called for the abolition of chartered corporations and banks, a return to hard currency, and a democratic system of higher education. As rural people, they lacked a tradition of solidarity comparable to that of urban artisans, and were generally ignored by radical journals. Nor could the valley's levelers follow the example of tenant farmers in the landlord-ridden western uplands of the Hudson River Valley, who turned readily to violence when landlords tried to evict them or to collect what they owed. Those people flirted with progressive ideologies during the Anti-Rent Wars of the 1840s, because they felt that they had yet to win the Revolution and to establish an open, democratic society (a feeling reflected in the rioters' decision to dress as Indians on many of the raids, in imitation of the patriots who held the Boston Tea Party). The valley's levelers, because they lived in an area of widespread proprietorship, could not blame their own lack of access to proprietorship on landlords who refused to sell farmland. It was also difficult for them to achieve intellectual independence and to translate their resentment into a political movement capable of realizing their egalitarian vision. Yet many had lost patience with moderate measures. Wealthy Democrats and Democratic editors did all they could to prevent these levelers from trying to transform the party into a progressive insurgency.[57]

The Democrats were as deeply divided on moral issues as on economic ones. Many leading Democrats, like Charles Eastman and the Eatons, were church and temperance society members who wanted to woo respectable citizens, while others, like Martin Flint of Randolph, a founder of the Antimasonic party, were abolitionists who wanted to attract advocates of human equality. Neither goal was easily met, for the Jacksonians had been identified in the minds of many former National Republicans and Antimasons with opposition to abolitionism and to the churchgoing community's initiatives. Democratic reformers tried to "correct" their views by pointing out that the Whig party was dominated by colonizationists and that many important Whigs were guilty of unrespectable conduct, from wine drinking to forcing themselves upon young women who worked in their mills. Democrats also came down hard on the Whigs' "hard cider and log cabin" campaign for William Henry Harrison in 1840.[58]

The reformers faced considerable opposition within the party. Democrats generally supported temperance and common school improvement, opposed slavery, and sympathized with efforts by the church to promote piety and moral seriousness. Half of all Democrats who voted supported local option no-license legislation (Table 7.2). But a number of Democrats privately expressed hatred of "the nigger business in any shape" and thumbed their noses at the valley's near-unanimous opposition to slavery and Indian removal. In Democratic towns like Cabot there were rallies at which the feats of Indian fighters were celebrated and minstrels with blacked faces entertained. Many Democrats also opposed the measures that reformers wanted to use to achieve their ends: anti-license laws, state-mandated improvements in district schools, and abolition of the state militia. Like C. P. Van Ness, a long-standing colonizationist, they resented the insults leveled at them by abolitionists and the efforts by leading Whigs, themselves largely colonizationist, to put them on the moral defensive. Pressure to improve the moral tone of the valley created angry resistance. Editor Edwin Church of Fayetteville printed inflammatory stories about female gossips and busybodies who plagued their innocent husbands and were blind to their own faults. Mary

Trask sympathized with the temperance movement, but not the no-license movement. She wrote her brother that "as soon as they began to use *compulsion* I flew off the handle and agreed that I would have no part or lot in the matter.... I'll be coaxed but I *won't* be *drived*." Trask promised to share a stiff drink with her brother when he next visited.[59]

Democratic political leaders had no choice but to follow the old Jacksonian course. They supported religious and moral movements only if they were not connected with politics, if they were "non-coercive" and did not impugn the decent men and women who declined to support them. Thus for the most part they opposed state-wide anti-license laws, abolitionist attacks on slaveholders, state-mandated improvements in district schools, and the abolition of the state militia, even though the great majority of Democrats shared the moral concerns of those who supported these causes. The party's position prompted many abolitionists and teetotalers to quit the party by the early 1840s, but leading Democrats patiently stood by the voluntarism, informality, and relative openness of former years and allowed others to see what they wished in Democracy.

That position did not satisfy the valley's most discontented citizens, many of whom by the late 1830s had come to detest churches, temperance societies, and the gospel of respectability. The Democrats found their most zealous partisans among failing young family men, wayward wage earners, and middle-aged eccentrics who did not belong to churches or reform societies and who found themselves at odds with or on the fringes of the respectable community. They were the real outsiders in town life; they had no power, no resources, and no prestige. They increased in numbers and in bitterness, caught between an economy that made it harder to get ahead and a society that impugned the moral worth of those who failed. Many, like Lester Johnson, the unsuccessful farmer from Peacham, complained that their misfortunes stemmed from persecution by their neighbors. Others defiantly flouted the standards of respectability. Ira Hoffman, a young farm laborer from the Caledonia County hill town of Sutton, who was destined for a migratory existence, used profane language and harbored an untoward hostility toward his employer, whom he described as "meaner than cat piss." He relished opportunities to scoff at community leaders and claimed to have bested them all in a local lyceum debate about the Democratic Party's position on Texas. His manner was calculated to frustrate and embarrass the respectable citizenry, who disliked crude speech and insolence, especially from a penniless upstart who enjoyed parading down Main Street in a fancy satin vest.[60]

Few Democrats were as full of hatred for the respectable community as Willard Stevens of Barnet, the eccentric, embittered brother of Henry

Stevens, who by 1837 had lost his property and been deserted by his wife. In the Democratic Party Stevens found a medium through which he could vent his spleen against everything he had come to hate, including Christianity, revivalism, evangelical societies, and the majority of institutions supported by "respectable" society. He was pleased that Democrats maintained a rigid separation between church and state and that Martin Van Buren had opposed the most recent efforts by Christians to rewrite the Constitution in accordance with the teachings of Christ. America's government had to be protected against Christians and Whigs, the self-righteous oppressors. Predictably enough, given his experience with marriage, Stevens had also turned against women, whom he considered agents of respectable society. His attitude toward them and toward religion was expressed in diatribes against Jesus' mother Mary, whom he described as a "whore" who gave birth to a "bastard."[61]

Stevens's distaste for religion and the respectable community was not unique. The unsuccessful and the unregenerate made themselves at home in the Democratic Party and urged their moral and spiritual views upon it. Stevens himself sent letters of advice to President Van Buren and former President Andrew Jackson every month. These outsiders seldom had the confidence or the connections to work effectively toward transforming the Democratic Party into a progressive insurgency against the revival and against the campaign toward a modified order in town life. Their presence merely exacerbated divisions within the Democratic Party and embarrassed leading Democrats, who found it difficult to placate them without alienating ordinary Vermonters.

The growing divisions among the valley's inhabitants over the economy, the revival, and the modified order in town life clearly threatened the unity and the survival of both the Whig and Democratic parties. The great majority of Vermonters, including party editors and orators, expressed dissatisfaction with the equivocations and electioneering tricks of both parties. They were dismayed at the kinds of zealots both had attracted, and at the violence of their competition, which to one D. Crane of Sharon presaged the struggle between "Gog and Magog."[62] Yet between 1836 and 1844 nearly everyone took sides. Turnout was strong at party conventions and over 70 percent of the electorate went to the polls in the early 1840s. In addition, diaries, letters, and voting returns (which showed steady patterns of party support at the town level from election to election) revealed an increasingly strong and stable identification with parties among both men and women.[63]

The parties' success stemmed in part from their ability to dramatize their conflict with intensive electioneering. They staged ever more imposing political rallies, sent cadres of organizers into every neighborhood, and inundated the valley with propaganda. More important, however, both parties were able to persuade voters of the danger posed by the minorities within their opponents' camp. Thus the Democrats explicitly attacked Whigs like Henry Stevens, while Whig propaganda focused on men like Stevens's younger brother Willard, who came to fulfill the popular picture of a Democrat that Henry had drawn years before in a poem entitled "Character of a Democrat."

> A Democrat's picture is easy to draw.
> He can't bear to obey, but will govern the law;
> His manners unsocial, his temper unkind,
> He's a rebel in conduct a Tyrant in mind.
> He is envious of those who have riches and power;
> Discontented, malignant implacable sour;
> Never happy himself he would wish to destroy
> The comforts and blessings which others enjoy.[64]

Party leaders also attracted voters by giving a new urgency to the "reformist" vision of history that had been articulated by the Jacksonians, the National Republicans, and the Antimasons. Neither the Whigs nor the Democrats offered much hope that the present "crisis" would soon end; indeed, both parties described the present as a time of perpetual crisis and danger. Both parties allowed the once potent hobgoblins of conspiracy and moral declension to sink back into their graves, making it clear that they intended to struggle openly for their views, not covertly, and that they held their adversaries, not a general moral decline, responsible for the valley's moral problems. Still, both parties gave their followers some reason to hope, just as they had in the early 1830s, by promising a future that would bring them even greater economic satisfactions than the 1820s, a future in which party conflict would be eliminated and Christian values would triumph.[65]

Politics in the valley became temporarily stable as Whigs and Democrats exploited new and long-standing social conflicts, and voters voted consistently, although as much against groups they feared as for a particular party. People tended to divide into Whigs and Democrats on the basis of the degree to which they were included or estranged from the mainstream in social and economic life. The Democratic Party, like the Jacksonians, was most attractive to voters who had an antipathy to the centers of wealth and power in the valley and who were themselves poorly positioned to capitalize on postwar economic growth. The Democrats also appealed to people who were reluctant to grant the government power over the valley's moral and spiritual life. They won the votes of roughly two-fifths of the members of egalitarian denominations and of nonmembers in areas first settled by moderates and Old Lights, and did

Table 7.11. Social, Religious, and Political Status of Party Voters, 1836-1844[a]

	National Republicans, 1834	Jacksonians, 1834	Antimasons, 1834	Nonvoters, 1834	R^2
Whigs, 1836-44[b]	.72 (.07)	.03 (.04)	.54 (.03)	.36 (.03)	.54
Democrats, 1836-44	.01 (.07)	.90 (.04)	.27 (.04)	.25 (.04)	.63
Nonvoters, 1836-44	.27 (.07)	.07 (.04)	.18 (.03)	.40 (.03)	.20

	Liberals, Calvinists[c]	Non-Calvinist evangelicals	New Light area nonmembers, Universalists[c]	Moderate and Old Light area nonmembers, Universalists[c]	Percentage in commerce and manu-facturing[d]	R^2
Whigs, 1836-44	.61 (.07)	.35 (.08)	.44 (.03)	.32 (.02)	.04 (.12)	.24
Democrats, 1836-44	.06 (.06)	.44 (.07)	.24 (.03)	.48 (.02)	-.06 (.10)	.55
Nonvoters, 1836-44	.34 (.05)	.21 (.06)	.32 (.03)	.21 (.02)	.02 (.09)	.20

[a] Standard errors of the coefficients are in parentheses. On statistical methods, see Appendix D. The estimates are calculated from the median proportions of Whigs, Democrats, and nonvoters in each town between 1836 and 1844.
[b] The slightly positive correlation between the Whig vote and per capita taxation and the proportion of males age sixteen and older engaged in commerce and manufacturing indicates perhaps a greater tendency of Whigs and Democrats to differ along economic lines than the members of previous parties. The inclusion of these variables in the equations, however, does not increase the precision of the estimates substantially or alter the pattern of crossovers between parties.
[c] Separate estimates of the proportions for religious liberals and Universalists are unstable because few towns had liberal churches and because the proportion of Universalists in each town must be estimated by a step variable. The inclusion of these denominations in the categories above causes the least instability in the estimates and does not alter other proportions substantially. The unstable estimates for religious liberals are close to those for Calvinists. The unstable estimates for Universalists are close to those for non-Calvinist evangelicals.
[d] The proportion of males age sixteen and older engaged in commerce and manufacturing ranged from 0.00 to 0.43, with a median of 0.12.

slightly better among all voters in poorer towns and in the countryside (Table 7.11). The evidence on political activists in towns studied intensively confirms this pattern, with the Democrats doing well among nonmembers and the members of egalitarian denominations, among subsistence farmers, and among businessmen, professionals, and master craftsmen in the countryside. They won few votes among Calvinists and religious liberals, and only a fifth of the votes of nonmembers in areas first settled by New Lights; and they found few supporters among commercial farmers or among businessmen, professionals, and master crafts-

Table 7.12. Religious Status
of Political Activists, 1835-1850: All Towns[a]

N's	Democrats	Whigs
Congregationalists	13	49
Baptists	8	14
Episcopalians/Unitarians	15	55
Associate Presbyterians[b]	5	3
Reformed Presbyterians[b]	2	2
Methodists/Freewill Baptists/Christians	12	10
Universalists	32	12
Nonmembers	112	82
N =	199	227

[a] Few political activists can be identified after 1847, when newspapers stopped printing the names of party leaders in each town on a regular basis.
[b] The aggregate data from all towns distort the meaning of the data on Associate and Reformed Presbyterians. They came exclusively from Barnet and Ryegate, where only 37 percent of all political activists identified were Whigs, as opposed to 53 percent in all towns.

men in the commercial and manufacturing villages in Windsor, Woodstock, and St. Johnsbury (Tables 7.12 to 7.14).

In contrast, the Whigs did well among voters in wealthy towns and in commercial and manufacturing centers and won roughly three-fifths of the votes of Calvinists and religious liberals and two-fifths of the votes of nonmembers in areas first settled by New Lights. They received only one-third of the votes of other nonmembers and members of egalitarian denominations (Table 7.11). Like the National Republicans, they appealed primarily to voters who looked favorably upon postwar economic development, who belonged to religious denominations associated with larger towns and with social prestige and who were less reluctant to use state power to improve public morals.

The parties played upon critical divisions like those among the various denominations, those between the descendants of the supporters and the opponents of Vermont's revolution, and those between rural people and people who lived in the centers of wealth and power, as well as divisions that had emerged since 1815 between "insiders" and "outsiders" as economic equality and opportunities for self-employment declined.[66] The parties also capitalized upon more recent divisions between the opponents and proponents of the great revival and the various reform movements of the 1830s. The lines that divided Whig activists from Democratic activists in Windsor and Woodstock were evidently drawn in the early 1830s, since they were most deeply divided in their attitudes toward

Table 7.13. Social and Religious Status of Political Activists,
1835-1850: Marketing and Manufacturing Towns*a*

N's	Democrats	Whigs
Marketing/professions	20	42
Manufacturing	23	44
Agriculture	17	18
Unknown	22	9
Nonproprietors	35	31
Upper decile of wealth	5	17
N =	82	113
Church members	40	81
Nonmembers	42	32
Pro-temperance	20	21
Anti-removal	5	22
Antislavery*b*	-	-
Sabbatarians	0	6
Anti-Sabbatarians	13	4
Abolitionists	1	0
Agricultural society	6	4
Anti-Texas	2	2
Educational reform	0	3
Pro-license	3	4
Jacksonians	2	1
Antimasons	3	5
Workingmen	3	3
National Republicans	10	22

a The data are from Windsor and Woodstock. Data on wealth are available only for Windsor, where 69 percent of all the political activists identified were Whigs.
b Windsor and Woodstock did not forward antislavery petitions.

Sabbatarianism, Indian removal, and the churches. All activists who had been Sabbatarians became Whigs, while three-fourths of the anti-Sabbatarians became Democrats. Twenty-two percent of the Whig activists had signed petitions against Indian removal in 1830 to uphold "Christian" standards of leadership, whereas only 5 percent of the Democrats had. Whig activists were more likely than Democrats to have been church members by a margin of three-fourths to one-half.

Clearly, the campaign to unify and mobilize the churchgoing community in a nonpartisan defense of the new order ultimately polarized people in Windsor and Woodstock in ways that manifested themselves most clearly in politics after 1835. Yet those divisions were evidently so firmly set by 1831 that the vital reform movements of the mid-1830s –

Table 7.14. Social and Religious Status
of Political Activists, 1835-1850: Agricultural Towns

N's	Democrats	Whigs
Marketing/professions	16	24
Manufacturing	25	17
Agriculture	56	60
Unknown	7	4
Nonproprietors	31	27
Upper decile of wealth	17	31
$N^a =$	104	105
Church members	45	63
Nonmembers	72	51
Pro-temperance	27	73
Anti-removal	13	17
Antislavery	17	13
Sabbatarians	9	10
Anti-Sabbatarians	1	0
Abolitionists	2	11
Agricultural society	3	15
Anti-Texas	7	23
Educational reform	0	3
Pro-license	2	13
Jacksonians	0	0
Antimasons	13	18
National Republicans	13	19
$N^b =$	117	114

a Ryegate is not included.
b Ryegate is included.

abolition and temperance – did not divide party activists significantly. Fears of disorder and of popular insurgency were by then so widespread among prominent citizens in these marketing and manufacturing towns that few in either party opposed temperance or favored immediate abolition. In fact, under Charles Eastman's leadership, Democrats in Woodstock established their own temperance society in the early 1840s and helped organize the local agricultural society to prove that Democrats were hostile neither to enterprise nor to morality, but only to crusading morality and religion in politics (Table 7.13).[67]

The controversies of 1830–31 did not polarize political loyalties in agricultural towns, which had been predominantly Antimasonic, in lasting ways. The campaign by the churchgoing community to save the social order through revivals and reform won widespread support in the general population and thus did not provoke anti-Sabbatarian, anticlerical, or pro-Jackson responses. Political divisions after 1835 reflected that fact: Church members, Sabbatarians, and opponents of Indian removal and slavery in the District of Columbia were almost as likely to be Democrats as Whigs (Table 7.14). Activists in the two parties had much in common on these issues.

Rural political activists were polarized instead over the issues of the mid-1830s: temperance and abolition. Anxiety over inequality and public morals became intense in rural communities by the late 1830s, but the inhabitants of those towns did not agree on ways of resolving these problems. The Whigs captured the support of most political activists who thought the solution lay in no-license laws, agricultural societies, and dedication to immediate abolition, while the Democrats won the allegiance of most activists who believed that immorality and inequality would disappear if common people had equal opportunity in the valley (Table 7.14). Divisions over reform appeared only after the demise of Antimasonry, which the people of these communities believed had offered the best hope of solving these problems.

It is important to emphasize that party loyalty was not a simple matter. Many Democrats were church members and temperance advocates or inhabitants of struggling marketing and manufacturing towns like Danville and Montpelier, just as many Whigs were nonmembers or inhabitants of hill towns who entrusted their fate to Whig economic schemes.[68] Patterns of political loyalty were complex, for people were trying to express a multitude of diverse concerns through only two parties.

The Whigs prevailed in every gubernatorial election from 1836 through 1844, though by an average margin of only 10 percent of all votes cast. They won because they received two Antimasonic votes for every one received by the Democrats (Table 7.11). The party's leaders had been able to persuade former Antimasons that they were the true defenders of egalitarian and communitarian values. Their strongest supporters, Calvinists and nonmembers in areas first settled by New Lights, were half again as likely as other nonmembers and members of egalitarian denominations not to vote, primarily because of their confidence in Whig victory, which gave them occasion to reveal the valley's continuing disdain for partisan conflict and compromise. (It had been the members of egalitarian denominations – the Antimasons' strongest supporters – who had voted least often in the mid-1830s, for the same reasons.)[69] But the Whigs won enough support among Calvinists and nonmembers in New Light towns to carry both former Federalist and former Republican strongholds in the New Light region, which overcame the advantage that the Democrats had won in other regions by surpassing the Whigs' strength in former Republican strongholds (Table 5.3). Vermont's revolutionary and New Light heritage thus kept the state in the Whig column, although the Democrats contested all but a handful of elections closely.

The antagonisms among the valley's inhabitants appeared too deep for political reconciliation. The prospect of perpetual strife did not distress professional politicians and journalists, like Cornelius Van Ness, Nahum Haskell, or Charles Eastman. Their livelihoods depended on party conflict, and they believed that the rivalry between the Whigs and Democrats improved the quality of government, giving voters an opportunity to decide important public issues and making it easier for them to weed out corrupt public officials. With the two parties continually vying for power, no one faction – moral, spiritual, or economic – could dominate government. In 1837, Joshua Dana, a popular rhymester from Calais, extolled the virtues of party conflict for just these reasons. In an election day ballad, he sang about an infidel miller who was running for office against a religious zealot, about adversaries in a local road-building controversy who were struggling openly for control of the town council, and about gubernatorial candidates who were at daggers drawn over the banking question. In Dana's opinion, these contests guaranteed that extremists would never control the government and that candidates, once elected, would do what they had promised, for "if they do not it is certain the Door they'll be shown."[70]

The valley's voters were amused by Dana's caricatures, but few really shared his sanguine attitude toward party conflict. For the most part voters still had common values and aspirations, and because of their unique character and political heritage they were dissatisfied with party politics. They believed that political parties fostered corruption and tyranny and subverted the popular will by making it difficult for citizens to discover their common interests. For a brief period, however, politics in the valley took on the aspect of politics elsewhere in America, with interest ranged against interest and partisanship the order of the day.[71]

Most people felt that all hope of stability, unity, and peace had been lost, but party conflict actually safeguarded the legitimacy of propertied men and the popularity of their economic schemes and preserved the stability of the political order by diverting existing social divisions into safe channels. Pursuing common ends in different but overlapping ways, the parties diverged enough to attract distinctive constituencies and to give people on opposite sides of the valley's social divisions hope of victory and a feeling that others shared their views and their plight, yet ensured that extreme solutions to the valley's moral and economic problems would not prevail. The parties were able to organize antagonistic geographical, economic, religious, and moral groups into two purposeful crusades that sustained the valley's faith in reform and development and won the loyal support of the great majority of citizens. At the same time, the parties enabled wealthy people and wealthy communities to maintain their hold on state and local offices.[72]

The modified order that appeared in town life and politics in the late 1830s and early 1840s did not reproduce the social and political equilibrium of the postwar order. It did not bring peace to the valley, nor did it prevent minorities — capitalists, freethinkers, professional politicians — from embracing liberal visions of society. Still, the vast majority of the valley's inhabitants stood by the ideals of their revolutionary forebears and did not embrace individualism, pluralism, capitalism, or partisanship. They were divided, however, over how best to pursue their enduring ideals. In politics, some were Whigs and some Democrats. In town life, some advocated that new precautions be taken to protect their families and communities against moral dangers, whereas others stood by older, more informal measures. These debates kept the valley in an uproar and offered people with liberal views occasion to press their arguments. Yet through these debates and the movements they brought forth, the valley's inhabitants reshaped their social and political order and thus contained, in ways they could neither foresee nor fully understand, the liberal forces working to change their society.

8

Boosterism, sentiment, free soil, and the preservation of a Christian, reformed republic

The modified order in town life and politics addressed the concerns of the valley's inhabitants in concrete ways, but it failed to restore the sense of purpose, the prestige, and the influence that were theirs when they stood as revolutionary frontiersmen in the vanguard of civilization. The valley remained incapable of providing sufficient opportunities for its inhabitants. Because of the disappointments of the revival, the churches had lost their early vigor, and the political parties proved unable to defend the valley's interests in national debates on the economy and the western territories, upon whose outcome the valley's fate seemed increasingly to depend. Its citizens were fated to be searching still for solutions to their problems at midcentury. Yet few Vermonters surrendered their dreams of economic independence and prosperity, and despite the failure of the modified order to recapture the social harmony and unity of purpose that characterized the 1820s, most of them believed that the new spirit of boosterism, the awakening of sentimental piety, and the campaign for free soil could reconcile the valley's divided inhabitants and revive their dedication to a Christian, reformed republic.

Economy and society

Charles Merrifield, editor of the *Vermont Journal*, complained in an editorial in 1844 that a "mental sleep" had enveloped the once bustling town of Windsor and that the town was in danger of becoming one of those places that time forgot. He insisted that Windsor was still "thriving and prosperous" and boasted of its hunting and trout fishing and its wholesome young people, but he knew that something was amiss and that if Windsor wanted to maintain its prosperity its citizens would have to come up with some bold new enterprise "to save our credit."[1]

Merrifield's editorial marked the arrival of a new spirit in the valley. Boosterism was not simply idle boasting about the valley's economic prospects or its quality of life. Nor was it merely a collection of promotional schemes to encourage tourism, immigration, and outside investment. It was a critical spirit that tried to identify the valley's problems and worked feverishly to surmount them.

Boosters were determined to extricate the valley from the economic doldrums and restore people's confidence in the future, but they differed from the postwar proponents of growth. Both groups focused on the economy and measured progress in quantitative terms, but boosters wanted everything to grow – industry, churches, schools, community spirit – and they left no stone unturned in their effort to arouse interest in their ideas and to bring communities together. Merrifield exhorted the Windsorites to action. "Let something be done," he wrote, "a dinner – a picnic – a dance – a temperance jubilee – ... anything."[2]

Unlike the postwar proponents of growth, boosters did not ask people to sanction the developmental schemes of entrepreneurs, financiers, and commercial farmers. Instead, they asked people to participate in those schemes. In Windsor, the sponsors of a project to construct a dam to provide water power for manufacturing firms solicited contributions from every proprietor. In Ryegate, Barnet, and St. Johnsbury, proponents of a railroad that would enable farmers and shopkeepers to ship goods overland cheaply to Boston and Montreal did likewise. The organizers of insurance companies and mutual savings societies (which paid lower dividends and interest rates than banks but promised greater security and financial stability) sought members throughout the valley, as did the large landowners who in 1849 organized a wool-marketing cooperative at White River Junction to meet the challenge of low-priced western wool.[3]

Boosters encouraged people to invest in projects that promised little or no direct profit and to forgo promising economic opportunities in more prosperous communities elsewhere, in hopes that their sacrifices would enable their communities to prosper. By 1845, the boosters' campaign for improvement had turned into a crusade. When the valley's entrepreneurs and financiers undertook the construction of railroads throughout the state, they staged public meetings everywhere, encouraging people to buy stock, and labored tirelessly to win over the doubtful and the apathetic. Resistance was not unknown, particularly in towns not served by proposed lines and in Barnet and Ryegate. There, according to railway agent James Gilchrist, the Scots were either too stingy or too cautious to invest in the railroads, although they were eager to bid for railroad construction and supply contracts. Railroad promoters succeeded in persuading scores of farmers and shopkeepers who lived near prospective routes to purchase railroad stock. The supporters of Windsor's mill dam persuaded ninety-five men, or half of the town's independent proprietors, including every important Whig and Democratic leader, to buy stock, even though few stood to profit directly from the dam's construction.[4]

Proponents of capitalism, like the editor of the *School Journal and Agriculturalist*, supported boosterism enthusiastically and played freely on fears of economic decline to win local financing for expensive enterprises and institutions that the state would not support with taxes or preferential legislation. They traded on the valley's sense of inferiority to the cities of southern New England and promoted a vision of the valley's largest towns as future urban centers. They did not speak for the great majority of boosters, and their grand talk alienated some people. In poor agricultural communities and in bypassed market towns like Danville, where previous corporate ventures had failed, people scoffed at expensive, visionary schemes for economic and community development. Some alleged that boosterism was just another capitalist plot against their property and independence.[5]

The supporters of boosterism never won the widespread approval the postwar proponents of growth had and were never as unified, either. Yet their frank talk about the valley's problems, its economic decline, and its increasing poverty eventually won the support of many people who had lost faith in the roseate postwar vision of growth. Boosters persuaded people that they only wanted to preserve the character of the valley's economy and communities, not to transform it, and they were quick to reassure the valley that they wanted to retain the virtues of small town and rural life and to keep out the evils of urban and industrial life. They sponsored drives in St. Johnsbury and other major communities to improve housing, clean streets, plant shade trees, and support edifying forms of recreation, like museums and lyceums.[6]

Boosterism could not solve the valley's economic problems, but it did help the valley's inhabitants take advantage of the national economic revival that began in 1843. Boosters instigated major improvements in finance, industry, and agriculture. Private banks and mutual societies improved credit. Factories produced a growing volume of woolens, paper goods, and machinery for the national market. Forty-five of these firms employed ten or more men and women by 1850. Among them were the textile works at Royalton, which employed 326 men and women, and the Kendall and Lawrence armory of Windsor, whose 155 employees produced rail cars, metalworking machines, and guns for the army. Smaller firms sold patented pumps, plows, lathes, scythes, and other machined devices. These goods could now be transported by rail, for by 1850 rail lines had been laid along the river as far north as St. Johnsbury and inland to Montpelier and Lake Champlain.[7]

Growing urban demand for agricultural products led farmers to step up production of cheese and butter (Vermont led the nation in per capita production of those foodstuffs); to increase production of root crops, soil-enriching legumes, hay and oats; and to adopt all kinds of new agricultural machinery, from hay rakes to threshers. Farmers also gave increased support to agricultural societies, through which they shared information and techniques, and to publications and prizes to promote scientific breeding of stock and seed.[8]

These developments brought particular prosperity to those best suited to capitalize upon them: to commercial farmers on good land and to financiers and entrepreneurs in marketing and manufacturing centers with regular rail service. Their enhanced power over production and exchange allowed them to reap the benefits of recovery and expansion. A mania for the latest consumer items took hold in the valley, especially in Windsor, Woodstock, and Brattleboro, where leading citizens had long identified with Boston and maintained a style that set them apart from other people in the valley. Pianos, organs, greeting cards, photographs, fine furniture, and housewares began to appear in many homes. Some of these things were purchased directly from Boston merchants, whose ads began to appear in local papers after 1845. Music lessons, concerts, and excursions to the city or local resorts became fashionable.[9]

Middle-income families also became more prosperous, and although they still spent most of their income on their shops and farms and on churches and schools, they set their sights on having some of the finer things of life. Rosamond Heaton, of a farm family in Cabot, asked her brother in Montpelier to help her furnish her new home. She wanted a looking glass "as good ... as you think I can afford to have in my parlour," a lamp "like Miriam's," clear white crockery ("unless you can get something more fashionable that you think I should like better"), and a china tea service. Farm families bought inexpensive, ready-made chairs to prepare their parlors for polite company. Musical instruments and music lessons became commonplace among middle-income people, and the cost of musical training or entertainments was borne without much thought. Joseph Knight, a Corinth farmer with an average acreage, paid to send his children to church-sponsored singing meets by rail.[10] That such expenditures became quite ordinary shows that some families weathered the recession successfully and were prospering as commodity prices rose.

The spending patterns of some middle-income families had changed considerably by the late 1840s. Sales of alcoholic beverages plummeted to insignificance by 1850, whereas corn-stalk dust brooms, fine soaps, and commercially produced washboards and clothespins sold briskly. Families bought whale oil in order to read by lamplight.[11] This "virtuous materialism" was a reflection of a populace that wanted to be cleaner, better educated, and more temperate. Even the seemingly frivolous expenditures on parlor furniture and music lessons furthered the drift toward respectability. Musical entertainments were an alternative to the inducements of tavern society, and one that men and women could enjoy together.

Like the wealthy and the middle classes, people who worked for wages in the machinery factories and woolen mills also fared well. Men who manufactured machined goods or repaired railroad equipment received an average of $40 per month, far outstripping, even with the inclusion of room and board, the $12 per month farm laborers received. Although there were marked differences in pay according to gender, skill, and seniority, men and women who worked in the mills also received relatively good wages by 1850: roughly $30 and $16 per month, respectively.[12]

The effect of prosperity on these workers remains unclear. They left few letters, and records do not differentiate them from others who worked for wages. Many young women undoubtedly had control over their earnings. Some won independence from household chores by boarding in mill villages and could explore new possibilities, as did young women who went to mills in southern New England. But it is likely that women who worked close to home or stayed at home remained part of the family economy. One woman who worked in a mill in Woodstock in 1841 had to go home on weekends to the neighboring town of Bridgewater to help her sick mother with the "washing, ironing, etc." She resented her double work load and felt that women who trekked to the mills of southern New England got away with something. When her sister ran off to Massachusetts, leaving her "entirely alone with all the work to do," she was furious.[13]

As for male factory workers, their tremendous advantage in earnings often enabled them to buy their own shops or farms. If they remained employees, their wages still provided their families with a comfortable living. Did they then surrender dreams of self-employment? The records through 1850 make it impossible to tell, although the few wage workers in St. Johnsbury and Windsor who listed themselves as machinists, mechanics, or moulders and may have been the more skilled operatives at the major plants and mills were older than other laborers and more likely to have been homeowners and household heads. Perhaps they had settled into lifelong employment, as had some before them who took their families to the Lowell mills. They may have had no taste for life as farmers or shopkeepers and may have preferred to focus their ambitions on their children and to spend discretionary income on household goods or entertainment: perhaps even in the ten-pin alleys that opened in the valley's factory towns in the 1840s. Public schools in Windsor, Woodstock, St. Johnsbury, and Brattleboro, the towns with the most factory workers, received widespread support, and there was no resistance in those towns to plans for grading the schools and introducing advanced courses. Factory workers put forward no opposition to entrepreneurial leadership, either. There were no strikes in the valley through 1850.[14]

Only 3 percent of men and women aged sixteen and over were factory or railroad workers in 1850, however. For men and women in the non-agricultural sphere who were not factory or railroad workers, earnings were inferior and prospects poor. Far more women were poorly paid domestics, teachers, or needle workers than factory workers. Craftsmen and day laborers also did poorly. Unskilled labor wages in the valley reflected the influx of Irish and Canadian migrant workers eager for work. Laborers earned roughly $20 per month without room and board, and rental costs in crowded marketing and manufacturing towns steadily increased.

Those who aspired to proprietorship as merchants and needle tradesmen faced a difficult future. Both occupations had declined in the hinterland, because merchants in railroad and shire towns now had a clearer edge in cost and selection and because ready-made clothing, shoes, and hats produced in southern New England were flooding local markets. The production by households and outworkers of newly popular consumer goods – like brooms, palm-leaf hats, and chairs – opened some new jobs, but these industries were centered in towns like Fitzwilliam, New Hampshire, or Hadley, Massachusetts, closer to the demographic center of New England and its trade network. As was already the case in farming and other small crafts, there remained in these occupations a fixed number of very costly proprietorships.[15]

Indeed, the maturation of the economy after 1835 created few new opportunities for men who aspired to proprietorship. Martin Van Buren Townsend, who found a poor-paying, unskilled job in a wire mill just across the Massachusetts border, still believed that "an industrious and economical person can do well anywhere" and that his brothers were "destined to be independent." For him, however, there was little hope. "The future always looks dark," he wrote. "Perhaps the fault is in myself." Joseph Stevens, who left his family with relatives in Connecticut and worked up and down the valley as a copperas miner from 1836 through 1850, was similarly frustrated. He could save little from his salary of $16 per month or from his off-season earnings as a wood cutter. He worked from an hour past sunup till seven at night, most of the time in the "swamp" at the bottom of the open pits. By 1849 he had had his fill of copperas mines and rooming houses, and after putting his son out to work "where he can earn his living," he began bargaining with his siblings to buy their shares of the family homestead on credit.[16]

Fear of dependence and the lure of great gain spurred men of ingenuity in the valley to invent new tools, machines, and weaponry and triggered a mania for get-rich-quick schemes. A few inventors were motivated by genteel curiosity, as was George Paine of Randolph, a wealthy landowner who spent his leisure time devising a pump to irrigate his garden, but most were searching for independence and security for their families and were willing to go to great lengths to achieve their ends. E. F. English of Hartland, who invented new dental instruments and a machine to attach boot heels more effectively, left home for Milford, Massachusetts, where he had been promised support from the firm of Godfrey and Underwood. He was dissatisfied with his employers, and at the urging of his wife, who was afraid that his employers were secretly using his machines "in some other part of the country," he returned to the valley in 1852. Eventually he succeeded with his inventions, setting up business with an in-law in Hartland and adding to his list of successful inventions photographic equipment, a hydraulic cement for underground water pipes, and improved steam engines. English was typical of a growing number of valley men who traversed the country to work on and improve machines for others, so that they might one day return and build their own plants at home. These men brought good-paying jobs to the valley. Yet they lessened for others the chance for the self-employment they had single-mindedly pursued for themselves.[17]

Of course, men with such skills and interests had an advantage over the great majority of wage workers in the valley, who were also taking risks and "thinking big" so that they might someday lead independent lives. William Wilson, who with his brothers Edward and Darwin left home in Lyndon upon the early death of his parents, was swept up in the migration toward the great cities of the coast, where he worked as a seaman and a globe maker. His dream in 1844 was to write a great narrative of his adventures at sea, and to that end, he signed on for a whaling voyage of four years. He and his brothers felt considerable guilt over leaving their sister to grow up with relatives in Lyndon, and he hoped that in the end they would be reunited at home. In 1850 the brothers were still locked in poor jobs, however, and had not seen their sister. Darwin remained lighthearted, perhaps because he occasionally vented his spleen by writing articles for Democratic newspapers. He consulted a phrenologist to see if his future held better things and was told he would not set a "river afire" and would never be president, but that he had the stuff in him "to do considerable" if he wanted and would become president of something some day.[18]

The Wilsons' sister Lucy did better. She went to Lowell to work in the mills and met and married another operative. With their accumulated savings they returned to Lyndon and opened a shop. Again, the industrial economy and willing relatives were the keys to success.

The Wilson brothers were not singular in their misfortunes or their lofty ambitions. They were like thousands of other hard-pressed young Vermonters, many of whom raced off to the gold fields of California in 1849 to get rich. Some organized companies to secure their passage west; others, like William Henry Harrison Hall of Chelsea, who at age twenty-six had tired of trying to pay off his parents' farm by teaching school, simply went off alone in search of excitement and cash to clear family debts. Their behavior certainly showed enterprise and the willingness to take risks that was crucial to success in a capitalist society, but it also showed, as the Reverend John Dudley of Windsor recognized, that they had lost faith in the patient, steady path to proprietorship their forebears had known in the valley and that they entertained "enchanted" pipe dreams out of desperation.[19] Vermonters had not fled in such numbers to the gold fields of Georgia in 1828. They were moved now by more than just a general desire for wealth, by more than the lure of the city, the sea, and the West.

The erosion of proprietorship opportunities also meant a further increase in the number of propertyless wage earners. Black people found themselves edged almost completely out of the economy, now that needy whites coveted the menial jobs into which they had been shunted. There were, however, other reasons why the valley's black population dropped from 329 in 1830 to only 192 in 1850. It was not easy to live in a sea of white Vermonters who perceived Afro-Americans largely in symbolic terms. It was true that black people were often the objects of kindness, when principles of liberty, equality, and Christian fellowship were involved, and that white Vermonters had on occasion since the 1820s sheltered fugitives from slave catchers and given them small plots of land. White people were often fond of dutiful, loyal black servants and charmed by the distinctive spirituals they sang. They opened their churches to black people, and a number of female servants and an occasional man of substance, like John Fitch, Windsor's premiere confectioner and barber, joined. The Methodists admitted a young black woman to their seminary in Newbury in 1842 and allowed her to room with a white student, as proof of their commitment to abolition.[20]

However, much of this interest was paternal or designed to make a point, and it was far overshadowed by the malicious attentions of other white Vermonters. Black servants were often harassed and abused; whenever they failed to please their employers, they were told that they were exhibiting the faults of their race. For the most part, they were not full-fledged members of their communities. Farmers who had lived and worked successfully in one town for decades, like Peter Nassau of Pomfret, were forced to mortgage their property to secure small loans for which most unpropertied whites would have been trusted. Black men generally did not join churches. The sudden intrusion of an alien form of evangelical religion into their lives during revivals probably created resentment, and it would have been natural for them to have mistrusted the requirement of public professions of faith, which would have forced them to humble themselves publicly before the white community. Blacks were also the butt of newly popular minstrel shows, and on occasion were the objects of violent racism. In 1835 a duly constituted posse of 500 men destroyed an academy in Canaan, New Hampshire, that dared enroll black students. Vermont's first racist law, passed in 1837, prohibited blacks from serving as militia officers, because they were perceived as incapable of conducting orderly trainings and as unworthy of having the power of life and death over white troops.[21] Black people held on in the face of hostility and declining opportunity only in towns of old wealth like Windsor and Woodstock, where the elite supported a black servant caste and where some former servants had prospered enough to create black communities of eight or ten families with a modicum of independence and had the courage and ability to speak out in public meetings. Elsewhere, most gave up trying to make it alone and joined the black migration to the cities.

The erosion of proprietorship opportunities forced the poorest, most recent migrants in the valley – Irish and French Canadian Catholics – almost wholly into the ranks of workers, where they joined black men and women in laboring and service jobs. Only one of the twenty French Canadians listed on the census rolls in 1850 in the towns studied intensively was a proprietor, and only two of the 297 Irishmen. Held back by terrible poverty, by educational systems in Ireland and Canada that had left more than half of them illiterate, and by linguistic barriers, the roughly 4,000 to 5,000 Catholics in the valley – many of them young men – stood little chance of success. Most led an itinerant existence, moving with the seasons to work on farms or railroads. Most lived in rude, jerry-built shanties on their employers' property for the duration of their service to that employer, because there was not enough housing for wage workers in the valley and many native employers were reluctant to bring these aliens into their homes.[22]

These workers, and the poverty and lack of opportunity that came to be associated with them, encouraged the valley's more prosperous citizens, especially those who lived near or employed the growing body of wage workers, to perceive their society increasingly in class and ethnic terms. Propertyless wage earners had always been a source of anxiety in the valley. The Reverend Converse of Weathersfield had noted that the population of the mill village of Perkinsville was disorderly and highly mobile. One parent had worried that "village boys" might corrupt his son if he worked on a large commercial farm. Yet prior to the 1840s people who were anxious about the working poor had seldom used terms of class, wealth, or national origin to classify those who troubled them. In 1846 a member of the wealthy Dana family of Woodstock complained that "there was not a virtuous woman in the neighborhood" of the local mills "and that all the working girls and factory girls were whores." Robert Harvey demanded assurances from the railroad that the Irish would leave once they finished laying track in Barnet. Harriet Hutchinson of East Braintree was "sick" of the whole railroad construction business, because she disliked seeing "so many Irishmen about" and thought their shanties a public nuisance. L. J. McIndoe, editor in 1847 of the short-lived *Northern Protestant and American Advocate* in Newbury, wanted all Catholics deported.[23]

Such people were undoubtedly confirmed in their opinions when three murders and several prostitution arrests occurred between 1848 and 1850 near railroad camps and in large towns. Life in the predominantly male construction camps was at times violent, and the decline of household government in the valley's boomtowns – Brattleboro, Windsor, Woodstock, St. Johnsbury, and Montpelier – made public supervision of morals, native or immigrant, difficult. Native Vermonters also feared the readiness with which immigrants accepted wage labor, and held conflicting beliefs about it. On the one hand, they were afraid that the immigrants' willingness to accept menial work reflected an inherent docility, servility, and dependency that made them the natural allies of conspirators against democracy and equality; on the other, they believed the immigrants took jobs that other Vermonters needed if they were to accumulate sufficient resources to establish shops or farms.

The political and spiritual traditions of the French Canadians and the Irish were also threatening to native Vermonters. Many immigrants were anti-English, anti-Protestant, and bitter about the misery and oppression of their homelands. The insults they suffered for their religion at the hands of "stage drivers, hostlers, and hangers on" in large villages and the mistreatment rail workers and miners endured from labor contractors, who usually drove the "Pads" and "Frenchmen" harder than their native-born employees and on occasion absconded with their wages, led to a number of riots and to a growing conviction that Yankees, for all their talk of tolerance and equality, were only Englishmen by another name.[24] Literate immigrants often read newspapers from Montreal or Boston, and interpreted American events by the light of European political traditions. Some were radical democrats, who cheered the revolutionary violence of the Canadian Patriote uprising of 1837 and the European revolutions of 1848. They denounced America's war with Mexico as an imperialist venture against an innocent, democratic people that was analogous to England's wars against French Canada and Ireland. The Reverend Jeremiah O'Callaghan, who ministered to northern Vermont in the 1840s and was a friend of William Cobbett, wrote and preached vehemently against usury, slavery, and capitalist exploitation.[25]

There were other immigrants who were arch-conservatives and had few kind words for democracy. The priests who took the *Boston Pilot* out of radical hands in 1851 abided by the dictates of the Vatican and extolled the virtues of hierarchy and religious uniformity. They condemned resistance to the fugitive slave law as "treasonable," denounced the antislavery movement, and lamented that the "red republic" that had loosed its violence on Europe in the Revolution of 1848 had not been "sent back to hell." It is not surprising that Protestant Vermonters believed Catholic immigrants endangered their Christian, reformed republic. They heard some Catholics questioning the decency of financiers and entrepreneurs, while others condemned immediate abolitionists and denounced democratic revolutionaries like Giuseppe Mazzini of Italy and Lajos Kossuth of Hungary as the latest leaders of the Protestant "rebellion" against order and authority. The fact that many immigrants supported the Vermont Catholic Total Abstinence Society from its inception in the early 1840s, attended church more regularly than they had back home, espoused the Democratic Party's tolerant, reformist ideology, and were making some progress toward self-employment was lost on many natives. Anxious for the moral, spiritual, and political future of the valley, they were eager to fix the blame for society's faults on immigrants.[26]

Class and ethnic prejudice was general. Yet most businessmen and commercial farmers spoke of people who worked for them, both native and immigrant, without fear or malice, and on occasion with some affection, as "our men," "our Frenchman," "our Irishmen." Factory owners like Erastus Fairbanks and Charles Paine were remembered kindly by their workers. They went out of their way to defend Catholics against abuse and helped them establish churches. Even for these people, however, the class and ethnic identities of working people took precedence over their individual identities. In addition, as many poorly paid jobs began to be filled almost exclusively by new immigrants, the status of certain occupations plummeted. Jobs that had once been thought to provide good training, especially for the rural young, were now spoken of with scorn; respectable people did not become kitchen servants or grooms.[27]

Prosperous citizens who lived in marketing and manufacturing centers often tried to deal constructively with the new "realities" they perceived in the valley. The prospectus of the *School Journal* declared in 1847 that "every class of people would share" the benefits of educational reform. The poor would receive "the priceless treasure" of knowledge, while the education of the poor would protect the rich "against the depredations of ignorance and of crime. It is the best insurance on property at the lowest premium." Horace Eaton, the State Superintendent of Common Schools, assured Vermonters that immigrants could learn American ways and that natives could be protected against foreign ways.[28]

Perhaps it should have struck this crop of Vermont reformers as odd to apply the rhetoric of class and ethnic conflict to the problems of Vermont. It was clearly more appropriate to the dangerous, dirty, blighted cities of Great Britain, or at least to the cities of southern New England. By the 1840s, however, propertied people in major towns were ready to perceive their society as divided by class and ethnicity into potentially hostile groups, even though the valley was still a place where proprietorship was relatively widespread, wealth was diffused, and the immigrant population was small. Their social vision had been transformed. They wanted to enter the wider world of capitalist civilization and were willing to view their society through urban glasses, yet they were anxious to forestall the importation of the evils of modern civilization.

In the countryside, conditions remained as they had been since the late 1820s. In 1850, only one farmer in ten could afford to hire more than an occasional nonfamily tenant or laborer. Only one farmer in ten could commit his resources entirely to production for urban markets. Land prices were still high relative to farm wages (Table 4.1). No new farms were created and most families found it impossible to establish all their children in the valley. The final clearing of land, the weak competitive position of the rural needle trades, and the insufficient number of jobs at small woolen mills left farm men and women with few outside sources of income.

Of course, those with sizable farms could have sold out at good prices and settled successfully on larger tracts in the West, but most chose not to do so. The mobility of farm owners remained low throughout the 1840s. Only a third died, retired, or moved during the decade; that was the same rate that had prevailed during the two previous decades. Farmers wanted to stay in Vermont. Those who could not compete with western wool tried to profit from the dairy revolution, even though many of them owned farms with rough terrain better suited to raising sheep and less supportive of sown grasses and feed grains. Neighbors worked together to perform the heavy tasks that agricultural improvement required. Farmers labored in twos or threes to pull heavier plows, spread manure, and build cattle-proof fences. Women produced what shoes and clothing they could on the putting-out market. In many households, women spun and wove their own flax, if no longer wool; and they tried weaving palm hats for sale in eastern cities in return for credit at the stores that furnished them with palm leaves. Family members searched for work as miners, lumberjacks, and farmhands or took up rude tenancies in hill towns.[29]

Achsah Wellman and her husband rented a small farm in Westminster. Mrs. Wellman wrote her brothers and sisters that the house was cold and that there were "many inconveniences here but on the whole I think we can do better here than perhaps in some other places. We work for a very good man who seems interested for our advantage as well as his own." Her husband Timothy planted and sowed for half the crop and was paid in cash for all the wall he could build. Achsah took in weaving. "I have as much as I can do through the fall and winter . . . [the work is] heavy but tolerable profitable. It is mostly [comforters] made of twine and rags wove similar to the old rag coverlets." Her brother, who owned a modest farm in neighboring Brookline, described the Wellmans' condition as "poor as poverty," but Achsah herself looked upon her good health and the abundant spinning work she got from neighbors as a blessing. She and her husband had faith in God and the valley's future. They named their newborn son after the Whig congressman, Horace Everett.[30]

These people made a virtue out of making do. Their pleasures were old ones. Maple sugar, fresh peas, and the jelly-like innards of cows' horns were still the ultimate delicacies to them. They treasured finely carved powder horns and ornate quilts that depicted family members or scenes from farm life. They hunted and fished, and visited neighbors. Advanced education was useless to them, and by 1850, when teacher certification tests and the feminization of the teaching profession had improved the quality of common school education, they withdrew their support from the school reform movement. If they wanted more than a rudimentary education, they sought it from books, newspapers, and discussions with friends and relatives, as many clearly did, for newspaper subscriptions were nearly universal and the size and number of personal libraries recorded in wills had increased. This was not a way of life restricted to the hill country or to the coarse eccentric and the impoverished. Letters and artifacts revealed that there were people everywhere in the valley who were still determined to abide by old values, to set themselves up as proprietors and live out their lives amid their kin.[31]

Those who wanted greater material advantages, more education, or greater adventure left by the thousands for the valley's major towns, the cities of southern New England, and the West. Most of them were young men, and in many cases their departures led to actual declines in the populations of agricultural and hill towns. The exodus grew so large that the valley's total population grew only 2 percent in the 1840s (from 146,000 to 148,000) and not at all in the ensuing decade. That exodus was hard on young women. Lucy Brown of Strafford declared that she could not read the census figures "without chagrin and a firm determination not to emigrate!" Brown resisted the arguments of a western friend, who sent her "glowing accounts of fruitful fields, fleet horses, prairie flowers – (never a word about the rattlesnakes) – caravans of hogs, and ruddy heaps of boys and hominy – (she mixes them just so)." She knew, however, that her chances of marrying grew slimmer each year because of the exodus of young men from the valley, and jokingly she appointed her friend Justin Morrill "president" of a society to find her a husband.[32]

By 1850, economic and demographic change had created a new society in the valley. Proponents of capitalism could point with pride to six or seven marketing and manufacturing towns that were outposts of a fully capitalist society. Those towns had firms that were oriented to national markets and amassed capital to a degree hitherto unknown in the valley, and elites that embraced the latest urban fashions and ideas. Most Vermonters did not share the vision of society that these towns represented, however. The large firms in these towns provided jobs but offered no solution to the crisis in proprietorship. They gave rise to what in later years became a three-tiered division of classes, based roughly on the differing market power of those who had capital, those who had skills, and those who could perform physical labor. Marketing and manufacturing towns in the valley remained more intimate than the cities of southern New England and Great Britain, but they shared increasingly in the evils of urban and industrial life that boosters had hoped to avoid – in new kinds of poverty and vice, and in class and ethnic feeling.

The older economy of marketing and manufacturing towns, based on small shops, put-out production, construction, and nonrail transportation endured and coexisted with the fully capitalist economy, and the massive exodus of young people from agricultural and hill towns led to a more equal society there. Agricultural and hill towns maintained steady levels of proprietorship, although they did so by providing few jobs for wage workers (a trend only partly offset by the ensuing dairy boom), by sending their offspring away to find work, and by surrendering their self-sufficiency to some extent. They now imported more goods, and their farmers now specialized more often in the production of crops for Boston, Springfield, and Hartford. The population of these towns grew older, more homogeneous, and more interrelated, since for the most part only relatives of present proprietors were able to acquire farms or shops, and few newcomers moved in.[33]

Through all these changes, the general level of prosperity in the valley increased. Proprietorship remained fairly widespread, at about 45 percent, because the valley's rough terrain, remote location, and lack of iron and coal deposits prevented the growth of heavy industry, cities, and labor-intensive agriculture. Exchange was still centered in protected markets in towns and neighborhoods, and that enabled many farmers and craftsmen to insulate themselves against competition. Yet the aspirations of the great majority of people to provide opportunities for their children at home and to control the course of society in the valley were frustrated. Their economic fate and their children's future lay more than ever in the hands of the cities and the West.

Religion

The movement of the valley toward economic maturity and the rise of the modified order in town life had ironic consequences for many church members who had looked forward eagerly to both. Revivals almost disappeared. Membership in evangelical denominations fell 26 percent between 1843 and 1850. The annual rate at which people joined Calvinist churches in the towns studied intensively fell from twenty per 1,000 inhabitants during the revival to five between 1844 and 1850. Calvinist beliefs and evangelical disciplinary practices eroded. That is not to say that the churches no longer stood at the center of community life or that faith was dying. Fifty Protestant churches (including fifteen Adventist churches) were founded in the valley between 1844 and 1850. Church attendance remained fairly steady and the valley's inhabitants expressed their faith in God in letters and diaries as frequently as they had before. The problem was that the churches now had to struggle to retain their place in town life, and that a new kind of piety – sentimentalism – better expressed the feelings, anxieties, and aspirations of those at the heart of the respectable community than evangelism did.

The temperance and educational reform movements bore some responsibility for the weakening of evangelical churches. Seth Arnold, a

Congregationalist minister near Westminster since 1817, noted disconsolately in 1848 that while school exhibitions were "crowded" and the Sons of Temperance were attracting great numbers, his prayer meetings were "thin." One meeting failed to draw a single soul. He joined the Sons of Temperance "prayerfully . . . seeing no other way in which anything could be done here effectually at present," but he was discouraged by his congregation's inattention to spiritual matters.[34]

Some reformers even attacked evangelical piety. The commissioner of public schools in Caledonia County, A. O. Hubbard, declared his impatience with town commissioners "whose most profound questions" concerning the qualifications of prospective teachers were "how many *verses* are there in the hundred and nineteenth psalm?" Vermont author Daniel Thompson assailed rural zealots who were reluctant to embrace modern educational ideas and methods, satirizing them in his novel *Locke Amsden* as primitive eccentrics who believed their talented new teacher had come to practice witchcraft on them.[35]

Usually reformers were more tactful, albeit no less firm, when they trespassed on what had been the churches' territory. Thomas Powers, the Woodstock physician, observed in a temperance address to the cadets of Norwich Academy in 1846 that while "the highest aspirations of the devoted christian are fully realized in his communings with God," the temperance crusader battled for every cause that helped maintain "the peace & quiet of the domestic hearthstone." Powers relegated religion to the private sphere and preempted the field of organized benevolence for temperance. Nor did he stop there. The war against sin, Powers claimed, was best fought by the temperance society. Using the rhetoric of evangelical discipline, he promised that the temperance society would keep "an unslumbering watch" and exercise "an unwearied supervision" over those who made "the vows of *Love, Purity*, & *Fidelity*." It would watch for "the slightest violation" of the temperance pledge and would see that guilty members did not escape detection. It would also furnish "the rescued victims of intemperance, whose appetites, if left alone might control their reason . . . with a refuge & a sanctuary."[36]

Temperance advocates like Powers, who was no longer a freethinker, but a Universalist and church clerk, bore no malice against the churches. Yet they assumed that the churches would no longer play the most important role in defending society and the family. The growing importance of temperance and education as signs of respectability may also have weakened the churches, particularly the evangelical churches, by making full church membership only one token of good character, and perhaps not the most reliable one. Again, there is no evidence that a majority or even a sizable minority of respectable citizens questioned the primacy of church membership or expected less than regular attendance of all decent citizens. The statistics on loans, partnerships, persistence rates, and social mobility reveal that church members retained a preferred position through the 1840s.[37] If surviving diaries can be trusted, however, it would appear that by the 1840s evangelicals were more concerned to record church attendance and support for temperance than their innermost feelings about God, and it is clear that credit agencies penetrating the valley ignored the religious activities and sentiments of those they investigated, dwelling instead on teetotal temperance, reports about manners and appearance, and credit records as signs of reliability.[38] As suspicion of enthusiastic converts and awareness of the importance of other movements in town life increased, people seemed to feel less pressure to join evangelical churches. They were discovering other ways to allay the anxieties that fueled the revival.

Changing economic circumstances further undermined the churches in marketing and manufacturing towns. There evangelical churches won almost no new converts among workers and immigrants and were sustained only by the influx of church members from neighboring towns. Only forty-one men and ninety-three women joined the Congregational and Baptist churches in St. Johnsbury, Windsor, and Woodstock in the seven years from 1844 to 1850. Membership in Episcopalian churches rose only 1 percent in marketing and manufacturing towns despite population growth. Of course, Catholic immigrants refused to surrender their faith; Irish and French Canadian Catholics organized six churches in the 1840s and a dozen more in the 1850s. Yet native-born factory and railroad workers, a highly mobile group, did not join existing churches, either. Nor were they much encouraged to do so. Church members in these towns did not venture far beyond their own class or ethnic group to find friends, business associates, or new members for their churches. They believed that the interests of the rich and poor, native and nonnative, were distinct and thought the temperance and educational movements more congenial vehicles for reaching workers and immigrants. In time Protestant workers in towns like St. Johnsbury and Windsor would create their own Methodist or Baptist churches. Such churches would thrive on the breakdown of the broader sense of community, of fellow feeling and mutual regard, that evangelicals had sought so earnestly to stimulate through the revival.

Finally, a revival of respectable social life outside the churches absorbed the energies of many who would in an earlier time have been completely absorbed in religious activities. Young people, especially in the wealthiest towns, indulged in an endless round of parlor visits, song fests, and sugar parties, enjoying a camaraderie that had once characterized community-wide events. To an earlier generation, much of their behavior would have appeared depraved. Card playing, parlor games and theatricals, open concern for fashionable clothing and possessions, flirtatious talk, and even kissing among unrelated young men and women were pervasive. To some extent respectable citizens had only imported urban manners into the valley along with urban goods in the 1840s. However, these changing standards of behavior also marked the increasingly unassailable confidence the respectable had in their own virtue and reputations.[39]

A few bold male spirits, sensing that social life outside the churches had now regained its legitimacy, organized Masonic and Odd Fellows lodges again. E. B. Rollins, the Antimasonic activist, sounded the alarm in a short-lived paper called the *Even Fellows Gazette*, but his newspaper interested few except the Sons of Temperance, who mobbed his office to protest his claim that no secret organization could be of benefit to society. (Unlike most temperance activists, the Sons and their auxiliaries, the Martha Washingtonians, maintained the secrecy of their disciplinary proceedings out of concern for their fallen brothers and sisters.) Organizations with reputations for rowdy behavior appealed to few at this time, however. Neither the Masons nor the Odd Fellows had more than five lodges in the valley in 1850. Respectable citizens had directed their energies toward polite amusements firmly integrated by sex; their standards of conduct for men and women were similar.[40]

Evangelical churches suffered from the sudden unwillingness or inability of their members to discipline sinners. Why discipline perished is difficult to explain. As with the demise of the enforcement of morals laws after the Revolution, no one openly favored the change. Disciplinary mechanisms remained in place and expulsion was still the ultimate sanction, but by 1860 evangelical churches made virtually no use of either.

Sinners may have undone discipline themselves by simply walking away from the churches. In Congregational and Baptist churches, the proportion of disciplinary cases dealing with the neglect of church rose from 11 percent prior to the revival to 34 percent during the revival, and to 61 percent from 1844 to 1859, after the revival had ended (Table 2.1). Revival converts, who made up the majority of these cases, often slid into spiritual indifference, but it is equally likely that everyone who fell into personal sin simply avoided worship services or left town. They may have been fearful of the damage their reputations would suffer if they made full confessions of their sins, and they probably realized that without confessing they would be expelled if they returned to church. So they stayed away. The zeal with which these churches upheld respectable standards of conduct may have ultimately undermined their ability to reclaim the fallen.

It is also possible that discipline declined because people were confident that a profound concern for personal reputation would hold most church members in line and that sinners would be sufficiently punished for their acts by being kept at arm's length by the respectable community. One class-conscious citizen was convinced that society should not be overly concerned about certain sins, especially slander. In 1845 he or she assured readers of the *Vermont Journal* that a propensity for sins like slander was endemic among the lower classes and in the end harmless, because people of low status did not have the power to injure anyone's reputation but their own.⁴¹ Such attitudes toward the fallen made church discipline irrelevant.

Calvinism itself, the predominant creed among evangelicals during the revival, fell victim to the forces of the modified order. Only a few Congregational and Baptist churches jettisoned the doctrine of predestination from their church covenants, but church members accepted the general assumptions that the campaign for respectability made about character, morality, and the human will. Their journals, sermons, diaries, and letters no longer dwelt on the metaphysical mysteries of salvation. They informally embraced free-will doctrines.⁴² In the countryside, a small but steady stream of Calvinists moved into Free Congregational, Freewill Baptist, and Christian churches, which explicitly embraced theological tolerance and diversity. Those churches regarded differences among Christians as inevitable and accepted other Christians who abided by the teachings of Christ and the maxims of respectability.

Free Congregationalists, who organized churches in Pomfret and Braintree, tried to reunite evangelicals and religious liberals. Like the rural Unitarians of southwestern New Hampshire who had gained strength in the 1820s among Old Lights (who in that stronghold of the standing order had refused to bury their differences with New Light Calvinists during the postwar revival), the Free Congregationalists kept themselves apprised of the latest theological ideas among Unitarians and romantics in Boston and Europe. Yet they approved of revivals and celebrated the pietistic, emotional side of the Unitarian revival then under way in the greater Boston area. The Freewill Baptists and Christians had added members in the late 1830s amid speculation about the Second Coming and the imminent reunification of all Christians. After 1843, they continued to grow (adding nine churches by 1850), but for different reasons. Their appeal was now similar to what it had been for some years in southwestern New Hampshire and much of southern New England. They attracted Christians in long-settled rural areas of the valley who believed in free will and moral accountability. Such people had learned through experience the value of neighborly tolerance and the inevitability of dif-

ferences among Christians. In small agricultural towns like Chelsea, Congregationalists and Christians united in one church, as did the Baptists
and Freewill Baptists, and simply ignored the theological differences that
had hitherto divided them.[43]

The movement toward ecumenical services was not confined to Calvinist denominations or their Arminian and liberal offshoots. The Methodist convention had to censure ministers in 1848 for holding joint
services with Universalists, so widespread had ecumenism become in rural
areas, especially among those who supported Union meetinghouses.
Christians were coming to believe that even differences over doctrines as
fundamental as spiritual rebirth and damnation should not keep them
apart at worship.[44]

The decline of Calvinism and the rise of latitudinarian denominations
cleared the way for the spread of a new doctrine of spiritual accountability, renewal, and harmony: the creed of sentimentalism. Sentimentalists, drawing inspiration from the Bible, the revival, the benevolent
crusade, and romantic novels and poetry, insisted that Christians could
fulfill themselves only by helping others and by being "sympathetic."
That capacity flowed from a sentimental sensibility, which enabled people
who possessed it to respond with thought and feeling to the plight of
others. A sentimental sensibility could be cultivated not only in the home,
where husbands, wives, and children learned daily about love, duty, and
compassion, but in schools and churches, and through literature – indeed,
through any medium that could promulgate the Christian message and
encourage people to extend the feelings they felt for their families and
friends to society at large.[45]

This new faith was for practical purposes inseparable from its public
rhetoric, which promoted a new community of feeling among Christians
and encouraged reverence toward God and God's creations. Sentimentalists felt that growing social and spiritual divisions and the tendency
of respectable citizens to hold themselves above the masses had imperiled
true Christianity. Some young sentimentalists stridently attacked the unchristian behavior of people who thought of themselves as Christians.
Poems like "The Town Pauper's Burial" by Charles Eastman of Woodstock and "The Young Immigrant" by Hannah Pitkin of Marshfield
reproached Christians for hurrying ungrieved the remains of the honest
poor into unmarked graves and for ill-treating young Irish girls who had
suffered so much in the potato famine. Emma Wood Smith of Windham,
an Episcopalian and a well-known poet, condemned people who denied
women educational opportunities, yet did not appreciate their sacrifices
or sympathize with their harsh lot, and forced them to pour out their
"wealth of love...on the dust." Joseph Brown, a recent graduate of

Dartmouth College, complained that it was all too common for Christians to divide society into classes and to pursue wealth while leaving others "the heirs of constant privation suffering degradation and sorrow." An anonymous mill girl asked whether it was Christian to prate about one's own respectability and declare the rest of mankind hopelessly lost? To care more about the figure one cut before the congregation on Sunday than before the Lord on Judgment Day? "Once perhaps the House of God was a place of worship, but it has degenerated into a place of idle show," she wrote.[46]

Like many urban young people, the Vermonters who made these complaints were at a dangerous crossroads. On the one hand were radical new initiatives to right social wrongs; on the other, sweeping disillusionment with human nature and organized religion.[47] These young sentimentalists were trying to make their own way by focusing on the plight of the oppressed and by confronting prosperous and respectable people with the way others (and by implication God) saw them.

Sentimentalists received encouragement from spokesmen for the oppressed, who played upon sentimental ideals to demand full membership in society. French and Irish-born priests, like the Reverend Hector Drolet of the Montpelier mission and the Reverend Jeremiah O'Callaghan of the northern Vermont circuit, spoke eloquently of the sufferings Catholic immigrants had endured in their homelands for their Christian faith and asked why Protestant Vermonters, with their taunts and outrages, were so eager to deny them a new home. Black abolitionist itinerants, like the Reverend Cato, railed against the abuse that was heaped upon black families and demanded that they be included in the sentimental circle of mutual regard and obligation. Reformed alcoholics spoke out against the tendency of temperance societies to persecute rather than try to reform heavy drinkers. They had organized divisions of the Sons of Temperance and the Martha Washingtonians in thirty-two communities by the late 1840s. Their societies treated drinkers sympathetically, extending charity to impoverished drunkards in the form of temporary lodging, loans, and employment to help them keep the pledge. They believed it was more Christian to work patiently with drinkers and to provide them with an active social life in temperance lodges than to hold them at arm's length and run roughshod over what little society they had.[48]

Most sentimental complaints were not related to social questions or to perceived failures of democratic spirit, however. Sentimentalists more often lamented the emotional and spiritual effects of the cold regimen of respectability on the respectable themselves. When Amanda Walker of Grafton waxed nostalgic about a pious "Old Parson" who could preach to the "heart," or when oft-quoted Massachusetts author L. M. Child remembered the days before "conventional forms" impeded "a free communion with other souls," they colored the past with their own desire to be free of conventional respectability. They felt that faith had been reduced to a stultifying set of rules and that "the fear of what Mr. Somebody will say" had made each person "afraid of [his] neighbor."[49]

Neither Walker nor Child would have been happy in the good old days, when parsons called down God's wrath upon sinners and condemned infants to hell and when a relative indifference to the opinions of others allowed some people to indulge in the sort of rough-and-ready revelry both found abhorrent. But that was unimportant, because Walker's old parson, who sometimes "forgot what the grammars said" and wore a coat "in fashion years before," and Child's old neighbors, who would invite each other over "without the slightest hesitation" and through intimate discourse share "their highest thoughts," were created not to reflect the past accurately but to grapple with contemporary problems, to break through the artifice of cultivated diction and stylish display, through the repressive power of public opinion, in order to create a community of sentimental Christian feeling.

When such sentimentalists addressed social questions, they usually did so not to attack the respectable community but to humanize it and legitimize its claims to predominance in town life. Thomas Powers, in his aforementioned temperance address, urged his audience not to denigrate the intemperate, but to love and pity them, for they were helpless victims of the "hydra-headed monster," alcohol. School reformers wanted teachers to have sympathy for the higher feelings of their students. The editors of the *School Journal* issued this injunction: "Never sneer at a tender conscience, nor laugh at the scruples or the weaknesses of a pious heart." Only compassionate teachers, who understood that most children's contempt for principle was merely "an affectation" and that their natural spirit and gaiety were not "vice," could nurse the delicate sensibilities of children to maturity.[50]

These proponents of the modified order wanted to persuade people who still stood outside civilized society that respectable citizens were motivated only by Christian love. Sentimentalism did not interfere with the campaign for respectability; it helped soften its edges and hasten its progress. The campaign's proponents were not deaf to the message of angry sentimental poems or sermons, for they did not want distinctions to erode fellow feeling across class and ethnic lines. They read such poems not as manifestos for social change, however, but as pleas that Christians treat the downtrodden with sympathy, in the name of a humanity that transcended all temporal distinctions.

Sentimentalists also wished to achieve a communion of spirit between men and women. They did not call for female equality or for alleviation of the burdens of women's work, as Emma Wood Smith had hoped, but for appreciation of the sacrifices women made for others. They wanted society to esteem women, in the words of the editors of Montpelier's *Green Mountain Freeman* in 1846, for their capacity "to soften firmness into mercy, and chasten honor into refinement; to be a compensation for hopes that are blighted... to exhibit on this lower world a type of love, pure, constant and ineffable, which, in another world, we are taught to believe the best of virtue." As wives and mothers, women would make sentimental love the respectable community's primary means of shaping "the character and habits of every member" of the human family. A few sentimentalists championed this female mission in order to restrict women's activities to the domestic sphere, to shut them out of the places they had taken as workers, reformers, and political activists. Yet most did so to justify a wide range of female activities on behalf of the family and moral causes and to make the family a more secure pillar of the modified order. They recognized, however, that extolling domesticity would do little to help the cause of women's equality.[51]

Sentimentalists were attempting, partly but not exclusively through this changed view of woman's mission to society, to foster a kind of love that could, when exercised wisely and benevolently, shape the behavior of others more reliably than fear or the conversion experience or any moral imperatives. Their ideal was well expressed by Daniel Thompson, the Montpelier novelist. Thompson discussed his family in detail in an 1835 letter to a friend. He doted on his children and allowed them a great deal of leeway, because he believed that their occasional intransigence stemmed more from innocent immaturity than from willfulness. When his daughter complained about school, Thompson allowed her to learn to read and write at home. She grew to love reading and eagerly returned to school. In the same patient way, he encouraged his youngest son to adopt the ambitions that his eldest (a thorough scholar at the age of thirteen) had already embraced. "Last year the youngest wanted to be a stage driver rather than governor of Vermont, and this year a farmer with a span of horses rather than President of the United States. He will be all right soon." To his friend he wrote with amusement at his own familial pride. "So you now see I have the handsomest wife, smartest children... in all Vermont. Ah! if you could be blest with such a power of vision in looking at things personal!"[52]

The spread of sentimentalism was not confined to wealthier families intent on preparing their children for advanced educations and elite careers. It affected poor families as well. Sentimentalism fostered new ways of speaking about love between husbands and wives that helped them to persevere in the face of poverty and family troubles. Couples like Cyrus and Anne Farnham of Bradford, who worked at various jobs throughout New England, sometimes together, sometimes apart, and Andrew and Mathilda Roberts of Walden, who were separated for two years while Andrew searched for gold in California, found strength in their sentimental love for each other. The Farnhams had neither money, nor home, nor their families' blessing for their traveling courtship and marriage, but their effusive declarations of love, their appreciation of each small gift and kindness, and their solicitousness for each other's feelings helped them stand together against the world. The Roberts, who married only months before Andrew left for California, likewise heaped love and kisses upon each other and tried to "communicate" their intimate "thoughts and feelings" through the mail. Mathilda understood the toll that gold digging and bad luck took on her husband. She heartened him by remaining patient, by telling him that the two dollars he had sent had done her "more good than a hundred dollars would have from anyone else," and by composing a poem on the spotless home, the hearty meal, the healthy son (who had yet to see his father), and the loving wife who waited faithfully. Andrew for his part appreciated Mathilda's sufferings, lamented her need to board with relatives and work outside the home to make ends meet, and bid her never apologize for her bouts with loneliness and despair. "Write all about the folks, all the news and everything you can think of except my unworthy wife. You need not write about her for I am not acquainted with such a wife." By encouraging husbands and wives to share their innermost thoughts and by fostering appreciation of the sacrifices and labors of both, the sentimental ideal generated a spirit of mutual dependence and cooperation that lightened the burdens of poor couples as they struggled toward independence, and helped them maintain their discipline and dignity.[53]

Sentimentalism did not leave the individual family to its own resources, however. Sentimental families were sustained by fellowship with other sentimental families; by new customs and habits, such as the exchange of Valentine's Day cards with loved ones and the tendency to anthropomorphize family pets; by the celebration of Christmas as an expression of love and commitment to family members and neighbors; by sentimental funerals, weddings, and christenings. There were sentimental books, prints, songs, poetry, and other materials and a host of other innovations imported from major eastern cities and from England. The poor had almost as much access to these materials as the rich, through friends and neighbors and through schools, newspapers, reprints, and lending libraries.[54]

Men and women in wealthier, polite circles in both town and country spread sentimentalism through existing churches, reform organizations, and political movements. These people, deeply divided over revivalism, discovered in sentimentalism a faith that smoothed over differences between evangelical and genteel Christians, that emphasized pious feeling but did not demand that it take a specific form. Theirs was a stylized rhetoric, congenial to those unused to expressing their sentiments without benefit of a rough draft, to those learned enough to appreciate allusions to religious, romantic, and classical works. It addressed the spiritual quandaries of a people who had gone too far even in their own opinion toward reducing Christianity to a doctrine of rote morality and toward creating a society more materialistic and contentious than Christian.

Sentimentalism spread so rapidly that by the 1850s it encompassed nearly all Vermonters. It bound respectable citizens together across political and theological divides in ways evangelism could not. That Leverett Lull, the Woodstock songwriter, could set to music poetry by Charles Eastman and dedicate the results to Mrs. Nahum Haskell and Mrs. Norman Williams shows the power sentiment had on an emotive, spiritual level to unite speculative theist, Universalist, and evangelical Congregationalist, as well as Democrat and Whig.[55] Sentimental writing also heightened the respectable community's awareness of and sympathy for the feelings and frustrations of many outsiders – the poor, the alcoholic, blacks, Catholics. That sympathy did not create real bonds or real understanding between these outsiders and the valley's more esteemed citizens. It did, however, encourage some outsiders to hope that sentimentalism would lead to a genuine recognition of their humanity and their rights and win them the name of respectability, after they furnished proof of their readiness to abide by certain standards: to be industrious, sober, pious, clean, and honest. In this way sentimentalism deepened the hegemony of respectable values in town life.

Ironically, it was the failure of the revival that created the possibility of greater religious unity in the valley. By rekindling unpleasant antagonisms between liberals and evangelicals, the revival had made people receptive to new doctrines that glossed over long-standing differences in theology and style and placed equal emphasis on thought and feeling, self-help and deliverance. The sentimental creed improved upon evangelicalism as a postrevolutionary theology by making Christian renewal a more sedate, manageable process, more dependent on the cultivation of sensibility than on spiritual rebirth, and by insisting that renewal concern itself as much with the social as the spiritual condition of sinners. That strengthened Christianity's appeal to the discontented and better enabled it to address the concerns of a people who persisted in believing their society to be in a state of crisis. Sentimentalists articulated their own afflictive vision of progress and demonstrated loyalty to the varied aims of Vermont's democratic revolution in their pronouncements on behalf of equality and community.

Sentimentalism fell short of establishing the community of feeling it sought, as had every previous spiritual movement in the valley, but it accomplished a subtler goal. Having drawn members of the respectable community into greater sympathy with the plight of people who stood beyond its bounds, the sentimental creed led them to believe that the adoption of tough new measures in the war against vice would help the poor, the downtrodden, the alcoholic, the ill-educated. Gone were concerns about coercion and repression, gone the reluctance to go beyond the informal pressures that had upheld community standards in the 1820s. Moved by the desire to help and uplift, great numbers of people enlisted in the temperance movement, the anti-militia crusade, and the fight for no-license laws and school supervision. A decreasing force of voluntarists was forced to explain why the lot of their brothers and sisters should not be improved by means of these compassionate measures. Together with the sustained pressure exerted by the modified order, sentimentalism drove nonchurchgoers and drinkers from the valley in vast numbers by 1850 and slowly broke individual and collective resistance to new standards of behavior. The general acceptance of those standards was evident in the late 1840s and early 1850s in the decline of gossip and slander in private correspondence, the demise of organized opposition to temperance and militia reform, and the acceptance by the vast majority of the population – perhaps three-fourths or more – of the need for teetotal temperance and improved teaching.

In practical terms, sentimentalism helped the modified order erode diversity, undermine individual assertiveness, and set new standards for mutual obligation and personal restraint among civic-minded citizens. As a creed, a matter of faith, sentimentalism satisfied the needs of those citizens, both prosperous and poor, who recognized the shortcomings of their society as it moved toward settled maturity. Inherent in it was an admission of society's failure to achieve Christian ends. Yet it too, like all the spiritual movements before it, promised to bring a truly Christian community into being, and that was a strong part of its appeal. The inhabitants of the valley had not yet wholly relinquished the quest for community.

Politics

The political parties of the 1840s were not troubled by the rise of class and ethnic consciousness. In comparison with southern New England or

New York, the valley was only dimly aware of the problems associated with class stratification and immigration, for there were as yet few full-fledged industrialists and few men who saw themselves as permanent members of a working class in Vermont, and Catholic men were generally too poor and mobile to vote. The growth and behavior of such groups elsewhere in the country occasionally worried the valley's citizens. Yet only a few, like Charles Merrifield, editor of the *Vermont Journal*, tried to politicize such concerns. Incensed by Henry Clay's defeat in the presidential election of 1844 at the hands of "ignorant foreigners" in New York and Pennsylvania, Merrifield called for an alliance between the Whig and Native American parties, and for a twenty-one year naturalization period for immigrants. He found little support for his ideas, however, and soon returned to the Whig mainstream, where he spoke out once again against prejudice.[56]

The parties were confounded, however, by an issue upon which they fundamentally agreed: slavery. Both parties had committed themselves to halting its spread into the West. Both expressed disapproval of slavery and promised to maintain the preeminence of the free states within the Union and to preserve opportunities for free men in the territories. But when the annexation of Texas and the war with Mexico nullified their efforts, Vermonters came to doubt the sincerity of party leaders and realized that the national parties would not follow their lead on the issue. Searching for an effective antislavery vehicle, 10 percent of the valley's voters bolted to the Liberty Party in 1844, 29 percent to the Free-Soil Party in 1848, and ultimately, in 1856, 78 percent would turn to the Republican Party. Voters had not lost interest in the issues that had divided them into Whigs and Democrats, but slavery came to overshadow them all. Vermont became the most antislavery state in the Union, and the political settlement of the late 1830s and early 1840s came entirely undone.

In the valley, people of every faith, party, and walk of life had long been hostile to the peculiar institution. Almost every Vermonter who visited the South, whether sympathetic to the planters or to the slaves, disliked slave society. Vermonters complained of the way slavery degraded labor and undermined incentives to work. Whites were idle and dissipated, expecting others to work for them, and blacks remained ignorant and "dilatory," having no incentive or opportunity to improve themselves. The South's "want of enterprise" had other baleful effects: drunkenness, ill-kept yards and households, and a lack of interest in education. It was not unusual for Northern observers to see in the South a reverse image of their industrious, disciplined, free society, but such perceptions were more intense among Vermonters because of the seriousness with which they regarded enterprise, respectability, and economic independence.[57]

Vermonters were also upset by the unchristian conduct of Southern whites. Not only did Southerners neglect the Sabbath and religion in general, they were violent and licentious. Vermonters were disgusted by duels and vicious fights accompanied by eye-gougings and stabbings, and they looked upon masters who imposed themselves on female slaves and sold their mulatto children for profit with horror. Most of all, they hated the punishment of slaves. C. Smith, a transplanted Vermonter, wrote his relatives back in Peacham that masters whipped their slaves "worse than any ugly horse." During a journey west in 1849, he saw a tavern-keeper beat a slave merely for warming himself by the parlor fire at five in the morning. Smith declared that even his dog was outraged. "Old Lyon... sprung at the Landlords throat and it was all we could do to keep him off."[58]

A few Vermonters dissented. Charles Fletcher of Lyndon, son of a prominent Democratic politician, rejected the prevailing view of slavery in Vermont. Fletcher wrote from South Carolina in 1837 that the slaves were "the happiest race of mortals" he had ever seen and that they took as much pride in keeping their plantations "neat & nice" as their masters did. He sneered at Whiggery and contrasted the "open hearted, liberal fine fellows" who governed the South with the "close fisted catch penney yankees" who dominated the North. Politicking with slavery was rare, however. Few Vermonters had the stomach for it. Even those who staunchly opposed abolitionism disliked slavery. John Henry Hopkins, bishop of the Vermont diocese of the Protestant Episcopal church, was one of the few Vermonters to deny slavery was a sin. He castigated abolitionists for rewriting the Bible as an antislavery text. Still, he reckoned slavery to be "an EVIL and a DANGER" that fostered idleness, immorality, and violence, and he believed it had to end for the good of the republic.[59]

Of course, the majority of Vermonters were not abolitionists. Like Bishop Hopkins, they believed that the federal Constitution prohibited interference in the internal affairs of the slave states. Most antislavery Vermonters doubted blacks could ever be equal with whites. Yet whenever proponents of slavery sought to claim another territory as a slave state, Vermonters responded angrily. Sixty-eight of the valley's 116 towns petitioned between 1837 and 1840 against the annexation of Texas as a slave state and the admission of any additional slave states before these issues won national prominence. Support within those towns came from both men and women, from colonizationists and abolitionists, and from members of all denominations (Table 7.1).

Some nonextensionists undoubtedly opposed the extension of slavery for ignoble reasons. There were racists who embraced free soil merely to keep the territories free of blacks. Yet most had loftier aims. Sentimentalists, who would make *Uncle Tom's Cabin* a bestseller in the valley in the 1850s, felt pity for the victims of slavery – slaves, masters, mistresses, overseers, and poor whites alike – and were eager to help them. Women sent petitions to Washington that proclaimed antislavery a "holy cause." Men's petitions stressed affronts to the republican ideals of liberty and equality, and pointed to the threat of an unjust war with the Republic of Mexico and the dangers that the addition of slave states (many feared six states would be carved out of Texas alone) would pose to free labor. "Such a result would probably lead to a DISSOLUTION OF THE UNION," warned petitioners from Barnet and Waterford. Of course, Vermonters petitioned not only for what they believed right, but to protect their political power, their country, and their way of life.[60]

These early petitions had a Whig bias. Only five of the sixteen towns that voted under 40 percent Whig in 1840 forwarded petitions, whereas all but two of the fifteen towns that voted over 75 percent Whig did so. The petitions were widely popular, drawing hundreds of signatures wherever they were circulated, especially among nonproprietors, people who were not church members, and rural voters. These people moved ahead of the valley's political and economic leaders on the free-soil issue. In 1848, the Free-Soil Party carried over one-third of the vote in agricultural and hill towns. Although less than a fifth of the voters in the valley's primary and secondary market towns deserted the major parties, rural voters listened attentively to the abolitionists and former Antimasons who led the Free-Soil Party. The Free-Soilers charged that the leaders of the major parties had conspired with slaveowners not only to perpetuate slavery, but to deprive farmers and shopkeepers of opportunities in the western territories, as a prelude to dispossessing free people altogether. "Our oath, as freemen," wrote a correspondent to the *Green Mountain Freeman*, a Free-Soil newspaper, "does not require us to act with these partisans."[61]

After the annexation of Texas in 1845, the beginning of the war with Mexico in 1846, and the drive by Southern interests for the creation of more slave territories from conquered Mexican lands in the Southwest, Democrats realized that the free-soil movement was not just another Whig attempt to embarrass Democrats, and they joined the crusade in great numbers. The Free-Soil Party did as well in Democratic as in Whig strongholds by 1848. In that year's election, the Free-Soilers resurrected the Antimasonic Party's coalition of egalitarian evangelicals, rural Baptists and Congregationalists, and nonmembers from New Light towns.[62]

Voters lost patience with Whig and Democratic leaders, not only because they could not stop the expansion of slavery, but because they could not prevent Southern interests from blocking the economic schemes that the parties had promised would alleviate the crisis of proprietorship in the valley. Because of the crisis, the parties' positions on national economic issues were no longer significantly different by the mid-1840s. Bipartisan proposals for higher tariffs on Vermont products and for plans to open vast territories in the Southwest to exclusively free settlement were defeated by slave interests. From the mightiest Whig manufacturer, who did little business with the South and whose woolens may have competed with Southern cotton goods, to the poorest Democratic hill country farmer, whose only hope for his children's future lay in cheap western land, everyone's path out of economic crisis seemed to be blocked by slavery. To people in the valley the campaign for free soil and free labor was more than a crusade against iniquity; it was a fight for economic survival.[63]

The valley's Whig and Democratic leaders, whose commitment to equality and benevolence was now generally doubted, finally abandoned their Southern allies. In 1849, Vermont's Whigs declared their party free soil, and the majority of Vermont's Democrats broke with their national party to organize the Free-Soil Democratic Party.[64] In 1850, the regular Democratic candidate for governor received only 9 percent of the vote. Ninety-one percent of the vote went to candidates pledged to free soil.

Whig and Democratic efforts to dissociate themselves from slavery did not revitalize those parties, however. Vermont's parties no longer disagreed on many important issues, and with each decision by national Whig and Democratic politicians to compromise or sacrifice Vermont's ideals or interests for the sake of party unity, voters became increasingly cynical about "party politics." Party loyalty and political conflict in the valley actually declined. Party rhetoric subsided in letters and diaries, Whig and Democratic town committees lost members and prestige, and voter turnout dropped from an average of 75 percent in gubernatorial elections in the early 1840s to 55 percent by the mid-1850s, as the gap between the parties on economic issues and on temperance diminished and as differences between the parties on the most important issue – free soil – disappeared.[65]

To some degree, the "free soil, free labor" campaign diverted attention from momentous economic and social changes within Vermont. Small property owners closed their eyes to the threat that population growth and rising capital costs posed to the ideal of widespread proprietorship. The activities of entrepreneurs and financiers menaced the economic independence of others, yet few people took note. Factory and railroad workers neglected the implications of their own dependence, and both workers and capitalists sidestepped the contradiction between the collective creation of wealth and the private appropriation of profit. Vermonters focused on free soil and free labor and shifted the blame for their continuing economic frustrations to their implacable adversary, the slave South.

The struggle against slavery did help Vermonters regain their sense of identity and purpose. For years they had watched Vermont and the valley lose ground to other states, other regions. They had received letters from relatives in Illinois or Wisconsin claiming that Vermont's soil was not one-tenth as good as theirs. They had seen mill girls return home from southern New England with "tasteful city dresses, and more money... than they had ever owned before."[66] Vermont's leading writers and public figures now made an effort to define and preserve the essence of its civilization and to restore its leading role in the world. Nature poets like Charles Eastman and Lucia Barton, historians like Abby Hemenway and the founders of the Vermont Antiquarian Society (established in 1838), and educators, journalists, and politicians like George Perkins Marsh, Daniel Thompson, and Governors William Slade and Carlos Coolidge produced sheaves of poetry, history, and public pronouncements after 1837 trying to give Vermonters a clear identity and a sense of renewed purpose.

They did not fully agree on who they were or where they should go. Yet male or female, Whig or Democrat, captain of industry or yeoman farmer, sentimentalist or rough-and-ready patriot, all concurred with the message of Daniel Thompson's heroic historical novel *Green Mountain Boys* (1839), that Vermont's greatest asset was the character of its people – industrious, decent, courageous, fiercely independent, enlightened – and that it was their duty to safeguard that character and fight for the values it represented. They might never achieve "a high degree of pecuniary prosperity, or political influence," as George Perkins Marsh wrote in 1843, but they would never cease trying to enlighten the rest of humanity. "In every good and noble undertaking," proclaimed Marsh, Vermonters would bring "their influence for good" to bear "not only on the rest of the United States, but upon the world."[67]

None of these historians, writers, politicians, or visionaries had the struggle against slavery in mind as they wrote, but the fight for free soil and free labor proved to be the mission they had hoped for. Through it Vermonters recaptured their purpose, transcended their political differences and racial prejudices, and renewed their hopeful, nonpartisan, independent spirit. By destroying slavery, they believed they could win for the nation the great battles for equality, Christianity, morality, material well-being, unity, and prestige that many felt they were losing, skirmish by skirmish, at home. Free soil subsumed all previous reform movements and encompassed all Vermonters' aspirations. The free-soil campaign was supported by boosters and bolstered by sentimentalists, for whom it was a crusade to redeem the souls of Americans both free and enslaved. Free soil thus led the valley toward political unity, much as boosterism and sentimentalism had led it toward economic and spiritual unity.

Vermont's sudden antislavery mania stunned one former Vermonter. John Wolcott Phelps had left the state before the troubles of the 1830s and 1840s, at a time when military service was still held in high esteem. He joined the army as an officer and served in the Mexican War, only to discover upon his return that people in his home state despised him for it and that his cousin, a judge in West Townsend and a Democratic candidate for the senate, had lost overwhelmingly because he called for an end to sectional bickering and for halting slavery not through nonextension, but through gradual, voluntary, state-compensated emancipation of the slaves. Phelps defended his cousin and spoke mockingly of the people who had repudiated him. "*He* is not for interfering with the governments of other states and kingdoms; *he* would not send a man to hell because he was foolish enough to drink liquor; *he* is not an abolitionist.... Why, he had no chance at all; *one* demagogue would have defeated a dozen of him – in such a *moral, holy* community as Vermont. Ah coz, we are too spiritually proud in Vermont; too holy – we thank God that we are not as other states are, extortioners, slaveowners: there's the rub." Phelps prayed that Vermonters might "arrive at that other state of mind in which with bowed necks we shall ask God to have mercy on us, miserable sinners," so that they in turn might "have some mercy on the slave-owner."[68]

It would not have mollified Phelps if he knew that Vermonters had chosen this course only after years of economic hardship, political rancor, and moral and religious struggle and that the inhabitants of other burned-over districts would soon join Vermonters in the free-soil vanguard. Phelps was right when he said that Vermonters showed little Christian sympathy for Southerners and when he accused them of being stubborn, impatient, and intolerant of opposition. Vermonters would not yield on slavery and focused intently upon its destruction.

The valley had changed by 1850, but the transformation was not a complete one. The improvement of the economy and the persistence of demographic growth had brought unprecedented riches for entreprèneurs and financiers and prosperity for many others, as well as a diminution of fellow feeling across class and ethnic lines in the principal marketing and manufacturing centers. The countryside depended increasingly on markets in southern New England and on goods and services from the valley's market towns. Yet these changes had not created a fully capitalist society in the valley, with class-stratified towns, an urban-oriented agricultural hinterland, consumption-oriented households, and a sharp division between male and female employments. Industry still had but a limited presence locally. Most farms and shops remained small and traded primarily in town and neighborhood markets. Most families spent little on luxury or display. Women retained a central place in local economic life and in the production of agricultural and manufactured goods, although more women in marketing and manufacturing towns now worked exclusively at domestic pursuits, keeping house and raising their children. Proprietorship remained the ideal and was still a possibility for most citizens. It was still the key to the valley's self-image, although it survived primarily because so many people ventured to the western territories to achieve it or to the cities to surrender it.

The valley's churches had lost members amid the eager search for "practical" solutions to moral problems, like temperance and educational reform. Yet that had not made the valley a secular or a pluralist society, wholly absorbed in a quest for worldly well-being and deeply divided over moral values and religious beliefs. Neither sentimentalism nor ecumenism had overwhelming power, but both exerted some influence over society, and church membership remained widespread. Churches remained at the center of town life, and although their place had been diminished by schools and temperance societies, they retained their capacity to unite people in a spirit of shared purpose and mutual obligation.

The major political parties failed to defend Vermont's interests on the national level or to stem its relative decline in prestige and power. Yet their failure did not drive the valley's citizens to sectional chauvinism, to greater partisan rancor, or to wheeler-dealer political pragmatism. Instead, Vermonters united across party lines and embarked on the most dramatic and widely supported crusade of the century, the crusade to end slavery and preserve free soil. It was marked by greater desperation than most earlier reform crusades and at times seemed to be merely a vehicle through which Vermonters could bring their peculiar interests and hatreds to the attention of the nation, and through which they vented frustrations at home. Yet those who participated in the crusade were undeniably acting in defense of an ideal and a way of life. The assertion of the valley's inhabitants that they were an independent people of singular spiritual and moral distinction clearly stood on shakier ground than it had in the recent past, but it still stood, not only on the continued vitality of their shops, farms, and churches, but on their enduring dedication to proprietorship, Christianity, and reform.

Conclusion

Religion, reform, and the problem of order in the Age of Democratic Revolution

The democratic revolution had promised to realize the aspirations of people throughout the Western world. Its adherents in the Connecticut River Valley of Vermont discovered that victory over aristocracy and established religion could not redeem that promise, however. Their aspirations were too complex and contradictory to be realized in any straightforward fashion, and democracy, far from alleviating popular discontent, often compounded it. The democratic revolution did not solve problems; it posed dilemmas. It forced the valley's revolutionaries, and indeed all of America's revolutionaries, to admit that they wanted a society dedicated to more than just the progressive values of freedom, equality, tolerance, competition, and popular government, and to recognize that democracy could threaten cherished traditions, expectations, and institutions as much as aristocracy and establishment.

The revolutionaries' only hope of resolving these dilemmas lay in constructing postrevolutionary orders that could sustain conflicting values and interests in the face of constant challenges. These postrevolutionary orders were nowhere alike. In southern New England, on the revolutionary frontier, in the slave states, and in the middle states, they varied according to the particular visions of order, justice, and harmony that each people sought to realize, according to the thoroughness of democracy's triumph over antidemocratic forces and according to the ways in which democratic ideas and institutions, as well as postrevolutionary economic and demographic change, impinged upon prerevolutionary society. Revolutionaries everywhere feared that the balance of opposed forces upon which these orders rested would come undone. That is why they shared a fascination with republican ideology and with institutions like the covenanted community and the standing order, which proffered hope that the dilemmas of democratic life could be resolved and stability achieved. Republican ideology could not provide revolutionaries with a template for the construction of a postrevolutionary society, however, nor did it guarantee the survival of stabilizing institutions or preclude the possibility of violent conflict between progressives and conservatives over fundamental rights, even in thoroughly democratic societies like Vermont. Each society had to make its own path, often unconsciously and with varying degrees of success, toward postrevolutionary order.

The order that emerged in the Connecticut River Valley of Vermont, and prevailed with some variations along New England's entire revolutionary frontier from western New Hampshire to the Western Reserve of Ohio, rested preeminently on voluntary churches and reform movements.[1] They were the means by which people of the valley created a dynamic order that could respond not only to the periodic conflicts caused by economic and demographic change, but to the ongoing problems of a democratic people who found it difficult to defend simultaneously the varied ideals and interests they embraced. They discovered, first in evangelical revivals and in an array of moral, benevolent, and social reform movements, and then in sentimentalism and the free-soil movement, ways of maintaining a social order that was in a constant state of disequilibrium and dissolution. These movements, together with a succession of complementary campaigns for economic and community development, helped Vermonters reshape family, community, and class relationships, revive their sense of moral community and political purpose, and achieve social stability, in ways that avoided or obscured the compromise of particular ideals and interests and that undermined protest. The dynamic order that emerged from these movements enabled the valley's inhabitants to secure their Christian, reformed republic against the liberal forces unleashed by the Revolution and ensured that the republic would not turn its back on the Age of Democratic Revolution and renounce the principles its founders had promised to uphold.

New England's revolutionary frontiersmen felt the democratic dilemma more deeply than other Americans, in part because they had to reconcile revolutionary imperatives with New England's ordered, hierarchical traditions, and because the frontier's openness undermined efforts to import time-honored ideas and institutions from southern New England at the same time that it encouraged people to interpret revolutionary imperatives in their most radical light. Churches and reform movements helped New England's frontiersmen confront these difficulties by giving them the intellectual and social resources they needed to reconcile their heritage with their democratic mission. Both churches and reform societies gained strength from the peculiar economic and demographic character of the burned-over districts. Revivals and reform movements were stronger, for instance, in marketing and manufacturing centers (like Windsor, Rochester, and Utica) than in commercial centers on major waterways that had little manufacturing (like Buffalo, Albany, and Troy). The growth of the regional economy and the decline of proprietorship did not create the kind of crisis in the relationship between shipping merchants and the unskilled laborers who worked for them that it did in the relationship between master craftsmen and their skilled workers, primarily because shipping merchants had never taken responsibility for the moral and spiritual development of their wage workers, who drifted in and out of town by the thousands. Merchants hired these job seekers by the day and did not board them in their homes or groom them for advancement, as they did their clerks, or retain their services when trade slowed each winter. For their part, laborers did not seem to aspire to the position of their employers. As a result they may have been less sensitive to the decline of proprietorship in commerce and more disposed to try to improve their economic circumstances by migrating to other cities in search of better jobs, rather than by bonding themselves more closely to employers through churches and other organizations, in hopes of being held in better favor and getting steadier work. In short, neither the shipping merchants nor the laborers seemed overly concerned about their impersonal relationship or its implications for the community, and that left them free of the anxieties that elsewhere propelled those engaged in manufacturing into churches and reform societies in great numbers. The churches and reform movements of the burned-over districts were thus blessed by the regional scarcity of ports and transportation centers.[2]

Revivals and reform movements were also weaker in areas of high tenancy, like the hill country southwest of Rochester and the uplands to the west and southwest of Albany, than in areas of low tenancy, like the Connecticut River Valley. Churches were weak in part because villages (which generally supported the strongest churches) were small and few and unable to grow because of the poverty of the surrounding tenants and farmers on whom they relied for custom. The problem probably stemmed to a greater degree, however, from the adversary relationship between landlords and their tenants. Landlords remained relatively aloof from their tenants, dealing with them primarily through retainers and making it clear that their major goal in the relationship was financial gain. Tenants hoped to earn money quickly and migrate to other areas where they could purchase farms outright. In consequence, landlords and tenants in the areas remained for the most part social strangers who cared little about the building of strong, stable communities. There was little sense of common purpose among them and few of the networks of mutual support that were to be found in the churches and reform societies of the burned-over districts.[3]

By contrast, the economy of the burned-over districts encouraged the growth of churches and reform societies. Employers and employees, as proprietors or expectant proprietors of small shops and farms, needed to work reliably and enthusiastically for each other if they wanted to improve or establish enterprises. Neighbors and townspeople, as producers and consumers who were by 1815 involved in a specialized, densely interwoven commercial economy, needed to exchange goods and services readily if they were to prosper. These relationships led of course to struggles for advantage. They also led to a strong sense of mutual dependence among townspeople and to the forging of economic bonds that cut across communal and class lines in ways that dampened antagonism. Economic relationships therefore encouraged contracting parties to search for means of assuring mutual concern and accountability and stimulated interest not only in campaigns for economic development, but in organizations like churches, reform societies, and reformist political parties, which encouraged people to recognize their mutual economic interests and obligations.[4]

The time of settlement of the burned-over districts also favored the growth of strong churches and reform movements. The region's small towns and rural communities were unique in the northeast in the 1830s and 1840s by virtue of the critical size of their populations. They were at the point at which the high expectations of their inhabitants (particularly high in this case because of the optimism generated by the postwar boom) were frustrated by a lack of opportunities for proprietorship for themselves and their children near home. As a result of crowding and its effects on the social order, townspeople were unable to uphold communal moral standards or maintain a rough equality. The decline in proprietorship was large enough to inspire fears of failure, conspiracy, and moral declension and yet small enough to avert confrontation between haves and have-nots. That partly explains why revivals and the more extreme political and reform movements, like Antimasonry and abolition, were less successful in areas of eastern New York and southern New England settled before 1763. Their residents had largely adapted to straitened circumstances by the 1830s and had accustomed themselves to preparing most of their children to leave town in order to establish themselves securely. The inhabitants of the burned-over districts made these adjustments, but only in the late 1840s and 1850s.[5]

Beyond matters of economy and demography were the peculiar ethnic traditions and experiences of the New Englanders who settled the revolutionary frontier. Towns settled by Yankees or their descendants, for example, sponsored stronger revivals than towns settled by the Scots or the Dutch. The strong communitarian tradition of the Scots of Barnet and Ryegate allowed them to respond more directly and collectively than their Yankee neighbors to the pressures of the times and thus to avoid the kinds of stress that forced Yankees in great numbers toward spiritual crises. On the other hand, an attenuation of fellow feeling and commitment to community may well have made the Dutch reluctant to engage in spiritual crusades. The Dutch had been a diverse people from the beginning of settlement in the New World; their communities comprised not only Netherlanders but Palatine Germans and French Huguenots, who adopted their language (but not necessarily their customs), and their Dutch Reformed churches harbored Calvinists, Pietists, Lutherans, and latitudinarians. Their diversity and their forced inclusion in the British empire in 1674 led the Dutch to prize tolerance and compromise on cultural and spiritual matters. Dutch civilization declined except in the less commercialized parts of the countryside, where the Dutch maintained their language, socialized with their kin and immediate neighbors, and remained apart from religious and reform societies and other social organizations, leaving politics and the wider world largely to Dutch patricians and the English.[6] The Scots of Barnet and Ryegate, by contrast, were fierce reformers, although they supported their favorite crusades, like Sabbatarianism, more to mark their separation from the Yankee world than to transform it.[7]

The history of the Dutch and the Scots suggests that the inhabitants of the burned-over districts were more likely than other people to join churches, reform societies, civic associations, and booster groups and to respond to crises through revivals in large part because of their peculiar habits as a people and their singular form of communal life, which they shared for the most part with other New Englanders. They clearly were not as close a people as the Scots of Barnet and Ryegate, or as parochial or family-centered as the Dutch. Their lives revolved to a greater extent around voluntary organizations, to which they turned for help in addressing economic and moral problems rather than to their families alone or to those of similar ethnic background.

The distinctive character of New Englanders and their experience as a people may thus have played a part in determining their approach to problems. Unlike the Dutch, New Englanders were anxious to attain proprietorship and to fashion their towns after a spiritual ideal. Unlike the Scots, Yankees for the most part had little awareness of a shared ethnicity. They did not have the degree of confidence that the valley's Scots did in their countrymen's character and benevolence, and their ambition in moral and economic realms made them more anxious for success than the Dutch. Voluntary organizations were thus more important to them than to either of the other groups. Those organizations offered New Englanders vehicles through which they could pursue their peculiar ambitions, through which they could meet a broader range of people on whose support they could rely in that pursuit, especially in times of crisis. Revivals were also more important to the Yankees. They were the last source of hope for New Englanders whose own individual and organized efforts had failed.

It is thus not surprising that churches and reform movements won their broadest support in the Connecticut River Valley of Vermont, the burned-over district in which proprietorship and Yankee ancestry were most widespread, in which the demographic crisis of the 1830s and 1840s developed most fully, and in which the revolutionary generation had the power, by virtue of Vermont's independence, to fashion truly democratic institutions and independent churches. It is important to remember, however, that the New Englanders who lived in the burned-over districts were unique not by virtue of the fact that they were the only people caught up in these crusades, but for the fervor with which they created and embraced them and for the way they exemplified the more general commitment of Americans to Christianity and reform. Their ambitions and circumstances may have been singular, but they were not remote from those of many other Americans.

Of course, Americans were not the only people to join churches and reform societies in extraordinary numbers during the Age of Democratic Revolution. Revivals and reform movements were as powerful in Great Britain as in America, particularly on Britain's "Celtic Fringe." That suggests that the difficulties of creating a stable, egalitarian postrevolutionary order cannot wholly explain the moral and spiritual enthusiasm of Vermonters. The democratic revolution was relatively unsuccessful and self-employment uncommon throughout Europe through 1850. But Great Britain, unlike the Protestant nations of the Continent, shared deeply in the same movements, and its Celtic Fringe was nearly as "burned-over" as New England's revolutionary frontier. The reasons for that pattern are complex. A comparison of Vermont with Wales and the Kingdom of Württemberg in southwestern Germany, each a predominantly rural land with strong pietistic traditions, suggests that Vermont's moral and spiritual distinctiveness may have followed as much from the distinctive character of prerevolutionary town life and politics in the Anglo-American world, of which Vermont again served as exemplar, as from the unparalleled success of Vermont's democratic revolution.

By comparison with their counterparts in Württemberg, townspeople and elites in Vermont and Wales possessed few formal means of protecting their values and interests. In Württemberg, peasant villages and market towns had the power to suppress immorality and divisive ideas and the ability to provide each citizen with an adequate living and to prevent individuals, especially outsiders, from expropriating land or trade other citizens needed to survive. Strict morals laws, mandatory attendance at the established Lutheran church, and prohibitions against marrying people deemed unfit kept the young and the wayward in line. Citizens retained their control of the town's economy by conferring citizenship and political rights only on their descendants and a select body of newcomers, by reserving patronage and government business for themselves, by restricting access to trades and to communal woodlots and pastures to official residents, and by forcing all tolerated strangers in market towns (people who came to perform menial or dishonorable but necessary tasks) to pay weekly residence fees.[8]

The power and economic well-being of the nobility and the Protestant clergy were also protected. The post-Napoleonic constitution of 1819 limited the power of the aristocracy and the establishment to a degree. It created a bicameral Parliament, enfranchised the wealthiest members of the middle classes (businessmen, professionals, and civil servants), freed peasants from feudal labor obligations, and guaranteed freedom of religion for Catholics and freedom of conscience for Protestants who attended worship and accepted confirmation in the state church. It forbade religious dissent, denied freedom of speech, granted the nobility and clergy veto power through the upper house of Parliament over the decisions of the popularly elected lower house, and guaranteed their rents and tithes, while declaring the king sovereign in most matters of church and state.[9]

These formal protections of the rights and privileges of townspeople and elites offered Württembergers powerful means through which to protect themselves against the common dangers of the revolutionary era: war, revolution, population pressure, and economic change. That is not to say that townspeople did not use gossip or informal discrimination to guard their businesses and communities against the wayward and dissident, or that they never sought comfort, fellowship, and assistance amid declining economic times through spiritual rebirth and entry into voluntary pietistic societies, which served as spiritual adjuncts to the established church.[10] Nor did the king, the nobility, the clergy, or wealthy members of the middle class remain altogether aloof from movements to distribute Bibles or discourage the use of alcohol. They were aware of the way those movements could enhance their prestige, particularly among rank-and-file pietists, at a time when some Continental radicals were proposing that all political and economic distinctions among men be abolished. Still, revivalism and reform remained secondary.[11]

Württembergers instead defended their families, values, and livelihoods directly, self-consciously, and collectively through 1850. Townspeople, who understood freedom primarily in corporate terms as the freedom of each community from external interference and exploitation, defied efforts by urban capitalists and civil servants to break their customary powers, move goods and people through them more freely, concentrate capital in the hands of entrepreneurs and financiers, ease restrictions on land sales and interest rates, and increase their economic and fiscal productivity. They drew the distinction between state and communal citizenship more clearly, closed their communities to outsiders (especially the poor and dispossessed), and asserted their right to choose, govern, and provide for their own members.[12] Nobles and clerics, terrified by the French Revolution and the Napoleonic reforms of 1806–13, spearheaded a conservative drive to marshal all elements of their seigneurial society against toleration and a broader democracy. Some of them wanted to preserve the status quo; others wanted to initiate their own reforms from above to avoid conflict and co-opt insurgents. There were even those who wanted to reconstitute the medieval order in all its imperial glory. All agreed that hierarchy, privilege, organic harmony, and some version of tradition had to be defended at all cost. These movements generated tremendous conflict. They set insiders against outsiders in each community and pitted conservatives against progressives in politics. Few believed, however, that revivals or reform movements could better reconcile warring factions or provide the foundation for a stable social order: not even moderate middle-class nationalists who, misunderstanding much of America's and Britain's success, spoke eloquently of the unifying, ennobling, enriching potential of liberalism, before a people to whom its values and methods were largely repugnant.[13]

Vermonters, unlike Württembergers and most other European Protestants, lacked direct means of protecting their economic positions and values and of shepherding their children safely to maturity. The towns of the valley were formally open by the 1820s.[14] Anyone could enter, set up a household, pursue his occupation, and live according to the dictates of his own conscience without encountering interference from the law or public institutions. By the same decade, the valley's politics were formally progressive.[15] Leading citizens wielded great power, yet they were ultimately at the mercy of the electorate and had no assurance they would retain their hold on political or clerical power or that the law would protect their economic interests. That made the valley's townspeople and elite in formal terms the most insecure in the world. Vermonters, like Württembergers, saw much to fear in an open, progressive society, but they had no institutions that could have rallied support for conservatism in politics and closure in town life, once the covenanted community and standing order had perished, nor could they create such institutions, given the commitments they had made to a democratic society in their public documents.

Still, the predicament of Vermont's townspeople and elite was not peculiar to formally democratic societies. In practical terms, their situation was not unlike that of their counterparts in Wales and much of Great Britain, who were equally insecure, though more from circumstance than design. The towns of rural Wales were nearly as open as those in the valley. The Anglican establishment, the spiritual arm of the English-speaking, culturally alien gentry, was losing its ability and authority to supervise the moral and spiritual life of the community by late in the eighteenth century. Settlement and poor laws were too weak to control migration and to apportion resources adequately among long-standing residents, as population pressure, rising rents, competition in commerce and manufacturing, farm enclosures, and periodic wars and crop failures made it difficult for the Welsh to make a living, let alone rent or own shops or farms – always a more remote possibility than in the valley.[16] The situation of Wales's indigenous elite, which was comprised largely of dissenting businessmen, professionals, and commercial farmers, was likewise precarious. These middle-class Welshmen were doubly besieged, by an Anglicized gentry and clergy that wished to deny them the power to govern Wales and by the Welsh people. Ninety-six percent of Welsh adult males were still disfranchised by property restrictions after the Reform Act of 1832, and they demanded with increasing urgency both the right to vote and limited recognition of Welsh sovereignty. Welsh elites thus had to fight for power in Parliament and defend their interests against popular challenges, while they tried simultaneously to establish themselves as the legitimate spokesmen for the aspirations of the Welsh people.[17]

The strength of revivalism and reform in Wales, which rivaled that in Vermont, suggests that churches and reform movements flourished in the valley not simply because they addressed the needs of a successful revolutionary people. Dissenting churches, teetotal societies, and Sunday schools grew strong in Wales, first in the market towns and then in the countryside, where these voluntary organizations drew their members into a somewhat separate world that marked "pobl y capel" from "pobl y tafern" (chapel people from tavern people) and conferred on members a solid reputation, a basic literacy in Welsh, and fraternal assistance, all of which helped them prosper and retain a sense of unity, self-sufficiency, and moral independence from the "corrupt" English world.[18] The dissenting, Welsh-speaking middle classes, searching for a safe way to serve simultaneously the ends of property, order, and justice and to secure their role in politics and the economy, embraced reform. They campaigned for abolition and temperance, as well as for a gradual extension of economic, political, and religious rights to the Welsh people, a gradual enactment of social legislation to alleviate suffering among the common people, and a gradual removal of the powers and privileges of the gentry and the established church.[19]

The point is not of course that similar circumstances in Vermont and Wales produced identical spiritual and moral results. Welsh dissenters, because of their antagonism toward Anglican religion and English domination, were generally unwilling to forge interdenominational or sentimental bonds with their adversaries, or to forsake evangelical religion. Churches in ports and industrial towns grew stronger in Wales than their counterparts in the burned-over districts, because the impersonal relationships they encouraged between Welsh workers and their usually Anglicized employers often fostered the feelings of national unity and distinctiveness from which Welsh churches drew their strength.[20] Reform did not unify men of property to the extent it did in the valley, nor did it forge as solid a moral consensus behind their leadership of the Welsh nation. The indifference of most Anglicized gentry and clergy to these crusades and their reluctance to part with their power and privileges at times stimulated political polarization between conservatives and progressives, and at times sparked violence and counterriots, as when the militia was sent out in the 1830s and 1840s, with no small degree of support from the Welsh-speaking middle classes, to put down riots against tollgates or poor houses.[21]

The similarities remain striking. The Welsh experience shows that the popularity of revivals, reform, and centrist political ideologies did not depend as much upon a successful democratic revolution or widespread proprietorship, which would have restricted their appeal to the northern United States, as upon a Protestant social order in which townspeople received little or no help from traditional institutions or customary rights as they tried to defend their interests and values, and in which wealthy entrepreneurs, financiers, professionals, and commercial farmers faced either no opposition or manageable opposition from an aristocracy or established church as they drove toward political and economic leadership. Under such an order townspeople and elites found themselves in a precarious position. They lacked strong formal or practical means of defending themselves against insurgents and outsiders, while at the same time they depended upon common people for their political and community power; and in Great Britain, they confronted the additional threat of domination or subversion by the gentry and establishment, which gave British moral and spiritual movements a more consistently insurgent tone. Both Americans and Britains thus had powerful reasons to join revivals and reform movements, especially where local circumstances or traditions made them particularly insecure, as happened both in the valley and in

Wales, and more generally on New England's revolutionary frontier, where America's prerevolutionary order collapsed completely, and on the Celtic Fringe, where England's government and establishment were most thoroughly discredited.

The similarities between the people of New England's revolutionary frontier and of Britain's Celtic Fringe became even more striking by the late 1840s and 1850s, as each made revivalism and reform central to its increasingly acute sense of regional and national identity. That self-consciousness stemmed in part from the failure of the European revolutions of 1848 and from the extension of slavery into the American Southwest. Most Celts believed that the British regime would never recognize willingly the legitimacy of their national, democratic aspirations, and most Yankees felt that the American Revolution had not been entirely successful in persuading the world, or even all Americans, of the superiority of the Yankee way of life. That self-consciousness stemmed from local failures as well. As inhabitants of the developed fringe of the capitalist world — facing continuing problems with economic growth and population pressure, finding themselves becoming economically dependent on and politically subordinate to the developed core of the Anglo-American world, and under pressure to accept urban, capitalistic values — both Yankees and Celts realized that their peculiar traditions and aspirations were threatened at home. They again found strength and unity in their Christian, reform traditions. As sentimental free-soilers, New England's frontiersmen sought to save their faltering revolution by remaking America and the world in their own image, while Celtic peoples sought to save their besieged nations by defending the rights of dissenters and dependent peoples everywhere against the claims of empire. The ironic fruit of the democratic revolution was thus a heightened sense of regional identity and loyalty, especially on the developed fringe of the Anglo-American world, as Yankees and Celts, realizing that revolution had failed to draw together the people of the world and that their own aspirations and interests were still in jeopardy, looked to their own traditions for new ways of realizing their parochial and cosmopolitian ambitions. They discovered in the 1850s and 1860s their greatest spiritual unity and their greatest political power, at the forefront of Republican and Liberal crusades that promised to save their ways of life by Christianizing and reforming the world.[22]

In the Age of Democratic Revolution, the problem of order appeared everywhere that revolutionary ideas and social change disrupted prerevolutionary society. Throughout the Anglo-American world, people looked to religious and reform movements for solutions to that problem. The people of the Connecticut River Valley of Vermont stood alone, however, both in the intensity of their commitment to moral and spiritual resolutions to the problems of revolutionary life and in their inability to combat disorder directly. As New Englanders on the revolutionary frontier, they came face to face with the central problem posed by the world's most successful democratic revolution — how to reconcile their commitment to the formally open, progressive, competitive society they had created with their equally earnest desire to protect their families, values, and spiritual beliefs; their shops, farms, and reputations; their wealth, power, and prestige (or the opportunity to attain those things). Unlike Europeans, they had to live with the success of their revolution, which threatened myriad interests and aspirations, some venal and selfish, but most not. They did not forsake democracy, but most found it hard to live with its full implications. Therefore they shaped a postrevolutionary order that, although it maintained their formal commitment to democracy, subtly lessened the dangers that they perceived in democratic life. It was not without cost, for it allowed no small degree of discrimination, elite rule, and collusion, and it permitted citizens to avoid a collective confrontation with the demographic and economic developments eroding the material base of their way of life, which diminished their ability to gain proprietorship and in the end undermined self-employment both as an ideal and a reality for them and their descendants. But their postrevolutionary order did, for a while, hold their conflicting values and aspirations in a creative tension and gave them confidence that they could indeed solve their problems, if only they remained the most dedicated Christians and reformers on earth.

Appendix A

Church records

The statistics in this study are drawn primarily from nine towns (Map 1). They are the only towns in the valley that have lost no more than one set of church records and were identified with the help of the inventory of Vermont church records compiled by the Historical Records Survey of the Works Progress Administration. The inventory indicates the contents of all records located by the survey and their location in 1940, and it lists all records known to have been lost or destroyed. The inventory is not perfect. A handful of unlisted records still exists, and several records have been lost or destroyed since 1940.

Almost all church records in the towns studied intensively have survived, and few of these are incomplete. Still, the use of these records poses several problems. First, evangelical denominations (Congregational, Baptist, Presbyterian, Methodist, Freewill Baptist, Christian) and nonevangelical denominations (Unitarian, Universalist) had different criteria for determining membership. Evangelicals distinguished between membership in a church, which was open only to those who experienced conversion, and membership in a religious society organized to support worship locally, which was open to all who attended church regularly and contributed a designated fee annually for support of the minister and maintenance of church property. Nonevangelicals, by contrast, had no separate "church" organization. People who attended regularly, paid religious levies, and joined religious societies were recognized as members.

These differences pose a problem: Who was a church member, and who was not? In the end each denomination's distinctive criteria for church membership were accepted: membership in a church for evangelicals and membership in a religious society for nonevangelicals. That left a problem only with Episcopalian churches. They were generally nonevangelical, which is to say that all who joined religious societies and supported worship financially were considered members.

Yet members of the religious societies who participated in communion, the most sacred sacrament of the church, retained a special place spiritually within these churches. Communion was not closed, as in evangelical churches, to all but those who could prove that they had experienced a work of grace. Prospective communicants were bound only to ask themselves whether or not they truly felt God's grace and to refrain from seeking communion until they were relatively certain of the state of their souls. Those who took communion were not subject to any special watch or discipline, and certain churches placed little emphasis on communion and its role in salvation (the St. James Episcopal Church in Woodstock had only one male communicant through the 1820s, despite the large male membership in its religious society). Communion was nonetheless an important spiritual exercise, emphasized particularly during the great revival, and it appears to have been customary to set communicants' names down on lists separate from those registering the names of all the society members. Unfortunately, most lists of communicants have been lost. Therefore society membership was accepted as the criterion for membership.[1]

A second problem is that of partial records. The records of the evangelical churches and of the Episcopalian religious societies are generally complete, but that is not the case for the records of the Unitarian and Universalist societies, which are nothing more than compilations of names. They do not indicate when individuals joined societies. That poses a problem: Should members be entered in mobility tables as "church members by 1827," recorded as "church members, 1827–43," or not entered at all? It was concluded after careful examination that they should be included as "church members by 1827," since their mobility characteristics were most like that group's and quite different from those of nonmembers. Their complete exclusion was not considered necessary, as it would not have altered the trends evident in the tables.

Meetinghouse records present a third problem. In South Woodstock Village and in Greenbush Village (Weathersfield), there were not enough people in the 1830s to support separate churches for each denomination, but there was enough enthusiasm to sustain regular worship. The members of various sects therefore joined to form religious societies for the purpose of establishing Union meetinghouses. Those houses sponsored preaching by ministers from a wide range of denominations on a regular basis. The records do not show denominational affiliation in Weathersfield (although most people were apparently Universalists, and those who were Methodists were recorded on class records for the area), and in South Woodstock it is not clear whether those listed as affiliated with evangelical churches were church members or only society members. The decision was made to consider society membership the criterion for membership in these cases, given the absence of other information.[2]

Finally, there is the problem of missing records. As the list that follows indicates, most of the towns studied intensively are missing at least one set of church records. Most of the problems created by those losses could be remedied. Only about thirty adult males belonged to the Freewill Baptist Church of Weathersfield and the Baptist Church of West Windsor, of whom four were identified from other sources – so their loss was not critical.[3] Meetinghouse records for the village of West Barnet were available as a crude substitute for the records of the West Barnet Associate Presbyterian Church, which have been lost. A substantial problem exists only in Peacham and St. Johnsbury, where Methodist church records have disappeared. Methodism was relatively weak in those towns prior to the great revival, but membership swelled in the 1830s. It is impossible to tell with certainty how many adult males belonged to these churches. Denominational statistics record only total male and female membership in religious societies. A reasonable guess would be that between forty-five and sixty-five adult males were full members of the church in St. Johnsbury by 1840, and from twenty-five to thirty-five in Peacham – of whom only twenty could be identified from other sources.[4] The names of the remaining fifty to eighty members are simply not available.

These losses mean that probably around 26 percent of the adult male taxpayers and household heads in the agricultural towns in 1827 were church members, rather than the 25 percent confirmed as church members on the basis of surviving records. They suggest too that about 38 percent of the same body of adult males were church members in 1843, rather than the 33 percent revealed in surviving records, because the Methodist churches whose records are missing made dramatic gains after 1827. In addition, this means that probably 3 to 5 percent of the 1,579 nonmembers recorded in the various mobility tables for the period 1830–40 were in fact church members who could not be identified. That would make nonmembers appear more persistent and successful over that decade, if the missing church members shared the attributes of other church members.

The following is a list of the church records of the towns studied intensively and a description of their condition.

Barnet
United Presbyterian, 1798–   Partial (gap, 1817–
                                              25)

Passumpsic Baptist, 1811–   Complete
West Barnet Presbyterian, 1820–   Missing
McIndoes Falls Congregational,   Complete
  1829–
Walter Harvey Meetinghouse,   Partial
  1831–

Peacham
Congregational, 1794–   Complete
Methodist, 1831–   Missing

Pomfret
First Congregational, 1783–   Complete
Freewill Baptist, 1803–14   Complete
Christian, 1817–   Complete
Free Congregational, 1843–   Complete

Ryegate
Reformed Presbyterian, 1798–   Partial (1824–37)
Associate Presbyterian, 1823–   Complete
South Associate Presbyterian,   Missing
  1843–

St. Johnsbury
First Congregational, 1809–   Complete
Universalist, 1813–   Complete
North Congregational, 1825–   Complete
Methodist, 1835–   Missing
East Congregational, 1840–   Complete

Weathersfield
Episcopalian, 1787–1835   Partial (1824–35)
Center Congregational, 1801–   Complete
Freewill Baptist, 1802–25   Missing
North Springfield Baptist, 1810–   Complete
  35
Methodist, 1822–   Complete
Perkinsville Baptist, 1835–   Complete
Greenbush Meetinghouse,   Partial
  1836–
Bow Congregational, 1838–   Complete

West Windsor
Second Congregational, 1775–   Partial (1775–1807)
  1823
Baptist, 1802–23   Missing

First Universalist, 1798–   Partial
Methodist, 1822–   Complete
Freewill Baptist, 1825–   Partial

Windsor
Old South Congregational,   Complete
  1768–
First Baptist, 1810–   Complete
St. Paul's Episcopalian, 1816–   Complete
All Souls Unitarian, 1835–   Partial

Woodstock
First Baptist, 1780–1809   Missing
North Congregational, 1781–   Complete
South Congregational, 1782–   Missing
  1825
Christian, 1806–   Partial (1843–)
Methodist, 1822–   Partial
St. James Episcopalian, 1825–   Partial
North Universalist, 1834–   Partial
South Chapel Society, 1839–   Complete

It is also difficult to identify every church organized in the valley between 1761 and 1850 and to determine the year in which each was founded. The study relies on the Historical Record Survey's inventory of church records, annual denominational reports, town histories, Abby Hemenway's *Historical Gazetteer*, Jeffrey Potash's enumeration of early Vermont churches, and histories of Vermont's major denominations, particularly Edith MacDonald's history of Universalism and Unitarianism.[5] It is even more difficult to determine total church membership in all the valley's towns. Annual reports of membership by town exist for the following denominations: Episcopalian (1819–), Congregational (1828–), Baptist (1834–), Freewill Baptist (1834–), and Methodist (1839–). That makes complete assessments of church membership by town impossible before 1839 and makes it necessary to estimate membership in many of the valley's Presbyterian, Christian, Reformed Methodist, Unitarian, and Universalist churches. Fortunately, the Historical Record Survey's inventory and MacDonald's history of Unitarianism and Universalism provide partial membership reports and assessments of the strength of local congregations, from which membership in these denominations can be estimated.

Appendix B

Types of towns

The towns in the valley that are suitable for statistical study do not represent a cross section of all towns in the valley. Two of the nine are major marketing and manufacturing towns, and the remainder are fully developed agricultural towns on good or fair land located near the Connecticut River (Map 1). That makes it necessary to examine the valley more broadly, to determine whether the towns studied intensively were representative of towns with similar settlement patterns and social structures and to learn how they differed in their behavior from dissimilar towns, especially those less developed and farther from the navigable parts of the Connecticut River.

For the purpose of such comparisons, the valley's towns were classified into four groups, two of which are composed of several subgroups.[1] Towns were classified primarily according to the date of their settlement, the density of their population in 1830 and 1840, the quality of their farmland, and the level of their mercantile, manufacturing, and professional activity in 1830 and 1840. However, towns that had banks, regular newspapers, or county seats were often raised to the status of secondary marketing, manufacturing, and professional centers, despite poor land, remote location, and limited nonagricultural economic activity (Map 2).

This system of classification was modeled after the systems used by Edward Cook in his study of political leadership in eighteenth-century New England, and by William Gilmore in his study of literacy and reading habits in the upper Connecticut River Valley from 1760 to 1830.[2] It is more detailed than that of Cook, who divides the towns of the eighteenth century according to their position in the hierarchy of economic and political influence, because the data on economic activity and population in nineteenth-century Vermont are more precise; but it is less detailed than that of Gilmore, who identifies different types of communities within townships, because the necessary data on economic activity, religious organization, and political behavior are available only at the township level.

1. Marketing and manufacturing towns (9)
   The valley's principal marketing, manufacturing, and professional centers. Each town was taxed over $400 on Vermont's Grand List in 1831 or 1841 for mercantile and manufacturing activity. St. Johnsbury and Springfield are included, although they remained predominantly agricultural until 1850.

2. Agricultural towns on good land (53)
   a. Secondary marketing and manufacturing towns (15)
   The valley's secondary marketing, manufacturing, and professional centers. Each town was taxed between $325 and $399 on Vermont's Grand List in 1831 or 1841 for mercantile and manufacturing activity, had sizable copperas mines or marble quarries (Barre, Strafford, and Tunbridge), or was an important local financial, administrative, or print center (Chelsea, Chester, Guildhall, and Newfane).
   b. Agricultural towns with mixed economies (24)
   Agricultural towns on good land with substantial mercantile and manufacturing activity. Most of that activity served local needs, although these towns occasionally had woolen factories that served broader markets.
   c. Agricultural towns with simple economies (14)
   Agricultural towns on good land with no substantial mercantile or manufacturing activity. By 1831, residents traveled to neighboring towns for many goods and services.

3. Agricultural towns on poor land (39)
   a. Agricultural towns with mixed economies (19)
   Agricultural towns on poor land with fairly dense populations and substantial mercantile and manufacturing activity. Much of that activity occurred in mill villages, where factories were built to take advantage of excellent water power sites.
   b. Agricultural towns with simple economies (20)
   Agricultural towns on poor land with fairly dense populations and no substantial mercantile or manufacturing activity.

4. Frontier towns (15)
    Sparsely populated towns in remote areas on poor land.
    All had fewer than 500 inhabitants in 1840 and no sub-
    stantial mercantile or manufacturing activity.

Appendix C

Occupational groups

For the purposes of statistical analysis, this study divides the adult male taxpayers and household heads of the valley into eleven broad occupational groups. These categories were drawn with an eye to classifying male inhabitants according to wealth, economic function, and occupation. Each category encompasses a diverse array of men, but the categories proved sufficient for almost every analysis, although it was necessary in a few instances to divide adult males into narrower occupational groupings.

The basic goals of the classification system were to distinguish self-employed proprietors from salaried and wage-earning employees, and to separate blue-collar workers in agriculture, manufacturing, and day laboring from white-collar workers in the professions, commerce, finance, and government service. An additional aim was to divide proprietors according to the size of their firms, the number of their employees, and the depth of their involvement in the regional economy. Because of the limitations of the economic information that has survived from the early nineteenth century, these goals could not be fully met. Separating white-collar employees from their blue-collar counterparts presented difficulties that were in most cases impossible to overcome.

Adult males were assigned to occupational groups primarily by means of tax lists. These lists, drafted annually by each town's assessors according to the exacting specifications of Vermont's tax laws, itemize real and personal property holdings, record the amount of money each individual had lent at interest or invested in bank and insurance company stock, and show the tax paid by self-employed professionals, merchants, and manufacturers on the basis of the volume of their business. The lists make it easy to distinguish proprietors from wage earners and to tell whether a proprietor was a farmer, master craftsman, businessman, or professional. The lists also make it possible to rank proprietors in commerce, manufacturing, and agriculture according to their wealth and the size of their businesses (although no indication is given of how many employees each had). They identify the self-employed and describe their enterprises better than ordinary antebellum tax lists (which are less detailed) and city directories (which cite individual occupations but do not distinguish proprietors from wage earners).

The tax lists do not, however, distinguish among nonproprietors according to occupation. It is therefore impossible, given the absence of city directories, to differentiate skilled from semiskilled or unskilled workers, or to divide with precision agricultural and white-collar employees from other wage workers. The only course open was to list all nonproprietors as journeymen/laborers, unless additional information from the census or other sources indicated they were clerks, farm tenants, or farm laborers. Heads of households listed on the federal censuses of 1820 and 1840 as agricultural workers or as professional or commercial workers were classified respectively as farm laborers and clerks. Nonproprietors who later became farmers or small proprietors or businessmen/professionals were also grouped respectively with farm laborers and clerks, although some were doubtless journeymen or laborers who became proprietors in nonmanufacturing pursuits. Nonproprietors who owned no agricultural land but were taxed for renting farmland were classified as farm tenants, and those who neither rented nor owned land, but owned spans of oxen or small herds of cattle or sheep, were classified as farm laborers. These methods identified the great majority of farm laborers, but probably left a good number of white-collar wage earners classified as journeymen/laborers.

The study employs the following categories:

1. Businessmen/professionals
   All self-employed attorneys, physicians, merchants who were taxed $40 or more per year on the volume of their business, and businessmen who were in the upper two deciles of wealth holding and derived their income primarily from investments, rents, and interest.
2. Master craftsmen
   All persons taxed for manufacturing (tailors, jewelers, cabinetmakers, etc.), except for those already classified as businessmen because they derived their income primarily from interest and rents, not from their own skilled manual labor.
3. Small proprietors
   Those taxed under $40 for conducting commercial enterprises.

4. Millers/taverners
   All persons who owned or rented mills or received tavern or innkeeping licenses from the county courts. Some taverners rented rather than owned their establishments.

5. Clerks
   All salaried white-collar employees (clerks, government employees, educators).

6. Journeymen/laborers
   All persons positively identified as laborers or wage workers in manufacturing, as well as all nonproprietors whose occupations could not be determined.

7. Commercial farmers
   All farmers who owned ninety or more acres of improved land (tillage, mowage, and pasture).

8. Family farmers
   All farmers who owned from forty-five to eighty-nine acres of improved land.

9. Subsistence farmers
   All farmers who owned ten to forty-four acres of improved land. Those with nine acres or less were not considered subsistence farmers, as they in all likelihood earned most of their income as farm laborers or as part-time craftsmen.

10. Farm tenants
    Farm operators who rented the land they worked. Each rented fifteen acres or more.

11. Farm laborers
    All wage workers engaged in agriculture.

Some adjustments were necessary in the assignment of a few individuals to occupational groups. First, a few mobile craftsmen were missed by the assessors, even though they advertised their shops in the newspapers, and blacksmiths in some towns were not taxed on their income from manufacturing, apparently in the interest of encouraging men to pursue that difficult, vital occupation. The former were listed as master craftsmen, as were the latter whenever local ads or deeds to forges served to identify them. Second, a handful of farmers who owned some land and rented substantially more, had much more livestock and cash on hand than one would expect from their own holdings in improved land. These farmers were placed in the category above the one they ordinarily would have been placed in on the basis of the acreage they owned outright, because they were obviously more involved in market agriculture and more likely to have hired extra workers than other farmers with the same amount of personally owned land. Otherwise, the criteria for assigning individuals to occupational categories were rigidly applied.

It should be noted that the tax lists are most suited to this system of classification between 1819 and 1841. Before 1819, farm owners rather than town assessors reported improved acreage, and that resulted in severe understatements. After 1841, mercantile and manufacturing firms were not taxed unless they owned commercial real property. That made the classification of farmers difficult prior to 1819, and the identification of some merchants and master craftsmen impossible after 1841 (thus, the study of mobility between 1840 and 1850 was difficult).

Tax lists have survived for all the towns studied intensively except Ryegate and Woodstock. The occupations of many inhabitants could be determined for Woodstock from other sources, but not for Ryegate. Also, the tax lists for Pomfret from 1817 to 1824 have been lost. Occupations in Pomfret in 1820 were estimated from the tax lists of 1816 and 1825.

Appendix D

Statistical methods

The analysis of the behavior of individuals in the nine towns studied intensively rests on tabulation. Significance tests are not reported for the various tables in the text. The data reported in these tables are complete rather than sampled from a larger body of data, so such tests are not directly meaningful. Each table was computed for each town separately, however, to ensure that the trends observed in the composite tables are not artifacts of compilation, but are visible in each town. Exceptions to trends are reported in the text. Not every trend in the tables is strong, nor does every table include a substantial number of cases, which makes interpretation difficult. These cases are also treated in some detail in the text.

Inadequate data pose several problems. The lack of tax lists from Woodstock and Ryegate makes it impossible to determine the proportion of the adult male population that belonged to a particular church or pursued a particular occupation in a given year. The tables on reformers and political activists, which include data from Woodstock and Ryegate, therefore describe the proportion of the members of each political or reform movement who belonged to a particular church or pursued a particular occupation, rather than vice versa. These tables compare the members of each movement with the members of other movements, but do not reveal how representative the members of each movement were of the entire population of the towns studied intensively. Reformers and political activists in the seven towns whose tax lists survived were compared in separate tables with nonreformers and nonactivists. The results of these tables are reflected in the text.

The loss of most district school records and the decision of the Vermont assembly prior to 1856 not to require registration of births or deaths make it impossible to assess statistically the impact of education, parental wealth, and family size on social and geographical mobility. The persistence and success of church members and temperance society members may have rested in part on their interest in education and family limitation, and on their ability to pass wealth and church membership on to their children. These possibilities are considered in the text, but they cannot be explored quantitatively.

The analysis of electoral data from the valley's towns rests on tabulation, two-way analysis, and regression. Because of the difficulty of inferring voter behavior from town-level data, the analysis focuses primarily on the behavior of towns. The two-way analyses measure the median vote over time for each party in each town, and the stability and consistency over time of each town's vote (see Chapter 2, note 59; and Chapter 7, note 63). [On two-way analysis, see John W. Tukey, *Exploratory Data Analysis* (Reading: Addison-Wesley, 1977), 331–400.] Tabulations and simple regression analyses reveal how the median town vote varied according to the social characteristics and past political behavior of each town (see Chapter 2, note 63; Chapter 8, note 62; and Table 5.3).

The analysis of electoral data focuses in certain instances, however, on the behavior of voters rather than towns. Because town-level data on church membership are available after 1834, it is possible to use ecological regression to estimate the proportion of the adult male members of each denomination who voted for a particular party in the 1830s and 1840s, and to examine how that proportion varied according to the social characteristics of the valley's towns and of their adult male inhabitants (Tables 5.4, 7.2, and 7.11). It is also possible to use ecological regression to estimate transitions of voters from party to party across elections. The elections must occur in close succession, however, so that migration and mortality do not dramatically alter the character of each town's population; and the results of the elections must not be highly correlated, so that the regression will not underestimate the proportion of voters who switched parties. These conditions hold only for the transitions examined in Tables 7.2 and Tables 7.11. [On the reliability of these estimates and the plausibility of the assumptions upon which they rest, see Randolph A. Roth, "Ecological Regression and the Analysis of Voter Behavior," *Historical Methods*, 19 (1986), 103–117; Hayward R. Alker, Jr., "A Typology of Ecological Fallacies," in Mattei Dogan and Stein Rokkan, eds., *Quantitative Ecological Analysis in the Social Sciences* (Cambridge: MIT Press, 1969), 69–86; and J. Morgan Kousser, "Ecological Regression and the Analysis of Past Politics," *Journal of Interdisciplinary History*, 4 (1973), 237–262.]

Notes

Abbreviations

A.A.S.	American Antiquarian Society
B.P.L.	Boston Public Library
D.C.L.	Dartmouth College Library
M.H.S.	Massachusetts Historical Society
N.H.H.S.	New Hampshire Historical Society
N.Y.H.S.	New-York Historical Society
N.Y.S.L.	New York State Library, Albany
U.V.M.	University of Vermont

Unless otherwise noted, all manuscripts are at the Vermont Historical Society. All towns referred to are in Vermont. The locations of correspondents are specified because the notes include references to letters not only from people in the Connecticut River Valley of Vermont, but from travelers and recent migrants from the valley.

On occasion the study uses evidence from western Vermont and western New Hampshire. Residents from these areas often had dealings with inhabitants of the valley. Evidence from these areas is also used when sources from the valley are too sparse to allow thorough study of a particular social group, as is the case with the rural poor in the 1830s and 1840s.

Introduction

1   On the region's extensive involvement in these movements, see David M. Ludlum, *Social Ferment in Vermont, 1790–1850* (New York: Columbia Univ. Press, 1939); Alice Felt Tyler, *Freedom's Ferment: Phases of American Social History from the Colonial Period to the Outbreak of the Civil War* (Minneapolis: Univ. of Minnesota Press, 1944); Whitney R. Cross, *The Burned-Over District: The Social and Intellectual History of Enthusiastic Religion in Western New York, 1800–1850* (Ithaca: Cornell Univ. Press, 1950); Paul E. Johnson, *A Shopkeepers' Millennium: Society and Revivals in Rochester, New York, 1815–1837* (New York: Hill and Wang, 1978), 4–5; Mary P. Ryan, *Cradle of the Middle Class: The Family in Oneida County, New York, 1790–1865* (New York: Cambridge Univ. Press, 1981), 11–17; and Glenn C. Altschuler and Jan M. Saltzgaber, *Revivalism, Social*

Conscience, and Community in the Burned-Over District: The Trial of Rhoda Bement (Ithaca: Cornell Univ. Press, 1983), 31–77.

2 Frank Thistlethwaite, *The Anglo-American Connection in the Early Nineteenth Century* (Philadelphia: Univ. of Pennsylvania Press, 1959), discusses the involvement of the Anglo-American world in revivals and reform movements. On religion and revivals in Great Britain, see W. R. Ward, *Religion and Society in England, 1790–1850* (New York: Schocken, 1973); Alan D. Gilbert, *Religion and Society in Industrial England: Church, Chapel, and Social Change, 1740–1914* (London: Longman, 1976); Ebenezer T. Davies, *Religion in the Industrial Revolution in South Wales* (Cardiff: Univ. of Wales Press, 1965); and William Ferguson, *Scotland: 1689 to the Present* (New York: Praeger, 1968).

3 For republican–liberal interpretations of revivalism and reform in America, see Gordon S. Wood, *The Rising Glory of America, 1760–1820* (New York: George Braziller, 1971), 1–22; John R. Howe, *From the Revolution through the Age of Jackson: Innocence and Empire in the Young Republic* (Englewood Cliffs: Prentice-Hall, 1973), 13–16, 123–125, 132–134, 137–143; H. Richard Niebuhr, *The Kingdom of God in America* (Chicago: Univ. of Chicago Press, 1937), 98–100; and Alexis de Tocqueville, *Democracy in America*, ed. Phillips Bradley (New York: Vintage, 1945), v. I, 310–326, and v. II, 21–29, 109–135, 215–221. The republican–liberal interpretation itself is discussed in Dorothy Ross, "The Liberal Tradition Revisited and the Republican Tradition Addressed," in John Higham and Paul K. Conkin, eds., *New Directions in American Intellectual History* (Baltimore: Johns Hopkins Univ. Press, 1979), 116–131; Robert E. Shalhope, "Toward a Republican Synthesis: The Emergence of an Understanding of Republicanism in American Historiography," *William and Mary Quarterly*, 3d ser., 29 (1972), 49–80; and Shalhope, "Republicanism and Early American History," *William and Mary Quarterly*, 3d ser., 39 (1982), 334–356.

See Ludlum, *Social Ferment*, 3–4; Cross, *Burned-Over District*, 54–109; and Altschuler and Saltzgaber, *Revivalism, Social Conscience, and Community*, 29–32, 37–39, for republican–liberal interpretations of revivalism and reform in the burned-over districts. See Johnson, *Shopkeepers' Millennium*, 8–10; and Randolph A. Roth, "Whence This Strange Fire? Religious and Reform Movements in the Connecticut River Valley of Vermont, 1791–1843" (Ph.D. diss., Yale Univ., 1981), 5–8, for a discussion of these interpretations.

4 For a discussion of liberalism in America prior to the Revolution, see Joyce Appleby, "Liberalism and the American Revolution," *New England Quarterly*, 64 (1976), 3–26; idem, *Capitalism and a New Social Order: The Republican Vision of the 1790s* (New York: New York Univ. Press, 1984), 1–23; and John P. Diggins, *The Lost Soul of American Politics: Virtue, Self-Interest, and the Foundations of Liberalism* (New York: Basic Books, 1984). Appleby and Diggins view liberalism as a product of the dissolution of the traditional European social order rather than of postrevolutionary change.

5 Definitions of liberalism are diverse. See, for example, Lance Banning, "Jef-

fersonian Ideology Revisited: Liberalism and Classical Ideas in the New Republic," *William and Mary Quarterly*, 3d ser., 43 (1986), 3–19; and Joyce Appleby, "Republicanism in Old and New Contexts," ibid., 20–34. The definition offered here encompasses the definitions of historians who use the term to describe and measure postrevolutionary social and cultural change. Some historians use the word "modernity" to describe and measure similar changes. See, for example, Wood, *Rising Glory*, 1–22; Richard D. Brown, *Modernization: The Transformation of American Life, 1600–1865* (New York: Hill and Wang, 1976), 3–22; and Joseph J. Ellis, *After the Revolution: Profiles in Early American Culture* (New York: Norton, 1979), xi–xiv, 21–38, 213–222.

6 Of course, some historians define liberalism and its constituent elements in ways that would make most Americans liberals in the late eighteenth and early nineteenth centuries. For example, Rhys Isaac defines individualism as a separation of the self from society, as a withdrawal by individuals "into a secluded realm" where "modes of silent thought developed." There evangelical Christians "faced alone the meaning of God's judgment" and readers confronted in isolation the "impersonal" world of printed discourse. *Transformation of Virginia, 1740–1790* (Chapel Hill: Univ. of North Carolina Press, 1982), 121–122, 171. Thomas J. Haskell associates capitalism with "the expansion of the market, the intensification of market discipline, and the penetration of that discipline into spheres of life previously untouched by it." "Capitalism and the Origins of Humanitarian Sensibility," *American Historical Review*, 90 (1985), 342.

By these definitions, Vermonters had always been individualists and capitalists. The settlers of Vermont sought inspiration and guidance in their private encounters with God and in their reading. They exchanged goods and services in neighborhood, town, and regional markets from the beginning of settlement, using both civil and ecclesiastical authority to enforce market discipline. They perceived noneconomic relationships among people in terms of mutually binding contracts called "covenants."

Such definitions of liberalism and its elements are popular among historians of eighteenth-century America, because they point directly to the disruptive, liberating movements and social developments that most historians believe lay behind the American Revolution, and because they suggest that the social changes caused by these phenomena – the privatization of thought and faith, the commercialization of human relationships – were progressive and irreversible, and that postrevolutionary America was becoming, inexorably, an increasingly modern, liberal society.

The problem for historians of postrevolutionary America is that the effects of literacy, evangelical Protestantism, deepening involvement in the market economy, and other "modern" phenomena are unclear. William J. Gilmore finds that most readers in postrevolutionary New England bought or borrowed printed materials from people they knew and belonged to communities of readers, printers, and booksellers who read selectively and discussed texts together. *Reading Becomes a Necessity of Life: Material and Cultural*

Life in Rural New England, 1780–1830 (forthcoming, Univ. of Tennessee Press). Paul Johnson shows that most evangelical Christians in antebellum Rochester, New York, not only worshipped, but lived, worked, and traded within communities of evangelical Protestants. *Shopkeepers' Millennium,* 95–115. These studies suggest that literacy and evangelical religion may have enhanced rather than diminished the ability of communities to shape individual thought and faith and may have bound self and society more closely, albeit in new kinds of communities.

James Henretta argues that involvement in the market economy did not mean that farmers and shopkeepers in antebellum America had to change their values or familial aspirations. Nor did it prevent them from using the market to sustain existing patterns of consumption and modes of production. "Families and Farms: Mentalité in Pre-Industrial America," *William and Mary Quarterly,* 3d ser., 35(1978), 3–32. Paul Johnson shows that Christians disciplined the market and transformed economic relationships in ways that enabled them to enlist commerce in their campaign to Christianize their communities. *Shopkeepers' Millennium,* 32–36. These studies present the possibility that postrevolutionary Americans may have shaped the market as much as it shaped them and suggest that an increase in the frequency or profitability of exchange may have little impact on the character of an economy or society, unless accompanied by simultaneous changes in production, consumption, or economic ambitions.

Because the effects of literacy, evangelical Protestantism, involvement in the market economy, and other potentially liberating social developments and movements are uncertain, historians of postrevolutionary America – including historians who adhere to the republican–liberal interpretation of postrevolutionary history – prefer definitions of liberalism that measure the impact of these phenomena on beliefs and behavior, rather than definitions that predict their effect on consciousness and society, or that imply that people bring little power or no community or family agendas to their encounters with markets, books, or evangelical doctrines. Definitions of the former sort, like those offered in this study, do not draw clear lines between traditional and modern societies, but they are subtler tools for measuring postrevolutionary change.

7 See, for example, Eric Foner, *Tom Paine and Revolutionary America* (New York: Oxford Univ. Press, 1976); Edward Countryman, *A People in Revolution: The American Revolution and Political Society in New York, 1760–1790* (Baltimore: Johns Hopkins Univ. Press, 1981); Alan E. Heimert, *Religion and the American Mind* (Cambridge: Harvard Univ. Press, 1966), 239–552; and Sean Wilentz, *Chants Democratic: New York City and the Rise of the American Working Class, 1788–1850* (New York: Oxford Univ. Press, 1984).

8 Donald A. Smith, "Legacy of Dissent: Religion and Politics in Revolutionary Vermont" (Ph.D. diss., Clark University, 1981).

9 J. G. A. Pocock, *The Machiavellian Moment: Florentine Political Thought and the Atlantic Republican Tradition* (Princeton: Princeton Univ. Press,

1975); and idem, "*The Machiavellian Moment* Revisited: A Study in History and Ideology," *Journal of Modern History*, 53 (1981), 49–72, argue for the persistence of republican ideology and aspiration.

10 See, for example, Wilentz, *Chants Democratic*; Foner, *Tom Paine*; Gary B. Nash, *The Urban Crucible: Social Change, Political Consciousness, and the Origins of the American Revolution* (Cambridge: Harvard Univ. Press, 1979); and Shalhope, "Republicanism and Early American Historiography," 336–346.

11 Robert R. Palmer, *The Age of Democratic Revolution* (Princeton: Princeton Univ. Press, 1959), v. I, 3–20.

12 Some historians may prefer to characterize the dilemma presented here as a republican dilemma, because republican ideology embraces the same contrary aspirations. My purpose is not to deny that New England's frontiersmen were republicans or that they sought inspiration and guidance in republican thought, but it was the settlers' progressive commitment to freedom, equality, tolerance, and popular sovereignty that made the dilemma difficult to resolve, and republican ideology could not resolve that dilemma. See Michael Kammen, *People of Paradox: An Inquiry Concerning the Origins of American Civilization* (New York: Random House, 1972), 216–220, on the contrarity of early American aspirations and on the likelihood that "the growth of democracy really was the central theme of early American history."

Chapter 1

1 Smith, "Legacy of Dissent," 119–278; Chilton Williamson, *Vermont in Quandary, 1763–1825* (Montpelier: Vermont Historical Society, 1949), 1–23; Harold A. Meeks, "An Isochronic Map of Settlement of Vermont," *Vermont History*, 38 (1970), 98; Charles E. Clark, *The Eastern Frontier: The Settlement of Northern New England, 1610–1763* (New York: Knopf, 1970), 334–338; and Jack M. Sosin, *The Revolutionary Frontier, 1763–1783* (Albuquerque: Univ. of New Mexico Press, 1967), 39–60.

2 Zadock Thompson, *History of Vermont* (Burlington: Chauncey Goodrich, 1842), Part II, 67–71; Williamson, *Vermont in Quandary*; and William M. Newton, *History of Barnard, Vermont* (Montpelier: Vermont Historical Society, 1928), v. I, 304–308.

3 Williamson, *Vermont in Quandary*; Smith, "Legacy of Dissent"; and Matt B. Jones, *Vermont in the Making, 1750–1777* (Cambridge: Harvard Univ. Press, 1939).

4 The information in the following town portraits is from *Vermont: A Guide to the Green Mountain State*, Federal Writers' Project, Works Progress Administration (Boston: Houghton Mifflin, 1937); Frederick P. Wells, *The History of Barnet, Vermont* (Burlington: Free Press, 1923); Edward Miller and Frederick P. Wells, *History of Ryegate, Vermont* (St. Johnsbury: Caledonian, 1913); Ernest L. Bogart, *Peacham: The Story of a Vermont Hill Town* (Montpelier: Vermont Historical Society, 1948); Henry S. Dana,

History of Woodstock, Vermont (New York: Houghton Mifflin, 1889); Henry H. Vail, *Pomfret, Vermont* (Boston: Cockayne, 1930); John L. Hurd, *Weathersfield: Century One* (Canaan: Phoenix, 1975); Edward T. Fairbanks, *The Town of St. Johnsbury* (St. Johnsbury: Cowles, 1914); Gilbert S. Williamson, "The Development of a Small Community: South Woodstock, Vermont, 1770–1900" (Honors thesis, Carleton College, 1974); William N. Hosley, "Architecture and Society of the Urban Frontier: Windsor, Vermont, 1798–1820" (M.A. thesis, Univ. of Delaware, 1981); and Abby M. Hemenway, *Vermont Historical Gazetteer*, 5 v. (Burlington: A. M. Hemenway, 1862–1882).

5   On the economic practices and aspirations of the early inhabitants, see Elias Smith, *The Life, Conversion, Preaching, Travels, and Sufferings of Elias Smith* (Portsmouth: Beck and Foster, 1816), 36–52, 78–101; Lora M. Wyman, *History of Athens, Vermont* (Ann Arbor: Edwards Brothers, 1963), 7–9; Rebecca C. Skillin, ed., "William Cheney (1787–1875): The Life of a Vermont Woodsman and Farmer," *Vermont History*, 39 (1971), 44–47; the reminiscences of Daniel Ransom; Fred Anderson, *A People's Army: Massachusetts Soldiers and Society in the Seven Years' War* (Chapel Hill: Univ. of North Carolina Press, 1984), 28–39; Bettye Hobbs Pruitt, "Self-Sufficiency and the Agricultural Economy of Eighteenth-Century Massachusetts," *William and Mary Quarterly*, 3d ser., 41 (1984), 333–364; Christopher Clark, "Household Economy, Market Exchange and the Rise of Capitalism in the Connecticut River Valley, 1800–1860," *Journal of Social History*, 13 (1979), 166–189; Henretta, "Families and Farms," 3–32; Michael Merrill, "Cash Is Good to Eat: Self-Sufficiency and Exchange in the Rural Economy of the United States," *Radical History Review*, 4 (1977), 42–71; Sosin, *Revolutionary Frontier*, 20–25, 172–192; Ryan, *Cradle of the Middle Class*, 18–31; and Nancy F. Cott, *The Bonds of Womanhood: "Women's Sphere" in New England, 1780–1835* (New Haven: Yale Univ. Press, 1977), 19–62.

6   Peter J. Coleman, *Debtors and Creditors in America: Insolvency, Imprisonment for Debt, and Bankruptcy, 1607–1900* (Madison: State Historical Society of Wisconsin, 1974), 65–73; and H. J. Conant, "Imprisonment for Debt in Vermont: A History," *Vermont History*, 19 (1951), 67–80.

7   Gilmore, *Reading Becomes a Necessity*; Wyman, *Athens*, 9–10; and Winifred B. Rothenberg, "The Market and Massachusetts Farmers, 1750–1855," *Journal of Economic History*, 41 (1981), 283–314.

8   On the practices of land speculators, see Florence Woodard, *The Town Proprietors of Vermont* (New York: Columbia Univ. Press, 1936); David M. Ellis, *Landlords and Farmers in the Hudson-Mohawk Region, 1790–1850* (Ithaca: Cornell Univ. Press, 1946), 1–65; Neil A. McNall, *An Agricultural History of the Genesee Valley, 1790–1860* (Philadelphia: Univ. of Pennsylvania Press, 1952), 17–65; Philip L. White, *Beekmantown, New York: Forest Frontier to Farm Community* (Austin: Univ. of Texas Press, 1979), 3–27; and Sosin, *Revolutionary Frontier*, 25–38.

9   On crowding in southern New England, see Kenneth Lockridge, "Land,

Population and the Evolution of New England Society, and an Afterthought," in Stanley N. Katz, ed., *Colonial America: Essays in Politics and Social Development* (Boston: Little, Brown, 1971), 466–491; Bruce C. Daniels, *The Connecticut Town: Growth and Development, 1635–1790* (Middletown: Wesleyan Univ. Press, 1979), 17–34, 43–44; and Gregory H. Nobles, *Divisions throughout the Whole: Politics and Society in Hampshire County, Massachusetts, 1740–1775* (New York: Cambridge Univ. Press, 1983), 107–131. On New Englanders' disdain for tenancy, see Ellis, *Landlords and Farmers*, 16–65; and White, *Beekmantown*, 19. On Nova Scotia, see John B. Brebner, *The Neutral Yankees of Nova Scotia: A Marginal Colony during the Revolutionary Years* (New York: Columbia Univ. Press, 1937), 27; and Gordon Stewart and George Rawlyk, *A People Highly Favored of God: The Nova Scotia Yankees and the American Revolution* (Hamden: Archon, 1972), xi, 3–23.

10 Williamson, *Vermont in Quandary*, 42; *Records of the Council of Safety and Governor and Council of the State of Vermont* (Montpelier: E. P. Walton, 1872–1880), v. I, 333; Smith, "Legacy of Dissent"; Countryman, *People in Revolution*, 42–45, 47–55, 154–159; John A. Williams, ed., *The Public Papers of Governor Thomas Chittenden, 1778–1797* (Montpelier: Secretary of State, 1969), 680–681; Newton, *Barnard*, v. I, 91–93; and David P. Szatmary, *Shays' Rebellion: The Making of an Agrarian Insurrection* (Amherst: Univ. of Massachusetts Press, 1980), 38–39, 59, 117–118. Such combativeness was absent only among those New Englanders who moved to the Nova Scotia frontier during these years, whose circumstances precluded the rise of rebellions. See Stewart and Rawlyk, *A People Highly Favored*, 3–44; and Brebner, *Neutral Yankees*, 291–300.

11 Lucius C. Matlack, *The Life of Reverend Orange Scott* (New York: C. Prindle and L. C. Matlack, 1847), 5–6; and Arthur M. Schlesinger, Jr., *Orestes A. Brownson: A Pilgrim's Progress* (Boston: Little, Brown, 1939), 1–7.

12 Justice Court records of Abel Stevens of Royalton, 1784–1796, at the Royalton Town Office; John W. Dana of Pomfret, 1784–1795, and John Throop of Pomfret, 1788–1801, at the Pomfret Town Office; and Vermont Supreme Court records (Windsor County), August 1802.

13 Smith, *Sufferings of Elias Smith*, 36–52, 78–101; Martin-Merrill Papers, 1800–1810; and the reminiscences of Daniel Ransom.

14 The data are from the mortgages recorded in the land records of Peacham, St. Johnsbury, and Weathersfield.

15 See especially Richard Bushman, *From Puritan to Yankee: Character and the Social Order in Connecticut, 1690–1765* (New York: Norton, 1967), 164–182, 196–220; Patricia J. Tracy, *Jonathan Edwards, Pastor: Religion and Society in Eighteenth-Century Northampton* (New York: Hill and Wang, 1980); William G. McLoughlin, *New England Dissent, 1630–1833: The Baptists and the Separation of Church and State* (Cambridge: Harvard Univ. Press, 1971), v. I; C. C. Goen, *Revivalism and Separatism in New England, 1740–1800: Strict Congregationalists and Separate Baptists in the*

Great Awakening (New Haven: Yale Univ. Press, 1962); and the works cited in note 9.

16   Smith, "Legacy of Dissent," 11–13, 27–41; Heimert, *Religion and the American Mind*, 27–236; Nobles, *Divisions throughout the Whole*, 75–106; Tracy, *Jonathan Edwards*; and Bushman, *Puritan to Yankee*.

17   See Goen, *Revivalism and Separatism*, 203; McLoughlin, *New England Dissent*, v. II, 791; and Smith, "Legacy of Dissent."

18   *The Church of the Baptised Brethren, Royalton, Vermont, A Record of Its Meetings, Conferences, and Councils for the Years 1790 to 1806* (Woodstock, 1919). See also the Articles of Faith of the Chester Baptist Church, drafted circa 1786; the covenant of the Springfield Congregational Church of 1781, in Thomas Mason Ross, "An Address Delivered at the Hundredth Anniversary of the First Church of Christ in Springfield, Vermont" (Montpelier: Chronicle, 1882); the 1792 articles of faith in the records of the Danville Baptist Church; the 1768 and 1778 covenants of the Old South Congregational Church of Windsor; and Paul Lucas, *Valley of Discord: Church and Society along the Connecticut River, 1636–1725* (Hanover: Univ. of New England Press, 1976).

19   James Hobart, "Confession of Faith and Covenant, Adopted by the Church of Christ in Berlin" (Randolph: Sereno Wright, 1803), 7–8.

20   Smith, "Legacy of Dissent," 27–37; Williamson, *Vermont in Quandary*, 20–21; Heimert, *Religion and the American Mind*, 27–236; McLoughlin, *New England Dissent*, v. I; and Nobles, *Divisions throughout the Whole*, 36–58, 72–74, 105–106.

21   For examples of Old Light universalism, Arminianism, and liberalism, see the records of the North Congregational Church of Woodstock, 1786–1796; the correspondence of James and Samuel Elliot, 1794–1810, B.P.L.; and the Craftsbury religious society compact, n.d., Crafts Family Papers, U.V.M. Most of the valley's Old Lights remained Calvinist, as did their church covenants.

22   McLoughlin, *New England Dissent*, v. II, 798ff.

23   Jeffrey Potash, "Welfare of the Regions Beyond," *Vermont History*, 46 (1978), 113.

24   Gershom C. Lyman, "A Sermon Preached at Manchester before . . . the Honorable House of Representatives" (Windsor: Hough and Spooner, 1784), 7–15.

25   Charles A. Jellison, *Ethan Allen: Frontier Rebel* (Syracuse: Syracuse Univ. Press, 1969); Smith, "Legacy of Dissent," 279–426; and Williamson, *Vermont in Quandary*, 20–21, 45–46.

26   See *Vermont Gazette* (Bennington), 24 October 1794. See also Samuel Whiting, "A Discourse Delivered before . . . the House of Representatives" (Rutland: Josiah Fay, 1797), 20–21; Dan Foster, "An Election Sermon Delivered before the Honorable Legislature of the State of Vermont" (Windsor: Alden Spooner, 1790); and Asa Burton, "A Sermon Preached at Windsor before . . . the Honorable House of Representatives" (Windsor: Hough and Spooner, 1786). It is impossible to determine with precision how many

people in the valley in the late eighteenth century favored state support of worship or deference to the governing elite. If silence and acquiescence reflected support, then the great majority supported the standing order. See McLoughlin, *New England Dissent*, v. II, 796; Smith, "Legacy of Dissent," 525–592; and David H. Fischer, *The Revolution of American Conservatism: The Federalist Party in the Era of Jeffersonian Democracy* (New York: Harper and Row, 1965), xii–xv.

27 McLoughlin, *New England Dissent*, v. I; and Charles B. Kinney, Jr., *Church and State: The Struggle for Separation in New Hampshire, 1630–1900* (New York: Columbia Univ. Press, 1955), 8–82, 145–151.

28 Smith, "Legacy of Dissent," 279–457, 684–804; and *Records of the Council of Safety*, v. I, 319.

29 Peter Powers, "Tyranny and Toryism Exposed" (Westminster: Spooner and Green, 1781).

30 Smith, "Legacy of Dissent," 279–339, 458–518; Heimert, *Religion and the American Mind*, 510–523; David Avery, "The Lord Is to Be Praised for the Triumphs of His Power" (Norwich: Green and Spooner, 1778); and "The People the Best Governors: Or a Plan of Government Founded on the Just Principles of Natural Freedom," in Frederick Chase, *A History of Dartmouth College and the Town of Hanover, New Hampshire* (Brattleboro: Vermont Printing, 1928), 654–663.

31 Aaron Hutchinson, "A Well Tempered Self-Love A Rule of Conduct toward Others" (Dresden: Padock and Spooner, 1779), 32–33; Nathaniel Niles, *Two Discourses on Liberty* (Newburyport: Thomas and Tinges, 1774), 23–27; and Heimert, *Religion and the American Mind*, 454–460.

32 Caleb Blood, "Sermon Preached before the Honorable Legislature of the State of Vermont" (Rutland: Anthony Haswell, 1792), 33–34; and Jellison, *Ethan Allen*, 220–221.

33 Allen Soule, ed., *Laws of Vermont, 1777–1780* (Montpelier: State of Vermont, 1964); and Blood, "Sermon," 33–34.

34 John A. Williams, *Laws of Vermont, 1781–1784* (Montpelier: State of Vermont, 1965), 195–197; McLoughlin, *New England Dissent*, v. II, 798–801; the Craftsbury religious society compact, Crafts Family Papers, U.V.M.; and the records of the Christian Catholic Society, organized in Windsor in November, 1789, to support nondenominational Christian worship, in the records of the Old South Congregational Church of Windsor. The Vermont constitution of 1777 had already upheld religion by tendering civil protection only to those who professed "the protestant religion" and by declaring that "every sect or denomination of christians ought to observe the sabbath, or the lord's day, and keep up, and support some sort of religious worship, which to them shall seem most agreeable to the revealed will of God." The authors of the constitution did not deprive non-Protestants of their rights or force citizens to attend church. The Act of 1783 changed state policy by requiring citizens to support religious worship, but church attendance was still not required, contrary to McLoughlin's claim (v. II, 796–797).

35 McLoughlin, *New England Dissent*, v. II, 796–797, 800–801; Jellison, *Ethan Allen*, 190; and Edwin P. Hoyt, *The Damndest Yankee: Ethan Allen and His Clan* (Brattleboro: Stephen Greene, 1976), 223–224.

36 Lyman, "A Sermon Preached at Manchester"; Ludlum, *Social Ferment*, 222–224; Clyde Fussell, "The Emergence of Public Education as a Function of the State in Vermont," *Vermont History*, 28 (1960), 179–196; and William J. Gilmore, "Elementary Literacy on the Eve of the Industrial Revolution: Trends in Rural New England, 1760–1850," *Proceedings of the American Antiquarian Society*, 92 (1982), 87–178.

37 McLoughlin, *New England Dissent*, v. II, 791, 799–803; Potash, "Welfare of the Regions Beyond"; and Newton, *Barnard*, v. I, 27–28. McLoughlin notes that Baptists gained important positions in state government and on the board of the University of Vermont.

38 Aleine Austin, "Vermont's Politics in the 1780's: The Emergence of Rival Leadership," *Vermont History*, 42 (1974), 140–142; idem, *Matthew Lyon: "New Man" of the Democratic Revolution, 1749–1822* (University Park: Pennsylvania State Univ. Press, 1981), 1–5, 14–44; Williamson, *Vermont in Quandary*, 165–186; and Smith, "Legacy of Dissent," 730–735.

39 Austin, *Matthew Lyon*, 45–54; and Smith, "Legacy of Dissent," 730–735.

40 Szatmary, *Shays' Rebellion*, 54–55, 78, 117–118; Austin, "Vermont's Politics in the 1780's"; idem, *Matthew Lyon*, 45–54; and Williamson, *Vermont in Quandary*, 165–186.

41 *Vermont Journal* (Windsor), 22 March 1791; Whiting, "Discourse," 20–21; and Dan Kent, "Electioneering for Office Defended" (Rutland: John S. Hutchins, 1796).

42 Niles, *Two Discourses on Liberty*, 26–27.

Chapter 2

1 Justice Court records of John W. Dana and John Throop, 1787–1800.

2 Wells, *Barnet*, 133; and Randolph A. Roth, "The First Radical Abolitionists: The Reverend James Milligan and the Reformed Presbyterians of Vermont," *New England Quarterly*, 55 (1982), 542–549. See William Nelson, *The Americanization of the Common Law* (Cambridge: Harvard Univ. Press, 1975), 6ff., on prosecutions in Massachusetts. Morals prosecutions persisted in Cheshire County, New Hampshire, until 1815. That was the first area of the valley settled, and the only portion of the valley in which an Old Light Congregational establishment and a standing order were firmly entrenched. Morals prosecutions died away to the north in Grafton County after the Revolution. Neither the Congregationalists nor the standing order ever obtained a secure foothold there. See the Justice Court records located at the Cheshire and Grafton County courthouses, and at the Dartmouth College Library.

3 Vermont's court records from this period have not all survived. The pre-revolutionary court records studied were the "Glouster County Court Records, 1770–1774," *Vermont History*, 13 (1923–1925), 141–192. Glouster

County became Orange, Caledonia, and Washington counties after Vermont gained its independence from New York. The revolutionary court records examined were in the "Journal of the Cumberland County Council of Safety, June 11, 1776 to September 3, 1777," in the *Records of the Council of Safety*, v. I, 344–370. Cumberland County became Windham and Windsor counties. The State Supreme Court records studied were of Windsor County, 1788–1815, and of Caledonia County, 1796–1815. Few Justice Court records have survived. Those studied were of Justices of the Peace: John W. Dana of Pomfret, 1784–1795; Abel Stevens of Royalton, 1784–1796; John Throop of Pomfret, 1788–1801; Enos Stevens of Barnet, 1792–1807; Thomas Prentis of Weathersfield, 1799–1830; Pardon Field of Chester, 1804–1805; Robert Whitelaw of Ryegate, 1812–1818; John Miller of Pomfret, 1812–1821; Henry Stevens of Barnet, 1819–1829; Reuben Washburn of Ludlow and Cavendish, 1824–1836; Walter Palmer of Woodstock, 1834–1836; Abner Field of Springfield, 1840–1850; C. C. Putnam of Middlesex, 1842–1850; William Nutting of Randolph, 1842–1861; and Moody Boynton of Danville, 1851–1852. The Supreme Court records are in the county courthouses, and the Justice Court records are at the University of Vermont Library and at the Vermont Historical Society, except for the records of Dana, Stevens, and Throop, which are in their respective town archives. The only morals case in the Supreme Court records occurred in 1794, when a case for blasphemy was heard. The verdict was not guilty. The Justice Court records listed here contain a number of cases concerning disturbing the peace, but no morals cases. See Merritt E. Goddard and Henry V. Partridge, *History of Norwich, Vermont* (Hanover: Dartmouth Press, 1905), for the only record of any morals prosecutions outside Barnet and Ryegate after 1795.

4 Supreme Court records (Caledonia County), October 1805.

5 Household heads were not prosecuted for immoral acts. Morals laws were not used to ensure that household heads abided by the moral code with which they were to imbue their dependents. See the Justice Court records of Thomas Prentice, 22 March 1804, and of Abner Field, 1843; and Martin Field in Newfane to Daniel Kellogg in Amherst, Massachusetts, 1 March 1812.

6 "Report of the Council of Censors" (Bennington: Anthony Haswell, 1807), 10.

7 Ariel Kendrick, *Sketches of the Life and Times of Elder Ariel Kendrick* (Windsor: P. Merrifield, 1850), 103.

8 Hemenway, *Gazeteer*, v. II, 79–80; and Smith, "Legacy of Dissent," 620ff. Only the Council of Censors of 1806 tried to explain the lack of enforcement of morals laws, which it attributed to neglect and depravity. There were denunciations from the pro-enforcement forces but their adversaries were silent, so there was no direct testimony to illuminate the absence of enforcement.

9 See Emil Oberholtzer, Jr., *Delinquent Saints: Disciplinary Action in the Early Congregational Churches of Massachusetts* (New York: Columbia Univ.

Press, 1956), for a demonstration of these trends. Oberholtzer does not explicitly break disciplinary cases into these categories, however. See also the records of the First Congregational Church of St. Johnsbury, November 1820; and *Church of the Baptised Brethren, Royalton,* November 1795.

10   Records of the West Windsor Congregational Church, October 1814; *Church of the Baptised Brethren, Royalton,* September 1795–November 1798; Danville Baptist Church, April 1820–May 1823; and First Congregational Church of St. Johnsbury, August 1823–January 1825. See also "H. N." in Woodbury to Anna Galpin in Woodbury, 17 September 1805, Martin-Merrill Papers; the letter from William Chamberlain in Peacham to an unknown person, May 1815; Benjamin Bell, "An Impartial History of the Trial of Benjamin Bell" (Windsor: Oliver Farnsworth, 1797); Eden Burroughs, "The Profession and Practice of Christians Held Up to View by Way of Contrast to Each Other" (Windsor: Hough and Spooner, 1784); Elijah R. Sabin, "A Discourse on Gospel Discipline" (Windsor: Alden Spooner, 1806); and Enoch Emerson, "A Series of Letters between Enoch Emerson and Joseph Boyce, Relative to the Excommunication of Said Emerson and Others from the Congregational Church in Rochester" (Windsor: Jesse Cochran, 1815).

11   Records of the Danville Baptist Church, December 1793.

12   Those who challenged the existence of church discipline generally left the Calvinist churches for nonevangelical churches that did not practice discipline. Most were not alienated by the outcome of particular cases, but by Calvinist theology and discipline.

The Revolution also seemed to encourage spouses to dispute the charges against them in marital arguments. Several couples with marital problems took out rival newspaper ads in which each partner blamed his or her spouse for the dispute and denied charges that had been leveled against him or her. Such arguments ended more often in divorce after the Revolution, especially because Vermont was the first state to recognize severity as grounds for divorce. See Betty Bandel, "What the Good Laws of Man Hath Put Asunder ...," *Vermont History,* 46 (1978), 221–233; Nancy Cott, "Divorce and the Changing Status of Women in Eighteenth Century Massachusetts," *William and Mary Quarterly,* 3d. ser., 23 (1976), 592–594, 613–614; and Linda K. Kerber, *Women of the Republic: Intellect and Ideology in Revolutionary America* (Chapel Hill: Univ. of North Carolina Press, 1980), 159–184.

13   Autobiography and diary of Henry Stevens, U.V.M.

14   Fairbanks, *St. Johnsbury,* 161, 159.

15   Miller and Wells, *Ryegate,* 223; Anthony Marro, "Vermont's Local Militia Units, 1815–1860," *Vermont History,* 40 (1972), 28–42; William J. Rorabaugh, *The Alcoholic Republic* (New York: Oxford Univ. Press, 1979), 19–20, 149–152; and Ian R. Tyrell, *Sobering Up: From Temperance to Prohibition in Antebellum America, 1800–1860* (Westport: Greenwood, 1979), 16–29.

16   These and the following passages are from the autobiography of Joel Winch.

See also Frederick P. Wells, *History of Newbury, Vermont* (St. Johnsbury, 1902), 137; and the narrative and diary of Abel Adams.

17 See, for example, Louis W. Flanders, *Simeon Ide: Yeoman, Freeman, Pioneer Printer* (Rutland: Tuttle, 1931), 24–25; the indenture of Harvey May to William Ashley of Hartland, 30 March 1822, Sabin Family Papers; and the indenture of Riley Chamberlain to E. C. Chamberlain, 13 May 1828.

18 Solon Currier, *The Wonderful Wheel of Fortune* (Laconia: John H. Brewster, 1867), 20–21; Kendrick, *Life and Times*, 12, 19–22; and Smith, *Sufferings of Elias Smith*, 23–25, 31.

19 Lois Leverett in Windsor to Louisa Morris in Springfield, 19 July and 4 October 1806, Wardner Collection; Smith, *Sufferings of Elias Smith*, 31ff.; and the autobiography of Joel Winch.

20 Records of the North Congregational Church of Woodstock, March 1782 and August 1783; Associate Presbyterian Church of Barnet and Ryegate, 1789–1816; and Old South Congregational Church of Windsor, June 1793. The trend toward the exclusion of baptized people from discipline and toward reluctance to press for youthful conversions did not stem from an effort by church members to preserve churches as havens for the truly elect. Such motives had indeed led Calvinists during the Great Awakening in southern New England in the 1740s to press for youthful conversions and to abandon the half-way covenant as scripturally unsound and a holdover from spiritually lax times; but no such motives were in evidence among Calvinists on the revolutionary frontier in Vermont.

21 Evidence from southern New England in the seventeenth and eighteenth centuries reveals that compared with earlier standards, both the average age at conversion for males and the proportion of women who were married at the time of their conversion were fairly high in the Connecticut River Valley of Vermont between 1790 and 1810, although not unusually high for periods of spiritual calm or lassitude. See Robert Pope, *The Half-Way Covenant: Church Membership in Puritan New England* (Princeton: Princeton Univ. Press, 1969), 279–286; J. M. Bumsted, "Religion, Finance, and Democracy in Massachusetts: The Town of Norton as a Case Study," *Journal of American History*, 57 (1971), 824; Gerald F. Moran, "Conditions of Religious Conversion in the First Society of Norwich, Connecticut, 1718–1744," *Journal of Social History*, 5 (1972), 331–343; James Walsh, "The Great Awakening in the First Congregational Church of Woodbury, Connecticut," *William and Mary Quarterly*, 3d ser., 28 (1971), 551; William F. Willingham, "Religious Conversion in the Second Society of Windham, Connecticut, 1723–1743," *Societas*, 6 (1976), 109–119; and Philip Greven, "Youth, Maturity, and Religious Conversion: A Note on the Age of Converts in Andover, Massachusetts, 1711–1749," *Essex Institute Historical Collections*, 108 (1972), 119–134.

22 Kendrick, *Life and Times*, 12–13; Joseph Lathrop in West Springfield to Paul Brigham in Montpelier, 26 July 1809, U.V.M.; and Burroughs, "Practice of Christians."

23 There is no evidence available, as there is in vital records and other sources

in other areas, to prove whether or not there had been an increase in the daily consumption of alcohol or in premarital pregnancy after the Revolution.

24 Ludlum, *Social Ferment*, 3–24; Donal Ward, "Religious Enthusiasm in Vermont, 1761–1847" (Ph.D. diss., Univ. of Notre Dame, 1980), 1–42; and Potash, "Welfare of the Regions Beyond," 113. Denominational rivalry was not confined to Vermont in these years. Established religions in southern New England and Great Britain confronted severe denominational challenges. Rival denominations arose, as they did in the valley, at least in part because of social stratification and the subsequent emergence of subcommunities with distinctive values, interests, and interpretations of Christian doctrine. See David W. Howe, *The Unitarian Conscience* (Cambridge: Harvard Univ. Press, 1970); Steven A. Marini, *Radical Sects of Revolutionary New England* (Cambridge: Harvard Univ. Press, 1982); Gilbert, *Religion and Society in Industrial England*; James Obelkevich, *Religion and Rural Society, South Lindsey, 1825–1875* (Oxford: Clarendon, 1976); Thomas W. Laqueur's review of Obelkevich in *Journal of Social History*, 12 (1979), 637–642; and McLoughlin, *New England Dissent*, v. II, 717–750.

25 Of the six towns with liberal churches before 1829, only Bethel did not have a Congregational church controlled or strongly influenced by Old Lights.

26 Thomas Thomas in Windsor to James Morse in Newburyport, Massachusetts, 8 June 1817, in the records of St. Paul's Episcopal Church of Windsor.

27 Elmer Townsend in Boston, Massachusetts, to Aurelia Townsend in Reading, 1 November 1827; and to William Townsend, Sr., in Reading, 30 June 1827, 11 May 1829, and 7 March 1836.

28 Elmer Townsend to Aurelia Townsend, 17 July 1832; and William Townsend in Boston, Massachusetts, to Aurelia Townsend, 4 April 1832 and 1 September 1833.

29 Flanders, *Simeon Ide*, 58–59.

30 Diary of Lucy Weston Gibbs, 16 August 1823–20 December 1824; Richard D. Shiels, "The Feminization of American Congregationalism, 1730–1835," *American Quarterly*, 33 (1981), 46–62; Nancy F. Cott, "Young Women in the Second Great Awakening," *Feminist Studies*, 3 (1975), 15–29; and Cott, *Bonds of Womanhood*, 126–146. The ministers of the Episcopal churches in Windsor and Woodstock periodically encouraged changes of heart as preparation for the receipt of communion, which only a minority (largely female) of the members of these congregations received.

31 Lois Leverett to Louisa Morris in Springfield, 19 July, 4 October, and 9 November 1806, and 16 September 1810, Wardner Collection.

32 On reading patterns, see Gilmore, *Reading Becomes a Necessity*; the correspondence of Daniel P. Thompson, 1816–1823; George F. Newbrough, "Mary Tyler's Diary," *Vermont Quarterly*, 20 (1952), 26–27; Samuel Crafts to Mary T. C. Hill, n.d.; Abby Waldo to an unknown person, 1811, John H. Hubbard Papers, N.Y.S.L.; and Boyd Wilson in Milton, Massachusetts, to James Wilson in Bradford, 11 July 1826, U.V.M.

33 Thomas Thomas to James Marsh, 1 April 1817, in the records of St. Paul's Episcopal Church of Windsor.

34 Records of the Old South Congregational Church of Windsor, 1834–1835; and the letter in those records from Elijah Rawson of Middlebury, 4 May 1835.

35 Correspondence between Daniel Kellogg of Newfane and Munnis Kenney of Putney, 1811–1848; Leon Brown in Newfane to Kellogg in Amherst, Massachusetts, 30 November 1811; Jeremiah Johnson, *Memoir and Correspondence of Jeremiah Johnson* (Cambridge: Riverside, 1873), 19–21; Solomon Stevens in Highgate to Enos Stevens in Barnet, 24 April 1805, U.V.M.; David Wing in Montpelier to Barnabas Doty in Rochester, 22 June 1792; Chester Bloss in Peacham to Messrs. Blanchard and Merrill at Dartmouth College, 18 November 1810, Martin-Merrill Papers; and Samuel A. Foot in Cheshire, Connecticut, to Horatio Seymour in Middlebury, 29 January 1801, Sheldon Museum.

36 William W. Newton, "Methodism in Eastern Vermont with Especial Reference to the Old Barnard Circuit" (TS, 1917), in the New England Methodist Historical Society Collection at Boston University; Edith F. MacDonald, *Rebellion in the Mountains: The Story of Universalism and Unitarianism in Vermont* (Concord: New Hampshire–Vermont District of the Unitarian–Universalist Association, 1976); and Marini, *Radical Sects*.

37 By 1815, the twenty-eight towns in Old Light–dominated Windham County had only nine egalitarian churches, circuits, and missions, whereas the remaining eighty-eight towns in the valley had ninety-six.

38 See Benjamin Shaw, *A New Selection of Hymns and Spiritual Songs: Designed for Prayer, Conference, and Camp-Meetings* (Woodstock: David Watson, 1830), 23, 11, 56–58; the diary of Joel Winch, 1803–1808; the diary of William Smyth Babcock, 1801–1811, A.A.S.; Matlack, *Orange Scott*; Kendrick, *Life and Times*; Gilbert A. Davis, *Centennial Celebration together with an Historical Sketch of Reading* (Bellows Falls: A. N. Swain, 1874), 64–65; Elias Smith, *A Discourse on Resurrection* (Windsor: E. Smith, 1806); and Gilmore, *Reading Becomes a Necessity*. See also the Newton Family Papers, N.H.H.S.

39 Hosea Ballou, *A Treatise on Atonement* (Randolph: Sereno Wright, 1805); Lucy Barns, *The Female Christian, Containing a Selection from the Writings of Miss Lucy Barns* (Portland: Francis Douglas, 1809); Sebastian Streeter and Russell Streeter, *The New Hymn Book, Designed for Universalist Societies* (Woodstock: Nahum Haskell, 1837), 3; and *Universalist Watchman, Repository, and Chronicle* (Woodstock), 16 April 1831. Many Universalists in the late eighteenth century were predestinarian Calvinists or Arminian evangelicals, who differed from the main body of Calvinists or Arminians only on the point of universal salvation. Nonevangelicals won control of the movement early in the nineteenth century.

40 Diary of Justin Morrill, 7 May 1830. Even though the Freewill Baptists first organized in the colonies in the 1770s in Nova Scotia, under the leadership of evangelist Henry Alline, most returned to the Baptist fold early in the nineteenth century; and the Methodists, who received substantial early support among settlers from Yorkshire, England, who had embraced Methodism back in Great Britain, did not prosper among Nova Scotia's Yankees.

See E. Arthur Betts, *Bishop Black and His Preachers: The Story of Maritime Methodism to 1825*, 2d ed. (Halifax: Maritime Conference Archives, 1976), 59–61, 65, 78; Maurice W. Armstrong, *The Great Awakening in Nova Scotia, 1776–1809* (Hartford: American Society of Church History, 1948), 35, 116, 131–138; and Stewart and Rawlyk, *A People Highly Favored*, 121–192.

41 Blanche B. Bryant and Gertrude E. Baker, eds., *The Diaries of Sally and Pamela Brown, 1832–1838*, 2d ed. (Springfield: William L. Bryant Foundation, 1979), especially 34, 37, 48, 82; the journals of Hosea Doton, 1840–1850, Pomfret Town Office; the diary of Justin Morrill, 1830; and Chapter 5, "The Rise of Political Insurgency," on Nahum Haskell, editor of the Woodstock *Workingman's Gazette*, and Benjamin Fellows, editor of the Chester *Vermont Phoenix*.

42 Shaw, *Hymns*, 21, 119–122. By the 1830s the Universalists were ridiculing evangelical attitudes toward conversion and innate depravity. See, for example, *Universalist Watchman*, 16 April 1831.

43 Streeter and Streeter, *Hymn Book*, 213, 243; and *Universalist Watchman*, 19 May 1832.

44 Ludlum, *Social Ferment*, 25–62; and Kenneth Silverman, *Timothy Dwight* (New York: Twayne, 1969).

45 Timothy Dwight, *Travels in New England and New York*, ed. Barbara Solomon (Cambridge: Harvard Univ. Press, 1969), v. II; Samuel Austin, "The Evangelical Preacher" (Peacham: Farley and Goss, 1799); Abijah Wines, "The Criminality of Vain Amusements Exposed" (Windsor: Alden Spooner, 1804); and *Vermont Christian Messenger* (Montpelier), 24 January, and 7 and 14 February 1849.

46 Roth, "Strange Fire," 80–81, 101–103.

47 Williamson, *Vermont in Quandary*; Ludlum, *Social Ferment*; McLoughlin, *New England Dissent*, v. II, 789–832; Austin, "Vermont Politics in the 1780's"; idem, *Matthew Lyon*; Smith, "Legacy of Dissent," 882–883; Judah Adelson, "The Vermont Democratic–Republican Societies and the French Revolution," *Vermont History*, 32 (1964), 3–23; and William A. Robinson, *Jeffersonian Democracy in New England* (New Haven: Yale Univ. Press, 1916).

48 Titus Hutchinson, "An Oration Delivered at Woodstock" (Windsor: Oliver Farnsworth, 1809), 2; the correspondence of James Elliot, 1795–1798, B.P.L.; William Fessenden, *The Political Farrago* (Brattleboro: William Fessenden, 1807), 3, 5–6; Cornelius P. Van Ness, "An Oration Delivered at Williston" (Burlington: Samuel Mills, 1812), 9–12, 48; and Chester R. Palmer, "A Political Biography of William Adam Palmer, 1781–1860" (M.A. thesis, Univ. of Illinois, 1953), 22.

See Karl Mannheim, "Conservative Thought," in *Essays on Sociology and Social Psychology*, Paul Kecskemeti, ed. (London: Routledge and Kegan Paul, 1953), 98–99, for the development of this definition of progressivism.

Vermont's leading Republicans were not typical of Republicans throughout the nation. They believed that the battle against Federalism was part of an ongoing war, begun during Vermont's struggle against New York, against oppressive standing orders and economic inequality in America. In states like Virginia and New York, where the Revolution had inspired less radical and widespread demands for change at home, prominent Republicans were more often ambivalent about political, social, and economic change and unwilling to uproot traditional institutions and social distinctions. They embraced ideologies that emphasized the need for reform or gradual modification of existing laws and institutions. These reformers were influenced more by the ideology of the Country Party of eighteenth-century England and by the thought of classical economists and political theorists than by the ideas of Thomas Paine and other progressive defenders of the French Revolution. See Lance Banning, *The Jeffersonian Persuasion* (Ithaca: Cornell Univ. Press, 1978); Richard V. Buel, Jr., *Securing the Revolution: Ideology in American Politics, 1789–1815* (Ithaca: Cornell Univ. Press, 1972); and Drew R. McCoy, *The Elusive Republic: Political Economy in Jeffersonian America* (Chapel Hill: Univ. of North Carolina Press, 1980). These studies slight regional differences in Republican thought and aspiration, and underestimate the number of radical Republicans.

49 Matthew Lyon, "Letter from Matthew Lyon...to Citizen John Adams," *Historical Magazine*, 2 (1873), 360–363; Hutchinson, "Oration Delivered at Woodstock," 3; Uriac Faber Republique (pseudonym), *Federal Catechism Metamorphosed: Or the Natural Spirit of Federalism Exposed* (Windsor: Alden Spooner, 1804); James W. Davidson, *The Logic of Millennial Thought: Eighteenth Century New England* (New Haven: Yale Univ. Press, 1977), 129–141, 270–280; the sermons and diaries of Joel Winch, 1803–1808; and the sermons and diaries of William Babcock, 1801–1811, A.A.S.

50 John Buell in Detroit, Michigan, to Paul Brigham in Montpelier, 22 September 1792, and Samuel Williams in Rutland to Brigham, 10 July 1793, U.V.M.; Isaac Tichenor to Joseph Farnsworth in Fairfield, 1 August 1798; and note 47.

51 Samuel Prentiss, "An Oration Pronounced at Plainfield" (Montpelier: Walton and Goss, 1812), 6, 28, 37–38. This definition of conservatism is developed in Mannheim, "Conservative Thought," 98–99. Federalist thought, like Republican thought, was less moderate and subtle in Vermont than in the nation as a whole. See Fischer, *American Conservatism*; Linda K. Kerber, *Federalists in Dissent: Imagery and Ideology in Jeffersonian America* (Ithaca: Cornell Univ. Press, 1970); and note 48.

52 Prentiss, "Oration Pronounced at Plainfield," 16; John Buell to Paul Brigham, 19 October 1798, U.V.M.; Isaac Tichenor to Joseph Farnsworth, 1 August 1798; Lewis R. Morris in Springfield to Timothy Pickering in Philadelphia, Pennsylvania, 1 June 1799, M.H.S.; *Vermont Gazette*, 27 February 1795; and Nathaniel Lambert, "A Sermon Preached...at Newbury" (Windsor: Alden Spooner, 1801). See also Ezra Sampson, *The Sham-Patriot Unmasked* (Peacham: Samuel Goss, 1804).

53 Richard Skinner in Manchester to Horatio Seymour in Middlebury, 27 March and 18 September 1801, Sheldon Museum; and Martin Chittenden

in Washington, D.C., to Jonas Galusha in Shaftsbury, 21 December 1803 and 7 February 1805. On deferential republican politics, see Gary Nash, "The Transformation of Urban Politics, 1700–1760," *Journal of American History*, 60 (1973), 605–632; J. G. A. Pocock, "The Classical Theory of Deference," *American Historical Review*, 81 (1976), 516–523; and idem, *Machiavellian Moment*.

54 Paul Brigham papers, 1793–1804, U.V.M.; the Bradley-Richard Family Papers, 1799–1816, L.C.; James Elliot to Samuel Elliot, 13 February and 24 April 1800, B.P.L.; Daniel Buck in Norwich to James Madison, 26 February 1808, 24 February 1809, and 4 July 1811, L.C.; and Lois Leverett to Louisa Morris in Warren, Ohio, 13 April 1808, Wardner Collection. See also Moses Robinson in Bennington to Thomas Jefferson, 17 November 1801, L.C.

55 Smith, "Legacy of Dissent," 886–889, using lists of leading Federalists and Republicans in Vermont compiled by Philip Lampi of the American Antiquarian Society, finds that 43 of 59 leading Federalists were Old Lights or Anglicans, and that 13 of the 24 leading Federalists in Windham and Windsor County who took a stand during Vermont's revolution sided with New York. Only 5 of 66 Republican leaders were Old Lights or Anglicans, and none had sided with New York.

56 McLoughlin, *New England Dissent*, v. II, 789–832; Smith, "Legacy of Dissent," 882–883.

57 "The Town Meeting," 1816, Crafts Family Papers, U.V.M.; untitled anticlerical poem from "The Poetical and Miscellaneous Writings of a Country Bard," anonymous MS; and Ignatius Thomson, "Review of New England Politics" (Pomfret, 1813). The town clerk of Peacham collected voluntary ministerial taxes for support of the Congregational church through 1839.

58 Hemenway, *Gazetteer*, v. II, 80; Isaac Tichenor in Bennington to Joseph Farnsworth, 24 September 1807; Lot Hall to Nathaniel Chipman, 1804; Richard Skinner in Manchester to Horatio Seymour in Middlebury, 27 March 1801, Sheldon Museum; Benjamin Smead in Bennington to Horatio Seymour, 4 December 1806, Sheldon Museum; and L. Whitney, Sr., to Phineas White in Putney, 2 July 1805, N.Y.S.L. See also Moses Robinson in Bennington to William Griswold, 3 August 1808.

59 The town-level data on Vermont gubernatorial elections come from official returns after 1813, on deposit at the Vermont Public Records Office, and from unpublished data collected by Philip Lampi of the American Antiquarian Society for the years 1796–1812. The pre-1813 data are incomplete. Data on at least four elections between 1800 and 1808 exist for sixty-five towns, and equivalent data on elections between 1808 and 1816 exist for 108 towns.

A two-way analysis of these incomplete electoral returns reveals that between 1800 and 1808 the percentage of votes won by the Republicans deviated by over 15 percent from the percentage of the previous year – once the effects of each town's long-term party preference and of the valley's deviation in each election from its long-term party preference were considered – in 145 of the 437 cases (33 percent) in which data are available for towns in adjacent years. (See Appendix D on two-way analysis.) The analysis reveals that between 1808 and 1816 such deviations occurred in only 13 of 592 cases (2 percent) outside Essex County, although they occurred in 15 of 53 cases (28 percent) in Essex County during those same years. After 1808 the percentage of votes won by the Republicans did not fluctuate widely from election to election in the valley as a whole, nor did voter turnout fluctuate widely in the valley or at the town level from election to election. The drop in townlevel deviations after 1808 thus reflected a stabilization of town-level voting patterns – which suggests, although it does not prove, that the political behavior of individual voters stabilized.

60 Gilmore, *Reading Becomes a Necessity*; James Elliot to Samuel Elliot, 10 September 1795, and John Chamberlain in Bangor, Ohio, to Samuel Elliot, 26 March 1806, B.P.L.

61 Samuel Elliot to John Chamberlain, 9 May 1806, and John Chamberlain to Samuel Elliot, 20 March and 22 July 1806, B.P.L.; W. Hall in Bellows Falls to John Hubbard in Washington, D.C., 12 February 1811, N.Y.S.L.; and Henry Stevens, "Practical Politics," 18 February 1810, U.V.M.

62 See note 59.

63 A simple regression analysis of the relationship between the median Republican vote in each town between 1806 and 1817 and the presence or absence of churches, circuits, or missions of the various denominations, reveals the following contribution of each religious organization to each town's Republican vote (the standard errors of the regression coefficients are in parentheses). (On statistical methods, see Appendix D.)

+.63	(.04)	Intercept term/no churches
−.33	(.05)	Old Light Congregational churches
−.18	(.04)	Moderate Congregational churches
−.10	(.06)	Presbyterian churches
−.03	(.07)	Unitarian or Episcopalian churches
−.01	(.03)	New Light Congregational or Baptist churches
+.06	(.02)	Methodist and Freewill Baptist/Christian and Universalist churches

R^2 is 38.8, adjusted for 101 degrees of freedom. The standard errors of the coefficients are large for the liberal and Presbyterian variables because of the small number of liberal and Presbyterian churches organized by 1815. The geographical relationship between liberal churches and Federalism is stronger than the equation indicates, because liberal churches were generally located in more heavily Federalist areas within townships, such as East Brattleboro and East Windsor.

The residuals are not correlated with town type or with the proportion of the adult male population engaged in commerce or manufacturing, the only socioeconomic variables available for the period. There may have been a tendency for farmers and poorer inhabitants to vote Republican within each town, but regression cannot reveal it, because of the high correlation between religious institutions, settlement patterns, and socioeconomic variables.

64 McLoughlin, *New England Dissent*, v. II, 789–832.

65 "Official Papers Containing the Speeches of the Respective Governors of Vermont in the Years 1808 and 1809" (Montpelier: Derick Sibley, 1809); the correspondence of J. H. Hubbard, 1811–1812, N.Y.S.L.; Palmer, "William Adam Palmer," 14–26; Royal Tyler in Brattleboro to Horace Janes in St. Albans, 25 May 1812; Jonas Galusha to Charles Phelps in Townsend, 29 August 1812; Charles Rich in Washington, D.C., to George Cleveland in Middlebury, 7 January 1814, Sheldon Museum; the Sandford Gadcomb Papers, 1811–1812, and James Fiske in Washington, D.C., to Paul Brigham in Montpelier, 18 January 1813, U.V.M.; Addison Smith in Chillicothe, Ohio, to Dudley Chase in Randolph, 7 September 1812, L.C.; Samuel Elliot in Brattleboro to James Fiske in Barre, 14 July 1814, B.P.L.; and *Green Mountain Patriot* (Peacham), 2 September 1809. See also the diary of David Sutherland, 4 May 1814 and 1 March 1815, N.H.H.S.

66 Gilmore, *Reading Becomes a Necessity*; William Slade to Matthew Carey, 4 April 1815, N.Y.H.S.; *Green Mountain Patriot*, 28 October 1806; Martin Chittenden, "Address ... on the Subject of War with Great Britain," MS; Van Ness, "Oration Delivered at Williston," 21–48; *Vermont Mirror* (Middlebury), 14 October 1812 and 27 October 1813; an untitled poem from "The Poetical and Miscellaneous Writings of a Country Bard," anonymous MS; *Proceedings of the General Assembly of the State of Vermont* (Montpelier: Wright and Sibley, 1813), 3–13, 36–37; "Protest of the Minority of the House of Representatives" (Montpelier: Wright and Sibley, 1813); and *The Centennial at Windsor, Vermont, July 4, 1876* (Windsor: Journal, 1876), 63.

Chapter 3

1 The Calvinist churches in Springfield and in the towns studied intensively are included in the calculation of Calvinist membership rates. On the revivals and the crop failure, see Joshua Bradley, *Accounts of Religious Revivals in Many Parts of the United States from 1815 to 1818* (Albany: G. J. Loomis, 1819).

2 John D. Post, *The Last Great Subsistence Crisis in the Western World* (Baltimore: Johns Hopkins Univ. Press, 1977).

3 On rates of admission by age, occupation, and marital status, see Tables 2.2, 6.1, and 6.2.

4 F. Gerald Ham, "The Prophet and the Mummyjums: Isaac Bullard and the Vermont Pilgrims of 1817," *Wisconsin Historical Magazine*, 56 (1973), 290–299; Ward, "Religious Enthusiasm in Vermont," 59; *Gospel Banner* (Woodstock), 6 October 1827; William Smith, "Reminiscences of Olden Times," D.C.L.; and Ludlum, *Social Ferment*, 239–240.

5 Adult male membership represents the proportion of household heads and taxpayers who were church members. (See Appendix A for the sources on religious organizations.) The estimate of the number of inhabitants per church or meetinghouse is lower than the estimate in Table 3, because it assumes that town meetinghouses served as houses of worship in most agricultural and hill towns.

6   The proportion of young people leaving the valley represents the net dif-
    ference between the number of young persons aged 10–19 in year X and
    the number of young persons aged 20–29 in town in year X + 10. All
    proportions were determined from the published returns of the U.S. Census.
    On the economy, see Chapter 4.

7   Gilmore, *Reading Becomes a Necessity*.

8   For illustrations of how partnerships worked, see Albert Townsend in Wind-
    sor and Bellows Falls to Albert Townsend in Reading, 1828 (no month)
    and 5 December 1830; Thomas Fullerton in Boston, Massachusetts, to
    Shubael Wardner in Windsor, 28 February 1840 and 31 May 1841; *Cen-
    tennial at Windsor*, 61; and Wells, *Barnet*, 512–513.

9   Philo Murray in Woodbury, Connecticut, to Aaron Mallery in Ascott, Lower
    Canada, 10 April 1805, Martin-Merrill Papers; the autobiography of Joel
    Winch; and James Lovell in Chester to William Jarvis in Weathersfield, 26
    April 1832.

10 Charles Fox in Windsor to Ebenezer Fox in Roxbury, Massachusetts, 2 May
    and 21 November 1815.

11 The data include members of the Congregational churches in Springfield,
    St. Johnsbury, and Windsor, and the Baptist church in Windsor. Other
    churches did not systematically record letters of recommendation for new
    and departing members. Fifty-six percent of those persons leaving churches
    between 1811 and 1828 remained in the valley, as opposed to 41 percent
    between 1790 and 1810. Sixty percent of those joining churches came from
    other churches in the valley, as opposed to 27 percent earlier. Roth, "Strange
    Fire," 118–119.

12 Albert Townsend to Alfred Townsend, 1828 (no month) and 5 December
    1830; Flanders, *Simeon Ide*; *Centennial at Windsor*, 61; and *Vermont
    Chronicle* (Windsor), 25 November 1831. See also William Slade in Wash-
    ington, D.C., to James Slade in Hinesburg, 25 February 1828, N.Y.H.S.

13 On the slow demise of the rhetoric of Christian love and intimacy, see Asa
    Lyon, "The Depravity and Misery of Man" (Middlebury: Timothy C.
    Strong, 1815), 10; the records of the Danville Baptist Church and the Old
    South Congregational Church of Windsor; and contrast the records of the
    Christian churches of Pomfret and North Springfield in the 1820s and 1830s,
    with the records of the *Church of the Baptised Brethren, Royalton* and the
    Freewill Baptists of North Springfield prior to 1815. The shift may have
    contributed to the heightened concern of Calvinist churches, after 1810,
    with personal sin, which affected people's reputations for reliability and
    self-discipline and reflected their decreasing interest in interpersonal sin
    (Table 2.1). On Restorationism, see MacDonald, *Rebellion in the Moun-
    tains*, 6.

14 *Woodstock Observer*, 11 January and 1, 15, and 22 February, 1820; and
    Oliver Smith, "An Oration Pronounced at Johnson" (Burlington: E. and T.
    Mills, 1826).

15 On voluntarism, see Lawrence Friedman, *Gregarious Saints: Self and Com-
    munity in American Abolitionism, 1830–1870* (New York: Cambridge
    Univ. Press, 1982), 102–111.

16 Flanders, *Simeon Ide*, 59–60; and Wyman, *Athens*, 19.
17 See the remarks of Joseph Tracy in the *Vermont Chronicle*, 30 April 1830, which reflect Tracy's prejudice against outsiders and his awareness that faith often spread along the lines of economic and marital alliances.
18 See note 12.
19 See Chapter 7, "A Modified Order in Town Life."
20 See Appendix A for sources.
21 Matlack, *Orange Scott*, 6–9; Skillin, "William Cheney," 43–50; William J. Gilmore, "Orestes Brownson and New England Religious Culture, 1803–1826" (Ph.D. diss., Univ. of Virginia, 1971); and idem, *Reading Becomes a Necessity*.
22 *Vermont Chronicle*, 30 April 1830.
23 Roth, "Strange Fire," 123–124, 169–170. In marketing and manufacturing towns, 39 of the 52 Masonic church members (75 percent) formed partnerships between 1811 and 1830, and 8 of the 13 Masonic nonmembers (62 percent). In agricultural towns, the proportions were 15 of 30 (50 percent) and 8 of 16 (50 percent) respectively.
   The number of Masons who received mortgages in Peacham, St. Johnsbury, and Weathersfield between 1821 and 1830 was quite small. Ten Masonic proprietors received mortgages, against an average of fifteen Masonic proprietors in those towns over the decade (67 percent), three nonproprietors out of an average of four (75 percent), and four new inhabitants in 1830 out of an average of fifteen (27 percent).
   The small number of Masonic mortgages poses problems of interpretation, because the trends visible in the data rest on few cases. Those trends should not be given too much weight, but they do have substantive importance in this instance. They rest on complete rather than sampled data, appear in each town studied, and are consistent with the trends visible in the data on Masonic partnerships.
24 On southern New England, see Dorothy A. Lipson, *Freemasonry in Federalist Connecticut* (Princeton: Princeton Univ. Press, 1977), 80–186.
25 Clark Brown, "The Utility of Moral and Religious Societies, and of the Masonick in Particular" (Keene: John Prentiss, 1814), 15–16; Bulkley Olcott, "Brotherly-Love and Friendship, Explained and Recommended" (Westminster: Judah P. Spooner, 1782); J. Roberts of Whitingham to Phineas White of Putney, 2 June 1827, N.Y.S.L.; and Lipson, *Freemasonry in Connecticut*, 200–213.
26 Brown, "Utility of Moral and Religious Societies," 15–16; Samuel Austin, "An Oration Pronounced before the George Washington Lodge at Strafford" (Randolph: Sereno Wright, 1810); and Hosea Ballou, "A Sermon Delivered at Wilmington, before the... Free and Accepted Masons" (Randolph: S. Wright, 1805). On Antimasonic feelings, see Chapter 5, "The Rise of Political Insurgency"; and Lipson, *Freemasonry in Connecticut*, 267–311.
27 Gilmore, *Reading Becomes a Necessity*; and note 54. See especially the diary of Lucy Gibbs, 1823–1828; Rebecca Thompson of Berlin to Josiah Pierce at Bowdoin College, 12 March 1817 and 10 March 1818; Salmon Chase at Dartmouth College to Mrs. Joseph Dennison in Royalton, 20 June 1826,

D.C.L.; William Chamberlain to Mellon Chamberlain in Castine, Maine, 30 August 1823; and Daniel Thompson in Fredericksburg, Virginia, to Josiah Pierce, 1 December 1822. See also William Slade to James Slade, 22 December 1827, N.Y.H.S.

28 Fairbanks, *St. Johnsbury*, 131–132; and Josiah Dunham, "Address . . . at the First Quarterly Meeting of the Windsor Sunday-School Union Society" (Windsor: W. Spooner, 1819).

29 Charles Marsh in Woodstock to James Whitelaw in Ryegate, 11 December 1812; Samuel Elliot in Montpelier to Stephen Greenleaf in Brattleboro, 29 October 1815; "Biographical Sketch of Daniel Chipman," Sheldon Museum; Marsh to J. H. Hubbard in Windsor, 11 January 1816, and H. C. in Cornish, New Hampshire, to Hubbard, 21 February 1816, N.Y.S.L.; Luther Jewett in St. Johnsbury to Samuel C. Crafts, 10 March 1818, U.V.M.; Shaw Livermore, *The Twilight of Federalism: The Disintegration of the Federalist Party, 1815–1830* (Princeton: Princeton Univ. Press, 1962), 82, 117–120, 231; and Clifford S. Griffin, "Religious Benevolence as Social Control, 1815–1860," *Mississippi Valley Historical Review*, 44 (1957), 423–444.

30 William C. Bradley in Westminster to Selma Hale in Washington, D.C., 5 February 1818, M.H.S.; Thomas D. S. Bassett, "The Rise of Cornelius Peter Van Ness, 1782–1826," *Proceedings of the Vermont Historical Society*, 10 (1942), 19; Addison Smith in Bloomington, Indiana, to Dudley Chase in Randolph, 13 July 1823, L.C.; and Roth, "Strange Fire," 141–142.

31 McLoughlin, *New England Dissent*, v. II, 877–911, 1065–1274; and Ronald P. Formisano, *The Transformation of Political Culture: Massachusetts Parties, 1790s–1840s* (New York: Oxford Univ. Press, 1983), 107–127, 149–170.

32 Membership lists are assembled from the annual reports of the Vermont Colonization Society, the Vermont Sunday School Union Society, and notices in various newspapers from 1813 to 1828.

33 Ward, *Religion and Society in England*, 12–17; Ludlum, *Social Ferment*, 25–62; Charles Roy Keller, *The Second Great Awakening in Connecticut* (New Haven: Yale Univ. Press, 1942); Silverman, *Timothy Dwight*; Sydney Ahlstrom, *A Religious History of the American People* (New Haven: Yale Univ. Press, 1972), 408–428; and William McLoughlin, *Revivals, Awakenings, and Reforms* (Chicago: Univ. of Chicago Press, 1978), 106–122.

34 William Chamberlain in Peacham to Mellon Chamberlain, 15 April 1817; and Robert Bartlett, "A Serious and Candid Examination of the Present Government of Sunday Schools" (Windsor: Simeon Ide, 1823), 4. Only the Reformed Presbyterians of Ryegate and Barnet refused to join reform organizations or to celebrate interdenominational harmony. See Roth, "First Radical Abolitionists," 540–563.

35 "An Address to the Inhabitants of the State of Vermont, on the Use of Ardent Spirits: By a Committee Appointed by the Legislature," in the *Vermont Intelligencer* (Bellows Falls), 17 November 1817; and Roth, "Strange Fire," 147.

36 Walter H. Crockett, *Vermont: The Green Mountain State* (New York: Cen-

tury History, 1921), 157ff.; *Journal of the Assembly of the State of Vermont* (Rutland: William Fay, 1821), 116, 183, 186; Josiah H. Benton, *Warning Out in New England, 1656–1817* (Boston: W. B. Clarke, 1911), 106–113; and Wells, *Newbury*, 43, 286.

37 See especially David Sutherland, "Christian Benevolence" (Windsor: Thomas M. Pomroy, 1812). On the link between benevolent activity and evangelical and latitudinarian religion, see Perry Miller, *The New England Mind: From Colony to Province* (Boston: Beacon, 1961), 397–398; Thistlethwaite, *Anglo-American Connection*; Michael Kraus, *The Atlantic Civilization: Its Eighteenth Century Origins* (Ithaca: Cornell Univ. Press, 1949); and David B. Davis, *The Problem of Slavery in Western Culture* (Ithaca: Cornell Univ. Press, 1967), 333–364, 385.

38 Crockett, *Vermont*, v. II, 156; and *Vermont Intelligencer*, 3 November 1817.

39 James A. Paddock to Samuel Crafts, 10 April 1820, Samuel Crafts to Eli Todd in Hartford, Connecticut, 28 January 1821, and "U.V.M. No. 4," 6 November 1816, MS, Crafts Family Papers, U.V.M.; *Woodstock Observer*, 18 January, and 14 and 28 March, 1820; J. Roberts to Phineas White, 2 June 1827, N.Y.S.L.; and George Frederickson, *Black Image in the White Mind: The Debate on Afro-American Character and Destiny* (New York: Harper and Row, 1971), 1–27.

40 Mary P. S. Cutts, *The Life and Times of the Honorable William Jarvis of Weathersfield, Vermont* (New York: Hurd and Houghton, 1869), 339.

41 On the contrast between urban and rural benevolence, see M. J. Heale, "Patterns of Benevolence: Charity and Morality in Rural and Urban New York, 1783–1830," *Societas*, 3 (1973), 337, 358; and Heale, "Humanitarianism in the Early Republic: The Moral Reformers of New York, 1776–1825," *Journal of American Studies*, 2 (1968), 161–175.

42 Stanley K. Schultz, *The Culture Factory: Boston Public Schools, 1789–1860* (New York: Oxford Univ. Press, 1973), deals with efforts by reformers in cities to bring new educational techniques, many of them from England, to bear upon New England's urban problems. Elie Halévy, *The Growth of Philosophical Radicalism* (New York: Kelly and Millman, 1949), 282–296; R. G. Cowherd, *The Politics of English Dissent* (New York: New York Univ. Press, 1956), 36–45; and David Wardle, *English Popular Education, 1780–1970* (Cambridge: Cambridge Univ. Press, 1970), 1–66, describe the contemporary educational reform movement in England.

Unlike urban reformers, the valley's reformers did not see the common schools as sources of disciplined factory workers, because industrialization had yet to arrive in the valley. Nor did they envision using the schools to assimilate aliens into American life, because immigration and ethnic conflict had not yet become pronounced. They thought of the common schools' contributions to social order in general rather than to human capital or socialization and envisioned them as cheap, effective literacy machines that could help children to appreciate the new nonsectarian moral and religious spirit that was to infuse the social order.

43 Dunham, "Windsor Union Sunday-School Society," 3.

44 "Political and Miscellaneous Writings," anonymous MS.

45 Data from Woodstock are included. The selectmen from these towns served 180 terms from 1808 to 1815, and 299 terms from 1816 to 1828. The data on the wealth of selectmen do not include the selectmen from Woodstock, because of the loss of that town's tax lists.

46 "Biographical Sketch of Daniel Chipman," Sheldon Museum; *Woodstock Observer*, 18 January 1820; Amariah Chandler, "A Sermon Delivered... before the Honorable Legislature of Vermont" (Montpelier: E. P. Walton, 1824), 19; Wilbur Fisk, "A Discourse Delivered before the Legislature of Vermont" (Montpelier: G. W. Hill, 1826), 22–25; and George G. Ingersoll, "A Discourse Delivered before the Legislature of Vermont" (Burlington: Chauncey Goodrich, 1830), 22–25.

47 George Leonard, "A Sermon Delivered at Windsor... " (Windsor: Ide and Aldrich, 1819); and idem, "A Sermon Delivered... before the Honorable Legislature of Vermont" (Windsor: Ide and Aldrich, 1820). On the post-Napoleonic reaction in Europe, see Post, *Last Great Subsistence Crisis*, 159–175; and R. K. Webb, *Modern England: From the Eighteenth Century to the Present* (New York: Dodd, Mead, 1970), 152–163.

48 *Woodstock Observer*, 14–28 July 1826; "Biographical Sketch of Daniel Chipman," Sheldon Museum; and Ingersoll, "Discourse," 24–25. Merrill Peterson, *The Jefferson Image in the American Mind* (New York: Oxford Univ. Press, 1960), 3–14, states that Jefferson was more highly regarded in the nation than Adams at the time of their deaths. That feeling did not prevail among the valley's reformers.

49 See the articles on Latin America and the Greek Revolution in the *Woodstock Observer*, 29 February, 7 March, and 13 June 1820, 25 February and 22 October 1821, and 1823; Humphrey Bennet of Danville to Samuel Crafts, 9 January 1819, U.V.M.; Bassett, "Cornelius Peter Van Ness," 19; Jonathan P. Miller, *The Condition of Greece in 1827 and 1828* (New York: J. and J. Harper, 1828); Daniel P. Thompson, *History of the Town of Montpelier* (Montpelier: E. P. Walton, 1860), 249–262; Livermore, *Twilight of Federalism*, 98–100; and Chandler, "Sermon," 6.

50 "First Annual Report of the State Superintendent of Common Schools" (Montpelier: Eastman and Danforth, 1846); "Report of the Board of Commissioners for Common Schools" (Woodstock: Rufus Colton, 1828); *Journal of the Assembly of the State of Vermont* (Woodstock: Rufus Colton, 1828), 11–13; Gilmore, "Elementary Literacy," 125–155; and Gilmore, *Reading Becomes a Necessity*.

51 From the records of the Overseers of the Poor of Windsor and Woodstock, in the respective records of those towns; and Wells, *Newbury*, 286.

52 Cutts, *William Jarvis*, 339.

53 Shaw, *Hymns*, 150–152; *Hymns and Spiritual Songs for the Use of Christians, Especially Methodists* (New Haven: I. Cooke, 1812), 14–15; and Robert Bartlett, "A Sermon Delivered... before the Honorable Legislature of Vermont" (Montpelier: E. P. Walton, 1825), 20. A number of Calvinists had difficulty accepting Universalists as political allies and social equals.

The appointment of a Universalist minister, Robert Bartlett, to deliver the election sermon of 1824 – a previously unthinkable move – drew violent objections from many Calvinists. The majority of the legislature stood by Bartlett and the cause of interdenominational harmony, and he delivered the sermon as scheduled. See William Gribben, "Vermont's Universalist Controversy of 1824," *Vermont History*, 41 (1973), 82–94; and Henry Stevens to Alexander Hackley in New York, 18 January 1832, U.V.M.

54   Rorabaugh, *Alcoholic Republic*, 7–10, discovers a drop in national alcohol consumption only after 1830. According to Thurston M. Adams, *Prices Paid by Vermont Farmers for Goods and Services and Received by Them for Farm Products, 1790–1871* (Burlington: Vermont Agricultural Experiment Station, 1939), purchases of rum from local merchants dropped drastically after 1815; and according to the "Third Annual Report of the Executive Committee of the New Hampshire Temperance Society" (Concord: Morrill and Chadwick, 1831), which presents less systematic data from surveys of production and consumption in various towns around the state, including many in the Connecticut River Valley, consumption of alcoholic beverages dropped from an estimated 4.5 gallons per person in 1825 to 2.5 by 1831. The 1825 level itself represented a drop from a level of perhaps 5 to 6 gallons circa 1820, which is at the lower end of the 6–10 gallon range of consumption that Rorabaugh found for the nation at large. The valley's inhabitants had a ready alternative to rum in potato liquor, which was produced in substantial quantities in Caledonia and Washington counties by 1810 or 1815. Most of that liquor was sold in Canada or southern New England for profit, however. Production dropped steadily in the 1820s, as did rum consumption, and informal support for temperance on the local level increased. See Hemenway, *Gazetteer*, v. IV, 32, 89–91, 171, 275, 774, on the history of liquor production and temperance in Washington County between 1810 and 1830; and Ludlum, *Social Ferment*, 65–67, on the various grass-roots efforts by local citizens in the 1820s to limit consumption.

   Numerous temperance societies did arise to the south in Massachusetts after 1813, gaining considerable popularity before declining in the mid-1820s. Their support came almost exclusively from Unitarians, Congregationalists, and Federalists, but both the rank-and-file and the elite were included in their ranks. The temperance movement in Massachusetts represented a popular mobilization of Federalists on behalf of that state's standing order, which did not collapse until 1833. Temperance was not a bipartisan, interdenominational, elite movement to restore order, political unity, and respect for authority. Robert L. Hempel, *Temperance and Prohibition in Massachusetts, 1813–1852* (Ann Arbor: UMI Research Press, 1982), 13–22; and Livermore, *Twilight of Federalism*, 117–119.

55   The number of men expelled rose from 25 of 255 to 64 of 263, and women from 31 of 553 to 37 of 433. The data for this and later statistics on expulsions include members from the following Congregational churches: Barnet, Peacham, Pomfret, Springfield, St. Johnsbury (First, Second, and

Third), Weathersfield, West Windsor, and Windsor. Also included are members from the following Baptist churches: Danville, Passumpsic, Windsor. After 1828, members of the Pomfret Christian Church are also included.

56 Vermont Bible Society, "Annual Report," 1813–1828; the records of the Missionary Society to the Indians, 1817–1819, in the records of the Associate Presbyterian Church of Barnet and the Old South Congregational Church of Windsor; and Cott, *Bonds of Womanhood*, 134–135. The twenty-nine women in the Barnet society were from every denomination in that town: Among them were two Baptists, four Congregationalists, and five Presbyterians.

57 Diary of Lucy Gibbs, 20 December 1824, and Gibbs's resolutions upon leaving home to become a wife; Lois Leverett in Haverhill, New Hampshire, to Louisa Morris in Poland, Ohio, 10 July 1827, Wardner Collection; and Cott, *Bonds of Womanhood*, 137–138. The most intense female activism during these years described by Cott, 132–159, and by Ryan, *Cradle of the Middle Class*, 83–127, occurred in more heavily settled and highly developed communities (especially cities). Such reform organizations were also popular in Connecticut, Massachusetts, and eastern New Hampshire, where they served as adjuncts to more narrowly Congregational or Unitarian campaigns to salvage the region's more powerful standing orders, rather than as interdenominational adjuncts to an informal reform campaign to improve the moral and religious tone of town life. Cott offers less evidence of activity in Rhode Island, where Congregational and Unitarian women had no established church to rally around.

Chapter 4

1 *Vermont Journal*, 10 December 1831; and Ludlum, *Social Ferment*, 200. See also Lance E. Davis, et al., *American Economic Growth: An Economist's History of the United States* (New York: Harper and Row, 1972), 1–60; Stuart Bruchey, *The Roots of American Economic Growth, 1607–1861* (New York: Harper and Row, 1968); Peter Temin, *The Jacksonian Economy* (New York: Norton, 1969); and George R. Taylor, *The Transportation Revolution, 1815–1860* (New York: Holt, Rinehart, and Winston, 1968).

2 "Memorial of the Citizens of Windsor County, Vermont, Opposed to the Removal of the Deposits, and in Favor of the Bank of the United States, May 2, 1834," to the Twenty-Third Congress, First Session, *Executive Documents* (Washington, D.C., 1835).

3 The determinants of antebellum economic growth are discussed in Thomas C. Cochran, *Frontiers of Change: Early Industrialism in America* (New York: Oxford Univ. Press, 1981); Davis, *American Economic Growth*, 1–60; and Gary M. Walton and Ross M. Robertson, *History of the American Economy*, 5th ed. (New York: Harcourt Brace Jovanovich, 1983), 165–184, 211–260. See Harold W. Fisher, *The Hill Country of Northern New England: Its Social and Economic History, 1790–1930* (New York: Columbia Univ. Press, 1936), 3–94; Paul W. Gates, *The Farmer's Age: Agri-*

culture, 1815–1860 (New York: Holt, Rinehart, and Winston, 1960), 23–29; and Lawrence D. Stilwell, "Emigration from Vermont, 1760–1860," *Proceedings of the Vermont Historical Society* (Montpelier: Vermont Historical Society, 1937), for discussions of the development of Vermont's economy. For discussions of changes in transportation along the Connecticut River, see the records of the Connecticut River Valley Steamboat Company, 1830–1832, D.C.L.; Cornelius Van Ness to Henry Dearborn in Boston, Massachusetts, 12 December 1825, M.H.S.; *Vermont Journal,* 25 November 1831; Fisher, *Hill Country*; Thomas D. S. Bassett, "The Urban Penetration of Rural Vermont, 1840–1890" (Ph.D. diss., Harvard University, 1952), 25–36; Margaret B. Pabst, *Agricultural Trends in the Connecticut Valley Region of Massachusetts, 1800–1900*, Smith College Studies in History no. 26 (Northampton, 1940–1941); and Clark, "Household Economy."

4   Data from Pomfret are not included in the data in this chapter on the towns studied intensively. Indicators such as improved acreage cannot be calculated for the year 1820, since the tax lists of that and adjacent years (from 1816 to 1824) have not survived.

5   Leo Rogin, *The Introduction of Farm Machinery in Its Relation to the Productivity of Labor in the Agriculture of the United States during the Nineteenth Century* (Berkeley: Univ. of California Press, 1931), 22–26; Fisher, *Hill Country*, 17–18; Gates, *Farmer's Age*, 163–169, 262–267; Clarence H. Danhof, *Change in Agriculture in the Northern United States, 1820–1870* (Cambridge: Harvard Univ. Press, 1969), 49–72, 181–250; White, *Beekmantown*, 355–362; Percy W. Bidwell and John I. Falconer, *History of Agriculture in the Northern United States, 1620–1860* (Washington, D.C.: Carnegie Institute, 1925); Bidwell, "Rural Economy in New England at the Beginning of the Nineteenth Century," *Transactions of the Connecticut Academy of Arts and Sciences*, 20 (1916), 214–399; Bidwell, "The Agricultural Revolution in New England," *American Historical Review*, 26 (1921), 683–702; and C. Benton and Samuel F. Barry, *A Statistical View of the Number of Sheep* (Cambridge: Folsom, Wells, and Thurston, 1837). See also J. Chamberlain in Burlington to Paul Brigham, 30 April 1814, U.V.M.; William Jarvis to Ward Woodbridge of Hartland, 7 February 1823; William Wheeler in Cambridge, Massachusetts, to Lucy and John Wheeler in Lebanon, New Hampshire, 5 September 1840 and 17 February 1842; Josiah Shedd in Fayetteville, Georgia, to Abigail Chamberlain in Peacham, 25 February 1841; Arthur W. Peach, "As the Years Pass – The Diaries of Seth Shaler Arnold (1788–1871), Vermonter," *Proceedings of the Vermont Historical Society*, 8 (1940), 124; Gilmore, *Reading Becomes a Necessity*; *New England Farmer* (Boston), 1822–1843; Thomas G. Fessenden, *The New American Gardener*, 11th ed. (Boston: Russell, Shattuck, and Company, 1836); Paul Jewett, *The New England Farrier*, 2d ed. (Salem: Joshua Cushing, 1807); and Samuel Deane, *The New England Farmer*, 3d ed. (Boston: Wells and Lilly, 1822).

6   The data are from the tax lists of the towns studied intensively. The actual number of master clothiers, tanners, sawyers, and carpenters rose in agricultural towns from 42 to 67, and in Windsor from 9 to 14.

7   Arthur F. Stone, "Vermont's Early Industries and Inventors," *Americana*, 24 (1930), 41–68; A. M. Saunders, "An Important Review of Pioneer Incidents," *Vermonter Magazine*, 38 (1933), 148–151; Marcus McCorison, "Patents Granted to Vermonters Prior to 1831," MS; Historical Records Survey, "Subject Matter Index of Patents for Vermont Inventions, 1790–1873," MS; Guy Hubbard, "The Influence of Early Windsor Industries upon the Mechanic Arts," *Proceedings of the Vermont Historical Society, 1921–1923* (Montpelier: Vermont Historical Society, 1924); and Hosley, "Architecture and Society." See also Gilmore, *Reading Becomes a Necessity*; Jacob Bigelow, *Elements of Technology* (Boston: Hillard, Gray, Little, and Wilkins, 1829); and Cochran, *Frontiers of Change*, 10–11, 14–16.

8   Gilmore, *Reading Becomes a Necessity*.

9   Roth, "Strange Fire," 181–184, 224; and Bassett, "Cornelius Peter Van Ness," 8–15.

10 *Vermont Intelligencer*, 26 October 1818 and 25 October 1819.

11 Bassett, "Cornelius Peter Van Ness," 9; *Journal of the Assembly of the State of Vermont...1824* (Bennington: Charles Dolittle, 1824), 112–113; and *Journal of the Assembly of the State of Vermont...1825* (Bennington: Darius Clark, 1825), 80–81, 116–117. On the changing attitudes of political leaders toward economic policy, see John Noyes in Washington, D.C., to J. H. Hubbard, 22 April 1816, N.Y.S.L.; Phineas White to Samuel Elliot, 25 October 1817, B.P.L.; Samuel Crafts to Eunice Crafts, 10 December 1820, U.V.M.; Palmer, "William Adam Palmer," 10–11, 22, 49–51ff.; and the correspondence of Charles Rich, 1814–1821, Sheldon Museum.

12 Roth, "Strange Fire," 179–181, 224.

13 Ibid., 223.

14 On changes in women's work, see Cott, *Bonds of Womanhood*, 19–62; Ryan, *Cradle of the Middle Class*, 21–51, 198–210; and Thomas Dublin, *Women at Work: The Transformation of Work and Community in Lowell, Massachusetts, 1826–1860* (New York: Columbia Univ. Press, 1979), 1–74.

15 The number of merchants in St. Johnsbury and Barnet rose only from sixteen in 1820 to eighteen in 1830, an increase of 13 percent. The number of merchants in West Windsor, Weathersfield, and Peacham declined from twenty-three to seventeen, a decrease of 27 percent.

16 On the exodus of population, see Stilwell, "Emigration from Vermont." See also Chapter 3, note 6.

17 The number of merchants and financiers rose in Windsor from 7 to 17. Roth, "Strange Fire," 188–189.

18 The federal censuses on manufacturing of 1810, 1822, and 1840, and the House of Representatives' survey of manufacturing of 1832, contain some information on investment and wages in manufacturing. See also Walton and Robertson, *History of the American Economy*, 240–242; Johnson, *Shopkeepers' Millennium*, 15–42; and Paul Faler, "Cultural Aspects of the Industrial Revolution: Lynn, Massachusetts, Shoemakers and Industrial Morality, 1826–1860," *Labor History*, 15 (1974), 367–394.

19 *Vermont Journal*, 22 September 1827; and Albert Townsend to his family

in Reading, 1 June and 21 October 1827, 1828 (no month), and 3 January 1830.

20 Report to the Twenty-Second Congress on *Manufactures in the United States* (Washington, D.C., 1833), v. I, 584.

21 Twenty-nine percent of the adult male inhabitants of Windsor were neither taxed nor enumerated as household heads, versus only 1 percent in agricultural towns. There was little difference in geographical mobility among nonproprietors listed on the tax or census rolls between those who lived in Windsor and those who lived in agricultural towns. Fifty-nine percent left Windsor during the 1820s; 57 percent left rural towns. The difference in transience showed in the far greater number of Windsor residents who appeared on neither tax nor census rolls.

22 Martha and Sarah Norton in Windsor to Reuben Norton in Lawrenceville, Georgia, 8 November 1831, 10 January 1833, and 17 May and 15 August 1837, Reuben Smith Papers, private collection.

23 See Gilmore, *Reading Becomes a Necessity*; and Stilwell, "Emigration from Vermont," on the economic underdevelopment of the backcountry.

24 Nell M. Kull, " 'I Can Never Be Happy There in among So Many Mountains' – The Letters of Sally Rice," *Vermont History*, 38 (1970), 52.

25 McNall, *Genesee Valley*, 195–244; Cross, *Burned-Over District*, 55–77; Johnson, *Shopkeepers' Millennium*, 15–61; Stilwell, "Emigration from Vermont"; and White, *Beekmantown*, 29–92. In none of these valleys did tenancy rates approach those in the Hudson-Mohawk region of New York.

26 Martin-Merrill Papers. See also Allen Hazen in New Orleans, Louisiana, to Lucius Hazen in Hartford, 4 October 1818 and 2 May 1819; and Lucius Hazen to Allen Hazen, 3 October 1819 and 6 March 1820.

27 On the rise of female academies and the feminization of teaching, see Cott, *Bonds of Womanhood*, 110–125; Thompson, *History of Vermont*, 143–144; and "First Annual Report of the State Superintendent of Common Schools." On mill work, see Dublin, *Women at Work*, 23–57.

28 *Vermont Chronicle*, 18 November 1835.

29 Recent studies of the northern United States and Canada suggest that the goals and activities outlined here were not atypical among rural and small town families in the early nineteenth century. See Henretta, "Families and Farms"; Michael Merrill, "Cash Is Good to Eat"; Clark, "Household Economy"; Robert A. Riley, "Kinship Patterns in Londonderry, Vermont, 1772–1900: An Intergenerational Perspective of Changing Family Relationships" (Ph.D. diss., University of Massachusetts at Amherst, 1980); and David P. Gagan, "The Indivisibility of Land: A Microanalysis of the System of Inheritance in Nineteenth-Century Ontario," *Journal of Economic History*, 36 (1976), 126–141.

30 Numerous studies indicate that rural families throughout the northern United States practiced family limitation as the availability of land decreased in their neighborhoods, although changing attitudes toward women and marriage also contributed to the declining birth rate. See Yasukichi Yasuba, *Birth Rates of the White Population in the United States, 1800–1860* (Baltimore: Johns Hopkins Univ. Press, 1962); Colin Forster, G. S. L. Tucker,

and Helen Bridge, *Economic Opportunity and White American Fertility Ratios, 1800–1860* (New Haven: Yale Univ. Press, 1972); Richard A. Easterlin, "Population Change and Farm Settlement in the Northern United States," *Journal of Economic History*, 36 (1976), 45–75; Don R. Leet, "The Determinants of the Fertility Transition in Antebellum Ohio," *Journal of Economic History*, 36 (1976), 359–378; Easterlin, "Factors in the Decline of Farm Family Fertility in the United States: Some Preliminary Research Results," *Journal of American History*, 58 (1976), 600–614; and Mary Beth Norton, *Liberty's Daughters: The Revolutionary Experience of American Women, 1750–1800* (Boston: Little, Brown, 1980), 232–235.

31 Hazen and David Merrill to Samuel Merrill, 18 October 1841.

32 Elmer Townsend in Boston, Massachusetts, to his family in Reading, 10 April, 10 May, and 11 July 1827.

33 The correspondence of Albert Townsend, 1837–1840; the correspondence of Alfred Townsend, 1836–1845; the correspondence of the Wilson family, 1837–1852; and Elisha Sabin to Louisa Sabin, 1 September 1845 and 9 April 1846.

34 Clarence E. Danhof, "Farm Making Costs and the 'Safety Valve': 1850–1860," *Journal of Political Economy*, 49 (1941), 317–359; Danhof, *Change in Agriculture*, 101–129; Robert E. Ankli, "Farm Making Costs in the 1850's," *Agricultural History*, 48 (1974), 51–74; and Gates, *Farmer's Age*, 51–98.

35 George Petrie in Griggsville, Illinois, to Eli English in Hartland, 27 November 1836; Timothy and Sabrine Humphrey in Conneaut, Ohio, to Nathaniel Goss in St. Johnsbury, 24 September 1841; Albert Townsend in Bellows Falls to Alfred Townsend in Reading, 22 September 1831; Mary Dodge in Little Osage, Missouri, to William Choate in North Montpelier, 10 January 1843; Charles Smith in Troy, Wisconsin, to David and Harriet Choate in Peacham, 10 December 1848 and 17 April 1849; Philander Chase to Addison Smith, 25 July 1833, L.C.; "To Get Established in the West: Letters to Windsor and Woodstock by Elisha Sabin," *Vermont History*, 41 (1973), 123–141; and "A New Englander in the West," *Minnesota History*, 15 (1934), 301–308.

36 These figures are derived from the Windsor tax lists and manuscript census rolls.

37 *Vermont Journal*, 16 January 1830.

38 *Vermont Chronicle*, 12 March 1835; and Dana, *Woodstock*, 324–327. The lack of mill records makes it difficult to identify and trace mill operatives. Of the seventeen Weathersfield men who identified themselves as spinners or manufacturers of wool on a Whig bank petition in 1834, only six could be located on the town's 1835 tax list, and all but two had left town by 1840. Only one joined a church.

39 These figures are derived from the tax lists and manuscript census rolls of Barnet, Peacham, St. Johnsbury, Weathersfield, and West Windsor.

40 *Weekly Messenger and Connecticut and Passumpsic River Valley Advertiser* (St. Johnsbury), 31 July 1828; and *North Star* (Danville), 22 January 1828.

41 Harriet Strong in Hardwick to Jane Shedd in Peacham, 16 August 1834.

42 The following story and interpretation are drawn from David Brion Davis, "Murder in New Hampshire," *New England Quarterly*, 28 (1955), 147–163.

43 The figures are derived from the tax lists and census rolls of Windsor. The situation in the valley was different from the situation in the cities described by Johnson, *Shopkeepers' Millennium*, 43–55, or Ryan, *Cradle of the Middle Class*, 146–155, where employers stopped boarding their workers in the 1830s.

44 *Vermont Journal*, 30 August and 17 September, 1828.

45 *Vermont Journal*, 9 January 1827; George Wales to William Jarvis, n.d. (c. 1828); and Simeon Ide to Jarvis, 2 October 1829.

46 *North Star*, 13 March 1827.

47 *Freedom's Banner* (Chester), 25 March 1829.

Chapter 5

1 "Memorial of the Citizens of Windsor County, Vermont, Opposed to the Removal of the Deposits"; *Vermont Luminary* (Randolph), 24 January 1829; *Workingman's Gazette* (Woodstock), 3 December 1830.

2 *Vermont Phoenix*, 25 November 1829; *Vermont Patriot and State Gazette* (Montpelier), 12 and 19 October 1829; C. P. Van Ness, "Appeal to the Unprejudiced Judgment" (1826); idem, "To the Publick" (Burlington, 1827); and *Proceedings of the Vermont Republican Convention* (Montpelier: G. W. Hill, 1828).

3 *Freedom's Banner*, 25 March and 22 April 1829; *Vermont Phoenix*, 25 March, 18 September, and 25 November 1829; and *Vermont Enquirer* (Norwich), 30 December 1830. The charges against Jarvis continued in the Jacksonian press for many years. See *Spirit of the Age* (Woodstock), 24 July, and 14 and 28 August 1840; and 1 April and 5 August 1842.

4 *Vermont Patriot*, 19 October 1829, 26 July 1830, 2 September 1831, 15 October 1832, and 4 April 1834; *Vermont Phoenix*, 18 September 1829; *Woodstock Observer*, 6 October 1829; and *Vermont Enquirer* and *Freedom's Banner*, 1829.

5 On the rise of the Jacksonians in Vermont and C. P. Van Ness's dislike of John Quincy Adams, see *North Star*, 27 January 1827; John Bailey in Milton, Massachusetts, to D. A. A. Buck in Montpelier, 7 October 1826, and Buck to Bailey, 18 October 1826 and 21 March 1827, M.H.S.; the correspondence of C. P. Van Ness and Martin Van Buren, 25 July 1820–22 February 1827, L.C.; William Bradley to Salma Hale, 16 August 1819, 18 January 1822, 5 May and 5 December 1823, M.H.S.; Horatio Seymour in Washington, D.C., to George Cleveland in Montpelier, 30 January 1823 and 11 January 1826, Sheldon Museum; and Horatio Seymour to Phineas White, 27 January 1827, N.Y.S.L.

6 *Freedom's Banner*, 25 March 1829; Russell Streeter, *Mirror of Calvinist Fanaticism, or Jedidiah Burchard & Co., during a Protracted Meeting... in Woodstock, Vermont*, 1st ed. (Woodstock: Nahum Haskell, 1835), 87;

Wells, *Newbury*, 161–162, 186; Chapter 4, "The Impact of Pressing Times on Household Government, Labor Relations, and Politics"; and Roth, "Strange Fire," 238–242.

7 McLoughlin, *New England Dissent*, v. II, 877–911; Livermore, *Twilight of Federalism*, 119–120, 192–193, 223–227; Donald B. Cole, *Jacksonian Democracy in New Hampshire, 1800–1850* (Cambridge: Harvard Univ. Press, 1970), 16–81, 106–108; Lipson, *Freemasonry in Connecticut*, 267–311; Gerald D. Foss, *Three Centuries of Freemasonry in New Hampshire* (Somersworth: New Hampshire Publishing, 1972), 51–55, 370–373; *Masonic Casket* (Haverhill, New Hampshire), May 1826; and Formisano, *Transformation of Political Culture*, 197–221.

8 Roth, "Strange Fire," 240–241; Jonas Clark in Middletown to Ebenezer Judd in Montpelier, 7 October 1832, and Ezra Meech in Shelburne to Charles Lindsley in Montpelier, 27 May 1833, Sheldon Museum.

9 *Vermont Luminary*, 10 and 24 January, and 25 February 1829; and *North Star*, 18 March 1828.

10 See Cross, *Burned-Over District*, 114–116; Ludlum, *Social Ferment*, 87–89; *North Star*, 27 February and 8 May 1827; the memorial from the inhabitants of Windsor and vicinity on the Burnham affair, 1 October 1829, in the Vermont State Papers; and *Woodstock Observer*, 29 September and 10 November 1829.

11 Reminiscences of Daniel Ransom; Ludlum, *Social Ferment*, 112–113; and *North Star*, 19 August 1829.

12 *Journals of the General Assembly of Vermont… 1830* (Woodstock: Rufus Colton, 1831), 26–28; *Journals of the General Assembly of Vermont… 1831* (Danville: Ebenezer Eaton, 1832), 42–46; "Proceedings of the Anti-masonic State Convention… 1831" (Montpelier: Gamaliel Small, 1831); "Proceedings of the Anti-masonic State Convention… 1833" (Montpelier: Knapp and Jewett, 1833); *North Star*, 22 February 1831, 27 May 1833, and 6 January and 30 June 1834; and *Vermont Luminary*, 10 January, 11 March, and 2 September 1829.

13 *North Star*, 26 August 1828; *Vermont Luminary*, 25 February 1829; and Lipson, *Freemasonry in Connecticut*, 188–193, 199–200, 329–338.

14 *Vermont Luminary*, 24 January and 4 March 1829.

15 *Vermont Luminary*, 17 January and 12 August 1829.

16 Palmer, "William Adam Palmer," 49–112; *Univeralist Watchman*, 1828–1829; T. Spaulding to S. Niles in West Fairlee, 11 May 1829; Ludlum, *Social Ferment*, 95; *Vermont Patriot*, 16 April 1827; Hemenway, *Gazetteer*, v. II, 1062; *Vermont Advocate* (Chelsea), 17 September 1828; and *Vermont Luminary*, 10 and 17 January, 8 July, 2 September, and 9 December 1829.

17 Arthur F. Stone, *The History of the North Congregationalist Church of St. Johnsbury, Vermont* (St. Johnsbury, 1942), 17; Miller and Wells, *Ryegate*, 230; Ludlum, *Social Ferment*, 106; and Roth, "Strange Fire," 260–262.

18 *North Star*, 4 August and 22 December, 1829; the Chauncey Richardson Papers, Woodstock Academy; miscellaneous Antimasonic essays, Niles Family Papers; and Roth, "Strange Fire," 262–265.

19 *North Star,* 26 August 1828; *Vermont Luminary,* 12 August 1829; the narrative of Abel Adams, 16; and Roth, "Strange Fire," 267–269. Thirteen Antimasonic former Masons from the towns studied intensively could be identified from testimonials printed in newspapers and from expulsion notices posted by Masonic lodges. Six (46 percent) were farmers and eight (62 percent) were church members. None were Episcopalians or Unitarians. Forty-eight Masons who remained fervently loyal to the organization amid the controversy could be identified in the towns studied intensively. Their names appeared in testimonials on behalf of Masonry and in church records where some were disciplined for refusing to renounce Masonry. Most lived in marketing and manufacturing centers. Only eleven (23 percent) were farmers. Only five (10 percent) were not church members, and thirteen (27 percent) were Episcopalians or Unitarians.

20 On the more radical views of Workingmen in urban areas, see Edward Pessen, *Jacksonian America: Society, Personality, and Politics,* rev. ed. (Homewood: Dorsey, 1978), 270–276; Walter E. Hugins, *Jacksonian Democracy and the Working Class: A Study of the New York Workingmen's Movement, 1829–1837* (Stanford: Stanford Univ. Press, 1960); John F. C. Harrison, *Robert Owen and the Owenites in Britain and America* (London: Routledge and Kegan Paul, 1969); and Wilentz, *Chants Democratic,* 172–216. Anthony F. C. Wallace, *Rockdale: The Growth of an American Village in the Early Industrial Revolution* (New York: W. W. Norton, 1978), 243–295, finds considerable radicalism in the countryside surrounding Philadelphia, perhaps because of Philadelphia's influence and radical heritage.

21 *Workingman's Gazette,* 29 March, 14 June, 23 September, 11 and 18 November, and 22 December 1830. See also the article on village aristocracy in *Liberal Extracts* (Woodstock), August 1829.

22 *Liberal Extracts,* January 1829.

23 *Liberal Extracts,* March–July, and December 1829; and *Workingman's Gazette,* 1 December 1830 and 21 June 1831.

24 *Liberal Extracts,* July 1829.

25 See note 21.

26 *Liberal Extracts,* March 1829; *Workingman's Gazette,* 23 September and 14 October 1830; and *Vermont Patriot,* 30 August 1830. Formisano, *Transformation of Political Culture,* 222–244, finds a similar pattern among small town and rural Workingmen in the Connecticut River Valley of Massachusetts.

Some Workingmen, in particular those who had been Free Readers, like Nahum Haskell and Thomas Powers, may also have feared the curtailment of their social and intellectual autonomy. The Free Readers were an irreverent, satirical group, who celebrated revolutionary fervor and camaraderie. They were afraid that crusading Christians and reformers would try to rid society of eccentricity and diversity and set bounds where there had been freedom. These sentiments were carried over into the Workingmen. Their committee in Woodstock included many men who prided themselves on being independent of the town's social and intellectual arbiters: a leading taverner, half of Woodstock's senior militia officers, and four of its book-sellers and printers.

27 Roth, "Strange Fire," 353–358; and *Workingman's Gazette*, 2 February and 21 June 1831.

28 The petition to the Senate and House of Representatives from the inhabitants of Wardsboro, Vermont, against the existence of slavery in the District of Columbia, 4 December 1828, National Archives.

29 The petition to the Senate and House of Representatives from the inhabitants of Norwich, Vermont, against the removal of the Georgia Indians, 17 March 1830, National Archives; and Charles Sheldon in Windsor to Reuben Norton in Newman, Georgia, 23 July 1831, Reuben Smith Papers, private collection.

30 Petition to the Senate and House of Representatives from the inhabitants of Windsor County, Vermont, against the removal of the Georgia Indians, 14 February 1831, National Archives; and *Vermont Chronicle*, 21 November 1828 and 5 March 1830.

31 *Vermont Journal*, 9 January 1830; *North Star*, 7 September 1830; and Benjamin Swift in Washington, D.C., to Phineas White, 12 February 1830, N.Y.S.L.

32 Roth, "Strange Fire," 311–318; *Journal of the General Assembly*, 1832, 42–46, on Governor Palmer's views; *Vermont Phoenix*, 18 September 1829; and *Vermont Enquirer*, 27 January 1831. The *Universalist Watchman* was sympathetic to Andrew Jackson on Indian removal (16 April 1831 and 22 January 1833). The *Watchman* did not, however, endorse Jackson, and many Universalists in St. Johnsbury signed the petitions. It should be noted that the Associate and Reformed Presbyterians of Barnet did not sign petitions in support of either initiative, but that may have been because the petitions did not appear in their towns, and not because of any antipathy toward the drives. Important members of both Presbyterian sects would soon play leading roles in the abolitionist movement.

33 On Sabbatarianism, see the petition from the inhabitants of Ryegate, Vermont, in opposition to the transportation of mail on Sundays, 25 December 1828, National Archives; Bertram Wyatt-Brown, "Prelude to Abolitionism: Sabbatarian Politics and the Rise of the Second Party System," *Journal of American History*, 58 (1971), 316–341; the petition from the inhabitants of Norwich, Vermont, in opposition to the transportation of mail on Sundays, 15 January 1830, National Archives; *North Star*, 19 January 1835; and *Vermont Chronicle*, 17 April 1829.

34 See Andrew Root in Woodbury to Ashbel Martin in Peacham, 15 April 1830, Martin-Merrill Papers; *North Star*, 22 January, 4 March, 17 June, and 28 December 1828, 29 June, 4 August, and 22 December 1829, and 8 February and 7 June 1831; *Vermont Journal*, 16 January 1830; *Vermont Republican* (Windsor), 19 September 1829, and 9 January and 10 April 1830; *Vermont Chronicle*, 20 October 1829 and 16 January 1830; and Albert Townsend in Windsor to Mrs. Orson Townsend in Reading, 2 February 1828.

35 *Vermont Journal*, 16 January 1830; *St. Johnsbury Farmer's Herald*, 2 December 1828; Rorabaugh, *Alcoholic Republic*, 7–10, 187–222; Tyrell, *Sobering Up*, 54–134; and Hempel, *Temperance and Prohibition*, 25–44. The newspapers that would later support the National Republican effort were frequently sympathetic to Sabbatarians and temperance activists. See *Vermont Journal*, 7 February 1828; *Vermont Republican*, 3 February 1829; and *St. Johnsbury Farmer's Herald*, 1828–1831.
36 *Vermont Republican*, 10 April 1830 and 26 September 1829.
37 Roth, "Strange Fire," 327–331.
38 The Congregationalist *Vermont Chronicle*, 19 December 1828, strongly favored Sabbatarian goals. The *Universalist Watchman*, 24 November 1832, strongly opposed them.
39 *Vermont Phoenix*, 6 January 1830; *Liberal Extracts*, January 1829 and January 1830; the petition from the inhabitants of Woodstock in favor of the transportation of mail on Sundays, 6 January 1830; and the petition from the inhabitants of Windham County, 12 January 1831.
40 *Universalist Watchman*, 17 August 1832; *Vermont Chronicle*, 1828–1835; *Vermont Republican*, 26 September 1829; *Vermont Patriot*, 31 September 1829; and Roth, "Strange Fire," 335–338, 378–379.
41 *North Star*, 8 February 1831; *Vermont Journal*, 17 September and 10 December 1831; *Vermont Republican*, 26 September 1829; Jeremiah Wolcott of Newport, New Hampshire, to William Sabin in Windsor, 13 July 1834; Charlotte Sabin in Keene, New Hampshire, to William Sabin in Windsor, 20 July 1833; *Vermont Chronicle*, 16 July 1830 and 8 July 1831; and *Weekly Messenger*, 23 October 1832.
42 *Vermont Republican*, 12 January and 11 August 1828; Samuel Elliot to Prof. Stuart, 22 February 1830, B.P.L.; Elliot, "A Voice from the Green Mountains on the Subject of Masonry and Antimasonry" (Brattleboro: George Nichols, 1834); anonymous pro-Masonic essay, MS, James Whitelaw Papers; and Ephraim Brown in Bloomfield to Silas Jennison, 13 August 1828, N.Y.S.L.
43 *St. Johnsbury Farmer's Herald*, 27 January 1830 and 15 July 1829; *Vermont Republican*, 8 August 1829; William Jarvis in Weathersfield to Coolidge, Poor, and Head, 7 February 1828; Simeon Ide in Windsor to William Jarvis in Weathersfield, 2 October 1829; William Jarvis to J. H. Harris, 25 November 1830, L.C.; William Hull of Bellows Falls to Silas Jennison, 25 August 1827, and D. Woodcock to Jennison, 27 April 1828, N.Y.S.L.
44 *St. Johnsbury Farmer's Herald*, 20 July and 7 September, 1831; and *Vermont Journal*, 27 January 1827.
45 *St. Johnsbury Farmer's Herald*, 17 February 1830; Timothy Tickle (pseud. of Benjamin F. Kendall), "The Doleful Tragedy of the Raising of Jo. Burnham, or, the 'Cat Let out of the Bag' " (Woodstock: W. W. Prescott, 1832); *Vermont Luminary*, 11 March 1829; Simeon Ide to William Jarvis, 2 October 1829; and Roth, "Strange Fire," 256–259.
46 *Vermont Journal*, 16 August 1833.
47 J. W. Vail to Phineas White, 25 June 1829, N.Y.S.L.; *Freedom's Banner*,

25 March 1829; and Horace Everett in Washington, D.C., to William Jarvis, 10 March 1830, M.H.S.

48 Roth, "Strange Fire," 339–340, 350. The *St. Johnsbury Farmer's Herald*, 20 January and 31 March 1830, defended Masonry outright. Thirty-five percent of the ardent defenders of Masonry in the towns studied intensively were identified as National Republicans. The Jacksonians did not do badly among Masons, however. Six of the fifteen Jacksonian activists identified in Pomfret, Weathersfield, West Windsor, Windsor, and Woodstock (40 percent) were Masons. The comparable figures for National Republican activists in the Windsor and Caledonia County towns were 30 percent and 29 percent, respectively.

49 *Vermont Journal*, 13 November 1830 and 24 May 1833.

50 *Vermont Journal*, 27 February 1834 and 27 March 1830; and *Vermont Chronicle*, 28 February 1834. See also *Woodstock Observer*, 25 August 1829. Such divisions appeared in the temperance movement nationally. See Tyrell, *Sobering Up*, 135–151; and Hempel, *Temperance and Prohibition*, 45–78.

51 *Vermont Chronicle*, 22 August 1834; and *Vermont Journal*, 28 August 1834.

52 *Vermont Journal*, 22 January 1834.

53 In 1827 and 1828, only twenty-eight religious and civic organizations voted funds for the support of the Colonization Society – 68 percent of them Congregationalist churches and 14 percent Masonic lodges. In 1830 and 1832, however, when the Masons were no longer in a position to donate much of anything, the number of contributing societies rose to seventy-nine. Contributions from organizations other than Congregationalist churches and Masonic lodges had risen from 16 percent of the total to 37 percent. See the "Annual Report of the Vermont Colonization Society" for the years 1824, 1827, 1828, 1830, and 1832.

54 "First Annual Report of the Vermont Anti-Slavery Society ... 1835."

55 *Vermont Watchman* (Montpelier), 25 September 1837; Oliver Johnson in Craftsbury to William Lloyd Garrison in Boston, Massachusetts, 4 June 1832, and Chauncey Knapp in Montpelier to Amos Phelps in Boston, Massachusetts, 17 August 1839, B.P.L.

56 Chamberlain Family Papers, especially Jane Shedd in Peacham to Harriet Strong in Hardwick, 3 December 1836; and Josiah Shedd in Augusta, Georgia, to Abigail Chamberlain in Peacham, 13 April 1841.

57 Ruth Buchman in South Woodstock to Parley Davis in Montpelier, 5 May 1840; Nancy B. Batchelder, "Growing Up in Peru (1815–1840)," *Vermont Quarterly*, 21 (1953), 6–7; Mary Worcester in Littleton, New Hampshire, to Jane Shedd in Peacham, 12 October 1841; the petition to Congress from the women of Jamaica and vicinity against slavery in the District of Columbia, 5 March 1834, National Archives; and Chauncey Knapp's offer to educate "young men of color," *Burlington Free Press*, 5 April 1833.

58 Erastus Fairbanks in St. Johnsbury to an unknown person, 28 February 1837.

59 William Porter at Dartmouth College to Luther Townsend in Fitzwilliam,

New Hampshire, 17 December 1839, D.C.L.; O. S. Murray in Montpelier to William Lloyd Garrison in Boston, Massachusetts, 11 October 1834, B.P.L.; and the memoirs of Charles Paine, 28. See *Vermont Chronicle*, 28 October, and 11 and 18 November 1831, 13 September 1833, and 16 February 1837, to chart the paper's growing antipathy toward immediate abolition.

60 See notes 58 and 59.

61 Whereas 79 organizations had donated in 1830 and 1832, only seventeen gave in 1836 and 1837, and the society's interdenominational base was by then almost completely eroded. "Annual Report of the Vermont Colonization Society," 1830, 1832, 1836, 1837.

62 Ludlum, *Social Ferment*, 147–151; *Herald of Freedom* (Concord, New Hampshire), 31 October and 14 November 1835, and 9 July 1836; Samuel J. May, *Recollection of Our Anti-Slavery Conflict* (Boston: Field, Osgood, 1869), 152–155; *Vermont Telegraph* (Brandon), 8 November 1837; and the antiabolitionist petition from Montpelier to the state legislature, 27 October 1835, in the Vermont State Papers, v. 69, 147.

63 On parallels with antiabolition riots in western Vermont and other areas in the northern United States, see Ludlum, *Social Ferment*, 147–151; and Leonard L. Richards, *Gentlemen of Property and Standing: Anti-Abolition Mobs in Jacksonian America* (New York: Oxford Univ. Press, 1970). The sources reveal little about the identity of the rioters or their motives, except in Montpelier, where the leading antiabolitionists were prominent Jacksonians: Timothy Hubbard, president of the Bank of Montpelier; George W. Hill, publisher of the *Vermont Patriot and State Gazette*; and J. T. Marston, an attorney who succeeded Hill as the editor of the *Patriot* in 1839. Samuel May, the abolitionist whose appearance they opposed, spoke at Montpelier's Presbyterian church, an indication May's supporters may well have been National Republicans, who stood at odds with the town's many Jacksonians.

Town elites were deeply and fairly equally divided politically in Newbury and Randolph, the towns where actual mob violence occurred. In Newbury it was the Jacksonians and in Randolph the National Republicans who may have resented the effort by their political rivals to bring in abolitionist speakers who would embarrass them on the slavery issue. Elites in Windsor and Woodstock, by contrast, were overwhelmingly National Republican, and that may have enabled them to close their churches to abolitionist speakers and thereby avoid the occasion for violence.

64 *Vermont Journal*, 15 March 1830.

65 Roth, "Strange Fire," 373–375.

66 In the towns studied intensively, selectmen together served 299 terms between 1816 and 1828, and 154 terms between 1829 and 1835.

67 Nathan Haswell, essay on slavery, MS.

Chapter 6

1 *North Star*, 19 October 1830.

2　See Chapter 3, notes 1 and 5, for the sources of these statistics. In the northern reaches of the valley membership in each type of town rose to nine-tenths of the levels it reached in more densely settled towns that were first settled by New Lights. Membership levels in towns first settled by Old Lights stood close to the median levels for the valley as a whole.

3　Ann Carter of Groton to Willard Stevens of Barnet, 29 April 1827, U.V.M.; and Andrew Root of Woodbury to Ashbel Martin of Peacham, 8 July 1827, Martin-Merrill Papers.

4　*Vermont Chronicle*, 10 October 1828; and Reuben Smith of Windsor to Reuben Norton in Greenfield, Massachusetts, 20 March and 9 July 1829, private collection.

5　Hazen Merrill of Peacham to Samuel Merrill of Indianapolis, Indiana, 23 September 1831; Reuben Smith to Reuben Norton in Lawrenceville, Georgia, 8 November 1831, private collection; James Wilson in Bradford to Boyd Wilson in Burlington, 13 January 1832, U.V.M.; and the diary of David Sutherland, 10 May and 3 September 1831, N.H.H.S.

6　*Universalist Watchman*, 19 November 1831; *Vermont Chronicle*, 1 May 1829; and Hazen Merrill to Samuel Merrill, 23 September 1831.

7　Anne C. Rose, *Transcendentalism as a Social Movement, 1830–1850* (New Haven: Yale Univ. Press, 1981), 28–37; Benjamin C. C. Parker of Woodstock to Benjamin Hill of Lebanon, New Hampshire, 25 February 1835, D.C.L.; the communion records of St. Paul's Episcopal Church of Windsor, 1831–1835; and Streeter, *Calvinist Fanaticism*.

8　Ann Niles, essay on Christian perfection, MS, Niles Family Papers; the diaries and meditations of Daniel Clark; Eben Spear in Ludlow to Norman Mason in Lowell, Massachusetts, 29 December 1838, Weaver and Mason Family Papers; and *Vermont Chronicle*, 1 April 1835.

9　See, for example, *Vermont Chronicle*, 30 April and 7 May 1830, and 27 May, 3 July, and 28 October 1831; and Streeter, *Calvinist Fanaticism*, 30–31.

10　Tobias Spicer, "Religion the Only Source of National Prosperity" (Montpelier: George W. Hill, 1833); and Friedman, *Gregarious Saints*, 96–126.

11　Horace Greeley, *Recollections of a Busy Life* (New York: J. B. Ford, 1868), 71–72; and Perry Miller, "From the Covenant to the Revival," in James W. Smith and A. Leland Jamison, eds., *The Shaping of American Religion* (Princeton: Princeton Univ. Press, 1961), 322–368.

12　Daniel O. Morton, *A Narrative of a Revival of Religion in Springfield, Vermont* (Springfield, 1834); and John J. Duffy and H. Nicholas Muller III, "Jedidiah Burchard and Vermont's 'New Measure' Revivals: Social Adjustment and the Quest for Unity," *Vermont History*, 46 (1978), 5–20.

13　Streeter, *Calvinist Fanaticism*, 10–11; Austin Chase in Lebanon, New Hampshire, to Mr. and Mrs. John Chase of Norwich, 1 April 1835, D.C.L.; and Duffy and Muller, "Jedidiah Burchard."

14　Morton, *Revival in Springfield*; Streeter, *Calvinist Fanaticism*, 30–31, 45, 126; *Vermont Chronicle*, 12 March 1835; and Austin Chase to Mr. and Mrs. John Chase, 18 April 1835, D.C.L.

15 Denominational records for the Congregationalists, Baptists, Methodists, and Freewill Baptists from 1837 to 1843 show that there were strong revivals outside major marketing and manufacturing towns, especially in towns along the border between Windham and Windsor counties and throughout Orange and Washington counties. The proportion of farmers and farm laborers among new members increased markedly in these same years in the towns studied intensively.

16 Diary of Abel Adams.

17 The decline in the median age at entrance into the churches is more remarkable, considering that the median age of the population rose steadily through the period. That rise was a product of the aging of the first settlers (most of whom were young or middle-aged people establishing their families), of the growing exodus of youths, and of the declining birth rate.

18 William Townsend, Jr., in Boston, Massachusetts, to Aurelia Townsend in Reading, 22 February and 1 September 1833, and to Mr. and Mrs. William Townsend, Sr., in Reading, 22 February and 8 May 1833. See also the diary of Horatio Chandler, September 1840–March 1841, N.H.H.S., on the spiritual life of a young married man who had yet to attain proprietorship.

19 William Townsend, Jr., to Aurelia Townsend, 1 September 1833, and to Mr. and Mrs. William Townsend, Sr., 18 September 1833 and 1 February 1834.

20 William Townsend, Jr., to Aurelia Townsend, 20 April and 26 May 1836.

21 Dennis Townsend in Plainfield, New Hampshire, to Mr. and Mrs. William Townsend, Sr., 21 December 1835, and to William Townsend, Jr., 24 July 1836.

22 *North Star*, 29 April 1828.

23 Kull, "Sally Rice," 52; and the Reuben Smith Papers, 1825–1837, private collection.

24 Diary of Nancy Taft, 1838–1840.

25 William How at Dartmouth College to Jacob Chapman in Lyndon, 26 July 1836, and Austin Chase to Mr. and Mrs. John Chase, 1 and 18 April 1835, D.C.L.; and the correspondence of Aurelia Townsend, 1827–1852.

26. The average improved acreage per farm in Barnet was only 45.6 acres in 1840, versus 63.3 acres in other agricultural towns; and 9.4 percent of those farms were organized as partnerships, versus only 5.5 percent in other agricultural towns.

27 In agricultural towns, master craftsmen rose from 1 percent of all new members during spiritually calm times to 5 percent during the great revival. Businessmen, professionals, and small proprietors fell from 5 to 3 percent of all new members; and farmers, millers, and taverners from 40 to 21 percent (Table 6.2). Master craftsmen did not make a similar proportional advance in marketing and manufacturing towns, but their percentage fell less far than those of businessmen, professionals, and small proprietors, from 18 to 14 percent, instead of from 31 to 10 percent (Table 6.1). These figures do not suggest that the revival's appeal was weak to proprietors other than master craftsmen. They merely suggest that the churches did not appeal as strongly to master craftsmen in spiritually calm times.

28 The census identified only household heads by name before 1850. Only the age, sex, and race of other household members were recorded. It is not possible to ascertain whether the people living in a household shared the same surname, let alone whether they were related to one another.

29 For example, "Group 1" master craftsmen from Windsor and commercial farmers who did not have households or youths in their households were just as likely to join churches during the revival as those who had households with youths in them. They were, indeed, the only groups of proprietors for whom the relationship between household composition and entry into the churches did not hold up.

That was understandable, however, because they had far more employees on the whole than other proprietors, given the size of their enterprises and the size of the markets in which they competed. Thus, they probably had youths in their employ even if those employees did not appear as members of their households, having to form independent households or find board elsewhere. They could have encountered difficulties with their employees even if (or perhaps because) their employees did not live with them. Johnson, *Shopkeepers' Millennium*, 102–115, 136–141, shows, for example, that the master craftsmen who joined churches in the greatest numbers in Rochester, New York, were not, as in Windsor, those who had the most journeymen and apprentices in their households, but those who had the fewest. The putting-out system developed so rapidly in Rochester that masters had far more employees than they could possibly board in their homes. The result was that a growing body of masters did not even attempt, like their Windsor counterparts, to squeeze as many employees as possible into their homes. Instead they sent them to live in working-class neighborhoods, while they themselves adopted a privatistic form of family life. In both cases, the masters' spiritual crises stemmed from difficulties they encountered in supervising and motivating their employees, which arose because the putting-out system undermined the practicality of household government and demoralized employees aspiring to proprietorship. The master craftsmen thus responded spiritually to the disruption of the same relationship, but it was disrupted for them in different ways.

30 Sophia Sheldon in Barnet to Charles Sheldon in Windsor, 12 October 1829, Willard Stevens Papers, U.V.M.

31 Correspondence of Daniel Thompson, especially the letters to Joseph Pierce, Jr., in Gorham, Maine, 10 April 1834, and 20 April and 17 July 1835.

32 James Wheeler in Burlington to Allen Hazen of Hartford, 12 March and 2 May 1836; and A. P. Marsh in Burlington to Allen Hazen, 13 August 1838.

33 Mary Williams of Woodstock to Henry Williams in Bellows Falls, 25 March 1831; Henry Williams to Mary Williams, 7 April 1831; Mary Williams to Henry Williams in New York City, 6 January and 10 June 1835, and 9 September and 14 November 1836; and S. Niles in Newburyport, Massachusetts, to Nathaniel Niles in West Fairlee, 9 February (c. 1830). Ryan, *Cradle of the Middle Class*, 60–144, finds that the response of Utica's women to social changes that affected the family was more important in causing the revival there than any problems the city's

employees encountered. Women in Utica may have had more power over spiritual life than their counterparts in the valley, however, because they were able, in an urban setting, to establish independent women's organizations (both ecclesiastical and extra-ecclesiastical) through which they could address their concerns.

34   The figures on corporate directors in agricultural towns understate the impact of the revival on rural corporate directors. Four of the eleven who did not join churches by the end of the revival lived in Barnet, where only one of five directors joined a church. Two who did not join churches in Weathersfield were woolen manufacturing agents, brought into town as experts by the Perkinsville Manufacturing Company to run the local mills. Each stayed in town only a year.

35   Hazen Merrill to Samuel Merrill, 23 September 1831; and Ruth Buckman of South Woodstock to Parley Davis of Montpelier, 29 March 1843.

36   Ward, "Religious Enthusiasm in Vermont," 59; the records of the Congregational Church at Weathersfield Bow, 1841; Wells, *Newbury*, 213; and Peach, "Seth Shaler Arnold," 8 (1940), 136.

37   See Chapter 2, "Denominational Rivalry"; Chapter 6, "The Causes of the Revival"; and the records of the Congregational Church at Weathersfield Bow, 1841.

38   The "N's" for male expulsion rates were: 74 of 337 from 1827–1833; 72 of 231 from 1834–1836; and 78 of 289 from 1837–1843. The corresponding rates for female converts were: 50 of 660; 63 of 387; and 48 of 476. Sources are noted in Chapter 3, note 55. Expulsion rates by the mid-1830s were three times those that had prevailed in spiritually calm times prior to the great revival.

39   *Vermont Chronicle*, 10 October 1828 and 1 May 1829.

40   Morton, *Revival in Springfield*.

41   Records of the West Windsor Methodist Church and of the Old South Congregational Church of Windsor.

42   *Vermont Chronicle*, 7 November 1834 and 1 April 1835.

43   Martha and Sarah Norton in Windsor to Reuben Norton in Lawrenceville, Georgia, 23 July 1831, 10 January 1833, and 15 August 1837, and Charles Sheldon in Windsor to Reuben Norton in Newman, Georgia, 28 July 1833, Reuben Smith Papers, private collection; and the Cowles Family Papers, 1832–1837, Columbia University Library.

44   Lois Leverett in Windsor to Louisa Morris in Springfield, 9 November 1806, Wardner Collection.

45   *Vermont Chronicle*, 1 January 1830.

46   Thomas Emerson in Windsor to Henry Cole in Detroit, Michigan, 1 August 1834. Palmer survived the epidemic and paid off the bond.

47   *Universalist Watchman*, 14 December 1834.

48. Jeremiah Wolcott in Newport, New Hampshire, to William Sabin in Windsor, 13 July 1834.

49   Streeter, *Calvinist Fanaticism*, iii–iv, 87; and Brenda C. Morrissey, ed., *Abby Hemenway's Vermont* (Brattleboro: Stephen Green, 1972), 134.

50 Streeter, *Calvinist Fanaticism*, back cover; and James Wilson to Boyd Wilson, 23 January 1832, U.V.M.

51 *North Star*, 6 April 1835.

52 Emerson Andrews, *Living Life, or the Autobiography of Emerson Andrews* (Boston: James H. Earle, 1875), 135–136; and James Wilson to Boyd Wilson, 23 January 1832, U.V.M.

53 *Vermont Chronicle*, 30 April 1830; and William B. Parker, *Life and Public Services of Justin Smith Morrill* (Boston: Houghton Mifflin, 1924), 14.

54 A note penned by George Thomas on the copy of Streeter, *Calvinist Fanaticism*, 70–71, U.V.M.; the Francis A. Freeman Papers, 1838–1842, N.H.H.S.; Austin Chase to Mr. and Mrs. John Chase, 18 April 1835, D.C.L.; and Hiram Orcutt, *Reminiscences of School Life* (Cambridge: Univ. Press, 1898), 34–41.

55 Streeter, *Calvinist Fanaticism*, 41–42, 10.

56 Ibid., 12.

57 Benjamin C. C. Parker in Woodstock to Benjamin Hill in Lebanon, New Hampshire, 25 February 1835, Nathan Lord in Lebanon, New Hampshire, to Charles Marsh in Woodstock, 25 April 1835, and George P. Marsh in Burlington to Charles Marsh in Woodstock, 29 December 1835, D.C.L.

58 Thompson, *History of Vermont*, 204.

59 Cross, *Burned-Over District*, 287–321; Ludlum, *Social Ferment*, 250–260; Ward, "Religious Enthusiasm in Vermont," 209–262; Ebenezer Spear in Ludlow to Norman Mason in Lowell, Massachusetts, 29 December 1838, Weaver and Mason Family Papers; Allen F. Davis, "The Girl He Left Behind: The Letters of Harriet Hutchinson Salisbury," *Vermont History*, 23 (1965), 277; and the diary of Abel Adams, February–May 1843.

60 William Miller, *Evidence from Scripture and History of the Second Coming of Christ About the Year 1843* (Troy: Elias Gates, 1838), 9, 262–278; Ludlum, *Social Ferment*, 253–254; Sylvester Bliss, *Memoirs of William Miller* (Boston: Joshua V. Hines, 1853); and the memoirs of Charles Paine, 69–70.

61 W. H. Eastman in Grantham, New Hampshire, to Charles Eastman in Woodstock, 6 January 1843; Chapter 2, note 38; the reminiscences of Daniel Ransom; Robinson and Southmayd in Castleton to Charles Eastman, 9 February 1843; *Midnight Cry* (New York), 12 December 1844; and Hemenway, *Gazetteer*, v. 5, 427. See also the Newton Family Papers, N.H.H.S.

62 *Universalist Watchman*, 17 August 1832 and 5 January 1833.

Chapter 7

1 Roth, "Strange Fire," 224; and Bassett, "Urban Penetration of Rural Vermont," 85–95.

2 Bassett, "Urban Penetration of Rural Vermont," 64–68; and Adams, *Prices Paid by Vermont Farmers*, 24–25, 30–39.

3 Francis Upham in Waitsfield to Gideon Chapin in Janesville, Wisconsin, 21 February 1843.

4   James Vaughn in Pomfret to Erastus [surname illegible] in Springfield, Wisconsin, 11 May 1845; and an entry in James Vaughn's notebook, n.d.

5   Thomas Emerson, *Account of His Trials, Troubles, and Distress Occasioned by the Financial Crash of 1837–8* (n.d.); F. E. Phelps in Windsor to Horace Everett in Washington, D.C., 5 April 1838, and Rufus Emerson to Everett, 5 April 1838, Wardner Collection; *North Star*, 14 April 1838; Austin Chase to Mr. and Mrs. John Chase, 18 April 1835, D.C.L.; and the records of St. Paul's Episcopalian Church of Windsor.

6   William Jarvis in Weathersfield to D. H. Sumner in Hartland, 9 March 1840; and *Spirit of the Age*, 1 and 8 October 1841.

7   Records of the Farmers' and Mechanics' Mercantile Company of Peacham, and of the Farmers' and Mechanics' Store Company of West Fairlee.

8   Twenty-three of the forty-five stockholders identified were church members. Most were Congregationalists. A quarter were former Antimasons and two-thirds were farmers.

9   These and the following passages are taken from various drafts of Stevens's temperance addresses, U.V.M. They are not dated, but all were written in the 1830s.

10 Enthusiasm for teetotal temperance had spread across the northern United States by the mid-1830s, and most temperance reformers adopted the teetotal position. See Tyrell, *Sobering Up*, 136–151; and Hempel, *Temperance and Prohibition*, 45–59.
    Laws against drunkenness were still enforced in the 1830s in Massachusetts, where the habits of the standing order endured. Massachusetts also passed a fifteen-gallon law in 1838, which until its repeal in 1840 forbade the sale of alcoholic beverages in small quantities. See Hempel, 33–34, 79–101.

11 On the relationship between temperance and concern for personal reputations, see Hempel, *Temperance and Prohibition*, 7–9, 25–44, 179–182.

12 Erastus Fairbanks in St. Johnsbury to P. H. White in Brattleboro, 13 July 1852. Fairbanks also used his position as a trustee of the Connecticut and Passumpsic Railroad to support religion and morals by giving religious leaders and temperance reformers half-fare passes for travel to state and district conventions.

13 See Tyrell, *Sobering Up*, 115, 125–131; and Hempel, *Temperance and Prohibition*, 57–58, for related interpretations of teetotal temperance. Hempel does not explore fully the social sources or implications of the cult of respectability, and Tyrell is content to classify temperance advocates as "improvers" or promoters of social change, disregarding or downplaying the diversity of their motives and the desire of many to protect older virtues, such as self-employment, strong families, and stable communities.

14 Records of the First Baptist Church of Windsor, December 1836; "Minutes of the Congregational General Convention in Vermont" (Windsor: Chronicle, 1835); "Proceedings of the Vermont Baptist Convention" (Brandon: Telegraph, 1837); "Minutes of the Vermont Annual Conference of the Methodist Episcopal Church... 1848" (Claremont: J. Weber, 1848); and the diary of Abel Adams, 8 May 1841.

15 Petitions to the Vermont State Legislature in Opposition to the Liquor License Law from West Windsor, Barnet, St. Johnsbury, and Weathersfield, October 1837, in the Vermont State Papers; *Vermont Journal*, 19 April 1845; and Bryant and Baker, *Sally and Pamela Brown*, 28–30. Women moved into the forefront of the temperance movement earlier in Vermont than they did elsewhere in the nation, where Tyrell, *Sobering Up*, 179–183, finds them a considerable force only after 1840.

16 Samuel Chipman in Brandon to George Mauser in Montpelier, 18 January 1839, Erastus Fairbanks Papers; *Vermont Republican*, 26 September 1829; *St. Johnsbury Farmer's Herald*, 15 June 1831; *Vermont Chronicle*, 27 August 1835; *Journal of the General Assembly* (Middlebury: Knapp and Jewett, 1835), 57–60; Marro, "Vermont's Local Militia Units," 28–42; and Ludlum, *Social Ferment*, 67–78.

17 Tyrell, *Sobering Up*, 272, maintains that support for the Maine law did not split along urban–rural lines, but it is clear that it did split in the valley along such lines. Support stood at a median level of 65 percent in prosperous agricultural communities and 55 percent in poor, well-settled agricultural towns.

18 Jeremiah Wolcott in Newport, New Hampshire, to William Sabin in Windsor, 13 July 1834; Bassett, "Urban Penetration of Rural Vermont," 66; and Edwin C. Rozwenc, *Agricultural Policies in Vermont, 1860–1945* (Montpelier: Vermont Historical Society, 1981). For an excellent description of an agricultural fair, see *Vermont Watchman*, 29 October 1858.

19 "First Annual Report of the State Superintendent of Common Schools... 1846," 6–21; and Ludlum, *Social Ferment*, 233–235. Ten of the remaining petitions came from agricultural towns on good land, two from agricultural towns on poor land, and none from hill towns. One of the other educational reform leaders was a master craftsmen, three were commercial farmers, and one was a subsistence farmer.

20 "Fourth Annual Report of the State Superintendent of Common Schools" (Montpelier: E. P. Walton, 1849), 11; and *School Journal and Vermont Agriculturalist* (Windsor), May 1847, pp. 6–7, 13–14, June 1847, p. 1, and September 1847, pp. 68–71.

21 Gilmore, *Reading Becomes a Necessity*; Alstyne Townsend in Reading to Eliza Townsend in Fitzwilliam, New Hampshire, 20 February 1846; the charges lodged in "Fourth Annual Report of the State Superintendent of Schools," 33–36; "Annual Conference of the Methodist Episcopal Church ... 1848"; and *Vermont Christian Messenger*, 19 and 26 January 1848.

22 "Annual Conference of the Methodist Episcopal Church ... 1848"; "Third Annual Report of the State Superintendent of Common Schools," 51–53; "Fourth Annual Report of the State Superintendent of Common Schools," 38–46, 53–56; *Vermont Journal*, 10 October 1845; and William Wheeler in Keene, New Hampshire, to Lucy Wheeler in Norwich, 7 April 1840, William Jarvis Papers.

23 Ludlum, *Social Ferment*, 222–237; *School Journal*, November 1847, p. 3, and June 1847, pp. 1ff.; and "First Annual Report of the State Superintendent of Common Schools," 42.

24 On the end of rum sales by the 1840s, see Adams, *Prices Paid by Vermont Farmers*; Tyrell, *Sobering Up*, 316–317; and Rorabaugh, *Alcoholic Republic*, 7–10. Bassett, "Urban Penetration of Rural Vermont," 355–356, suggests that illicit liquor sales endured, although at an undetermined level.

25 The identity of most temperance activists in Windsor and Woodstock in the 1830s could not be determined. Of those identified, none were nonmembers in Windsor and only three in Woodstock. No temperance society records exist for any of the towns studied intensively for the 1840s. Short lists of society leaders did, however, appear in newspapers, and every town studied intensively except Windsor and Woodstock sent a temperance petition to the state legislature in 1837.

26 Church members comprised 105 of the 192 adult male taxpayers and household heads in Windsor in 1840 (55 percent), and 61 of the 82 who were still in town in 1850 (74 percent).

27 Church and temperance society members accounted for 921 of the 2,261 adult male taxpayers and household heads in the agricultural towns in 1840 (41 percent), and 604 of the 1,127 who were still in town in 1850 (54 percent). Church and temperance society members were more successful than nonmembers in every occupational group between 1840 and 1850. Sixty-eight of the 159 church and temperance society members who appeared as household heads or taxpayers for the first time in 1850 were proprietors (43 percent), versus only 290 of the 1,878 new nonmembers (15 percent). Excluding immigrants from Catholic countries, the proportion of proprietors among new nonmembers rose to only 288 of 1,562 (18 percent).

   Church members were not more successful than nonmembers among agricultural proprietors over age forty (Table 7.7). The number of people in the subcategories here is so small that the significance of such a finding is questionable. However, these members did have children coming of age in the 1830s, children who had to be established and whose fates worried their parents deeply. Such circumstances may have led new members to conversion and may also have meant that there was a drain on their financial resources that made a net loss of land, or a deferral of plans to expand operations, more likely.

28 See Chapter 6, "The Causes of the Revival"; and Wells, *Barnet*.

29 George Cowles to Mary Bradley, 27 January and 12 December 1835, Columbia University Library.

30 Isaac Ewell in Peacham to Hazen Merrill in Peacham, 17 November 1845.

31 Henry Cutts in Hartland to William Jarvis in Weathersfield, 31 August, and 5 and 23 September 1834.

32 Diary of Arthur Bennett, 20 and 21 May 1844, A.A.S.; and Alvah Sabin, et al., in Montpelier to George P. Marsh in Burlington, 16 October 1844, U.V.M.

33 Sarah Hill to Ann Brainherd in Troy, New York, 19 February 1838, Smith Family Papers, U.V.M.; John Henry Hopkins, *The Primitive Church, Compared with the Protestant Episcopal Church of the Present Day* (Burlington: Smith and Harrington, 1836), 126–152; and Tyrell, *Sobering Up*, 147–151.

34 On the fluctuations in the temperance vote, see Ludlum, *Social Ferment*, 78ff.

35 *Citizen Soldier* (Norwich), 28 May 1841; and *Vermont Courier and Farmer's, Manufacturer's, and Mechanic's Advocate* (Woodstock), 20 October 1836.

36 On the anti-teetotal temperance struggle, which was especially intense in Windsor County, see *Vermont Mercury* (Woodstock), 29 November 1844, and 3 and 10 March 1845; *Vermont Journal*, 7 July 1844; and Tyrell, *Sobering Up*, 293–305.

37 The net proportion of young men in agricultural towns on poor land who left the valley between 1830 and 1840 stood at 34 percent, the same rate that prevailed in agricultural towns on better land, and a higher rate than prevailed in marketing and manufacturing towns. On tenancy in hill towns, see Gilmore, *Reading Becomes a Necessity*.

38 Skillin, "William Cheney," 44–45; and Greeley, *Recollections*, 38, 48–50, 58–60, 79–80. Because of the scarcity of sources on hill towns and the life of the rural poor in the valley, this section draws on nonquantitative evidence from both Vermont and New Hampshire during the early nineteenth century.

39 Batchelder, "Peru," 6; Greeley, *Recollections*, 41, 51; the memoirs of Charles Paine, 86–87; and Helen H. Flanders, ed., *The New Green Mountain Songster: Traditional Folk Songs of Vermont* (Hatboro: Folklore Associates, 1966), 167–171, 219–221. "The Woodsman's Alphabet" tells of the woodsman's self-reliance and the "Hog-Thorny Bear" of his reliance on his own resources rather than on God when in danger. See also William J. Tucker, *My Generation* (Boston: Houghton Mifflin, 1919), 26.

40 Greeley, *Recollections*, 42–47, 56.

41 Ibid., 42–47; Adeline Reed to Ann Brainherd, 12 January 1836, Smith Family Papers, U.V.M.; and the diary of Damaris Foster, 1844.

42 Greeley, *Recollections*, 78–80; and Calvin Hulbert, "Reminiscences of Northern Vermont," 61, Houghton Library, Harvard Univ.

43 For prejudicial comments on backcountry views of education, see George Dennison in "Jigger Village" to James Dennison in Connecticut, 9 January 1852, L.C.; the diary of G. A. Davis, December 1851; and Chapter 8, "Religion."

44 George Parker in Montpelier to J. S. Hollinbeck in Burlington, 8 August 1836, and Martin Flint in Randolph to William Niles, et al., in West Fairlee, 8 February 1836, Nathaniel Chipman Papers; H. F. Janes in Waterbury to Samuel Crafts in Craftsbury, 6 July 1835, U.V.M.; William Jarvis to David Crawford in Putney, 7 February 1836; William Slade to Heman Allen in Burlington, 7 July 1835, and Hiland Hall of Bennington to Allen, 21 July 1835, N.Y.S.L.; William Slade to Myron Holly, 8 March 1834, to an unknown person, 12 December 1834, to Abigail Slade, 24 January 1836, and to Thurlow Weed in Albany, New York, 9 April 1836, N.Y.H.S.

45 *School Journal*, May 1847, pp. 6–7, 13–14, and September 1847, pp. 68–71; *Vermont Mercury*, 19 October 1849; and Daniel W. Howe, *The Political*

Culture of the American Whigs (Chicago: Univ. of Chicago Press, 1979), 96–122.

46 Olivia Flinn to Dudley Smith in Bloomington, Indiana, 11 February 1831, and Paul Flinn to Smith, 15 February 1831, Dudley Chase Papers, L.C.

47 Carlos Coolidge to Charles Williams from Windsor, 21 July 1836, D.C.L.; *St. Johnsbury Caledonian*, 21 August 1838; and *Vermont Mercury*, 19 May 1837.

48 Coleman, *Debtors and Creditors*, 65–73.

49 *Vermont Journal*, 30 November, and 7 and 28 December 1844; the memoirs of Charles Paine, 8–9, 23; Clark Rich in Shoreham to Silas Jennison, 14 November 1841, N.Y.S.L.; William Slade to A. A. Phelps, 12 January 1839, N.Y.H.S.; Samuel Crafts to Mary T. C. Hill, n.d., U.V.M.; Chapter 5, "Alternatives to Political Insurgency"; and Chapter 7, "A Modified Order in Town Life."

50 Erastus Fairbanks to Albert Whittemore in Montpelier, 26 October 1843; Mary Williams to Henry Williams, 19 November 1838; Justin Morrill to E. P. Walton in Montpelier, 13 November 1844; Howe, *American Whigs*, 60–68, 150–180; and Tyrell, *Sobering Up*, 261–264. For evidence of silence on specific reform proposals, as well as the annual gubernatorial addresses of Whig governors, 1837–1843, see *Vermont Journal, Vermont Mercury*, and *St. Johnsbury Caledonian*, 1835–1843.

51 Ruth Buckman to Parley Davis, 3 June 1841.

52 *North Star*, 13 June, 26 September, and 12 December 1836, and 22 July 1837; *Spirit of the Age*, 8 May 1840; Charles Field to Charles Eastman, 18 November 1843; Samuel Price in Windsor to Eastman, 17 October 1843; and Andrew MacMillan in Barnet to Eastman, 14 June 1839.

53 *North Star*, 22 July 1837; Gilbert Grant in Windsor to Charles Eastman, 28 May 1839 and 7 July 1842; *Spirit of the Age*, 8 May, 24 July, and 28 August 1840; Andrew MacMillan in Danville to Eastman, 14 June 1839; and Charles Field in Newfane to Eastman, 18 November 1843.

54 *North Star*, 22 and 29 July 1837; and *Spirit of the Age*, 15 May 1840.

55 Gilbert Grant in Windsor to Charles Eastman, 28 May 1839 and 7 July 1842; and two letters from Lester Johnson to Hazen Merrill in Peacham, n.d., Martin-Merrill Papers. See also George Barstow in Yarmouth Port, Maine, to James Rix in Lancaster, New Hampshire, 2 January 1836, N.H.H.S.

56 Davis, "Harriet Hutchinson Salisbury," 276; the memoirs of Charles Paine, 62; and Bassett, "Urban Penetration of Vermont," 72–74, 197–203, 303.

57 Joshua M. Dana, "Calais Election Song," 5 September 1837, MS. On the Locofocos, see Hugins, *Jacksonian Democracy*; and Carl N. Degler, "The Locofocos: Urban 'Agrarians,' " *Journal of Economic History*, 16 (1956), 322–333. On the rent wars and landlord–tenant relationships in New York, see Paul D. Evans, *The Holland Land Company* (Buffalo: Buffalo Historical Society, 1924), 364–415; McNall, *Genesee Valley*, 195–209; and Ellis, *Landlords and Farmers*, 225–312.

58 *Spirit of the Age*, 10 July 1840, 5 August 1842, 29 August 1844, and 9

January 1845; *Vermont Mercury*, 19 July 1844 and 3 March 1845; and T. B. Ransom in Norwich to Charles Eastman, 14 and 25 August 1843.

59 Robinson and Southmayd in Castleton to Charles Eastman, 8 June 1842; Charles Field in Newfane to Eastman, 1 September 1845; N. Robinson in Norwich to Eastman, 1 June 1841; the diary of Willard Stevens, 5 August 1837, U.V.M.; C. P. Van Ness in Burlington to Charles Lindsey in Montpelier, 4 April 1840, Sheldon Museum; Gilbert Grant in Newmarket, New Hampshire, to Eastman, 11 May 1844; *North Star*, 12 August 1837; *Mountain Democrat*, 11 March 1836; *Spirit of the Age*, 9 October, 18 December, and 4 September 1840, 19 November 1841, and 16 January 1845; Mary Trask in Farmington, Connecticut, to William Trask in Windsor, 26 February 1840, Green Family Papers; and William Nye in Columbus, Indiana, to Ezekiel Nye in North Montpelier, 7 October 1846, Nathaniel Chipman Papers.

60 Ira Hoffman in Sutton to Henry Hoffman in Holliston, New Hampshire, 28 February 1848.

61 Willard Stevens to Martin Van Buren, 1837, and the diary of Willard Stevens, 1834–1843, U.V.M.

62 D. Crane in Sharon to Mary Crane in Burlington, 16 November 1836, George P. Marsh Papers, U.V.M.; Jonas Clark in Middletown to Ebenezer Judd in Montpelier, 7 October 1832, Sheldon Museum; *Vermont Mercury*, 9 April 1837; *Spirit of the Age*, 8 May 1840; Howe, *American Whigs*, 43–68; and Ronald P. Formisano, "Political Character, Antipartyism, and the Second Party System," *American Quarterly*, 21 (1969), 683–709. For evidence of electioneering and unsavory campaign practices, see J. R. Fairbanks in Lower Waterford to J. P. Fairbanks, 9 September 1837; Erastus Fairbanks to an unknown person, 28 February 1837; Josiah Shedd to Erastus Fairbanks, 9 April 1840; E. C. Chamberlain in Peacham to Erastus Fairbanks, 13 February 1849; Henry Stevens in Bradford to Erastus Fairbanks, 7 July 1836; and Erastus Fairbanks to Albert Whittemore in Montpelier, 26 October 1843. See also Isaac Fletcher in Washington, D.C., to E. B. Chase in Lyndon, 17 July 1840, D.C.L.; Carlos Coolidge in Windsor to Norman Williams in Woodstock, 21 July 1836, D.C.L.; Charles Hopkins in Windsor to Erastus Fairbanks, 15 June 1839, in the Vermont State Papers; Jabez Sargeant in Windsor to Charles Eastman, 3 January 1839; T. B. Ransom in Norwich to Eastman, 27 August 1841; and S. H. Price in Windsor to Eastman, 26 September 1843.

63 A two-way analysis of town-level voting from 1837 to 1844 shows deviations greater than 15 percent from the predicted median vote for each town in each year in only 2 percent of all cases. (See Appendix D on two-way analysis.) On the partisanship of women, see V. Town in Norwich to Lucy Wheeler in Lebanon, New Hampshire, 21 September 1840, William Jarvis Papers; the diary of Arthur Bennett, 26 June 1844, A.A.S.; Ruth Child in Bethel to Ann Brainherd, 7 January 1836, Smith Family Papers, U.V.M.; Davis, "Harriet Hutchinson Salisbury," 276; the diary of Jonathan Tenney, Jr., 15 April 1840, D.C.L.; Ruth Buchman to Parley Davis, 2 June 1837;

Mary Williams to Henry Williams, 21 November 1837; and Lucy Wilson in Lyndon to Mary Ann Waterman in Bradford, 13 July 1844, U.V.M.

64 Henry Stevens, "Character of a Democrat," 7 November 1828, U.V.M.

65 Howe, *American Whigs*, 69–95, 210–237; and Major L. Wilson, *Space, Time, and Freedom: The Quest for Nationality and the Irrepressible Conflict, 1815–1861* (Westport: Greenwood, 1974), draw important contrasts between Whig and Democratic conceptions of time and space, but it is important to note that these contrasts, like that between Howe's "historic" Whigs and "abstract theoretical" Democrats, were not as clearly marked in the valley as in southern New England or on the eastern seaboard generally, where Howe and Wilson focus most of their attention. On the party contest, see Pessen, *Jacksonian America*, 149–260; Ronald P. Formisano, "Toward a Reorientation of Jacksonian Politics: A Review of the Literature, 1959–1975," *Journal of American History*, 63 (1976), 42–65; and idem, *The Birth of Mass Political Parties: Michigan, 1827–1861* (Princeton: Princeton Univ. Press, 1971).

66 For an overview of the literature on the social sources of party affiliation, see Howe, *American Whigs*, 11–22; and Formisano, *Transformation of Political Culture*, 5–8. Carl H. Peterson, "The Politics of Revival, 1783–1815" (Ph.D. diss., Stanford Univ., 1974), 46, 50–51, 287, 301, finds that Baptists voted Democratic in most areas in the United States, but not in Vermont and throughout most of the Yankee belt, where Baptists, Congregationalists, and Presbyterians were less at odds than elsewhere.

67 Still, it is likely that more Whig activists were pro-temperance, given that so many more of them belonged to the Congregational and Baptists churches of those towns. Those churches imposed total abstinence on their members. The poor temperance lists from Windsor may create the illusion of less difference over temperance than actually existed.

68 The median Whig vote was slightly higher in marketing and manufacturing towns (62 percent) than in hill towns (49 percent).

69 Formisano, "Antipartyism," identifies nonvoting and antiparty attitudes with evangelicals in general. Such attitudes, however, were clearly common among nonevangelicals and nonmembers as well as evangelicals in the valley. Nonvoting apparently depended more on the likelihood of victory than on the strength of antiparty attitudes among religious groups.

70 Dana, "Calais Election Song."

71 On the rise of partisanship elsewhere in the nation in the 1830s and 1840s, see Formisano, *Transformation of Political Culture*, 268–320; and Joel H. Silbey, *The Partisan Imperative: The Dynamics of American Politics before the Civil War* (New York: Oxford Univ. Press, 1985), 33–84.

72 The proportion of terms served by lawyers in the governorship, the United States Senate, and the House of Representatives, rose from 79 percent between 1815 and 1829 to 91 percent between 1837 and 1851. The proportion of terms served by inhabitants of major market and manufacturing towns rose from 54 to 72 percent. The proportions were similar between 1837 and 1851 for both Democratic and Whig office holders.

By contrast, the proportion of terms served by citizens in the upper decile of wealth as selectmen (N = 166) fell from 56 percent between 1815 and 1828 to 47 percent between 1835 and 1843, as farmers took a greater proportion of seats on town councils. The proportion of terms served by nonmembers held steady at one-third.

Chapter 8

1 *Vermont Journal,* 20 June 1844; *St. Johnsbury Caledonian,* 7 January 1845; and *North Star,* 10 March 1845.

2 *Vermont Journal,* 20 June 1844.

3 Account of Stock, Ascutney Mill Dam Company, 15 August 1843, D.C.L.; the correspondence of Erastus Fairbanks, 1845–1847; and Bassett, "Urban Penetration of Rural Vermont," 65, 85–87.

4 On support for the railroad subscription campaign, see the correspondence of Erastus Fairbanks, 1845–1847; Henry Cutts to William Jarvis, 29 August 1845; and *Vermont Christian Messenger,* 28 February 1849. On resistance to the subscription campaign, see James Gilchrist to Erastus Fairbanks, 16 January 1845 and 28 April 1847; and Josiah Shedd to Fairbanks, 5 April 1847. In 1843, 28 percent of all Whig activists (35 of 123) and 28 percent of all Democratic activists (16 of 56) identified in Windsor and West Windsor between 1835 and 1850 held shares in the Ascutney Mill Dam Company.

5 *School Journal,* 1847–1850; Ebenezer Eaton in Danville to Erastus Fairbanks, 11 July 1836; William Mattocks to Fairbanks, 18 September 1845; and Josiah Shedd to Fairbanks, 5 April 1847.

6 On town improvement, see John S. Garner, *The Model Company Town: Urban Design through Private Enterprise in Nineteenth-Century New England* (Amherst: Univ. of Massachusetts Press, 1984), 37–38, 65–72.

7 Bassett, "Urban Penetration of Rural Vermont," 72–80, 85–111, 239–263; Hubbard, "Early Windsor Industries," 159–183; and the manuscript records of the "United States Census of Manufacturing," 1850. On railroad construction, see Raymond E. Bassett, "A Study of the Promotion, Building, and Financing of the Vermont Central Railroad to July 1, 1853" (M.A. thesis, University of Vermont, 1934); E. C. Kirkland, *Men, Cities and Transportation: A Study in New England History, 1820–1900* (Cambridge: Harvard Univ. Press, 1948); William J. Wilgus, *The Role of Transportation in the Development of Vermont* (Montpelier: Vermont Historical Society, 1945); "Proceedings of the Convention of the Northern Lines of Railway" (Boston, 1850–1851); *Vermont Journal,* 19 April and 17 May 1845; and *St. Johnsbury Caledonian,* 7 January 1845. The *Vermont Journal,* 4 January and 22 March 1845, tells of the revival of regular freight service on the Connecticut River.

8 Bassett, "Urban Penetration of Rural Vermont," 64–68; Holman D. Jordan, "Ten Vermont Towns: Social and Economic Characteristics, 1850–1880" (Ph.D. diss., University of Alabama, 1966), 35–39; and Hal S. Barron,

"Their Town: Economy and Society in a Settled Rural Community; Chelsea, Vermont, 1840–1900" (Ph.D. diss., University of Pennsylvania, 1980).

9 Bassett, "Urban Penetration of Rural Vermont," 312–320, 374–388; and the advertisements in the Windsor *Vermont Journal,* the Woodstock *Vermont Mercury,* and the *St. Johnsbury Caledonian,* 1845–1850.

10 Rosamond Heaton to Polney Heaton, 24 April 1842; and the diary of Joseph Knight, Jr., 2 July 1849, private collection. See also the essay on living conditions in the 1840s and 1850s, Newton Family Papers, N.H.H.S.

11 Adams, *Prices Paid by Vermont Farmers,* shows the rise in purchases of whale oil and the end of purchases of alcoholic beverages. On other consumer trends, see Gregory H. Nobles, "Rural Manufacturing and Urban Markets: A Case Study of Broommaking in Nineteenth-Century Massachusetts" (paper presented at the annual meeting of the Organization of American Historians, 1983); Jordan, "Ten Vermont Towns," 38–42; Tyrell, *Sobering Up,* 316–317; and Rorabaugh, *Alcoholic Republic,* 7–10.

12 Wage levels were reported in the manuscript records of the "United States Census of Manufacturing," 1850.

13 Unknown person in Woodstock to Mrs. Carlos French in Northumberland, New Hampshire, 31 August 1847, Choate Family Papers; and Dublin, *Women at Work,* 23–57.

14 Dublin, *Women at Work,* 175–176; and George Gary Bush, *History of Education in Vermont* (Washington, D.C.: Government Printing Office, 1900), 22–23.

15 "United States Census of Manufacturing," 1850; Barron, "Settled Rural Community," 87–97; Jordan, "Ten Vermont Towns," 39–42; Nell M. Kull, *History of Dover, Vermont: 200 Years in a Hill Town* (Brattleboro: Book Cellar, 1961), 47–49; Nobles, "Broommaking"; Thomas Dublin, "Women and Outwork in a Nineteenth-Century New England Town: Fitzwilliam, New Hampshire, 1830–1850," in Steven Hahn and Jonathan Prude, eds., *The Countryside in the Age of Capitalist Transformation: Essays in the Social History of Rural America* (Chapel Hill: Univ. of North Carolina Press, 1985), 51–69; and Riley, "Londonderry," 167–169.

16 Martin Van Buren Townsend in Worcester, Massachusetts, to Aurelia Townsend, 9 August 1851; and the Stevens Family correspondence, especially Joseph Stevens in South Strafford to Jacob Stevens in Chatham, Connecticut, October, 1836.

17 Albert P. Paine, *History of Samuel Paine, Jr.* (Randolph, 1923), 137; the Eli English Papers, 1848–1852, especially Mrs. English in Hartland to Eli English in Milford, Massachusetts, 3 October and 19 December 1852; the diary of Arthur Bennett, 13 April 1845–11 May 1846, A.A.S.; and Villette Townsend in Washington County, Iowa, to his parents in Reading, 4 December 1855.

18 Wilson Family correspondence, 1837–1852, especially William Wilson in New York City to Laura Wilson in Lyndon, 27 September 1844, and Darwin Wilson in New York City to Laura Wilson in Lowell, Massachusetts, 20 January 1850.

19 Eric Schneirsohn, ed., *The Private Letters and Diaries of Captain Hall, an Epic of an Argonaut in the California Gold Rush* (Glendale: London Book, 1974); *Vermont Journal*, 26 January 1849; *North Star*, 23 February 1850; "Letters from the Past," *Vermont Quarterly*, 20 (1952), 45–50, 125–132, 208–214, 295–303, and 21 (1953), 38–46; "Footnotes to Vermont History," *Vermont Quarterly*, 21 (1953), 51–52; John Wheeler in New Bedford, Massachusetts, to Lucy Wheeler in Lebanon, New Hampshire, 7 November 1843, William Jarvis Papers; John Dudley, "A Discourse on Means of a Revival" (Windsor: Chronicle, 1849); and Stilwell, "Emigration from Vermont," 211–213.

20 Wilbur H. Siebert, *The Underground Railroad from Slavery to Freedom* (New York: Russell and Russell, 1967), 36, 80–81, 106–107, 130–131; Lois Leverett to Louisa Morris, 6 September 1811, Wardner Collection; "Footnotes to Vermont History," *Vermont Quarterly*, 21 (1953), 141–142; "Anti-Slavery Action in 1838: A Letter from Vermont's Secretary of State," *Vermont History*, 41 (1973), 7–8; Newton, *Barnard*, 181; and Wells, *Newbury*, 213. See also the diary of Silas Cummings, 1851, N.H.H.S.

21 Munnis Kenney to Daniel Kellogg, "Sunday after Meeting," n.d.; the memoirs of Charles Paine, 13; William Townsend, Jr., to Dennis Townsend, 1 February 1834; Wells, *Newbury*, 213; and Marro, "Vermont's Local Militia," 28–42.

22 Robert H. Lord, John E. Sexton, and Edward T. Harrington, *History of the Archdiocese of Boston* (Boston: Pilot, 1945), 3 v.; Ralph V. Dominic, "Immigration of French Canadians to New England, 1840–1900: A Geographical Analysis" (Ph.D. diss., Univ. of Wisconsin, 1968); Oscar Handlin, *Boston's Immigrants, 1790–1880*, rev. ed. (New York: Atheneum, 1968); Donald H. Akenson, *The Irish Educational Experiment* (London: Routledge and Kegan Paul, 1970), 376–385; and K. H. Connell, *The Population of Ireland, 1750–1845* (Westport: Greenwood, 1975).

23 On class prejudice, see Chapter 6, "The Course of the Revival" and "The Causes of the Revival"; and the records of the North Congregational Church of Woodstock, February 1846. On the rise of nativism, see Bassett, "Urban Penetration of Rural Vermont," 127–129, 356–364; Robert Harvey to Erastus Fairbanks, n.d. (c. 1846); Davis, "Harriet Hutchinson Salisbury," 281; *Northern Protestant and American Advocate* (Newbury), 23 August and 22 September 1848; and Wells, *Newbury*, 316–317.

24 "Memoranda of the Archdiocese of Boston," 13 February 1850, Archives of the Archdiocese of Boston; Joseph Stevens to Jacob Stevens, October 1836; Lyman Benson in South Royalton to Nathan Haile in Montgomery, 8 November 1852; and *Boston Pilot*, 1 July 1848.

25 *Le Patriote Canadien*, 7 August 1839; Jeremiah O'Callaghan, *Usury, Funds, and Banks* (Burlington, 1834); idem, *A Critical Review of Mr. J. K. Converse's Calvinistic Sermon* (Burlington, 1834); and *Boston Pilot*, 29 January, 5 February, and 4 March 1848.

26 *Boston Pilot*, 24 August 1850, and 4 January and 20 December 1851; and newspaper subscription list for Ludlow and Plymouth, Vermont, New York

Public Library. On political moderation and cultural assimilation, see the memoranda book of Bishop DeGoesbriand and "Records for Historical Sketches of Parishes," Archives of the Archdiocese of Burlington; *L'Avenir*, 16 and 28 July 1847; Vincent A. Lapormarda, *The Jesuit Heritage in New England* (Worcester: Jesuits of Holy Cross College, 1977), 62–63; and *Boston Pilot*, 6 January 1844 and 5 May 1849.

27 Erastus Fairbanks to P. H. White, 13 July 1852; "Historical Sketches of Parishes," St. Johnsbury, Archives of the Archdiocese of Burlington; "Roman Catholicism in Northfield, Vermont, 1856–1977," MS; Paine, *Samuel Paine*, 93, 103; Luther Jewett to Luther Jewett, Jr., in Lafayette, Indiana, 29 April 1855, L.C.; and Daniel P. Thompson, *Locke Amsden, or the Schoolmaster* (Boston: Benjamin B. Bussey, 1853), 180. Josiah Shedd in Fayetteville, Georgia, to Abigail Chamberlain of Peacham, 25 February 1841, refers to his hired man in Peacham by his last name, "Dubois," as does Henry Cutts in Hartland to William Jarvis, 23 September 1834, who in addition refers to his hands as "light" or "heavy" according to their ability to perform physical labor.

28 *School Journal*, May 1847; and "First Annual Report of the State Superintendent of Common Schools...1846," 35–36.

29 Bassett, "Urban Penetration of Vermont," 64–68; Hal S. Barron, "The Impact of Rural Depopulation on the Local Economy: Chelsea, Vermont, 1840–1900," *Agricultural History*, 54 (1980), 318–335; the diary of Joseph Knight, 1849–1850, private collection; Dublin, "Women and Outwork"; and Nobles, "Broommaking."

30 Achsah Wellman in Westminster to Mrs. Nathan Haile in Montgomery, 3 February 1839; and Amos Haile in Brookline to Nathan Haile in Avery's Gore, 27 May 1838.

31 See, for example, the Stevens Family Correspondence, 1834–1851, especially Julia Ann Stevens of South Strafford to Jacob Stevens of Chatham, Connecticut, 31 July 1836; the Tarble and Haile Family Papers, 1836–1852; Jane C. Beck, ed., *Always in Season: Folk Art and Traditional Culture in Vermont* (Montpelier: Vermont Council on the Arts, 1982); and Gilmore, *Reading Becomes a Necessity*. On the persistence of older familial aspirations, see Barron, "Settled Rural Community"; Riley, "Londonderry"; and Williamson, "South Woodstock."

32 Lucy Brown to Justin Morrill, 10 January 1848, L.C.

33 Riley, "Londonderry," 120, charts an increase in the proportion of new household heads in a given census year who were related to persons who were already household heads at the time of the previous census, from 13 percent in 1810 to 60 percent by 1830 to a peak of 84 percent by 1850. On the aging, homogenization, and increasing stability of the rural population, see Riley, "Londonderry"; Barron, "Settled Rural Community"; and Williamson, "South Woodstock." The patterns they trace were not as pronounced in most of the towns studied intensively in this study, which were generally more highly developed economically and closer to major trade and travel routes.

34 Peach, "Seth Shaler Arnold," 180–186. On other tensions, see Tyrell, *Sobering Up*, 145–147, 191–199.
35 "Fourth Annual Report of the State Superintendent of Common Schools," 33–36; and Thompson, *Locke Amsden*, 107–122.
36 Thomas Powers, "Address to the Sons of Temperance of Northfield, 1846."
37 On the limitations of the data on mobility in the 1840s, see Appendix C.
38 See, for example, the diaries of Arthur Bennett of Woodstock, 1844–1846, A.A.S.; G. A. Davis of Rockingham, 1851–1852; and Joseph Knight, Jr., 1848–1851. See also the correspondence of Gilbert Wood, 1846–1850, and the diary of Marion Hopkins, 1851–1855, N.H.H.S. On the nostalgia of older church members for spiritually intense times, see Peach, "Seth Shaler Arnold," 170–185; and the diary of Abigail Baldwin of Ludlow, 1853–1854. See also the credit reports in the Dun and Bradstreet Collection, Windsor County, 1843–1860, and Caledonia County, 1839–1860, Baker School of Business, Harvard University.
39 See, for example, Paine, *Samuel Paine*, 137–139, 149, 153; the diary of Arthur Bennett, 21, 22, 28, and 29 March 1844, A.A.S.; the diary of G. A. Davis, 28 January and 10 February 1852; Peach, "Seth Shaler Arnold," 139; Lucy Brown to Justin Morrill, 10 January 1848, L.C.; Sarah Ann Hill to Ann Brainherd, 19 February 1836, Smith Family Papers, U.V.M.; and Samuel Elliot, *An Humble Tribute to My Country* (Boston: Otis, Brodders, 1842), 89–95. On musical conventions and bands, see the diary of Hosea Doton, 1840–1843, Pomfret Town Office. See also Hattie Bellows in Walpole, New Hampshire, to A. Herbert Bellows, 23 July 1847, N.H.H.S.
40 *Green Mountain Eagle and Even Fellows Gazette* (Wilmington), 9 and 16 February, and 21 March 1850; *North Star*, 6 January 1845; "Proceedings of the Most Worshipful Grand Lodge of Vermont" (Burlington: C. Goodrich, 1849); Bassett, "Urban Penetration of Rural Vermont," 145–146; and Tyrell, *Sobering Up*, 212–214. The Methodists advised their ministers not to become Odd Fellows and warned them that they would be relocated without their consent if membership rendered them "unacceptable among the people," but they did not prohibit membership. "Annual Conference of the Methodist Episcopal Church . . . 1848."
41 *Vermont Journal*, 29 March 1845.
42 "The Articles of Faith, Covenant, and Rules of Church Government Adopted by the Second Congregational Church in Brookfield, Vermont" (Windsor: Chronicle, 1850), 4, shows that the congregation apparently rejected predestination when the church organized in 1848. They believed that men and women perished for their sins "by their own wilful rejection" of God's freely given grace and implied (without stating it flatly) that individuals had the power to accept or reject God's grace. No other Calvinist covenant went that far. For forthright reaffirmations of Calvinist doctrine during these years, see the "Articles of Faith and Covenant adopted by the First Congregational Church in Guilford, Vermont . . . 1855" (Boston: T. R. Marvin and Son, 1858); and "Articles of

Faith and Covenant of the Congregational Church, Rochester, Vermont
...1842" (Windsor: Chronicle, n.d.).

43 See the records of the Free Congregational Church of Pomfret, 1843–1850;
    Barron, "Settled Rural Community," 166; and Cad Wilson in Lyndon to
    Laura Wilson in Lowell, Massachusetts, 17 March 1848.

44 "Annual Conference of the Methodist Episcopal Church...1848."

45 Walter E. Houghton, *The Victorian Frame of Mind* (New Haven: Yale Univ.
    Press, 1957), 273–281; Karen Halttunen, *Confidence Men and Painted
    Women: A Study of Middle-Class Culture in America, 1830–1870* (New
    Haven: Yale Univ. Press, 1982), xvii, 56–58; George B. Forgie, *Patricide
    in the House Divided: A Psychological Interpretation of Lincoln and His
    Age* (New York: Norton, 1979), 4–5; Rose, *Transcendentalism*, 28–37;
    Ann Douglas, *The Feminization of American Culture* (New York: Avon,
    1977), 143–309; and Elliot, *Tribute*, 85–89.

46 Charles G. Eastman, *Poems* (Montpelier: Eastman and Danforth, 1848),
    24–25; Abby M. Hemenway, ed., *Poets and Poetry of Vermont* (Rutland:
    George A. Tuttle, 1858), 188–189, 70–74; Joseph Brown in Brooklyn, New
    York, to Marianna Ward in Rindge, New Hampshire, 7 October 1846,
    Raymond-Ward Papers, N.H.H.S.; Loriman S. Brigham, ed., "An Inde-
    pendent Voice: A Mill Girl from Vermont Speaks Her Mind," *Vermont
    History*, 41 (1973), 143; Roswell Farnham, Jr., "The Scrap," MS, U.V.M.;
    and the memoirs of Charles Paine, 88–99, 110–111. See also the diary of
    Silas Cummings, especially 6 May 1851, N.H.H.S.

47 On the urban sources of the transcendental, romantic, and feminist
    movements, see Cott, *Bonds of Womanhood*, 204; Rose, *Transcenden-
    talism*; and Douglas, *Feminization of American Culture*, 313–395. On
    the rise of spiritual doubt, see James Turner, *Without God, Without
    Creed: The Origins of Unbelief in America* (Baltimore: Johns Hopkins
    Univ. Press, 1985).

48 Jeremiah O'Callaghan, "St. Mary's Church (1839)," in Thomas F. O'Con-
    nor, ed., "The Catholic Church in Vermont," MS; "Historical Sketches of
    Parishes," Montpelier, Archives of the Archdiocese of Burlington; Peach,
    "Seth Shaler Arnold," 136; *North Star*, 25 November 1841; *Vermont Mer-
    cury*, 24 November 1848; and *Proceedings of the Grand Division of the
    Sons of Temperance of the State of Vermont* (Montpelier: Ballou, 1849).

    The Sons of Temperance and Martha Washingtonians were not as strong
    in the valley as they were in southern New England or in cities, both because
    the valley's mainstream temperance societies extended greater sympathy to
    drunkards than did comparable societies elsewhere and because the class
    tensions that drove primarily working-class and lower-middle-class people
    to form separate temperance organizations in long-settled areas were not
    as powerful in the valley. No membership lists survived from the towns
    studied intensively, but there is little evidence to suggest that the valley's
    Sons differed in social standing from the men in the valley's mainstream
    organizations. The Sons' leadership was heavily ministerial and professional.
    In 1850, 4 percent of the valley's adult males belonged to the Sons of
    Temperance. See Tyrell, *Sobering Up*, 159–224; and Hempel, *Temperance
    and Prohibition*, 103–146.

In 1850, 4 percent of the valley's adult males belonged to the Sons of Temperance. See Tyrell, *Sobering Up*, 159–224; and Hempel, *Temperance and Prohibition*, 103–146.

49 Hemenway, *Poetry of Vermont*, 427–428; and *Vermont Mercury*, 12 January 1849. See also "The Casket," especially 2 February 1850, MS, and the Raymond-Ward correspondence, 1843–1852, N.H.H.S.

50 Thomas Powers, "Address to the Sons of Temperance"; *School Journal*, May 1847, p. 5; and Adeline Reed to Ann Brainherd, 12 January 1836.

51 *Green Mountain Freeman* (Montpelier), 23 May 1846. See Cott, *Bonds of Womanhood*, 158, 197–206.

52 Daniel Thompson to Josiah Pierce, 6 July 1847; the correspondence of Peter and Almira Washburn, 9 October 1839–11 September 1842, U.V.M.; and the diary of Damaris Foster, 1844.

53 Anne White in Lowell, Massachusetts, to Cyrus Farnum in Boston, Massachusetts, 1 October 1843, Farnum to White, 10 November 1843, Cyrus Farnum in Haverhill, Massachusetts, to Mrs. Roswell Farnum in Bradford, 4 January 1844, and Anne Farnum to Roswell Farnum, Jr., 15 July 1844, U.V.M.; "Letters from the Past," 20: 128, 210, 212, 297, and 21: 38, 42–43; and the diary of Arthur Bennett, 13 April 1845, A.A.S.

54 See Haltunnen, *Confidence Men and Painted Women*; David E. Stannard, *The Puritan Way of Death* (New York: Oxford Univ. Press, 1977), 171–188; and Dudley, "Means of a Revival."

55 Leverett A. Lull, "The Farmer Sat in His Easy Chair" (Boston: Stephen W. Marsh, 1847), and idem, "I've Thrown Them All Away" (Boston: Stephen W. Marsh, 1848).

56 See Barron, "Settled Rural Community," on class and ethnic tensions; *Vermont Journal*, 14 and 23 November 1844; Jane Shedd in Andover, Massachusetts, to Lydia Shedd in Peacham, 4 September 1834; and Justin Morrill in Strafford to E. P. Walton in Montpelier, 13 November 1844. On the strength of political nativism elsewhere in the nation, see Pessen, *Jacksonian America*, 279–283; Benson, *Concept of Jacksonian Democracy*, 114–122, 213–215; Formisano, *Transformation of Political Culture*, 329–343; and Tyrell, *Sobering Up*, 268, 321.

57 George Wheeler in Covington, Kentucky, to Lucy Wheeler in Croydon, New Hampshire, 6 February 1818, William Jarvis Papers; Allen Hazen in New Orleans, Louisiana, to Lucius Hazen in Hartland, 2 May 1819; Daniel Thompson in Fredericksburg, Virginia, to Josiah Pierce, 20 January 1821; Boyd Wilson in Gainesville, Alabama, to Mary Ann Wilson in Bradford, 15 July 1838, U.V.M.; Louisa Chamberlain in Gainesville, Georgia, to Jane Shedd in Augusta, Georgia, 14 March 1841; Josiah Shedd in Augusta, Georgia, to Abigail Chamberlain of Peacham, 13 April 1841; V. Town in Portsmouth, Virginia, to Lucy Wheeler in Croydon, New Hampshire, 20 April 1842, William Jarvis Papers; and Eric Foner, *Free Soil, Free Labor, Free Men: The Ideology of the Republican Party before the Civil War* (New York: Oxford Univ. Press, 1970), 40–72.

58 See note 57; Albert Townsend in Carthage, Mississippi, to Sarah Townsend in Norwich, 6 July 1840; and C. Smith to his sister Mary, 17 April 1849, Choate Family Papers.

59 J. Kevin Graffagnino, "Vermont Attitudes toward Slavery: The Need for a Closer Look," *Vermont History*, 45 (1977), 31–34; and John H. Hopkins, "Slavery: Its Religious Sanction, Its Political Dangers, and the Best Mode of Doing It Away" (Buffalo: Phinney, 1851).

60 "Petition of Laura Belknap and 89 others, women of Windsor County, Vermont, for the immediate abolition of... the slave trade in the United States," 23 August 1837, and "Remonstrance of L. P. Parks of Barnet and 15 others... against the admission of Texas into the Union," July 1837, National Archives. On sympathetic responses among whites to the plight of blacks in slavery, see Frederickson, *Black Image in the White Mind*, 1–42, 97–164; Joseph Poland in Montpelier to Paul Dillingham in Washington, D.C., 16 December 1845; and Newton, *Barnard*, 181. On a tour of the valley by black abolitionist Henry Highland Garnet, see *Vermont Mercury*, 30 March 1846.

61 *Green Mountain Freeman*, 18 May 1848; *Voice of Freedom* (Montpelier), 21 March 1840; *Vermont Freeman* (Norwich), 18 March, 1 April, and 1 July 1843; and Joseph Poland to Paul Dillingham, 16 December 1845.

62 A regression of the Free-Soil proportion of the three-party vote in 1848 on the median Whig and Democratic proportions of the two-party vote between 1836 and 1844 ($R^2 = .18$), yields the following results:

	Whigs, 1836–1844	Democrats, 1836–1844
Free-Soil, 1848:		
Essex County towns	−.03	.06
	(.18)	(.11)
Primary marketing and manufacturing towns	.21	.22
	(.16)	(.24)
Other towns	.29	.33
	(.05)	(.06)

Essex County fell increasingly within the political orbit of Coos County, New Hampshire, from which its settlers and newspapers emanated. The voters of Coos County rejected the Free-Soil Party overwhelmingly.

It is impossible to separate clearly the contributions of denominational affiliation and per capita wealth to the Free-Soil vote. The Free-Soil vote depended heavily not only on these variables, but on a third variable – town type – which is highly correlated with per capita wealth and denominational affiliation. The high correlation among the independent variables produces unstable estimates of the desired proportions. (See Randolph A. Roth, "Ecological Regression and the Analysis of Voter Behavior," *Historical Methods*, 19 (1986), 103–117; and Appendix D.) The most stable equations suggest that Baptists, egalitarian evangelicals, and nonmembers in areas settled by New Lights voted disproportionately Free-Soil – the same groups that voted disproportionately Antimasonic.

63 On the economic platforms of the parties and the frustration of party leaders in carrying them out, see *Vermont Journal*, 2 and 30 August 1845, and 26 June 1847; *Vermont Mercury*, 12 May 1843, and 4 April and 12 November 1844; *St. Johnsbury Caledonian*, 22 February 1842 and 25 August 1845; *Spirit of the Age*, 30 April 1846; and *North Star*, 1 February 1845 and 20 April 1850.

64 On the move by leading Whigs toward free soil and anti-Southern attitudes, see *Vermont Journal*, 20 June 1844, 1 and 15 February, 5 April, 12 July, and 10 October 1845, and 28 July 1848; *Vermont Mercury*, 28 April 1837, 22 November 1844, 21 November 1845, 29 January 1847, and 19 October 1849; and *St. Johnsbury Caledonian*, 10 March 1845, 29 May 1847, 29 January 1848, and 2 June 1849. On the parallel move by leading Democrats, see *North Star*, 2 September 1845 and 2 February 1850; *Spirit of the Age*, 22 February and 8 August 1844, 26 January 1846, and 12 July 1849; G. W. Nichols in Brattleboro to Charles Eastman, 3 July 1848; Ira Davis in Norwich to Eastman, 10 May 1849; Erasmus Plimpton in North Wardsboro to Eastman, 22 May 1849; Joseph Fuller in Danville to Eastman, 5 July 1849; William Slade in Middlebury to E. A. Stansbury, 18 September 1848, L.C.; and Bassett, "Urban Penetration of Rural Vermont," 434. On voting patterns, see Bruce L. Bigelow, "Abolition and Prohibition: For An Historical Geography of Vermont, 1841–1850" (M.A. thesis, Pennsylvania State Univ., 1970).

65 Party rhetoric persisted in Whig and Democratic newspapers, but Whig and Democratic rhetoric faded from letters and diaries after 1843. Free-Soil newspapers listed proudly the members of town committees, but Whig and Democratic newspapers halted the practice for the most part after 1848, when the sectional controversy produced massive defections and enthusiasm flagged. Voter turnout in presidential elections fell below 60 percent after the election of 1856.

The argument here does not refute the claim by most political historians that partisanship persisted in the 1850s in most Northern states. But it suggests that political historians may claim too much when they argue for the persistence of partisanship in northern New England, Michigan, Wisconsin, and other areas settled predominantly by New Englanders after the Revolution. Sibley, *Partisan Impulse*, 45, supports the argument for persistence with voting data gathered only from southern New England, the middle states, Ohio, Indiana, and Illinois. Formisano, *Transformation of Political Culture*, 329–343, may overstate the case for the persistence of partisanship in Massachusetts as well, by classifying the antipartisan Know-Nothing Party as a "social movement" and by presenting no quantitative evidence of partisan behavior from the 1850s. The inhabitants of the valley may not have been the only New Englanders not to become partisans.

66 Chapter 4; and Thompson, quoted in Dublin, *Women at Work*, 55.

67 Daniel Thompson, *The Green Mountain Boys* (New York: Lovell, Coryell, 1839); George Marsh, "Address to the Philomathesian Society of Middle-

bury College," U.V.M.; Elizabeth Allen, *Sketches of Green Mountain Life* (Lowell: Nathaniel Dayton, 1846); Eastman, *Poems*, 26–48; Hemenway, *Poetry of Vermont*, 514; and Daniel Chipman, *Memoir of Warner and Allen* (Middlebury: L. W. Clark, 1848).

68 Phelps Correspondence, especially John Phelps in Fort Brown, Texas, to James Phelps of West Townsend, 11 February 1851; John McClaughry, "John Wolcott Phelps: The Civil War General Who Became a Forgotten Presidential Candidate in 1880," *Vermont History*, 3 (1970), 263–266; and William Nye to Ezekiel Nye, 7 October 1846, Nathaniel Chipman Papers.

Conclusion

1 Roth, "Strange Fire," 545–551. On the postwar rise of interdenominational revivals and nonpartisan reform movements in western New Hampshire, the Champlain Valley, and western New York, see Cross, *Burned-Over District*, 11, 24–29, 115–116; Ludlum, *Social Ferment*, 50–55, 89–94; White, *Beekmantown*, 122–125, 155–156, 162–163, 169; Johnson, *Shop-keepers' Millennium*, 15–36; Ryan, *Cradle of the Middle Class*, 53–54, 60, 75–77, 83–98, 108–111; Heale, "Patterns of Benevolence," 337–359; McLoughlin, *New England Dissent*, v. II, 898–911; Benson, *Jacksonian Democracy*, 4–11; Livermore, *Twilight of Federalism*, 69–79, 113–120, 192–193, 223–235; and Cole, *Jacksonian Democracy in New Hampshire*, 31–45. These works suggest that new orders arose after 1815 in every burned-over district, although New York's socioeconomic diversity and the enduring controversy over New Hampshire's standing order made it impossible for New England's revolutionary frontiersmen to achieve political unity as fully in these states as they did in Vermont.

On the appearance of pressing times in other burned-over districts in the 1830s and 1840s, and on the connections between economic and demographic change and social movements, see McNall, *Genesee Valley*, 109–244; Cross, *Burned-Over District*, 55–77; Stilwell, "Migration from Vermont," 151–213; White, *Beekmantown*, 71–92, 309–313; Yasuba, *Birth Rates of the White Population*; Forster, Tucker, and Bridge, *White American Fertility*; Johnson, *Shopkeepers' Millennium*; Ryan, *Cradle of the Middle Class*; and Judith A. Wellman, "The Burned-Over District Revisited: Benevolent Reform and Abolitionism in Mexico, Paris, and Ithaca, New York" (Ph.D. diss., Univ. of Virginia, 1974). Recent studies of communities in western New York caution that the nature of support for religious and reform movements varied from town to town, as it did in the Connecticut River Valley of Vermont. However, Cross, *Burned-Over District*, 75–77, 116–125, 211–226; Ludlum, *Social Ferment*, 68–85, 101–113, 134–166; and Bigelow, "Abolition and Prohibition," indicate that the movements of the 1830s and 1840s tapped the same geographical and denominational bases of support at the regional level in western New York and the Champlain Valley that they did in the Connecticut River Valley of Vermont.

2 For descriptions of this pattern, see Cross, *Burned-Over District*, 75; Johnson, *Shopkeepers' Millennium*, 137–138; Tyrell, *Sobering Up*, 113–115; and Stuart M. Blumin, *The Urban Threshold: Growth and Change in a Nineteenth-Century American Community* (Chicago: Univ. of Chicago Press, 1976), 63–74, 166–189.

3 The following discussion of landlord–tenant relationships draws on Evans, *Holland Land Company*, 364–415; McNall, *Genesee Valley*, 195–209; Ellis, *Landlords and Farmers*, 225–312; and Cross, *Burned-Over District*, 71, 269–272.

4 Linda K. Prichard, "The Burned-Over District Reconsidered: A Portent of Evolving Religious Pluralism in the United States," *Social Science History*, 3 (1984), 243–266, finds that by 1850 churches were strongest throughout the northeastern United States in commercial farming towns and in marketing and manufacturing towns with few factories. See also Cross, *Burned-Over District*, 75–77, 211–217; Ludlum, *Social Ferment*, 68–85; and Bigelow, "Abolition and Prohibition."

5 See Cross, *Burned-Over District*, 353–357; Riley, "Londonderry"; Barron, "Rural Depopulation," 318–335; and Stilwell, "Migration from Vermont," 196–213, on the stagnation of the economy and the demise of spiritual and moral enthusiasm after the revival. Ellis, *Landlords and Farmers*, 118–158, discusses the troubles the inhabitants of the Hudson-Mohawk region encountered beginning in 1808, and their efforts to adjust to population pressure and competition from other agricultural areas.

6 Dixon Ryan Fox, *Yankees and Yorkers* (New York: New York Univ. Press, 1940), 66–71; Blumin, *Urban Threshold*, 42, 44–49, 185–189; Irving Elting, "Dutch Village Communities on the Hudson River," in Herbert B. Adams, ed., *Municipal Government and Land Tenure* (Baltimore: Johns Hopkins Univ., 1886), 1–68; Albert E. McKinley, "The English and Dutch Towns of the New Netherlands," *American Historical Review*, 6 (1900), 1–18; Patricia U. Bonomi, *A Factious People: Politics and Society in Colonial New York* (New York: Columbia Univ. Press, 1971), 201–203, 211–216; Alice P. Kenney, *Stubborn for Liberty: The Dutch in New York* (Syracuse: Syracuse Univ. Press, 1975), 50, 76–77, 88–89, 112–113, 116–117, 122–123, 129–136, 140–143, 175–177; and Michael G. Kammen, *Colonial New York: A History* (New York: Scribner's, 1975), 293–295, 228–231.

   Carl Nordstrom, *Frontier Elements in a Hudson River Village* (Port Washington: Kennikat, 1973), 36–39, 52, 55–60, and 92, largely neglects ethnicity, but charts the same pattern of isolation, persistence, and close ties among kin among the early Dutch settlers. Nordstrom and Blumin observe that reform movements took shape in both Orange and Kingston in the 1850s, when many migrants from New England arrived. Blumin shows that migrants from New England were prominent among Kingston's reformers and civic leaders. Both authors maintain that the Dutch entered politics primarily to advance or protect economic interests, not to reform society.

   The behavior of the Dutch may have been typical of many ethnic groups in New York, New Jersey, and Pennsylvania. Michael Zuckerman, "Puritans, Cavaliers, and the Motley Middle," in *Friends and Neighbors: Group Life in America's First Plural Society* (Philadelphia: Temple Univ. Press, 1982), 3–25, observes that the "milling pluralism" of these colonies led often to narrow familism or a clannish persistence in old ways, to ethnic accommodation or antagonism, both of which frustrated efforts to pursue a communal ideal and contributed to a "feebly principled pursuit of profit" and a narrow political concern with economic issues.

7 Roth, "First Radical Abolitionists," 540–563; and Chapter 7, "A Modified Order in Town Life."

8 Mack Walker, *German Home Towns: Community, Estate, and General Estate, 1648–1871* (Ithaca: Cornell Univ. Press, 1971), 34–142, 185–279; and Wolfgang v. Hippel, *Die Bauernbefreiung im Königreich Württemberg* (Boppard am Rhein: Harald Boldt, 1977), v. I, 544–577. See also Walker, *German Home Towns*, 11–142; Walker, *Johann Jakob Moser and the Holy Roman Empire of the German Nation* (Chapel Hill: Univ. of North Carolina Press, 1981); James A. Vann, *The Swabian Kreis: Institutional Growth in the Holy Roman Empire, 1648–1715* (Bruxelles: Editions de la Librarie Encyclopédique, 1975); Christopher Friedrichs, *Urban Society in an Age of War: Nordlingen, 1580–1720* (Princeton: Princeton Univ. Press, 1979); and John G. Gagliardo, *Reich and Nation: The Holy Roman Empire as Idea and Reality, 1763–1806* (Bloomington: Univ. of Indiana, 1980). These studies describe the Holy Roman Empire as an "incubator" of particularism and communal defensiveness, in which the inhabitants and rulers of the many communities, territories, and jurisdictions that made up the Empire identified liberty with preservation of their customary rights and freedom from external interference.

9 Walker, *German Home Towns*, 248–279; Ernst Marquardt, *Geschichte Württembergs* (Stuttgart: J. B. Metzlersche, 1961), 271–285; James C. Hunt, *The People's Party in Württemberg and Southern Germany, 1890–1914* (Stuttgart: Ernst Klett, 1975), 15–16; Dieter Langewiesche, *Liberalismus und Demokratie in Württemberg Zwischen Revolution und Reichsgrundung* (Dusseldorf: Droste, 1974), 27–40, 71–77; Rosemarie Menzinger, *Verfassungsrevision und Demokratisierungsprozess im Königreich Württemberg* (Stuttgart: W. Kohlhammer, 1969); Harmut Lehmann, *Pietismus und Weltliche Ordnung in Württemberg vom 17. bis zum 20. Jahrhundert* (Stuttgart: W. Kohlhammer, 1969), 142–146, 176–187; Jerome Blum, *The End of the Old Order in Rural Europe* (Princeton: Princeton Univ. Press, 1978), 29–79, 357–400; and Hippel, *Bauernbefreiung*, v. I.

10 Lehmann, *Pietismus und Weltliche Ordnung*, 117–119, 136ff., finds that pietistic meetings and sects gained strength beginning in the 1780s as the old order of guilds and noble societies decayed. He believes that they gave many middle-class and lower-class men and women an alternative source of identity and community. However, they never attracted more than 2 percent of the total population of Württemberg, or about 5 percent in the predominantly Protestant territories within the kingdom, between 1820 and 1860. (Lehmann, 254–256.) Franz Schnabel, *Deutsche Geschichte im Neun-*

zehnten Jahrhundert, 2d ed. (Freiburg: Herder, 1951), v. IV, *Die Religiöse Kräfte,* v, 379–492, emphasizes the inability of the pietistic awakening across Germany to transform German society, although Koppel S. Pinson, *Pietism as a Factor in the Rise of German Nationalism* (New York: Columbia Univ. Press, 1934), believes it contributed to the rise of German nationalism. Most Protestant Württembergers remained dutiful if uninspired Lutherans, who viewed the established church as another traditional defender of communal values.

11 Reform organizations were not unknown in Württemberg. Societies to distribute Bibles, to spread pietistic doctrines, and to halt consumption of liquors did take shape after 1815. The leaders of these societies were aware of similar movements in Britain and the United States and eager to import their ideas and organizational techniques. Their movements may well have filled some of the same needs for their supporters that they did in the valley. They had a particular appeal for pietists, state officials, and middle-class citizens in general, who sought emancipation from the old order and hoped to shape a new one. These reform societies also won the support of a number of elite citizens, including the king.

Reform societies did not gain considerable support outside pietistic circles, however, and were never a major force in shaping the post-Napoleonic order. Most pietists remained aloof from politics, or allied themselves politically with conservative or progressive movements, which left reform without an effective political voice or institutional base. Elite citizens who supported reform movements were usually, like the king, conservative non-pietists who wished to encourage the spread of pietism, which spoke generally for conservative values and encouraged obedience to the government. They did not share the pietists' religious enthusiasm, however, or their belief that Bible or temperance societies could solve social problems. They defended their regime as conservatives, not as reformers, and sought primarily political, constitutional solutions to its problems. See Lehmann, *Pietismus und Weltliche Ordnung,* 147–150, 165–173, 188–195, 202–212, 215–231, 256–266; T. Nipperdey, "Verein als soziale Struktur in Deutschland," in *Gesellschaft, Kultur, Theorie: Gesammelte Aufsätze zur neueren Geschichte* (Gottigen: Vandenhoeck und Ruprecht, 1976), 174–205; and Langewiesche, *Liberalismus und Demokratie,* 48–220.

For a warning against overstating the differences in social and political development between Germany and Great Britain, see David Blackbourn and Geoff Ely, *The Peculiarities of German History: Bourgeois Society and Politics in Nineteenth-Century Germany* (New York: Oxford Univ. Press, 1984), especially 190–225. Blackbourn argues that historians have underestimated the importance of voluntary associations in German politics and community life. The studies that Blackbourn cites in support of his assertion, however, reveal that few voluntary associations existed in Germany outside cities prior to 1848 and that relatively few German associations were involved in moral reform or spiritual uplift. On voluntary associations in southwestern Germany, see Ernst M. Wallner, "Die Rezeption stadtbürbürgerlichen Vereinswesens durch die Bevölkerung auf dem Lande," in Günter Wiegelman, ed., *Kultereller Wandel im 19. Jahrhundert* (Göttingen: Vandenhoeck und Ruprecht, 1973), 160–173; Wolfgang Kaschuba and Carola Lipp, "Zur Organisation des Bürgerlichen Optimismus," *Sozialwissenschaftliche Informationen Für Unterricht und Studium,* 8 (1979), 74–82; and Werner Boldt, *Die Württembergischen Volksvereine von 1848–1852* (Stuttgart: W. Kohlhammer, 1970).

12   Walker, *German Home Towns,* 288–404; Hippel, *Bauernbefreiung,* v. I, 485–498, 544–577; David Blackbourn, *Class, Religion, and Local Politics in Wilhelmine Germany: The Center Party in Württemberg Before 1914* (New Haven: Yale Univ. Press, 1980), 63–74, 77–81; Peter Borsheid, *Textilarbeitershaft in der Industrialisierung: Soziale Lage und Mobilität in Württemberg* (Stuttgart: Klett-Cotta, 1978), 297–300, 355–356, 442; and Langewiesche, *Liberalismus und Demokratie,* 48–50, 55–58, 199–220.

13   Klaus Epstein, *The Genesis of German Conservatism* (Princeton: Princeton Univ. Press, 1966), 3–32; Marquardt, *Geschichte Württembergs,* 223–271, 285–292; Langewiesche, *Liberalismus und Demokratie,* 27–225; Theodore S. Hamerow, *Restoration, Revolution, and Reaction: Economics and Politics in Germany, 1815–1871* (Princeton: Princeton Univ. Press, 1958), 3–195; Walker, *German Home Towns,* 145–431; Walker, *Germany and the Emigration, 1816–1885* (Cambridge: Harvard Univ. Press, 1964), 42–174; and Blackbourn, *Politics in Wilhelmine Germany,* 63–74, 77–81. Horst Dippel, *Germany and the American Revolution, 1770–1800* (Chapel Hill: Univ. of North Carolina Press, 1977), 329–364, traces Germany's political polarization to the response of the German bourgeois to the French Revolution. These works reveal that many middle-class citizens – farmers, artisans, bureaucrats, intellectuals, entrepreneurs, and financiers – found themselves at odds with both progressive and conservative activists, but unable to find common ground among themselves or redirect the course of politics. James J. Sheehan, *German Liberalism in the Nineteenth Century* (Chicago: Univ. of Chicago Press, 1978), especially 1–76, 272–273, argues persuasively that liberalism, defined as a movement toward individualism, pluralism, capitalism, and partisanship, held little appeal for the disaffected. Like their counterparts in Vermont and Wales, many Germans looked to constitutional reform, education, and economic development for deliverance. But these initiatives won relatively little support outside cities. Sheehan attributes their failure not only to the difficulties presented by German political and community institutions, but to the reluctance or inability of middle-class reformers in Germany to act as their counterparts in Great Britain and America did – to embrace popular government and religion, to include peasants and townspeople in their voluntary associations, to work at persuading artisans and farmers that economic development would increase rather than decrease self-employment, and to establish popular sovereignty over the monarchy, the aristocracy, the army, and the established church.

14   The distinction between "closed" and "open" communities draws upon Eric

R. Wolf, "Types of Latin American Peasantry," *American Anthropologist,* 57 (1955), 452–471; and G. William Skinner, "Chinese Peasants and the Closed Community: An Open and Shut Case," *Comparative Studies in Society and History* 13 (1971), 270–281.

15 The distinction here between progressive and conservative political thought stems from Karl Mannheim, "Conservative Thought," in Paul Kecskemeti, ed., *Essays on Sociology and Social Psychology* (London: Routledge and Kegan Paul, 1953), 74–164.

16 On the weaknesses and strengths of the Anglican establishment, see David Williams, *A History of Modern Wales,* 2d ed. (London: John Murray, 1977), 127–138; Geraint H. Jenkins, *Literature, Religion, and Society in Wales, 1660–1730* (Cardiff: Univ. of Wales Press, 1978), 305–309; and Evan D. Evans, *A History of Wales, 1660–1815* (Cardiff: Univ. of Wales Press, 1976), 26–41. On social problems, see Williams, *Modern Wales,* 177–200, 213–235; Evans, *History of Wales,* 127, 189, 257–261; David W. Howell, *Land and People in Nineteenth-Century Wales* (London: Routledge and Kegan Paul, 1977); David Thomas, *Agriculture in Wales during the Napoleonic Wars* (Cardiff: Univ. of Wales Press, 1963); A. H. Dodd, *The Industrial Revolution of North Wales,* 3d ed. (Cardiff: Univ. of Wales Press, 1971); and A. H. John, *The Industrial Development of South Wales* (Cardiff: Univ. of Wales Press, 1950).

17 Williams, *Modern Wales,* 163–176, 200–212, 231–261; and Evans, *History of Wales,* 210–230.

18 On the rise of dissent, see Williams, *Modern Wales,* 139–157; Evans, *History of Wales,* 36–37, 88–96, 108–114; Gwyn A. Williams, *The Search for Beulah Land: The Welsh and the Atlantic Revolution* (New York: Holmes and Meier, 1980); Williams, *The Merthyr Rising* (London: Croom Helm, 1978), 7, 10–13, 39–50; and Michael Hechter, *Internal Colonialism: The Celtic Fringe* (Berkeley: Univ. of California Press, 1975), 167–191. Social historians have only begun to investigate Welsh religious life during the Age of Democratic Revolution. The best studies of the spiritual history of Welsh communities are anthropological. See Williams, *Modern Wales,* 155–157, 166–175; and Evans, *History of Wales,* 210–230, on the relationship between religious dissent and Welsh national identity. Dissenting churches gained strength in Wales among middling, propertied groups, as they did in the valley. Old Dissent, which tended toward religious liberalism, gained strength in villages and large towns, whereas New Dissent, which was predominantly evangelical, won most of its support in the countryside. On villages, see Evans, *History of Wales,* 36–37; David Jenkins, "Aber-Porth: A Study of a Coastal Village in South Cardiganshire," in Elwyn Davies and Alwyn D. Rees, eds., *Welsh Rural Communities* (Cardiff: Univ. of Wales Press, 1960), 49–55; Emrys Jones, "The Sociology of a Market Town in Central Cardiganshire," in Davies and Rees, *Welsh Rural Communities,* 89–109; Williams, *Beulah Land,* 14–31; and Williams, *Merthyr Rising,* 23, 72–75. On the countryside, see Evans, *History of Wales,* 90–94; T. Jones Hughes, "Aberdaron: The Social Geography of a Small Region in the Llyn

Peninsula," in Davies and Rees, *Welsh Rural Communities*, 164–173, 181; Trefor M. Owens, "Chapel and Community in Glan-Llyn, Merioneth," in Davies and Rees, *Welsh Rural Communities*, 185–190, 197–218; Alwyn Rees, *Life in the Welsh Countryside: A Social Study of Llanfihangel Yng Ngwynfa* (Cardiff: Univ. of Wales Press, 1951), 100–108, 128–141, 162–170; and Williams, *Beulah Land*, 34–35.

On the relationship between church membership, reputation, and success, see Jenkins, "Aber-Porth," 10–56; Owens, "Chapel and Community in Glan-Llyn," 231–245; and Rees, *Welsh Countryside*, 142–146.

19 On reform, see William R. Lambert, *Drink and Sobriety in Victorian Wales, c.1820–c.1895* (Cardiff: Univ. of Wales Press, 1983); Gwynne E. Owen, "Welsh Anti-Slavery Sentiments, 1790–1865: A Survey of Public Opinion" (M.A. thesis, Univ. College of Wales, Aberystwyth, 1964); Evans, *History of Wales*, 96; and Williams, *Beulah Land*. On parallels with reform in Scotland, see C. Duncan Rice, *The Scots Abolitionists, 1830–1860* (Baton Rouge: Louisiana State Univ. Press, 1981). On politics, see Williams, *Modern Wales*, 163–176, 200–212, 231–261; Evans, *History of Wales*, 210–230; Rees, *Welsh Countryside*, 154–159; Williams, *Merthyr Rising*, 90, 132–133, 226–229; B. G. Owens, "Hugh William Jones: A Chapter in the History of Tabernacle Baptist Church, Carmarthen," in Tudor Barnes and Nigel Yates, eds., *Carmarthenshire Studies* (Carmarthenshire: Carmarthenshire County Council, 1974), 215–216; David J. V. Jones, *The Last Rising: The Newport Insurrection of 1839* (Oxford: Clarendon Press, 1985), 3–4, 46–84, 217–218, 225–229; and Ieuan Gwynedd Jones, *The Dynamics of Politics in Mid-Nineteenth Century Wales* (Cardiff: Univ. of Wales Press, 1971), 22–26. On parallels with reform politics in Scotland, see William Ferguson, *Scotland: 1689 to the Present* (New York: Praeger, 1968), 266–317.

20 Dissenting churches were strongest in iron and coal mining communities, where churches gave the largely Welsh working class a social and spiritual home in an alien setting. Before 1850 these churches had few ties with the predominantly Anglican owners of the works and mines; nor did they have many middle-class members, because industrialized towns contained few shops that were not owned by local mines or mills. See Ebenezer T. Davies, *Religion in the Industrial Revolution in South Wales* (Cardiff: Univ. of Wales Press, 1965); John, *Industrial Development of South Wales*, 70–74; and Williams, *Merthyr Rising*, 47–64, 80–87.

21 On popular protests outside the electoral process, see David J. V. Jones, *Before Rebecca: Popular Protests in Wales, 1793–1835* (London: Allen Lane, 1973); idem, *Last Rising*; Williams, *Merthyr Rising*; David Williams, *The Rebecca Riots: A Study in Agrarian Discontent* (Cardiff: Univ. of Wales, 1959); Williams, *John Frost: A Study in Chartism* (Cardiff: Univ. of Wales Press, 1939); and Davies, *Religion in the Industrial Revolution*, 76–92.

22 Jones, *Politics in Mid-Nineteenth-Century Wales*, 26–32; Kenneth O. Morgan, *Wales in British Politics, 1868–1922* (Cardiff: Univ. of Wales Press, 1970), 1–27, 297–314; Stephen E. Koss, *Nonconformity in Modern British*

Politics (London: B. T. Batsford, 1975), 16–54; Hechter, *Internal Colonialism*, 167–191; Williams, *Modern Wales*, 269–275; and Ferguson, *Scotland*, 317–329.

Appendix A

1   Only a small portion of the communicant list of St. Paul's Episcopal Church of Windsor survives. It runs from 1829 to 1834 and records too few communicants to bear detailed study. Still, those who appear on it were much like others who joined churches between 1829 and 1843, and very much like those who joined that church's religious society during those same years. The loss of the communicant lists may not have been critical, if the communicants were indeed much like society members in general.

2   A separate statistical analysis of the members of these societies was made. Their characteristics were similar to those of others in their towns who joined churches between 1827 and 1843, and unlike those of nonmembers. Their inclusion as new members in the text thus did not alter the statistical picture that would have appeared if they had been excluded entirely.

3   Denominational records show between fifty-five and sixty male and female members in the West Windsor church over the 1830s. It was estimated that 38 percent of those members were male (from the average male/female ratio among members of other evangelical churches) and at most 90 percent of them were aged twenty-one or older. That produced the estimate of twenty adult male members.

4   The upper estimates were constructed by estimating that 45 percent of the members of the religious societies were adult males and that half of them might have been church members. The lower estimates were derived by considering the possibility that fewer than half the society members were church members, or that society membership totals included children as well as adults.

5   John M. Comstock, *The Congregational Churches of Vermont and their Ministry, 1762–1914* (St. Johnsbury: Caledonian, 1915); Henry Crocker, *The History of the Baptists in Vermont* (Bellows Falls: P. H. Gobie, 1913); and Edith F. MacDonald, *Rebellion in the Mountains*.

Appendix B

1   For the purpose of the study, several small or short-lived towns were joined to larger towns from which they separated or to which they were later annexed. Acton was joined to Townshend, Baltimore to Cavendish, and Stannard to Wheelock. That left 116 townships in the valley, excluding townships that still had under eighty residents in 1840. Those townships were considered "not settled."

2.   Edward M. Cook, *The Fathers of Their Towns: Leadership and Community Structure in Eighteenth-Century New England* (Baltimore: Johns Hopkins Univ. Press, 1976); and Gilmore, *Reading Becomes a Necessity*.

Index